The *Metamorphoses* of Ovid

The
Metamorphoses
of Ovid

TRANSLATED FREELY INTO VERSE
BY DAVID R. SLAVITT

The Johns Hopkins University Press
Baltimore and London

© 1994 The Johns Hopkins University Press
All rights reserved
Printed in the United States of America on acid-free paper
9 8 7 6 5 4 3

The Johns Hopkins University Press
2715 North Charles Street
Baltimore, Maryland 21218-4363
The Johns Hopkins Press Ltd., London
www.press.jhu.edu

Part of this poem appeared in the following magazines, to which the
translator and the publisher extend their thanks: *Boulevard, Grand Street,
Michigan Quarterly Review, New England Review/Breadloaf Qurarterly,* and
Texas Review.

Library of Congress Cataloging-in-Publication Data will be found at the
end of this book.

A catalog record for this book is available from the British Library.

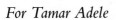

For Tamar Adele

CONTENTS

PREFACE

Publius Ovidius Naso—Ovid—wrote this poem roughly between A.D. 2 and 8, which was about twenty years after the death of Virgil. In other words, this is an epic written in the shadow of Virgil's *Aeneid*, then and still the most official epic in literature. People who like the Stazione Centrale in Milan adore the *Aeneid*, with its earnest if rueful celebration of piety and the glory and manifest destiny of Rome. To attempt another large poem that would, in its rather different way, presume to engage history and cover everything from the creation of the world to the late news must have been, for Ovid, both inevitable and dismaying.

Rome—the civilized, literary Rome of wealth and power—was a relatively small town. Ovid wasn't exactly a buddy of Augustus Caesar's, but because Ovid's third wife was Livia's cousin, he was probably on the B list for palace parties. (This was what got him into trouble and, eventually, exiled to Tomis, at the mouth of the Danube, where he died.) One must remember, though, that Augustus had been Virgil's patron, too. What we must try to imagine, then, was not just some theoretical instance of the "anxiety" of literary influence, but a constant comparison, the burden of which must have weighed on Ovid all the more heavily as his reputation grew with the successes of the early courtly poems. As he became "the" poet, he must have come to feel Virgil's shadow more and more palpably; it persisted, grew, and loomed over the Roman hills.

It is not impossible for a poet my age to understand at least a little of what this must have been like. I can remember the odd atmosphere of the fifties in which poets such as James Merrill, Richard Wilbur, and Howard Nemerov made their debuts. The successes of their early books were occasions for celebration not only because these were collections of impressive and accomplished poems from writers of great talent but also because, in a more general way, these successes demonstrated that it was possible to go on from the achievement of Eliot, Pound, Joyce, and the modernists. The work of these younger men was liberating because now other, if perhaps smaller, kinds of excellence were . . . imaginable.

As Ovid reports, himself, in the *Tristia* (4, 10), remembering how he became a poet:

> I was lucky, at least in the timing of the choice I'd made. Macer
>   was old then but I knew him well and heard him
> read often of birds and snakes and healing plants
>   from that long didactic poem of his. Propertius
> was a close friend. We enjoyed poetry, conversation,
>   and a friendly glass with Bassus, who used to write
> iambics, and Ponticus, famous now for his epics, and Horace,
>   whose odes we heard him read with the ink still
> damp on the page. I saw Virgil once at a party
>   but didn't have the nerve to go up to speak
> to the great man.

A complicated business, we can allow, a potpourri of admiration, envy, pride, reverence, modesty, and ambition. There was also the expectation—from Rome, perhaps from Augustus himself—that the mark of success in a poet's career was an epic that might stand on the shelf alongside Virgil's. But how was a poet like Ovid, with a more intimate, livelier, funnier, and more self-mocking sensibility, to attempt such a thing? The epic form was not, I think, immediately congenial, and my guess is that Ovid recognized this himself. Accordingly, he transformed the epic, playing against its grain a lot of the time, and escaping its severe organizational and thematic demands by transforming it into something altogether different. The first metamorphosis, then, is of the idea of the epic itself.

Virgil's is a highly conscious, elegantly artifactual poem of the waking mind; Ovid's is a dream poem in which one story blossoms into further stories, some of which are tangential, others of which are enfolded and enveloped. The speakers shift and shimmer, giving way to speakers within their tales and sometimes to speakers within those. (I have never before had occasion to use three different levels of quotation marks.) Ovid acceded to Virgil's metrical approximation of the Homeric hexameter, but with a quite different set of strategies and, therefore, quite different results. As L. P. Wilkinson puts it, in *Ovid Recalled,* "The gravity, variety of rhythm and expressiveness of Virgil's verse were due largely to heavy elision, but also to variation of pauses in the line and to free use of spondees, whereas Ovid dispensed as much as possible with elision, tended to pause at the caesura or at the end of the line, and in general was more dactylic, sacrificing everything to lightness and speed." There is a footnote that points out, with wonderful scholarly exactitude, that A. Siedow declared in 1911, in *De elisionis usu in hexametris Latinis*, that Ovid has 15.6 elisions on average for each hundred hexameter lines, while Virgil has 50.5.

So what? Think of the differences between Milton's pentameter lines and Dryden's, or the difference between Dryden's and Pope's, and you get the general idea. Ovid's metric calls attention to itself, and only now and then will he allow the drama of a story to interfere with the dancing-master precision of his performance.

My own experiment here is in the assertion of the possibility of English hexameters, even though there are not many successful precedents. Longfellow's Acadian jog-trot sounded in my ears like a bell buoy, warning me off that treacherous reef. And yet, there was Lattimore's Homer, which is in hexameters and which works well. (It remains my favorite modern translation of Homer and is the only one that suggests both the metrical stateliness and the syntactical muscularity of the Greek.) I wanted, moreover, not just to be more contemporary than Horace Gregory and Rolfe Humphries, but to attempt something that had not been done before, something that might stand comparison with Arthur Golding's work of 1567, and George Sandys' (1632), and even Dryden's brilliant fragments. Both Sandys and Dryden used heroic couplets, and Golding's version (Ezra Pound called it "the most beautiful book in the language,") is in fourteeners—the metrical pattern of "Mary Had a Little Lamb"! So why not hexameters? They might perhaps give some sense of the formality of Ovid's Latin, that constraint he could tighten or relax as the rhetorical occasions prompted.*

The poem, I think, is known more in its pieces than as a whole, perhaps because the separate stories are so conveniently excerptable. This is the *locus classicus* for a great number of myths, after all, and people have consulted this text the way they have consulted Lemprière's classical dictionary. (It is also true that, in a fourteen-week term, a poem of this length tends to get assigned in pieces, like the *Faerie Queene,* for example.) At 12,015 lines, the *Metamorphoses* is longer than the *Aeneid* (9,896) or the *Odyssey* (10,912) and almost as long as the *Iliad* (15,600). As a translator, I take all kinds of liberties, but I am strict in my observation of length and scale, which I take to be significant artistic decisions that any new poem ought to respect and re-create. The sweep of this work, the change in its moods and rhythms, the way in which the

---

*As an act of homage, I have used Sandys' rhymes for the last dozen lines of the poem, although the lines I am rhyming are hexameters, of course. My other expropriation is the Cyclops' song, which I took from John Gay's elegant libretto for Handel's *Acis and Galataea*.

heart of the poem turns out to be in the transitions, some of them quite arbitrary and fortuitous, are what have impressed me and what I have tried to convey.

A translation, after all, is an account of a reading. Each person's encounter with any text amounts to a translation, for each of us supplies a context, a frame of reference, an emotional environment, and an individual history that is unique and that the author could not possibly have imagined or tried to predict. The miracle is that any writer's text can resound in the mind, heart, and soul of any other reader. This is the great mystery of literature. It is also what allows me to imagine that what I have been doing may be of some possible use. My enthusiasm for Ovid's work and my delusion that I have understood his poem, that I have seen it and seen through it to these new words, are brash but necessary, and no more implausible, after all, than that first impossibility of any reader's leap of sympathy, intuition, understanding, and, finally, collaboration.

I do not propose therefore to discuss the poem or to attempt to analyze or explicate it. My translation is my commentary. But I can recommend that those who are interested may look at Wilkinson's *Ovid Recalled* and at Sarah Mack's *Ovid*. Both of these are reliably informative and provide useful bibliographies that will enable further reading.

The *Metamorphoses* of Ovid

BOOK I

Bodies, I have in mind, and how they can change to assume
new shapes—I ask the help of the gods, who know the trick:
inspire me now, change me, let me glimpse the secret
and sing, better than I know how, of the world's birthing,
the creation of all things from first to the very latest.
　　Before there was water and dry land, or even heaven and
　　　　earth,
Nature was all the same: what men imagine as "chaos,"
that jumble of elemental stuff, a lifeless heap,
with neither Sun to shed its light, nor Moon to wax
and wane, nor earth poised in its atmosphere of air.　　　　　　10
If there was land and sea, there was no discernible shoreline,
no way to walk on the one, or swim or sail in the other.
In the gloom and murk, vague shapes appeared for a moment,
　　loomed,
and then gave way, unsaying themselves and the world as well.
Cold and hot contended, as wet warred with dry,
soft battled with hard, and buoyance with weightiness
in default of reason and order, until, at the last, a god
sparked, glowed, then shone like a beam of light to define
earth and the heavens and separate water from hard ground
and clear crystalline air from the shifting masses of cloud,　　20
freeing the muddled elements and letting them each become
for the first time its own distinguishable self.
Then, in a further work of wonder, in combination,
he bound them all together to make the harmonious cosmos
in which we can live, on which we all have to rely.
Upward the aether flowed, as is its nature to do,
forming the vault of the sky; the air we breathe collected
over the stolid earth; and water, learning its heft
and weight, began to flow downward, spilling into seas
that seemed to hold in embrace the masses of pristine land.　　30
That god, whoever he was, once he had sorted the chaos

into its various parts, molded the earth he'd made
into a huge ball, rounded on every side,
and the waters heaved and spread in waves, currents, and tides
over which like currents of air blew in freshening winds.
Springs bubbled up, and ponds and still pools, and the rivers
flowed down from the uplands in babble or roar to the greater
lakes and on into distant and endlessly restless seas.
At his divine order, the plains stretched out and the valleys,
bosky groves, and woods sprang up and into leaf,   40
and craggy mountains arose with their curtain walls of rock.
The scheme of the god informed the way the vault of the sky
divided itself into two zones on the left and right
with a fifth zone in the middle—just as the earth divides
in exactly the same way, with unendurable heat
in the center, and impossible cold at each end with snowdrifts
and dismal expanses of ice, but between these unwelcoming places
are two more temperate regions, mixing the heat and cold.

　　　Think of the intricate way matter sorted itself,
the relative weights of the elements sifting to form the patterns   50
we take for granted—with fire lighter than air, and water
lighter than earth. By such contrivances was the god
able to arrange the way in which mists can form
and turn into clouds, which crash to produce great peals of
　　　　thunder
and jagged flashes of lightning that fill the air as they filled
the mind of the maker first, which is why they do not reduce
the world to smithereens. The quarrel, fierce as it seems,
is yet fraternal, familiar, a controversy of brothers—
East Wind lives with the Arabs and sometimes sojourns in Persia;
West Wind settled himself where the Sun goes down every night;   60
North Wind claimed for himself the barren Scythian steppes;
and South Wind chose what was left, the region of fogs and
　　　　rainstorms.
Over them all is the dome of utterly weightless aether
the god put there to contain them, like a dream of purity.

　　　Once these distinctions were made and matter began to
　　　　behave,
the sky displayed its array of stars in their constellations
the murk had hitherto concealed, a twinkling template
of order. The sea upon which they shone quickened with fish,
and the woods and meadows with game, and the air with
　　　　twittering birds,
each order of creature settling into its home.   70

A paradise, it would seem, except that the word was lacking,
as all words were, for the last creation had not yet happened—
of the one who should understand his dominion over the rest.
Man was born: some say the god perfected the world,
creating of his divine substance the race of humans;
others maintain that we come from the natural order of things,
the aether having left some trace of its heavenly self
for Prometheus to mix with new-fallen rain water
and mold into a shape not unlike that of the gods.
But one way or another, man arose—erect,   80
standing tall as the other beasts do not, with our faces
set not to gaze down at the dirt beneath our feet
but upward toward the sky in pride or perhaps nostalgia.
In such a way was the earth, so lately a rough-and-tumble
affair, changed, transformed to an intricate, ordered marvel
on which for the first time mankind was able to walk,
looking about himself in wonder and gratitude.
        That first age was golden: all was then fresh and new
and so arranged that out of spontaneous goodness, men,
without the compulsion of laws or fear of punishment, kept   90
their faith with one another, behaving with decency,
fairness, justice, and generosity. Plaques of bronze
with their formal legal phrases and barely veiled threats
were as yet unimagined. There were no benches with judges
        glaring
down at the crowds of perpetrators and victims, angry,
fearful, or sullen, but suppliants every one. The tall
pines grew undisturbed: no shipwrights came to cut
and hew them into masts for ships to plow the distant
and treacherous seas. In those days, men remained at home
in pleasant cities that needed neither walls nor moats,   100
no straight trumpets or curving horns to summon troops
to take up arms. There was never occasion for soldiers. Men
lived entire lifetimes in peace and ease, as earth,
without the scratching of plows or prodding of hoes, produced
whatever they needed for sustenance. Gentle creatures, they
        roamed
abundant meadows to gather the fruits, berries, and nuts
that hung from the boughs of bowers of a bliss they took for
        granted.
Jupiter's mighty oak trees showered the earth with acorns,
and spring with its temperate promise extended throughout
        the year.

Gentle winds from the west tussled the meadows of flowers   110
that popped up, unprompted as the laughter of small children.
Wheat grew wild in the fields; streams flowed with milk
and nectar; and honey dripped like sap from hives in the trees.
     When Saturn died and Jove succeeded as ruler, the silver
age began with another race of men, lesser
than those of the golden age that was gone—but they were better
than those of the age of bronze that followed in time's declension.
Now there were four seasons, with parching summer heat
and the biting cold of winter with a glitter of ice and a howling
of winds that seemed malevolent. Men began to seek shelter   120
not in caves and thickets but now in wattled huts.
They learned from their desperation to sow small seeds in furrows
and toil behind the bullocks that strained under heavy yokes.
     Next came the age and the race of bronze, of sterner stuff,
hard men ready to take up the weapons of war, crude,
even savage fellows and yet by no means wicked.
The age of iron came last, and with it came pouring forth,
as from a smelter's fire, a river of molten evil.
Modesty fled the earth; truth was rare; and honor
disappeared. In their places were snares, deceit and greed,   130
and violence everywhere, with envy egging it on.
Men spread sails to the winds to cross the heaving water
on keels of pines that had lorded it over their mountainsides.
The earth itself, which before had been, like air and sunshine,
a treasure for all to share, was now crisscrossed with lines
men measured and marked with boundary posts and fences.
Dissatisfied now with the yield from the plowshares' surface
          scratchings,
mankind began to attack the earth with picks and shovels
to delve down in her innards for gold the gods had hidden
as deep sometimes as the Styx itself. It was greed that dug   140
with iron tools, and then took up the weapons of iron
in a blood lust after loot, and the gold ran red with gore.
Men discovered brigandage, lived by banditry, stole
and killed—strangers of course, but also their own houseguests.
Fathers-in-law were right to fear their daughters' husbands,
and brothers as often as not were at their brothers' throats.
Husbands strangled their wives for dower money, and wives
dreamt—not always idly—of the deaths of wealthy husbands.
Stepmothers in kitchens cooked up their deadly potions,
and sons consulted with seers to discover how much longer   150
they had to wait before their sires would leave the estate.

Decency had become a memory, even a joke,
and Justice, the last immortal, gathered her robes about her,
knowing she had no place here, and fled the blood-soaked earth.
    This was the time the giants decided to make their assault
on the high gods, piling the hugest mountains skyward
even up to the stars—until the almighty father,
hurling thunderbolts earthward, smashed their impiety, shattered
Olympus, and then dislodged Pelion from Ossa
and onto their mangled bodies to bathe the ground in gore.   160
From the soaked and reddened soil sprang up a race of men
contemptuous of the gods and altogether unruly,
passionate, and bloodthirsty, being the children of blood.
    Then Saturn's son, the father of gods, looked down from
        his seat,
groaned aloud in disgust, and recalled Lycaon's feast,
the infamy of which was yet new in the world.
What to do? How should the wrath of mighty Jove
express itself in a worthy way? He called a council
of all the gods, and promptly they came to attend upon him.
When the sky is clear, you can look and see their glittery path   170
we call the Milky Way. On this *allée* their procession
passed in state to the royal dwelling places of him
they call in awe the Thunderer. To left and right were the halls
of the gods of the first rank, their porticoes now crowded
with lesser deities craning to watch how they all assembled
for their conclave on what we might call heaven's Palatine Hill.
    The gods had taken their places within the marble chamber,
when the king of the gods seated himself on his lofty throne
and, leaning upon his scepter, shook his head three times,
his hair fluffing each time as below earth's skies and seas   180
trembled in their response. And yet once more, and then
the god spoke: "Lords, there was a time when giants
with dragons' feet assaulted our fortress here in the sky.
That was a terrible time, but the present danger is worse,
coming from every corner of earth that Ocean enfolds.
The race of men is become vile, and I am resolved
to destroy them, every one. This I swear, by the Styx
and the other rivers that run deep in the underworld.
This is a dreadful prospect, but when there's no hope of cure
for a gangrenous limb, the surgeon's knife is the better choice   190
than to watch the infection spread. Fauns, satyrs, nymphs,
and demigods deserve our care and solicitude.
We have not allowed them places here with us in the heavens;

let us therefore protect their groves and mountainsides,
where they may continue to live in a measure of peace and quiet—
a small thing to ask, but most unlikely to happen
so long as the likes of Lycaon live. They are but small game
to those who know no limits and even plot against me,
the master of thunderbolts and lord of all the gods."

    At this there was clamor and babble of outrage and dismay,   200
and calls for justice and vengeance. As here, when a crew of
      madmen
and rogues conspired to blot the name of Rome with Caesar's
blood, and we all felt horror as well as fear—for great
Augustus first but also each man for himself
in the general wreck of things (Augustus, you must have delighted
in your countrymen's show of affection); so was Jupiter moved
and even pleased. He raised his hand in signal for silence
into which he spoke: "Be not afraid. Lycaon is punished.
What he did and what I thereafter did I will tell you.
It had reached my ears that the men of this new age were evil.   210
To confirm these reports and judge for myself, I descended to
      earth
in human form and wandered from place to place, my anger
first welling up and then giving way to grief, grief
at what I saw on all sides in the countryside and towns,
wretchedness and meanness. The reports had been understated.
In something close to despair, I approached the royal seat
of Arcadian kings, a place with a terrible reputation,
and there put off my disguise and announced myself a god.
Some of the common people thereupon did me reverence,
but Lycaon, their king, was scornful and mocked their simple
      prayers: 220
'Do not be quick to believe. I shall determine, myself,
whether he be an immortal and one of the gods, as he boasts,
or only an arrogant faker.' His plan, at the start, was
      straightforward—
to kill me and demonstrate I was clearly and merely mortal.
But then it grew complicated, as such undertakings do.
He took a Molossian hostage, butchered him there on the spot,
and threw his flesh into kettles and onto the grill to roast.
These were the dainties he served at the welcoming banquet
      he gave
to celebrate my arrival—and also his own departure,
for this was where I destroyed the table, house, and household.   230
Lycaon fled to the woods, in terror more than shame,

and there he howled and howled, tried to speak . . . but could not.
Imagine how foam flecks at his jaws, and his body hair
thickens and mats. His hands deform, and his arms are twisted
into a wolf's forelegs. Lycaon turns into a beast
but with still recognizable eyes, and the same expression he had,
only now his cruel glare is directed perforce at sheep.
But the fall of one royal house is only a gesture, an omen,
when everywhere is fury and rage reigns supreme.
Let them all suffer severe and immediate penalty. Let them   240
feel the pain they have each and all so well deserved."
     When he had spoken, some voiced approval, while others,
          struck
by his terrible meaning, gave their assent in solemn silence,
which may have allowed for at least a degree of the grief they felt
for the loss of the race of men. What would become of the world
without these creatures to bring incense to their holy altars?
Would there be only beasts now running wild on the prairies
and plains? The master of gods commanded them all to keep faith
and trust as much in his mercy as they relied on his justice,
reassuring that what he had once made he could make   250
again but different and better—a new order of men.
     He took up his thunderbolts and had already raised his arm,
but then, staying his hand, worried that such a great
blast might even endanger the heavens, that everything could
go up at once in that general conflagration the Fates
had said would bring an end to the universe he loved,
he lowered his arm, put aside the Cyclopean thunderbolts,
and decided on yet another way to inflict his will,
destroying the human race with rain that fell from the sky
in torrents and waters that rose in answer from out of the sea.   260
     First he shuts North Wind into Aeolus' cave with all
the winds that scatter the clouds. Then he lets South Wind loose
to fly with soppy wings over darkening skies, his beard
dripping with moisture, as water flows from the hair on his head
and his wings and garments drip. He squeezes the ripened clouds
with his huge hands, and they crack and then gush forth their
          juice
to pour down rain on the land that lies exposed below.
Iris, goddess of rainbows and Juno's messenger, draws
the moisture up to replenish the rapidly emptying clouds,
and down on the earth the rain pelts and batters the crops,   270
ruining all that the farmers have worked and prayed to achieve.
The ripening grain in their fields is flattened into the mud,

and the work of a whole year is gone in a couple of hours.

Jove is not content with the waters that his own skies
can sluice down but asks his brother who rules the seas
to add what he can with waves that now batter the shores.
The river gods he summons to attend in his council chamber,
and there he issues his orders, commands them to open their
     doors,
overflow dikes and levies, and let their currents run free,
racing wherever they will to tear toward the turbulent sea.   280

Neptune raises his trident and smashes it down on the earth,
and waters gush, as the rivers leap like flying fish
up and into the air, over their banks and bounds,
to frisk in the wide meadows and play in the plains, orchards,
and kitchen gardens, and then, to try the doors and windows
of barns and houses, of temples and shrines, sweeping away
tools, toys, and precious heirlooms as refuse and junk.
The flimsier houses wash away; the sturdier stand
fast as the water rises up to their eaves and gables,
submerges them, and hides them, beneath its impassive surface.   290
Ocean extends its shores, which after a time meet
and disappear as everywhere is awash with water.

Here is a man who has taken refuge on top of a hill,
a rapidly dwindling islet; here is a man in a boat,
rowing with oars in the very place he was recently plowing;
here a man in a dinghy sails over the roof of his barn,
and trolls his line for fish caught in the top of his elm.
Where plowshares once had furrowed the meadows, anchors tore
the bottom's clods. Grapevines climbed toward the keels of boats.
Where kids had frisked, now seal, walrus, and sea calf lolled.   300
Nereids swam in wonder through gateways, over towers,
and in and out of the windows of deserted buildings of men.
Dolphins romped in the woods and darted like huge birds
from branch to branch of trees, above which, in the flood,
desperate wolves were swimming alongside helpless sheep.
Lions and tigers, living and dead, drifted at random,
with the swift stags and the sturdy boars . . . all swept away.
From black skies the weary birds, scouting a perch,
fell exhausted at last into that endless sea
that in its greed had devoured entire mountain ranges.   310
Whoever hadn't drowned outright—here and there, some sailors
survived in their boats—perished inexorably of hunger.

Between the lands of Boeotia and Oeta, somewhere in
     Phocis—

or actually it would have been somewhere *over* Phocis, afloat
on the waters that washed Parnassus, all but submerging its twin
peaks—in a little skiff, Deucalion and his wife
came aground on almost the only ground there was,
for which that couple gave thanks to the nymphs and mountain
       spirits,
and to Themis, the goddess who, from her shrine, foretold the
       future.
In all the world, before the deluge, there was no better   320
man than this, nor as upright, nor was there a woman more
respectful of the gods. Only this man remained
of the myriads that once had defiled creation; only
this woman was left. And Jupiter looked down,
saw them as innocent, worthy, reverent, and rent the skies
to free North Wind and have him disperse those vengeful clouds
and restore a gentler blue. The turbulent sea subsided
at once, as the lord of ocean laid his trident down
and calmed the swell. From the froth, he called forth mighty
       Triton,
his shoulders thick with mollusks and seaweed, to blow his all   330
but deafening conch to signal the rivers' and streams' retreat.
He lifts the spiral shell to his lips, and the roar resounds
from its widening whorls to reach the horizon and even beyond
to the shores of the rising and setting Sun. The waters hear
and obey, and the sea has shores again, and rivers banks,
and the waters run in accustomed channels, revealing once more
hilltops and then whole hills, and then the upland meadows,
in islets that expand and join. At last there are crests
of trees, still covered by underwater slime that the flood
has left, and their branches, and then, once again, the bark of their
       trunks.   340
    The world was restored, but empty. Deucalion looked
       about him,
heard the oppressive silence, and burst into copious tears.
With effort he addressed Pyrrha, his wife, saying,
"O my dear wife, the only woman alive in the world,
our ties of blood and the marriage couch have joined us together,
as has our misfortune also—we have survived, but alone.
The others are gone, washed away . . . as we may be ourselves,
for I do not yet altogether trust this relenting. Our perch
may prove to be a further torture, raising our hopes
only to dash them again when the rains recommence to float us   350
free and onward to death to join the rest of mankind.

And yet, it could have been even worse than it is. Imagine
yourself on this strand in this same boat, but all alone,
without my help or my consolation. And for my part,
had I survived to this moment but without you, I should plunge
into the depths to follow and rejoin you, quite unable
to bear without you the scrap of a widower's empty life.
Prometheus, my father, would have known what to do to restore
the nations of earth, breathe life somehow into inert clay,
and repair the disaster. But only we remain, the relicts   360
of all our kind. The will of the heavenly gods is harsh—
and should we survive, how can we not imagine those things
that might have come to pass?" He broke off speaking and wept,
again, and they wept together and resolved to appeal to the
          heavens
and learn from the oracles what to think and what to do.
They went to Cephisus' stream, turgid still but confined
more or less to its former banks, and they sprinkled its holy drops
upon their heads and clothing, having done which, they turned
to the shrine of the goddess, fouled with moss and seaweed, its
          fires
dead of course, but they fell prone on the steps and kissed   370
with reverent lips the stones and prayed the prayers of the
          righteous:
"Themis, tell us, is heaven's terrible wrath abated?
What must we do, o gentle and merciful goddess? Tell us,
how may we look to restore a world that is overwhelmed?"
     The goddess was moved and spoke: "Go from this place,
          with heads
covered and robes thrown open, and fling the bones of your
          mother
behind you as you walk." What? They look at each other,
speechless, appalled. It is Pyrrha who breaks the astonished
          silence.
"My mother's bones? Assuming that I could retrieve them, how
could I dare defile them so? What can the goddess's words   380
have meant? Not what they seem! The heavens sport with us yet."
They mull over the puzzle, trying to read aright
the difficult text, and at last, the son of Prometheus soothes
Epimetheus' daughter with comforting words: "What it has to
          mean—
for the gods would never command us to do so wicked a thing—
is that we must look down at the earth, which is mother to one
          and all,

and take up stones, which are bones of the earth's body, and
    throw them
behind us as we go." Pyrrha wants to believe him,
but what good will it do throwing stones over their shoulders?
It's another imposition the heavens have conjured up   390
to turn the last moments of human life to farce.
But what's to lose? They cover their heads, open their robes
as they were bidden, and walk, flinging pebbles and small
rocks behind them. They do not see (and who would believe it,
did we not have our ancient tradition to reassure us?)
the stones hitting the ground, losing their shape and hardness,
and growing in softness and size to a blobbiness first and then
a vaguely humanoid presence, like statues not yet completed,
but roughly blocked in marble—save that the marble is soft,
its damper parts even fleshlike, or fleshy or, say, flesh!   400
There seems to be a mollification, a kind of relenting,
and whatever was solid is now become hard bone, and the veins
in the rock, retaining their names and nature, are still veins
but now in arms and legs of people who move and speak,
albeit stiffly at first, and slowly as if in amazement.
The stones Deucalion flings behind him take on the shape
of men, as likewise the stones from Pyrrha assume the form
of women. And from this circumstance it came to pass
that there is a hardness in humans, or hardiness and endurance,
for we are the children of stones whose origin speaks in us still.   410
    And the other forms of life, the richly various fauna?
What of them? They are here. The earth somehow produced them
out of its own substance, as the rays of the Sun baked dry
the muck and slime of the flood, and the marshes basked in a heat
intense enough that the air shimmered and solid shapes
danced in the middle distance, dreams of themselves. From
    the mud,
all manner of creatures were spawned. They say that each year
    the Nile
floods its valley and then, in season, returns to its bed,
leaving the farmers to turn the newly fertilized earth
in their rich fields. They plow and they see how the new mud   420
teems with animate creatures, sluglike, blind, unfinished,
but wriggling into existence, having appeared from the union
of moisture and heat in the nuptial bed of the rich earth.
In this way all that moves and breathes came into being,
for fire and water are hostile—as lovers sometimes can be—
but out of their union there comes a miraculous teeming of life.

So, when the Sun shone down on all that alluvial muck,
it brought forth the countless forms of the creatures we see
flitting, darting, lumbering, or creeping hither and thither,
some of them much the same as those that had come before,   430
but others, in the ebullient creation, or call it a frenzy,
novel and strange, or even terrifying. Consider
the Python, that huge serpent that struck fear in the hearts
of those newly created men. With what possible purpose
would the earth produce from itself a monstrosity like that?
But there it of course was, coiling its scaly length
around whole mountainsides as if it would swallow them up.
The archer god, Apollo, whose accustomed targets were deer
or now and again a chamois, emptied his whole quiver
into this dreadful beast, whose blood and venom mixed   440
as they seethed into the ground. To keep alive the fame
of this exploit of his in the minds of men, the god in his grace
gave sanction to sacred contests called, from the name of that
      dread
serpent, the Pythian games. At these meets, victorious
youths in boxing or running or chariot-racing are given
garlands to wear on their brows, woven of leaves of the oak,
for the usual laurel we now award to our champions did not
then exist, and they had to make do with what there was.
      Apollo, you will remember, was smitten with love for
         Daphne,
the beautiful daughter of Peneus (he was a river god).   450
It was not merely a chance infatuation, but rather
the mischief—and some say more, the positive malice—of Cupid,
enraged by the boasts and unseemly taunts of his Delian colleague.
Apollo, still in the warm glow of his triumph, having
recently slain the Python, saw Cupid bending and stringing
his bow and said: "That's a cute toy—not unlike my own.
The difference comes from the shoulder it sits on and arm that
      draws it
back. I have killed great beasts, game of the forest, and now
the amazing Python, that animate plague that sprawled across
      whole
fields and mountainsides, and all of its length was a-sprout   460
with numberless arrows, for mine is the greatest bow. You, sir,
merely trifle with yours as an icon or clever symbol.
But do not therefore persuade yourself that you are an archer."
The reply of the child of Venus was pleasant enough: "Sir,
your arrows can bring down anything; mine can bring you down.

If glory comes from the grandeur of what one bags, then mine
must surely exceed yours, if you are one of my trophies."
Having thus replied, he took wing, as the god
is able to do, and ascended into the air to alight
on the peak of Parnassus, where, in a pleasantly shaded recess,   470
he drew from his quiver arrows of opposite magic powers:
one having a gold tip—it is razor-sharp—
and causing attraction and kindling love; the other, dull,
crude, and tipped with lead, producing extreme distaste.
This latter shaft he fitted onto his bow and fired
into the heart of Peneus' daughter. And then, with the gold
arrow, he smote Apollo, piercing the god to the marrow.
He burned at once, with passionate ardor; regrettably, she
was not disposed to respond. Indeed, she fled from the thought
and name of love, retreating into the woods to live   480
in quiet and solitude, a devotée of Diana,
a hermit-huntress. Suitors presented themselves, but she
fled them and raced on familiar paths, her hair flowing loose
and bouncing brightly behind her. Marriage? Her father
      complained
that she owed him a son-in-law, that she owed him grandchildren.
    She blushed and lowered her eyes, or threw her arms round
      his neck
and pleaded with him, "Papa, allow to me what Diana's
father has given to her; let me stay as I am,
a maiden, and my own woman." What father could have refused?
He granted her wish—but the world and Nature had other
      notions,   490
for what man can ignore a breathtaking beauty like hers?
That double-edged gift undoes her, for Phoebus sees her and
      promptly
longs for her, to have her, marry her, possess her!
He knows better, his mantic gift not having left him. . . .
But still he longs, and therefore hopes, and therefore believes
the impossible. As a cleared field is set afire
and the stubble bursts into flame, or as hedges ignite from a
      traveler's
torch that has brushed its branches and blaze up into the night,
so does the god burn, is consumed by the fires of passion,
his heart sizzles, his brain fries in the fat of his rapture   500
and vain hope. He watches as that ponytail of hers
whips the innocent air, and he all but cries out in pain.
He sees her eyes, her lips, her marvelous fingers, her wrists

tiny and lovable, gazes, thirsts for the vision he sees
but can't get enough of. He longs for what he's unable to see. . . .
She runs away, as fast as the wind itself, and he follows
and calls her name, but she does not stop or even look back.
"O nymph, daughter of Peneus, I am no enemy! Hear me,
I mean you no harm. Please, believe me! Wait! You run
as the lamb runs from the wolf, or the deer from the ravening lion,   510
or the dove on the wing flees the circling eagle above.
So each creature flees its predators and hunters,
its enemies. I am not one of those, but a lover, a friend,
who means you no harm. I wish you well and fear you may fall
or that some bramble or burr may scratch your beautiful body.
This is rough country. Let's both slow down. I promise to follow
at a decent distance, and you can ask whomever we pass
to tell you who I am—no shepherd or rustic bumpkin,
but a son of Jove, a god, the lord of Tenedos, Delphi,
Claros, and Patara. I am master of prophets and seers,   520
patron of music, god of all the archers but one
(whose aim is surer even than mine and has struck my heart,
which up until now flew free as any bird). I am god
of medicine but cannot cure myself, no herb
or poultice I know can assuage the grievous hurt I have
     suffered. . . ."
He would have gone on, but the nymph had bolted, was
     running away,
and he was left with his words hanging in air like the wisps
of the spiderwebs she had broken. He saw how the wind whipped
the fringe of her skirt, the sleeves of her tunic, her streaming hair.
(Oh, lovely!) He followed, running as fast as he could   530
and seemed to catch up—as a whippet races a scampering hare
across an open field and almost has it, but then
it feints and cuts to one side or the other, the snapping teeth
of the dog grazing its heels but closing somehow on air.
So it was with them, the girl and the god behind her.
Fear gave her a strength she'd never had, but he
was driven by love, which is strong as fear and has no mercy,
which gave her no time to rest, and took its fuel from the air
her hair had stirred, or that streamed over her shoulders shiny
with sweet sweat. Crazed, he followed, his heart pounding   540
loud in his ears, and she, now at the end of her strength
and courage, and pale with terror, and seeing the banks of the
     stream
over which her father reigned, cried out in desperation:

"Father, help me. If you are a god, if your waters are holy,
save me! Destroy this beauty that is my curse. Spare me!"
The words had scarcely faded away when she felt in her limbs
a weight and numbness, a languor, a drugged indifference.
        Her soft
skin began to crust and turn into bark, her hair
burst into bud and leaf, and her arms ramified to branches.
Her toes took root where she stood, as she was changed to a tree,   550
a beautiful tree—her beauty was all that remained, a constant,
and this beauty Apollo still loved. His hand
he placed on the trunk and felt the heart of the girl yet beating.
He stroked her branchlike forearms and pressed his lips to
        the wood,
which shrank from his kisses still. The god wept and exclaimed,
"You would not be my wife; yet you shall be my tree.
My hair, my lyre, and my quiver shall always bear the laurel,
which shall be my emblem and sign. With laurel shall generals
        wreathe
their triumphant brows, and laurel shall stand at Augustus' door
to keep watch and to gentle the grove of imperial oaks.   560
Because I am immortal and my hair cannot turn gray,
you shall be like me, with foliage ever green."
The Paean god fell silent. The laurel rustled her branches
and nodded her leafy crown in assent to the world's winds.
        In Thessaly, there is a place, a valley, steep and wild—
people call it Tempe—there, from Pindus' foothills,
a river flows, the Peneus, with white waters and falls
that send up mists and sprays to the tops of trees and fill
the air with continual roaring. This is a special place,
and here, in a cavern of wet, black, overhanging rock,   570
the river god sat in state, ruling his watercourses
everywhere. To this place, all the rivers came
to attend their lord and condole—and offer congratulations
to the father of Daphne. Nearby streams were the first to appear:
Sperchios with his fringe of poplars; Enipeus,
the nervous one; Apidanus, venerably old;
gentle Amphrysos and Aeas. And then came more distant rivers
that flow, by whatever whims of topography and soil,
wearily to reach at last the welcoming sea.
They all were there . . . but one. Inachus is hidden away   580
in his deepest cave, weeping, adding his tears to the flow
of his dark water as, wretched, he laments the loss of *his* daughter,
Io. His precious Io! Is she alive or dead?

He has no notion, having searched and failed to find
a trace of her anywhere. His soul is full of dread
either of death or whatever it is that is worse than death.

What had happened was Jupiter noticed the girl on her way
from her father's stream—noticed, and more than noticed. He
    called
out to her: "Young lady, permit me to say you are lovely,
will make some husband happy, are worthy even of Jove's   590
ardor. You are on your way into the shady woods"—
and here he made a welcoming, proprietary gesture—
"but have no fear of the wildlife. You are under a god's protection,
and not just any god's, but as you walk the paths,
know that your safety lies in the hands of the Lord of Heaven.
I who hold the scepter and hurl the thunderbolt
am watching you. . . . Oh, do not flee from me." But she
had already bolted and in her haste and far behind
left Lerna's pleasant pastures and the rich Lyrcean woodlands.
Jupiter covered the land with a thick duvet of cloud   600
under which he enfolded the maiden. And then the god raped her.

Juno, looking down, noticed those clouds in their sudden
agglomeration in an otherwise perfectly clear sky,
like a patch of night that has wandered into a bright afternoon.
A billow of river mist? Some swamp's dank exhalation?
Most unlikely! She looked to see where her husband was,
for she knew his tricks and had caught him often enough before.
Gone! Nowhere to be seen. "Unless I am wrong," she said,
"I am being wronged." Forthwith, from the sky's summit she
    plunged
earthward to disperse that improbable clump of cloud.   610
Jupiter, ever-ready, heard her approach and changed
Io into a milk-white heifer—poof! like that.
But still lovely. Juno, puzzled, noticed the beast,
and could not help but admire. Still suspicious, she asked
what it was, and whose, and where it had come from. Jove
shrugged, smiled, and announced it had sprung up out of the
    earth
marvelously, which was almost true, after all. But Juno,
taking him at his word, asked him to give the heifer
to her as a present. What could he do? How could he not
hand over the girl he adored without letting Juno know   620
what he'd been up to? His shame warred with his heated passion
(pride perhaps played a part, and possibly also fatigue).
Juno, his wife, who was also his sister, won in the end.

He could not refuse. He handed the remarkable creature over.

    Juno, not yet complacent, was unwilling to trust her triumph
and led whatever it was away to give in charge
to Argus, son of Arestor, who could watch the marvelous beast.
Who in all the world could keep an eye on it better?
Or a hundred eyes, for that was what he had, set around
his head, and they took their rest only two at a time,   630
while all the others were peeled. He therefore could watch in all
directions, front and back, both day and night, keeping Io
close, letting her graze in the daytime, but shutting her up
at night with a crude cowherd's halter as ornament
on her delicate neck. The maiden had to make do for food—
or let us be blunt and call it fodder—with leaves of bushes
and trees and bitter grasses and weeds. Instead of her comfortable
couch, she had to lie down at night on the hard cold ground.
Water she had to drink from muddy streams and puddles.
She would have stretched out her arms like a suppliant to
      Argus. . . .   640
But what arms? And with what voice could she make complaint?
She tried to speak but only managed an inarticulate
lowing, plaintive but nonetheless absurd. She was wholly
appalled. She ambled down to the bank of the stream over which
her father presided, that stream where once she had played as
      a girl,
and looked to see reflected in the water's surface a gaping
jaw, huge eyes, and horns growing out of her skull.
She fled in terror. The other naiads looked on in blank
incomprehension of who she was. Even her father,
Inachus himself, was a stranger. She sought him out and mooed   650
piteously beseeching his aid, or at least attention,
a touch of comfort and reassurance. He held out hay.
She licked his hand and even tried to purse her lips
to a kiss, but could not. The tears rolled down the hairs of her
      cheeks.
She bawled. And then at last, with a hoof, she wrote in the dust
her name with its two letters, the straight line and the circle,
at which her father groaned aloud. "Oh, woe. O Io!
My daughter! You? I have searched the whole world over, my
      heart
utterly broken. But finding you thus is a greater grief.
You cannot answer in words; sighs and sobs are enough,   660
and groans that are much like mooing. I'd thought one day to
      prepare

a wedding for you and hoped for a son-in-law. Must I look
to the barn for such a one? Will my grandchildren someday
join the herd in the meadow? Such great grief commends
death to mortal men, but I cannot look for relief
even through that dark door. My pain will continue forever,
unabated and unrelenting, immortal as I am."
The father thus bewailed his daughter's plight and his own,
as Argus came to herd the child away to safer
pastures, where he could perch on a mountain peak from which   670
he could see for miles in all directions and keep his watch.

    Jupiter, having now seen all that has happened, is wracked
by pains he can no longer bear. Mercury, he dispatches
to kill Argus. His son, whom the dazzling Plead bore him,
puts on the wingèd shoes and takes his wand in his hand
that induces sleep. He puts on his magic wingèd cap,
and thus arrayed he bounds from the heavens down to earth,
where he puts hat and shoes aside, and with only his wand,
in the guise of a goatherd, drives a flock along the paths
that happen to lie adjacent to Io's pasture. He plays   680
a panpipe as he goes, an oddly attractive tune
that catches Argus' attention. "You, with the pipe," he calls,
"come, sit here by me. Nowhere is better grass
for your flock than here. Enjoy the shade of these pleasant trees."

    Mercury, son of Jove and grandson of Atlas, sits,
and they talk of this and that. Mercury plays on his pipe
a slow, languorous air. Argus feels his lids
heavier by the moment and struggles to keep awake,
to keep at least a few of his hundred eyes open.
To interrupt the spell of the music, he asks his companion   690
how the flute was invented, and the god tells him the story:
"Once in Arcadia's mountains, on a hill they call Nonacris,
there lived a pretty nymph whom all the gallants adored.
Her name was Syrinx. Over and over, she'd barely escaped
from satyrs and even gods who had set their sights on her beauty.
She preferred Diana's chaste kind of life, and dressed herself
to look, at least from a distance, just like the goddess. The telltale
difference was that her bow was of horn rather than gold.
One day, on his way from Mount Lycaeus, Pan, with his head
crowned with jaunty sprigs of pine, encountered the nymph. . . ."   700
He would have gone on to explain what the god had said, what
    the nymph
replied, and how she had fled through the woods and thickets to
    Ladon's

sandy banks. He could have told how Pan was approaching,
and the nymph implored the river to come to her aid and change
her form, and then how Pan, catching up at last with Syrinx,
held out his arms to clutch her, but found himself holding . . .
      reeds,
nothing but reeds in his arms, and sighed in his disappointment,
and the wind in the reeds in answer made sounds of sad reproach,
which were better, the god decided, than nothing at all. This
      response
he treasured, and, joining the pipes, he made the first instrument,   710
to which the maiden's name attaches still. He would
have said all this, but Argus' eyes were all closed in sleep.
Mercury now falls silent, and deepens the other's slumber
by passing his wand above the hundred closed eyelids.
The wand, and then the sword, for with one quick blow at the
      neck,
he takes off the head and sends it rolling down to defile
the defile of rocks below with its copious gouts of blood.
Argus is dead, and the light of all those eyes extinguished
replaced by the single darkness to which the universe tends.

    Juno took the eyes and set them as a memento   720
on the tail of her pet bird, to make the peacock grand
with astonishing jewels. But angry, angrier now than ever,
she drove poor Io forth, with threats and insults, hounding
the beast from place to place, to the very ends of the earth.
At last, at the banks of the Nile, her journey came to an end.
She reached that stream exhausted, knelt down to drink and pray,
and, with head thrown back, she raised her face and voice to bawl
complaint to the stars. In tears she begs great Jove to end
her endless torment. He hears and feels contrite, and throws
his arms around Juno's neck, and pleads with her for mercy: 730
"You have nothing to fear from Io. By the Styx, I swear this oath,
that she will never again be occasion to you of grief."

    The wrath of the goddess is gentled, and Io is retransformed
to what she was before. Her hair falls away, her hide
softens, her horns disappear, and her great round eyes grow
      smaller.
Her mouth narrows, her shoulders and arms return, and her hands.
Her hoofs once again are feet, with toes and five dainty nails.
Her heiferness now is gone, except for the singular whiteness
her body has. She stands on two feet. She still fears
to speak, not wanting to moo. She clears her throat, and words   740
with all their grace and power miraculously return.

Io now is a goddess; her enthusiasts, in linen
robes, intone their prayers to her majesty. A son,
Epaphus, was born to her—we suppose the fruit of her union
with Jupiter. In her temples are also altars to him.
When he was a young boy he had a playmate and friend,
Phaëthon, whom he sometimes teased, as boys will do.
Phaëthon, then, got huffy, put on airs, and boasted
that his sire was Phoebus Apollo. Epaphus was unimpressed:
"You believe every silly story your mother tells you? You think   750
that you are the son of the Sun? Tell me another!" His playmate,
purple with rage, ran home to Clymene, his mama, to say
what the other boy had said, and ask what he could have
            answered.
Ashamed, insulted, he wanted proof of his noble birth,
something both for himself and to flaunt in the other's face.
"Prove it!" he said, and threw his arms around his mother's
neck. In the name of all that is holy, he begged her to make it
better, make the pain go away. And the mother heard him,
was moved by the boy's distress, and perhaps as well by the insult
to her own person. She stretched her arms up toward the sky   760
and invoked the Sun: "Hear me, my child. In all his glory,
your father looks down upon us. By his splendor, I swear
that you are his truly begotten son, that fiery orb
you see crossing the sky each day and whose heat enlivens
and enables the world and orders our days and nights is indeed
your sire. Believe me, my darling! For if I do not speak truth,
I pray that I never again may behold the light of the world,
which is his alone." She looked down at her son, in whose
            small face
some embers of doubt still guttered. "Do you need further proof?
You are welcome to seek it from him. Go to your father's house   770
and ask him yourself. The place where he rises is easy to find.
If you are disposed to do so, go," she says and smiles
to see him smile. Indeed, he's beside himself with excitement
and joy. He leaps up, imagines the heavens, and instantly sees
himself striding across the sky. He has heard her words.
Forthwith he sets out eastward to make his father's acquaintance
trekking across the expanses of Ethiopian grassland
and reaching at last the Indus Valley, which lies adjacent
to the place where his father, the Sun, commences his daily round.

BOOK II

The great hall of the Sun is lofty with sweeping columns
and bright with shining gold and bronze polished like fire.
The pediments are paneled in ivory; the portals
are silver buffed to a high sheen. Everywhere you look,
the craft is splendid and rarer than any precious metal
or gemstone. Consider the doors with their intricate bas-reliefs,
Vulcan's work, a map that shows the ocean surrounding
the island of earth, that holy circle above which a column
of cloud rises to heaven. In the sea are the gloomy masters
of waves and the great tides—Triton, who sings his chanteys;   10
the sly chameleon, Proteus; burly Aegaeon, whose arms
can wrestle the greatest whales; and Doris and all her fifty
nereid daughters who swim, or bask on the rocks and comb
their long green hair, or joy-ride on porpoises' backs or
      dolphins'—
and each had a distinct and recognizable face,
although you could tell they were sisters. In the representation
      of land,
there are cities, fields, flora and fauna, men and beasts,
as well as the demigods who rule over rivers. Above
in the sky are the planets and stars, with all the constellations
of the zodiac represented, six on each of the doors.   20
     The approachway is steep, and Phaëthon climbed its
      imposing height
boldly until he reached the house of the Sun—his father's
house, if what he'd been told was true. He entered the hall
and beheld at last his father's face, although at some distance
for the radiance was all but blinding. Decked in a robe
of imperial purple, the great god Phoebus sat on his throne
that shone with precious emeralds. To left and right were
      attendants—
Day, Month, Year, and Century. Hours hurried
this way and that on their endless tasks while the statelier Seasons

conversed among themselves: Spring in her diadem
of blossoms; Summer with sprigs of grain as her emblem; Fall
gay with her splotches of trodden grape juice; and chilly Winter
with tousles of long white hair and a cascade of matching
     whiskers.
    From the center of this, the Sun, with dazzling eyes that see
at once into every soul, beheld the terrified youth
who stood there gawking at all this majesty. "My son,"
he said, reassuring the lad with his first words, "you are welcome,
but tell me what brings you here to my dwelling place. Whatever
is in your heart, confide in me. Speak, Phaëthon, to your father."
"O light of the world," he answered, "if only you will allow me   40
so to address you, I come to hear you acknowledge me
and let me have some proof that you indeed are my sire.
Reassure my troubled mind and let me know
the story my mother has told me, however far-fetched, is
     the god's
truth." His father removed his radiant crown and invited
the youngster to come closer, embraced him, and then said:
"You are, indeed, my son. Clymene has spoken the truth.
And to give you the proof you ask for, let me grant you a favor—
whatever you ask shall be yours. I take my solemn oath
by the Styx on this—or whatever the gods swear on, for I   50
have never myself beheld that fabulous watercourse.
Ask, and it shall be given." The son requested his father's
car, that splendid chariot, and the right to drive his amazing
team of wingèd horses, if only for one day.
The father, sorry he'd made such a promise and sworn the oath,
shook his radiant head three times and a fourth and said:
"Your words have demonstrated that mine were vain and foolish.
I cannot retract my promise, but I ask you to name another,
any other favor in all the world. What you here
request is ruinous, mad. You have not the strength and skill.   60
A mortal, you want more than even the gods themselves
would dare imagine. None but myself has the mettle to drive
those fiery steeds. Consider the words of a loving father
who wishes you well. Not even the god of thunder, lord
of all the gods, would presume to take those reins in his hands.
Understand what I say. The road at first is steep, and the horses,
strong as they are and fresh at the start of the day's journey,
can barely make their way as we mount into the sky.
Then, when it levels off, the course is so high that one looks
down at the mountaintops and glittering seas and feels   70

THE METAMORPHOSES

giddy. I do it daily but never without some fear
when my heart quakes and the backs of my knees begin to quiver.
But the last part is the hardest, the sudden and steep descent.
One takes one's life in one's hands along with the heavy reins.
I come down to meet with Tethys, who receives me into her
      waters
and every day is worried lest I overturn and fall
headlong into the sea. And all this time, the heavens
are spinning, whirling in constant motion that carries along
everything in the skies except myself and my car.
Only I can maintain a contrary motion against   80
the tide of time itself. Suppose you took my place.
Would you stand there and endure the dizzying spin of the world?
If I can barely survive its buffets, would it not sweep
you away altogether? And why would you want such a thing?
Do you imagine pleasant vistas? Attractive sights
upon which you may gaze in the course of your journey? It is
      nothing at all
like that, no groves of trees, no temples, no charming prospect
of cheerful exotics offering interesting gifts and mementos,
but a rough track in a dark jungle where fierce beasts
of prey are lurking—the raging bull, the hungry lion,   90
the pinching crab, and the scorpion with deadly poisonous barb.
The horses are not what anyone would think of as tame; they
      breathe
flame from their mouths and nostrils as their huge muscular necks
fight against the restraints of harness and reins. I cannot
change my mind or retract, but you can withdraw your request
and make another and better. You ask for a fatal gift.
If I were not truly your father, why would I speak to you so
with a parent's concern and love? Look at my face, in my heart
that breaks to think of his child and how the world's rich gifts
may never be yours. The treasures of earth and sea and sky   100
are there for the taking. Only this one thing, I implore you
not to ask. It's a gift more like a curse if only
you understood what's in store should you hold me to my
      promise."
      The young man heard his father's words, but did not hear
      them,
paid no heed, and insisted on what the god had sworn to.
He wanted to drive that fiery car. Slowly, with dread,
the father led his son to the chariot Vulcan had made
for him with its gorgeous golden axle and intricate golden

wagon tongue. Its wheels had tire hoops of gold
and silver spokes. The horses' yoke, thickly set with jewels   110
and chrysolites, reflected the radiance of their driver.
Phaëthon gazed in wonder at the splendor of this machine,
as in the East Aurora threw open her purple gates,
and the stars faded away in a slowly brightening sky,
with the morning star the last to quit its celestial watch post.

    The Sun god saw the dwindling horns of the Moon tumble
down from view and ordered the Hours to yoke the horses.
This the goddesses did and led the steeds from their stalls
snorting smoke and flame. They buckled the bridles on
and harnesses. Then, with a magic ointment, the father anointed   120
the face of his son to protect it from searing in those hot flames.
Then, despite himself and with soul-wracking sighs, he placed
the dazzling diadem on the youngster's head and said:
"At least, take my advice and profit from what I have learned.
Never use the whip, but take it slow and steady,
keeping as tight a rein as you can on these spirited creatures.
They'll give you a lively enough ride, I warrant. Your course
is slantwise through the zones of the heavens, or more like an arc
that never extends as far as the northern or southern extremes.
Follow the tracks you'll see that the wheels have already marked   130
and try not to go too high, which would set the skies on fire,
but neither dip down too low, for that would ignite the earth.
Keep to the middle, and try not to swerve too much to the right,
where the Serpent is, or the left, where heaven's altar lies
so low in the skies. Fortune perhaps may come to your aid
in this foolhardy business. Do not compound your folly
but keep your wits about you. Night has come to its end,
and it's time. The dawn is here, chasing the last shadows.
Are you sure you want to do this? Take my advice and love
instead of this mad ride. You stand here on firm earth,   140
and nothing compels you to climb up into that terrible car.
Spare yourself and me. Let me do what I do
everyday, bringing light for you and the world to bask in."

    But Phaëthon wouldn't listen. He had already ascended
and gathered the reins into his eager hands. He stood
proudly as if he were posing, waved a cheerful salute
to his smiling, heartbroken sire to thank him for this great gift.

    The team, whinnying, restless, was pawing the earth,
       impatient
to go, go. . . . The four, Pyroïs, Eoüs, Aethon,
and Phlegon, charged the air with their wild animal spirits.   150

When Tethys, the great sea goddess who had borne Clymene,
        opened
the gates wide as she'd done a thousand times before,
she had no idea her grandson was standing there in the car.
The horses charged together, with a thunder of hoofs and a
        flashing
that glazed the clouds in their path. The chariot rose up into
the air, overtaking and then passing East Wind and rising
higher and faster. The horses could feel the weight of the car
but less than on other days. As ships on the sea will skitter
without their usual ballast, yawing and rolling, the Sun's
chariot bounces along, unstable, a bobbling plaything   160
of physics' slightest impulse, as if there were no one driving.
Given thus their heads, the horses enjoy themselves,
romp, run free, frisk, and break to unfamiliar
regions that always tempted on all their unvarying journeys
before. The young man is now in the grip of panic; his will
has fled, as he would have liked to do himself, but he cannot
dismount, cannot escape. The reins hang slack in his hands.
He has no idea where he is, where he wants to go, where he wants
not to go. The constellations are roused. The Great
and Lesser Bears that had dozed in the cold awake and try   170
to cool off in the sea. The Serpent, which stretches in polar
skies, is warmed and writhes into life. Even the clumsy
Boötes in his lumbering oxcart is startled and flees
in a haste that would have been funny to see, but Phaëthon's eyes,
elsewhere, are wide with fright as he sees how far below now
earth's mountains and valleys lie. His knees are weak
with the knowledge that he will fall. Blinded in all that light,
all he can see now is his huge and dazzling wrongness,
his folly and pride, his repentance that he ever came anywhere
        near
this infamous team of horses, this dreadful vehicle. Crazed   180
and desperate now, he wishes he never asked his father's
name and fame. His mother might better have told him Merops
had been his sire, that father whose sons refused to listen
to the good advice he gave them—and then Diomedes killed
        them.
Death is clearly his lot. He looks behind at the empty
space he has already traveled, and then ahead at the larger
distance yet to go. In dismay. It is simply hopeless,
as, when a ship is abandoned, or the pilot is washed away
and the useless rudder wavers purposelessly in the sea,

there is not even the hope that the gods may playfully nudge it   190
to safety or hearken to desperate prayers of those yet on board.
He would call out to the horses but cannot remember their names,
and to left and right he can see the menacing beasts of the heavens.
There, Scorpio flexes his barbed tail to strike
as any scorpion would, but huge, blotting out the sky,
and the tip of the barb shines with the deadly venom the creature
exudes—and the very sight of it paralyzes the youth.
His wits are dulled, his will drains, and the reins fall
from insensate hands. The horses, feeling their freedom, exult
and, with nothing to check their fervor, run wild into the strange   200
quarters of air they have always eyed on their ordered rounds.
Wherever their whim prompts, they rush now in a transport,
rattling over the smaller stars and careening madly,
the axle bouncing, the wheels erratically showering sparks
as they climb higher, higher, then wheel and plunge down again.
The Moon watches in wonder as her brother's chariot scorches
clouds and thunderheads, and the earth bursts into flame,
the crests of the mountains first, and then, as the moisture
          of rocks
comes to a sudden boil, in loud, random explosions.
Trees are consumed, and grain in an instant ripens to ash.   210
Try to imagine entire cities consumed in a moment,
the nightmare of whole nations flashing, charring, gone.
The woodland is burning, and mountains are smoldering logs in
          a huge
hearth that is the world—Athos, Taurus, and Tmolus.
Oeta goes, and Ida, her springs gone dry, is burning.
Helicon now is ablaze, and Haemus burns like Aetna,
which is double bright and doubly ruined. Parnassus is gone,
and Eryx, Cynthus, and Othrys. The snows of Rhodope melt
and boil away. Mimas and Dindyma go, and sacred
Cithaeron liquefies into fire. The distant Scythian   220
ranges smolder and blaze, the Caucasus lie beneath
a thick pall. The craggy Alps and the cloud-shrouded
Appennines go. Ossa, Pindus, and even mighty
Olympus are burning. He looks at the general conflagration
and feels the heat of the air searing his lungs. His car
is a furnace now. The floor is hot beneath his feet,
and the smoke and sparks are a dreadful whirl on all sides as
          heaven
turns into hell, and the horses are running faster than ever,
although they can't see either. Phaëthon's eyeballs fry,

and his lids are all but seared together, but, could he open 230
his eyes, it would do no good in the choking soot and smoke.
It was then that the Ethiopians, up until then like us,
were blackened by the intense heat, and Libya turned
from a garden spot to the desert we see there now as her rivers
and lakes were boiled away. The nymphs of our springs and pools
tore their hair, bereft, as Dirce dried up in Boeotia;
in Argos, Amymone no longer bubbled up and sang;
the Pirenian spring in Corinth gave out. And the world's great
         rivers
shrank in their beds and died, the Don, Peneus, Caïcus,
and quick Ismenus . . . gone. The Eremanthus and Xanthus 240
disappeared, and muddy Lycormas, and crooked Maeander,
which lolls and writhes in its plain. The Melas and the Eurotas,
Euphrates, Orontes, and Thermodon, the muddy Ganges, the
         Phasis,
the Danube, and Alph the sacred river . . . all of them vanished.
The Sperchios' banks are burning, and the wide Tagus dries up
in distant Lusitania. Water birds, serene
on the Cayster's gentle waters out in Maeonia, poach
as if the lake had turned of a sudden into a great
bain-marie. The seven mouths of the Nile choke
with dust and die. In Thrace, the Hebrus as well as the Strymon 250
dry up and disappear. The Rhine, the Po, the Tiber
are nothing but empty ditches in a world that cracks and yawns
as ghastly chasms gape and the bright light of the fire
cuts through the underworld's habitual murk to frighten
Pluto, his consort, and all their kingdom of shadowy wraiths.
The ocean itself, enraged, skulked off to leave behind it
an enormous desolation of cooked fish in the baking
mud. There were brand-new islands, hitherto submerged
but now towering high in the nightmare landscape, mountains
where the only game was the upturned bellies of dead dolphins. 260
Nereus and Doris, who had lived in the blue Aegean,
perspired in their cave, and all their fifty daughters,
who had sung and danced in the sea in choruses around them,
shrieked in fear and pain. Neptune, himself, was roused
to defend his kingdom and came three times to the surface to raise
his arms against this threat, but each time turned away,
unable to bear the heat of the air that was now on fire.
       Earth, having nowhere to hide, felt how her streams were
            dying
and turned her scorched face to the skies in pain to complain,

raising her hand to shield her eyes so mountains trembled.   270
In broken and piteous tones, she implored the celestial gods:
"If it be your will that I should perish thus, I demand
to know what I have done. And why, if I am fated
to die, o king of the heavens, should it not be by your own
hand? What lesser fire than yours should burn me so?
I suffer, but let me know the justice of my fate.
Make manifest the true necessity for this dreadful
end! If I must perish, enfold me in your wisdom
and stern love. . . ." She coughed, choked, begged the pardon
of the august gods, and continued: "See how my hair is burning.   280
Ashes are hot in my eyes and stinging my face and shoulders!
Is this my proper reward for the good service I've done,
bearing the wounds of the curved plow and the sharp pick,
pestered from season to season, and always abundantly giving?
Those creatures you have entrusted to me I nurtured, providing
food for them and their beasts. For their sacred rites, I supplied
incense with which they offered thanks to the high gods.
But even if somehow, without having known it, I have sinned,
what has my brother Ocean done to deserve your wrath?
His waters recoil, his third of the universe bubbles and shrinks   290
from an angry sky and its searing flames. The heavens themselves
smoke and smolder. Have pity, if not on land and sea,
at least on the sky, where you yourselves live in lofty splendor.
From pole to pole there are nothing but arcs of billowing fire.
Your sacred dwelling places cannot be safe for long.
Atlas can scarcely endure the heat of the weight he carries
and shudders in pain. If earth and sea and sky all go,
chaos will come again in all its incoherence,
supplanting the orderly cosmos that deserved your pity and care."

        So Earth spoke and, exhausted and agonized, fell silent,   300
retreating into herself as far as the borderlands
of the world of shadows. But Jove has heard her plaintive cry,
and the mighty father summons the other gods to witness,
and especially him who had given the fiery car into
the care of another, that unless he exert himself and offer
urgent help, all life would perish in this disaster.
Jupiter then ascends to the parapet of heaven,
from which he covers the earth with clouds, hurls thunderbolts,
and sends down rains from the skies. But nothing is there at hand.
There are no clouds to spread, nor rains with which to shower   310
the burning everywhere below. He takes a bolt
of lightning, hefts it high beside his ear, and hurls it

down with precise aim to that charioteer in the air,
fighting fire with fire. The horses, maddened further,
rend their traces and scatter. The chariot, now careening
crazily, wrecks, its axle broken, its wheels destroyed,
their spokes flying in all directions, while Phaëthon,
his hair ablaze, is thrown free, plummets down through the air,
leaving a neat contrail of fire and smoke behind him.
As a shooting star that seems sometimes to fall from a clear   320
sky and makes its momentary punctuation,
so Phaëthon fell, and fell, and landed at last,
far from his native place, in the river Eridanus,
which received his broken corpse and bathed the ruined face.
The nymphs thereupon performed the solemn rites of interment
for the charred flesh, which was all that remained of the
          handsome lad
after the thunderbolt's devastation. They carved on a stone
an epitaph to mark the site and note the life:
IN · THIS · PLACE · PHAËTHON · LIES · WHO · ROSE · IN · HIS · FATHER'S · CAR
WITH · A · DARING · BEYOND · HIS · STRENGTH · OR · WISDOM—
          AND · FELL · FAR.   330
That father, stricken, grieving, covered his face and wept,
and, if we believe the stories we have heard passed down from
          those times,
there was once an entire day when the Sun never appeared,
and the only light was the garish glare from those still burning
fields and woods. In that dreadful dreamscape, sooty and rank,
Clymene wandered, mute with woe, her clothing torn
where the woman had plucked and rent it, in search of her
          son's body.
At length she reached the banks of that river in Italy, found
the tomb, and fell on the ground to weep and kiss the stone
and hug it to her breasts. Joining her now, her daughters,   340
the Heliades, pour out their bitter lamentations
at their brother's death and what it implies—the limitation
each of us must learn for himself on what a man
may dare to dream. The world is different now, and smaller,
hardly worth their notice. They stay there by the tomb
days and weeks on end. Months, and they have not moved,
and then one day the eldest, Phaëthusa, complains
her feet are cold and heavy. Lampetia, her sister, comes—
or tries to—but she, too, is held fast now. Her toes
have rooted into the ground. A third, seeing this awful   350
thing that has now afflicted her sisters, raises her hands

to tear her hair in grief and anger, but finds there leaves
growing out of her head. Another looks down at legs
that are turning wooden, at arms that are twisting into branches.
Bark closes around their slender waists, their breasts,
loins, shoulders, and necks . . . but their lips, still lips, cry out
to a mother who runs to them, frantic and quite unable to help.
All she can do is kiss those not yet transformed lips. . . .
But what is the good of that? She tries to tear off their bark,
to break the twigs from their fingers, but her daughters cry out
        in pain   360
as each one feels the wounds her unwitting mother inflicts:
"Don't! Mother, it hurts me. Please! You are tearing my body,
which still, within this tree, feels all the pains of the flesh.
Mother, mother, farewell. . . ." And the bark closed over the
        speech
to leave a roughened and silent loss in the air. And tears,
for the tears of the girls still flowed for their poor brother, their
        mother,
and for themselves now, too. Those tears hardened to amber
as the Sun glanced down at his daughters, who were changed then
        to a grove
of miraculous weeping trees. The amber glistened and hardened
into the jewels the pretty brides of Rome now wear.   370
        Their cousin Cygnus, who'd come to mourn at Phaëthon's
        grave,
saw this miraculous change and, there at the banks of the river,
gave himself over to keening and lamentation, for pain
is contagious, engendering pain, as we see in the plight of one
the sorry condition of all. His wailing was high, shrill
and higher still, and his hair turned white and fluffed to feathers.
His neck stretched and thinned, and his reddened fingers grew
webs. His arms were increasingly alar, and his mouth
decidedly beakish. Thus did Cygnus turn into a new
bird: the swan, which dislikes the upper air, where Jove   380
makes free with his thunderbolts, and prefers the lakes' and
        ponds'
cool water, which is fire's complement and foe.
        Apollo, meanwhile, huddles in deep mourning, his light
cloaked as if eclipsed by grief. He hates himself
and the world he once illumined. In sorrow and anger he sulks,
refusing to do service to a world he now despises.
"Weary, sick of it all, I am done. Let anyone else
who dares attempt my route and drive my damnable cart

across the sky. If no one volunteers, so be it.
Let all the gods confess the task is beyond their strength.   390
Let Jupiter try it himself, and while he fights those beasts
and tries to hold the reins, let him forswear those weapons
that undo foolish sons and destroy innocent fathers.
When he has tried it himself and failed, let him know the boy
did his best and therefore did not deserve to die."

The other gods surround him and plead for him to restore
the light of the world. Jove, himself, apologizes—
gruffly, but that is the way of the mighty Lord of Heaven.
Phoebus rounds up the team, yokes them, trembling still,
into the chariot's harness, and with fierce strokes of the whip   400
lashes the wild and hateful beasts that killed his boy.

Now the mighty Father, making his rounds of the walls
of heaven, inspects the fortifications and checks the damage
the fire has done, but the splendid muniments stand firm.
He then descends to earth to assess the damage and see
how what remains of mankind is faring, with special attention
to the Arcadian lands he loves. Her springs and rivers that
          languish,
he brings again to life. He restores grass to her fields,
outfits her trees again with their proper raiment of green
leaves, and repairs the devastation of woods and forests.   410
Occupied thus in this work—involved, engaged—he encounters
quite by chance a certain nymph and, as it happens,
is in an instant struck to his very marrow, her beauty
impossible to behold and not to have. She was
Callisto, lovely indeed, but hardly a flirt or coquette,
not at all a girl who devoted whatever attention
she had to her coiffure. Her severe gown was held
by a plain pin, and her hair tied back with a simple hank
of utilitarian ribbon. She was one of Diana's women,
with a spear and bow in her hands. Nowhere on all Maenalus'   420
slopes was there any nymph the goddess loved any better.
But even that turned out to be not enough. The Sun
was high in the sky when the maiden entered a grove of ancient
trees to lie down and rest. She unstrung her bow and stretched out
on a grassy knoll, her quiver doubling there as her pillow.
Jove, beside himself with eagerness and delight,
smiled as he guessed that his wife might never find out—and
          then,
on second and more realistic thought, reflected that this
would be well worth the price he'd have to pay if she did.

He put on the guise and dress of that goddess Callisto loved,   430
and said, as Diana herself would have said: "My dearest young
          woman,
where have you hunted today, and how have you fared?" The girl
replied with delight and awe: "Hail, glorious goddess!
I greet you with greater love than I bear even for Jove,
which is what I should say even if he were here to hear me."
Jove grinned, entertained to be loved more than himself,
and kissed her, but not with the kiss of a goddess, nor yet the kiss
one woman gives another. The nymph, confused, babbled on
about where she'd been and what she had bagged, but he
          interrupted
and copped an abrupt and unambiguous feel, which betrayed   440
his imposture. The maiden, alarmed and confused, struggled
          against him
as hard as she could. Had Juno seen how she fought him,
the anger the goddess later directed at her might have been
much less severe. The girl did her utmost, but mighty Jove,
stronger by far, did more, did what he would, undid her,
and then went back to his home in the sky. The girl, disgusted,
fled the grove that had been the scene of her defilement,
that had been, itself, defiled. Hating the place, she ran,
almost forgetting to pick up the quiver and bow she'd put by.

          Diana now approaches, sees the girl, calls out,   450
but Callisto flees in fear that it's Jove returning for more,
except that she sees the rest of the nymphs, that band which she
          joins—
or would but cannot now. She has changed and is sure the goddess
is able to tell. The nymphs can see that she's clearly different
but say nothing. In silence and shame she resumes her place
in the happy throng, but worries, day to day and month
to month, as it starts to show, that they'll learn her secret. At last,
on a hot afternoon, at the banks of a cool stream where they all
decide to go for a swim and begin to disrobe, it happens.
She cannot take off her tunic. They insist. At last she complies,   460
and at once they see her shameful state. Diana orders
the mortified girl: "Go! You pollute our sacred pool."
She withdraws to bear, alone, the child with which she is
          pregnant,
a boy, whom she names Arcas. Juno, biding her time,
having known all for all this while, and having nursed
her rage, looks down to see that the wrong is now compounded
by the birth of a son, a reward to her rival and also a proof

of her humiliation. Grabbing the nymph's hair,
the goddess shrieks in rage: "Now shall you surely suffer
as you deserve to do. That beauty of yours, I will take   470
away so it never again may occasion trouble. Proud
and full of yourself, are you, for having attracted a god?
But pride must fall," she cries and flings her prone to the ground,
where she lies with arms stretched out to the goddess praying
        mercy,
only to see them turn suddenly shaggy with rough
hair, and her hands are tipped with curved claws and becoming
paws. Her dainty lips enlarge, and her jaw is longer.
She has grown a kind of snout. Her power of speech is lost,
and all she can now produce is a hoarse and frightening growl.
Her feelings, her sense of herself, were still human; her body   480
was that of a great she bear. She reared up on hind legs,
extended her paws to heaven, and lumbered about in a comic
circle, groaning aloud to Jove of the great injustice
she's suffered. Having no answer, she slunk off into the woods
to flee where she once pursued, and hide where she had hunted.
If humans were enemies now, beasts were hardly friends.
She feared other bears and dreaded the packs of ravening wolves
even though her father, Lycaon, was one of those now.
Her son, Arcas, meanwhile grew up, unaware of his mother's
story, in time went into the woods, a young man learning   490
to hunt, and encountered—of course—his mother, who stared
        at him
in recognition and horror. Struck by those liquid eyes
that gazed so strangely upon him, he felt an irrational fear.
Slowly, the bear approached, and, terrified, he raised
his spear and was ready to drive its sharp point into her shaggy
breast, when at last Jupiter answered Callisto's prayer,
stayed his hand and prevented the crime, removing them both
from a sordid world. A sudden whirlwind arose to carry
the two of them up and into the sky as adjacent stars.
      Juno's wrath was hotter than ever, now that her rival,   500
thus promoted, was given eternal life. Complaining,
she descended to Tethys and Ocean, whom the gods all hold in
        reverence,
and explained to them what had happened: "Another queen in
        heaven
usurps the place that is properly mine alone. Look up
in the night sky and behold new constellations that blemish
the firmament and my honor! See where they shine in the place

of honor up near the pole. For the rest of time, all those
who may contemplate actions offensive to Juno will blithely
     suppose
there is little risk. It is *lèse-majesté* and contagious.
Where is my dignity now? My power? And where is the fear   510
I ought to inspire? Did I turn this slut into a beast
for her to become a goddess? What can my husband do now?
Will he turn her back from a bear, restoring her human form
as he did with Io? What new indignities can he devise
to make my existence a torment? Why not take her to wife,
and install the appalling upstart in my room and my bed?
Replaced, displaced, disgraced, perhaps I shall be divorced.
Jove could marry her then and be son-in-law to Lycaon,
that swine in wolf's clothing. It would serve him right and
     confirm
the general beastliness to which everything sinks at last. . . ."   520
Her tirade ran on, ran down, and then ran out. Exhausted,
she subsided at last and implored Tethys and Ocean to give her
what small comfort they could—at the least to deny those two
a welcome within their realm. "Other stars rise and set,
and appear to dip into the sea. But turn that whore away!
Don't let those arrivistes come near to pollute your waters."
     The gods of the ocean granted Juno's prayer. She expressed
her thanks, withdrew, and mounted into her gaudy car,
which was borne up into the air by her team of improbable
     peacocks,
who carried now the elaborate blazon of Argus' eyes.   530
This was a lively time in the bird-watching business. Ravens,
which up until then had been all milk-white, the rivals of swans,
doves, or the snowy geese that would one day sound the alarm
on Rome's Capitol Hill, had become suddenly black
as jet, through the fault of their tongues. Their silvery white glory
was the forfeit they paid for the gossip that blackens men's
     reputations
and women's, too. It is said that in Thessaly, in Larissa,
a young woman lived, a stunningly beautiful girl named Coronis,
whom Apollo adored—madly, truly, deeply, with all
the usual ideation and idealization. Wrong,   540
in this case at least, as the god's familiar, the bird, had seen
with his own eyes, the whole sordid affair, *in flagrante*—
and was coming now to report to his master. But on the way
he encountered his cousin the crow, who asked where he was off to
in such a rush. The raven explained his purpose. The crow

croaked out her dismal warning: "Do not expect any good
to come of this business. Take my advice or, better yet,
learn from my own sorry experience. See what I am,
consider what I once was, and try to be smarter. Don't let
it happen again." And the crow recounted the following story: 550
"There once was a baby, a poor motherless waif whose name
was Erichthonius. Pallas hid him away in an intricate
reed casket she gave to the three daughters of Cecrops,
the half-human, half-serpent, founder and first king
of Athens, with clear instructions—never to look in the box.
From high in a tree, I could watch to see how two of the girls,
Pandrosos and Herse, did as the goddess had ordered. The third,
Aglauros, scorning her virtuous sisters and calling them cowards,
opened the catch and lid to behold a child with a viper
uncoiling beside him. This I reported at once to Minerva 560
and, for my good deed, was stripped of my rank and dismissed
from her service. Ask her yourself. She'll tell you it happened thus.
Don't be the little birdie from whom people say they heard
whatever it is. You'll risk ruin, as I did, the daughter
of kings . . . or didn't you know? My father was the great
      Coroneus
of the land of Phocis, and I was rich and lovely, had more
suitors than I could count. But my beauty undid me. One day,
as I walked on the sandy beach, the lord of the ocean saw me,
liked what he saw, and made advances, as gods often do.
I wasn't receptive, but he couldn't have cared any less. 570
What charm and persuasion did not effect, he decided to take
by brute force. I ran. He chased me. And on loose sand
running is very strenuous. Soon, I wearied and called
to men and the gods for help, but nobody answered. I pleaded,
desperate now, and a virgin goddess heard a virgin's
cries and came to my aid. As I stretched out my arms to heaven,
I felt them change and darken, sprouting pennate projections—
feathers? Indeed! And my arms and hands were turning to wings.
My feet on the sand no longer slipped but now flew along
lightly, on top of the ground, and then up into the air, 580
soaring, floating, wheeling. . . . Thus, I became Minerva's
acolyte and companion, and thought it a wonderful honor—
until I heard how Nyctimine, Nycteus' daughter and lover,
had earned by her crime the same transmogrification, from girl
to flying bird. An owl, she still crisscrosses the sky,
although she avoids the glare of daylight and its stern judgments,
preferring, as one might expect, to hide her sins in the shadows."

To these divagations, the busy raven made curt reply:
"These are preposterous stories you tell, and of doubtful bearing
on my present errand and situation. I beg you to keep   590
your advice to yourself until asked—which I don't recall having
       done.
Good afternoon," he said and continued on to his master,
Apollo, to make his report about what he had seen Coronis
up to, down to, and into, with Ischys, that Thessalian
beefcake. Apollo, hearing what the raven said, grew pale.
The laurel fell from his brow, and the lyre pick from his hand,
and after the first moment of shock had passed he reached
for his deadly bow of horn, strung it, fitted an arrow
onto the bowstring, and fired an unerring shot to strike
the bosom he'd loved to fondle and press to his own. The girl   600
groaned in surprise as the hot sharp pain grew into a torment.
She pulled the arrow out and saw the great gush of blood
that drenched her now. "O Phoebus, I did indeed deserve this,
but you might have waited. Our child had no part in my sin,
and you have destroyed us both." She coughed, gurgled, and died,
and the lover, crazed, bereft now, felt his rage turn into
remorse and hated himself for having listened to that
damned bird. He despised the bird, which ought to have kept
its big beak shut. He hated the bow, hated the arrow,
and his own hand that had taken the fatal shot. He touched   610
that hand to the corpse, the rubbery flesh beyond all feeling
and any help. He fondled the girl he loved. He tried
to revive her but couldn't. It's too late for that now. The hurt
is beyond all healing arts—even his. He orders the pyre
piled high for the rite for her poor beautiful body,
and groans aloud in his torment, such inconsolable groans
as a cow might produce as she watches her darling suckling calf
ambling toward the altar and sees how the cudgel is raised
to crash down near the ear and shatter the delicate skull.
The god pours aromatic incense onto her senselessly   620
senseless breast, gives a last caress, and intones the proper
prayers. . . . But he interrupts himself and his sorry service,
for he cannot bear it, cannot endure that his son should also
die this way. He slashes the womb open, delivers
the unborn child, which he saves from death and the fire, bears it
away, and gives it over for safekeeping to Chiron,
the centaur who is half-man, half-horse. Meanwhile, the raven,
hopping from foot to foot and waiting for his reward,
the god disappoints. His glare is bleak and black as he turns

the bird to the ominous color it has had to wear ever since.   630
     The centaur was altogether delighted to have this cuddly
baby, and also honored by the god's commission. His daughter
Ocyrhoë had feelings one would have to say were mixed.
She came, looked down at the child, the infant Aesculapius,
and started to croon, intoning as the inspiration seized her
a prophecy from the depths of her troubled soul: "O child,
you shall bring health to the world, and many men shall owe
their lives to your skill. Some you shall even succeed in redeeming
from death's dominion, and Pluto, cheated thus, will complain,
whereupon Jove will blast you with one of his thunderbolts,   640
but you shall become at last a god and will live again.
And you, my father, who now are immortal, shall feel such pain
from the Hydra's blood as will make you pray for the knack of
          death
and Jove shall hear your prayer and cut the endless cord
that binds you." There was more. Perhaps there was everything
that she could see, but tears welled up in her eyes, and her voice
choked with the grief of things. "I cannot go on," she gasped.
"I am forbidden. . . ." She moaned. "I regret I ever acquired
this awesome gift. Its cost is excessive. I long for peace
and grass. To graze the grass of pleasant meadows! " She saw   650
her shape changing, her human portions resorbing, her horseness
dominant now and growing. She was no longer like her father,
but more and more mere mare. Her words tumbled together
and gave way to a neigh, higher with now and again
emphatic and spirited snorts as punctuation. Her arms
were forelegs, and wrists, fetlocks; her nails came together and
          thickened
to hoofs; her mouth enlarged; her neck stretched out; and her
          gown's
train turned into a tail as her hair became a mane.
And as her form was changed, so was her name changed also
from that day on to Euippe, which signifies "goodly mare."   660
Chiron, the half-divine son of Philyra, wept
to see what had happened, and understood that his dear daughter's
equine regression implied the end of his line and kind,
and the closing off of the dream of the unity of life,
or at the least the end of the ancient horse cult. He despaired
on his own account, remembering what she had prophesied,
but also for a world that was sadly diminished now,
and he called on Apollo for help, in the hope that the powerful
          god

might be disposed to continue his favor, but no reply
came from the lord of Delphi, who either could not defy   670
the power of Jove's decree, or was elsewhere and otherwise
occupied at the moment. In fact, the god was away
in Elis, where he was busy pretending to be a cowherd
with one of those shaggy cloaks, a rustic wooden staff,
and even a syrinx of seven properly tuned reeds.
He was playing a melancholy song and thinking of love
and how, for all its promise of bliss, it often produces
misery—while his herd was wandering off to other
pastures, grazing its way from Messenia to Pylos,
where the son of Jove and Maia, clever Mercury, took   680
the cattle and hid them away in a shady grove. No one
had seen him do this underhanded thing but Battus,
an old codger whose job was to look after Neleus' splendid
pedigreed mares. The god contrived to ensure the fellow's
silence with a small—or not such a small—present.
"Keep what you've seen to yourself," he said, "and also this
          handsome
cow, which is yours. If anyone asks for a missing herd,
your answer is silence, right? And a blank look, which shouldn't
be hard for you to arrange? A deal?" Battus agreed
and pointed to a rock by the road. "I am as mute as that   690
stone," he promised, accepting the cow. And Mercury left,
but then, not altogether convinced of the other's good faith,
returned in a different guise, and to speak in another accent
and test the man. "I say, I seem to have lost some cows.
You haven't noticed a herd that came wandering by here, have
          you?"
There wasn't a yes or no, so Mercury pushed him a little.
"There's something in it for you. You help me find that herd,
which is only the decent and right thing for a person to do,
and you can pick out a bull and a cow to match. How's that?
Sporting? Fair? Have you seen those cattle of mine?" The payoff   700
was twice as good as before, and Battus nodded and pointed.
"They're down in that bottom land," he said. And Mercury
          laughed.
"Villain! Crook! You're worse than I am. Bought and paid for,
but no damned good, as I thought from the first moment I
          saw you."
And he looked at that stone by the road Battus had promised to
          match
in reticence, and made that promise good by transforming

the man abruptly to flint, which is sometimes used as a touchstone
to verify the claims of men one may not trust
that what they offer for sale is, as they warrant, gold.

　　Mercury then took off and alit in the port of Munychia,　　710
that region Minerva favors, and the people there give thanks
with festivals in her honor. The wingèd god looked down
to see the parade of maidens on the way back from her temple,
where they had brought their baskets covered with flowers and
　　　　filled
with ritual gifts. In a graceful spiraling swoop, Mercury
descended. Much as a kite or falcon turns and hovers
in the hope of food as he watches the priests about to perform
a sacrifice where there's promise of the guts they'll be discarding,
so did Mercury hover around that Athenian hill
waiting for his moment and all but licking his lips　　　　720
at the gorgeousness below him. In the sky at early dusk,
the evening star is brighter than any other, but then
the Moon comes up, and it and the others fade away;
by so much did the lovely Herse outshine her companions.
Imagine one of those missiles they shoot from a Balearic
sling, where the lead heats up as it flies through the clouds. It lands
burning hot from the friction—so was Mercury heated
high in that balmy air, stricken, done in by her beauty.
Startled, he came to earth, considered some sort of disguise,
but then decided not. He'd trust to his own handsome　　　730
looks, perhaps from a sense of fair play, or the simple
wish to be loved for his true self. Nonetheless, he smoothed
his hair with his palms and adjusted his robes to hang and flow
as well as they could to show off their rippling gold border.
He took his elegant wand and emblem that brings but can also
prevent sleep, or rather, say, he sported it, wore it
as officers sometimes wear their swagger sticks. And he scuffed
the dust from the magic sandals that shod his slender feet
so as not to mar the fine first impression he wanted to make.
Inside the house, in rooms inlaid with tortoise shell　　　740
and pieces of ivory carving, the daughters of Cecrops lived:
on the right, Pandrosos; on the other side, Aglauros; and Herse,
in the room between. Aglauros, the first to see the handsome
figure approaching, asked his name, his line, and his business.
"I am the son of Jupiter, messenger of the gods.
I am here for the sake of love. Be you faithful and true
to your sister, and you shall become an adored aunt to my
　　　　children.

I have come for Herse," he said with a smile. Hearing
the god, her heart sank as his sentence reached its conclusion,
and envy filled her being. It was just as it had been before   750
when she'd flouted Minerva's command and opened the osier box
to look inside. The wicked girl demanded gold,
a bribe for her help, and ordered him meanwhile to begone.
       Aglauros was not unobserved. Minerva saw and heard
and remembered how this was the girl who had disobeyed her
          before.
Was this the way to behave? Would that brazen girl succeed,
get Mercury's gold, be rich, and have as a brother-in-law
one of the gods? To fix that hussy's wagon, the goddess
went down to the cave of Envy, a dismal place in a dank
valley where no breeze blows away the lingering stench   760
of gore, no fire burns, and no light can penetrate
the thick miasma that clings to the place. She appeared at the door
but could not bring herself to enter the foul hovel.
She pounded the butt of her spear on the door, which opened.
       There stood
Envy gobbling vipers' flesh, to nourish her own
venom. Minerva felt her bile suddenly rising,
turned away, took a breath. The other rose and, leaving
the nasty mess behind her, came to greet her guest
with slow and grudging steps. She beheld the glorious goddess,
and groaned in distress at her beauty, frowning as if in pain.   770
She sighed a weary sigh and rudely glared at Minerva.
Her face is pale and drawn, her body shriveled and bent.
Her eyes are crossed, and the few teeth she has left are greenish
as if with mold. Her skin is covered with sores, some crusted
with scabs, and others fresh and running. Venomous spittle
drips from her glistening lips, which gleam whenever she
          smiles—
a rare event that is prompted by others' pains and troubles.
It is said that she never sleeps but lies there calculating
the triumphs of those she detests, the better to gnaw on the bitter
marrowbone of spite, for the only satisfaction   780
she has ever learned to take from the world's array of treasures.
Minerva stared at this creature, suppressed her distaste, and said,
"Sting with your poison Aglauros, one of the daughters of
          Cecrops.
You will not, I warrant, find her immune to your deadly venom.
This, I command you." She turned and fled the creature's
          presence,

banging her spear on the ground and bounding into the air.
　　The crone mutters in rage at somebody else's triumph
and the part she must play in this business. She takes up her
　　　　thorny stick
and puts on her cloak of murk to set forth on her errand.
The grass withers wherever she steps, and the flowers die　　　790
as she passes by. The trees shudder as if in a storm,
and wherever she goes she infects houses, villages, nations,
with a morbid taint. At length she approaches the city of Athens,
that center of wealth and culture, peace and good fortune,
　　　　and weeps
at the sight of so many people who have no cause for tears.
She ascends to the palace, enters the room of Princess Aglauros,
and does what the goddess commanded, touching the girl's bosom
with a razor-sharp fingernail. In the girl's breast there are thorns
that grow and fill her heart with their deadly spikes. Now Envy
exhales her poison into the young girl's nostrils, which quiver　　　800
as the venom enters her bloodstream and seeps into her marrow.
Then, as the capstone to all her mischievous work, she enlists
the girl's own imagination, letting her think
of her sister, happy, adored by the god and revered by mortals,
powerful, rich, fulfilled, blessed . . . and she hates it, hates it,
knowing it isn't her own good fortune but somebody else's.
She wastes away like a person in whom there's a cancer growing,
gnawing away from inside. She is haggard. Her skin is clammy,
as if she were not quite there to receive the warmth of the Sun's
golden rays. She's consumed by jealousy of her sister's　　　810
happy condition and burns, as a pile of weeds can burn,
hot but without any visible flame. She longs to die
so as not to have to see such affronting displays of delight
as her sister's life provides. She thinks of what she can do
to stop the torment, prevent the union. . . . Tell their father?
But that's no good. She is crazed, can't think of anything else,
and sits herself down at the threshold to object, indeed to become
an immovable object. She says she will never move, and the god
assents and holds out his wand. The door behind her flies open.
Aglauros tries to get up, but cannot. Her knees are stiff,　　　820
and her body is suddenly heavy. Her muscles don't work:
　　　　her mind
issues commands that the limbs no longer obey. Her hands
and feet are cold, and her flesh is suddenly bloodless as clay.
Her breath is shallow, labored, and her heartbeat, irregular.
　　　　Speech

is beyond her absolutely—she can't think of words anymore,
or even make simple noises by which to express her fear
as the clay of her flesh sets to brick, hardens to rock.
Her neck has gone to stone, and her face is stony. . . . Not white
marble but black as granite, stained by her mind and soul.

  She had no way of knowing the god was called away, flew up   830
to heaven to answer his father's summons and do his bidding.
Jove does not confide the reason for this commission,
but orders his son to proceed to Sidon, way to the East.
Mercury knows where it is. "Go then," the lord of Olympus
instructs. "You will find on a hillside a herd of cattle grazing,
rare and wonderful cattle, the king's, in fact. Drive them
down to the shore where a spit of land extends to make
a cove." He did not have to specify further where
the king's daughter took the air with her maidens-in-waiting.
But that was the place and purpose he had in mind, that young   840
and unbearably beautiful girl he had seen. The grandeur of gods
is all very well but makes for awkwardnesses in love.
The delicate (or sometimes indelicate) business is further
muddled—as Jupiter's lessons had so often demonstrated.
The august god therefore put down his lightning-bolt
trident and stowed away the impressive paraphernalia
of power, assuming instead a different and most unlikely
guise, getting himself to look, for the nonce, . . . like a bull,
handsome as bulls go, but one of the herd. He lowed
like all the rest as he grazed, nibbling delicate morsels   850
of grass. He was snowy white, dazzling, and his strength
was eloquent in the carved musculature of his neck
and shoulders. A noble dewlap hung down under his chin,
and the elegant twist of his horns suggested some mannerist artist
had carved them as his idea of what might adorn a bull.
His expression was altogether gentle and tranquil. Agenor's
daughter Europa noticed—could not help it—the striking
creature and felt drawn to hold out a timorous hand.
Frightened, of course, by his size and presence, she nonetheless
was fascinated. She offered clover for him to nibble   860
and felt the enormous lips that nuzzled her open palm.
The bull frisks like a calf on the sand, rolls on his back,
allows her to pat him and deck his horns with the blossoms she's
      braided
in garlands. It is a dance, their small steps forming a pattern
that seems in retrospect fated, her little forays, his responses,
the way she is bolder and clasps with delicate arms his huge

neck, which is yet so soft and tame. . . . She lolls on his flank,
and thrills to the silky steel of a power she's never imagined,
exhilarating and making it hard to breathe for her laughter—
or whatever it is that bubbles up from the depths of her spirit.   870
She climbs on the bull's back, and he ambles gently along,
taking the girl into shallow water and then farther out,
and faster, and, terrified now, she looks way back at the distant
shoreline and holds on tight to the great beast's horn as the wind,
freshening, whips her tunic, which streams into pennants
        behind her.

BOOK III

At Crete, he came ashore, wading out of the surf
not as a bull any longer, but naked, himself, a god!
Back in Sidon, King Agenor had no idea
what had become of his daughter and ordered his son Cadmus
to go in search of his lost sister—and not to return
without her. So crazed with grief was the king that no one
    could say
whether he was a doting father or cruel beyond
belief. Surely Cadmus could not, who traveled the world
trying to learn details of Jupiter's love life, a daunting
task. At length he admitted defeat and became an exile,   10
hating his father's anger and land, and now ready to settle
wherever the god's whim might dictate. Therefore he went
to a sacred cave in Castalia, close to Phocis, to seek
the oracle's suggestion. There Phoebus gave him this answer:
"Where you will meet a heifer that never has worn the yoke
or drawn the crooked blade of the plow, but ambles free,
there you will go and follow wherever she leads until
she pauses to graze and lies down to rest. That will be the place
to build your city, which you shall name, after the heifer:
Boeotia." Thus he spoke, and Cadmus left the grotto   20
to blink in the midday glare and rub his eyes . . . for there
a heifer ambled by as the god had specified.
Her neck bore no sign of a yoke or tether. He offered thanks
to the heavens and followed the beast wherever she wanted to go,
this way and that, as the vegetation and lay of the land
prompted, across the fords of Cephisus, over the fields
of Panope, where she paused, lifted her head toward the sky,
bellowed, and then sank down into the succulent grass.
Cadmus also knelt and kissed the ground with his lips,
greeting the mountains and plains that had signified thus their
    welcome.   30
    In gratitude for the gods' gift, he resolves to offer

appropriate thanks and tells his companions to search out a spring
with the waters of which they may offer libations according
    to pious
custom. There, in a grove of the virgin forest no axe
has ever touched, they notice a cave covered with vines,
dense with greenery, rich in that promising loamy smell.
It is, indeed, a spring that bubbles up in a grotto
that is almost like a shrine beneath its natural arch.
This breathlessly tranquil place, they soon discover, is home
to a mighty reptile sacred to Mars, a fearsome creature   40
with a gaudy crest on its head, eyes that gleam in the darkness,
and a body that coils on itself like the twined roots of a banyan.
Its forked tongue flashes out in the gloom, and its mouth gapes
to show an astounding array of serried and poisonous fangs.
The Phoenician adventurers had lowered their buckets into
the spring, and the clank of the metal had roused this drowsing
    monster.
It moved, yawned, flicked its tongue, and hissed, chilling
their blood in horror, freezing their muscles and nerves, which
    at once
surrendered, for nothing was clearer than that they had met their
    death.
In a merciful trance they watch as the creature writhes and coils,   50
rears and prepares to strike. It's as high as a fair-sized tree,
and mortality is its crop. It poses, looms for an instant,
and then it moves, a violent blur with a spoor of gore
of those it has bitten, those it has crushed in its powerful coils,
and those whom the venomous droplets of its exhalations have
    slain.
    Cadmus, growing impatient, wonders where they have gone
and why they are taking so long. He takes up his lion-skin
shield, his javelin, and a spear with its head of iron forged
and then honed—but the rarest and best weapon of any
hero is valor, and this he has in abundance, and needs it,   60
for quickly he finds the wood, the grotto, the corpses, and then
that serpent or lizard, or dragon, which now is sunning itself
on the broken bodies, its trophies and also its feast. He sees
how it licks their blood with a greedy tongue, laps it like nectar,
and he groans aloud and swears to avenge his friends or else
join them there where they lie on the bloody ground. In rage,
he seizes a stone, a massive boulder really, hefts it,
and heaves it toward the monster. It lands with such a thud
as one hears on battlement walls of a city that's under siege,

and the soldiers in towers quake at the sound of the mangonels   70
and then inspect for damage. The serpent is not even bruised,
those scales on its skin are hard as armor plate. Now Cadmus
takes his javelin, hurls it, strikes in one of the folds
where the scales meet, and pierces its point deep in the side
of the flailing dragon. Mad with pain, it writhes, bites
at the javelin shaft, and tears it out, but leaves the point
still in its flesh, embedded and hurting. In fury, the creature
hisses and spits a spray of deadly froth, which flecks
its jaws and spatters out, tainting the air around it.
The earth resounds as the creature heaves, thrashes, coils,   80
and suddenly stretches out like the spring of some deadly
          machine,
except that it's huge and turns tall trees in the wood to toys,
which it knocks down in its frenzy, sidewinding in pain
and hate. Cadmus retreats, astonished. The serpent charges,
its scales resounding upon the taut lion skin of his shield.
Cadmus holds out his spear, and the serpent snaps at it, bites
but in vain, and there's purple blood gushing out on the grass.
The serpent now gives way, and Cadmus advances, pressing
whatever advantage that spearpoint in the monster's palate can
          give him,
until there's a trunk of a tree, and the serpent can't retreat further,   90
but the iron spearpoint continues, going through flesh now and
          pinning
the beast by his throat to the trunk. It writhes and lashes. The tree
waves in the air like the frond of some delicate river reed,
and the wood groans, or is it the serpent? But then they are still,
the tree, the dead beast, and the man, who stands there breathing
hard and not quite sure it's over. From thin air he hears
a voice that tells him: "Cadmus, why do you stand there gloating?
You shall be that one day, a serpent for men to gaze on."
His hackles rise in terror, and the blood drains from his cheeks
at the very thought. He looks down in despair and loathing,
          but then   100
Minerva, his faithful protectress, descends from the air to
          help him.
She tells him to plow the earth and sow it with dragon's teeth,
which will grow up into men. He can't understand but dare not
disobey the goddess and does as he's bidden. A farmer,
he puts in his curious planting, and then—miraculous!—watches
as the furrows begin to quiver and tiny spearpoints emerge

like the first leaves of a crop coming out of the ground; then
    helmets,
with colored plumes that wave in the gentle breeze; then heads
and shoulders of men in arms, and all with the weapons of war.
Just as on our feast days, when we go to the theater and see   110
the curtain that hangs across the stage and is taken down
for the action, we see first heads, then shoulders, torsos, and legs,
so did Cadmus watch as these characters little by little
appeared before him. Friends or enemies, were they? Uncertain,
he drew his sword to prepare for the worst, but one of them
    told him,
"Keep your distance. Our quarrels have nothing to do with you."
Turning away, he raised his sword and then, with a mighty
blow to the man beside him, sliced his head in two,
whereupon a bloodied javelin point abruptly
bloomed out of his chest, the result of someone's stroke   120
from behind. The man with the javelin heaved a satisfied sigh
that became a fearsome râle as he felt a spearpoint ending
his own brief life. They were all savage and crazed as they hacked
this way and that in a frenzy that littered the ground with corpses.
Here and there a mortally wounded soldier twitched
and quivered or beat with a weakening fist on his mother, the
    earth,
which welcomed them gravely home—all but the last five.
Echion, one of these, Minerva commanded to stop,
drop his weapons, declare a truce, and arrange a peace.
Cadmus and this quintet should establish the city Apollo   130
had by his oracle promised. And this was the founding of Thebes.
    A happy man you might call him, even in exile: he married
Harmonia, daughter of Mars and Venus, a noble and lovely
wife who bore him children, pledges of love and the gods'
benevolence, and, in time, grandsons and granddaughters, too.
Still, one can never be sure, and a man's life is at risk
even until the end (as Cadmus would later learn).
But Actaeon, a grandson of Cadmus, first came to grief, and
    the story
was dreadful for him to hear of what had become of his child's
child. . . . Even we who recite the marvel must feel some small   140
frisson of his dread as the words sunk in of the dogs
that turned on their master, tore him limb from limb, and lapped
his pouring blood. It was not his or anyone's fault
but one of those terrible things that simply happens. The youth,

having done well on the hunt, dismissed his companions, and
    sent them
home again with their game, anticipating a feast.
The men, of course, obeyed, and Actaeon, left alone,
sought refuge from the midday heat, and perhaps a drink
of spring water. His quest brought him into a grove
of cypress and pine, a magical place we call Gargaphie,   150
a haunt Diana herself was fond of, to take her ease
after her own hunts. It looked like a place a clever
gardener might have designed, but this was Nature's own
extravagance, the arches of stone, the grotto, the brook
as pleasingly disposed as if by some master craftsman.
The brook emptied into a small protected pond the goddess
from time to time would grace with a quick, refreshing plunge.
And there she is, having given her paraphernalia over
to her armor bearer to hold, the bow, quiver, and spear.
To another companion she hands her tunic. A third receives   160
her sturdy sandals. A fourth, Crocale, repairs her coiffure,
binding into a knot those tresses the exercise
of the chase has disarranged, and the other nymphs attend her,
Hyale, Rhanis, Psecas, Nephele, and Phiale,
scooping up the cool water in ewers to sluice
over their mistress' body as she stands, calf-deep in the pool,
gracefully posed, indeed heartbreakingly gorgeous. Actaeon,
having by fate or merely chance and misadventure
come to that grotto, and at that particular moment, stands there
astonished, enraptured by what he sees, as the water beads   170
like diamonds to deck the breasts of the goddess. The naked
    nymphs
have seen him, are horrified, and throng about their mistress
to hide her body with theirs (or perhaps the youth from Diana's
wrath?), but it's too late. The goddess has noticed him, stands
tall and proud, advances in the dazzled young man's direction.
Without her quiver of arrows, she makes do with splashing
    his head
with water she kicks in his direction in playful anger—
or is it real? He has no idea! His wits have left him.
Utterly dumb, he can barely comprehend her words
as she speaks to him: "Now, that you've seen a naked goddess, go 180
and tell whomever you will, or whomever you can. . . ." On
    his head,
where the water drops landed, his horns are already sprouting out
in a rack of impressive antlers that spread out from the crowns

of mature stags. His ears are sharpening into pointed
excrescences, while his hands are pointing, becoming hoofs,
and his arms are turning to forelegs. His skin is a hide, and
    his heart
is cold with terror. He looks down into the water's surface,
sees what he has become, then turns in panic and runs
faster than he has ever been able to run. He attempts
to vent his rage at what's happened, give voice to his woe,
    but words   190
fail, have fled. . . . He has no more, can only groan
and weep, and feel the tears run down his cheeks or muzzle.
He startles and keeps on running. . . . But where? To the palace,
    or woods?
He pauses, stops as if snared in the net of his fear and shame,
and sees his familiar pack of hunting dogs approaching—
Blackie* and Swiftie first, with Scarfer and Oryx close
behind them. (Oryx, bred in Crete, runs like an oryx,
or maybe the idea was that it and its kind could bring down
one of those rare gazelles.) There is also Tenzing, the climber,
and Mauler, who named himself by what he once did to a fawn.   200
Stormy comes next with Nimrod, and then there are darting
    Birdie
and Snark (who'd been given that name in the hope he'd turn
    out to be
an aggressive hunter). Woody comes bounding along, the noble
mastiff whose wounds are not yet healed where a boar has
    gored her
with savage tusks. The wolf-dog, Valley Girl, with her two
pups, as yet unnamed; Old Shep; and Julius Seizer,
thin in the flanks but strong and never seeming to tire;
and Munson (called that because it seems able to catch almost

---

*Ovid gives the dogs' names in Latinized Greek: they are, in order, Melampus
(i.e., Blackfoot), Ichnobates (Trail-follower), Pamphagus (Omnivore), Dorceus
(Gazelle), Oribasos (Mountain-ranger), Nebrophonos (Fawn-slayer), Theron (Hur-
ricane), Laelaps (Hunter), Pterelas (Winged), Agre (Hunter), Hylaeus (Wood-
creature), Nape (Glen), Poemenis (Shepherd), Harpyia (Seizer), Ladon (Catcher),
Dromas (Racer), Canache (Gnasher), Sticte (Spot), Tigris (Tigress), Alce (Strength),
Leucon (White), Asbolos (Sooty), Lacon (Spartan), Aëllo (Whirlwind), Thöos
(Swift), Lycisce (Wolf), Cyprius (Cyprian), Harpalos (Grasper), Melaneus (Blackie),
Lachne (Shaggy), Labros (Fury), Agriodus (White-tooth), Hylactor (Barker), and,
mentioned a few lines later, Melanchaetes (Black-haired), Theridamas (Beast-killer),
and Oresitrophos (Mountaineer). I have tried to suggest an equivalent series of plau-
sible dog names.

anything); and Numbers (this one's a runner) follow
in impressive phalanx. Then Gnasher and Slasher come tearing by,   210
and, just behind, Damned Spot (who always wants to go out).
These are splendid dogs, each one a trusted companion.
There are Tigris, Brutus, Blondie, Smokey, and Whirl-away;
there are Harpy, and Schwartz (another black dog with a white
           blaze
on his forehead) and Yipper and Gipper, the crossbred pair from a
           Cretan
dog and a Cyprian sight-hound bitch; there is Mad Max,
who is not quite reliably tame, and his litter-mate White Fang.
This enormous pack has roamed these woods and highlands
           for years,
the best collection of hunting dogs in the world, and Actaeon
runs for his life, fleeing his old and adoring friends,   220
sprinting on rocky ground that isn't likely to hold
much of a scent, or splashing upstream and then crossing back
the way he came to try to confuse the leaders, who know
all the tricks of the wiliest quarry. He's spent his life
teaching these dogs their art, which he realizes will be
the death of him now. He wants to turn back, stand, and call out
to let them all know: "I am Actaeon, your master!
You recognize my voice!" But there is no voice, and words
are gone, have abandoned his spirit, and the woods are loud with
           the baying
of those excellent, relentless, and splendid—those dreadful—dogs. 230
They are closing, are on him. The first, Ebony, leaps on his back,
bites, and holds on; and Butcher is there, sinking his fangs
into the meat of his haunch. It's agony. He feels another
searing pain as Montagnard mounts to his shoulder and mauls him
pitilessly. These three had taken a kind of shortcut,
were ahead of the pack, but they held him as the other dogs
           approached,
belling and barking, to bury their teeth in the gory flesh.
He groans aloud with a sound no deer has ever produced.
It fills the hills and valleys, which echo with grief and the pain
of how things are. He is down, his legs having given way,   240
and he looks with shock and love at his best friends in the world,
which are turning back to look for their master, him whom
           they love
and would willingly die for, even as he knows he's going to die.
They're barking now, their signal for him to come and dispatch

the beast they've brought down. They're puzzled that he is not
     here, as he
is puzzled himself to be here in this terrible guise, and they harry
and wound him further and even to death in Diana's wrath,
of which they are unaware. At last, she is pacified.
    In the corridors of the heavenly buildings, talk was divided:
some suggested her rage and the punishment she had demanded   250
had been perhaps excessive; others maintained the fairness
of what she caused to happen, considering what he had done.
The debate went this way and that among the great gods, but Juno
remained aloof, was strangely noncommittal, delighted
that something appalling had happened to a member of that house
she so much despised—for Europa's brother Cadmus was
     grandsire
to poor Actaeon, which made the goddess happy indeed.
It was, as a matter of fact, a trying time for Juno,
her latest burden being that Semele, too, was pregnant,
a daughter of Cadmus, gravid with the seed of Jove. Her husband,   260
she knew, was out of control, but the hope remained that he
might attempt on his own to restrain and govern his errant lusts
if she could inspire some fear of the consequence of his action
and appeal to the pity he ought to feel for some of these women
whom she could cause to suffer extravagantly—as now.
It wasn't just the affair, but that it had had a result,
and there would be yet another heir. The wife and sister
of Jove could not abide this affront, this condescension
of his that diminished herself. This mortal was overreaching,
trusted too much in her beauty and what it might merit, and Juno   270
would teach her a lesson. Her knuckles were white on the
     diamond-studded
scepter she carried, her emblem of rank and power, a weapon
not altogether tamed to a symbol. She raised it high
and swore that she would extract an intricate, elegant, swift,
and perfectly just retribution. Jove would be made to destroy
this upstart himself in a reassertion of cosmic order.
    Resolved, she arose and put on a shimmering saffron cloud,
descended to earth, and at Semele's doorstep put on a new guise—
that of an aged beldam with wrinkled skin and white hair,
tottering, bent, and squeaky of voice—the perfect double   280
of Beroë, Semele's nurse and companion from Epidaurus.
She seated herself and rambled, gossiping, just like the nurse,
doing the voice and the gestures, enjoying the turn, and arriving

at last at the proper business: "He says he's a god, but that story
is easy enough to tell. One ought to have something substantial
as proof of so grand a claim. The world is crowded with
        tricksters,
mountebanks, and seducers who'll think up their far-fetched
        stories
to get what they're after. If I were you, I should ask him—force
        him—
to show me his heavenly self and come to you as he is
when he puts on his glory to visit the queen of heaven's chamber." 290
        Along with the tiny doubt the goddess had planted, the girl
was curious, even excited, as she thought about that glory,
and she asked her lover to grant her a favor. He smiled, nodded,
and promised whatever she wanted. By the Styx, he swore he
        would grant it.
Happy, beaming, she asked him to be as he was with Juno,
to come to her just as he came to the goddess. Jupiter groaned
as her words formed themselves and flew like deadly weapons
he could see as they darkened the air. Compelled by his sacred oath,
he ascended to heaven, put on his regalia of lightning and thunder,
mists and typhoons . . . the least impressive, the oldest, the
        mildest.   300
The huge bolts of the kind he'd used when he'd battled Typhoeus
he left untouched, and took up the miniatures, the toys,
the harmless flashes of summer lightning he sometimes employed
to signal those who needed some minatory prompting—
and all the time he knew it was hopeless, hopeless. In mourning
for what was about to happen, he returned to the palace of
        Cadmus,
entered Semele's room, and came to her bed. Her body,
under that heat and weight and energy, sizzled, shrank,
and was vaporized. But the god, at the last instant, had seized
the unborn child from her womb and inserted it into his thigh,   310
where he could keep it safe as it grew to term. At last,
when the child was born—a boy, the infant god Bacchus—
Jove gave it over to Ino, his mother's sister, to rear.
She in turn entrusted the baby to Nysa's nymphs,
who hid him away in a cave, where they gave him milk to drink.
        In heaven, peace had returned, or at least a truce, and Jove,
relaxing one evening and drinking a bit more wine than he
        should have,
got into one of those odd discussions—this one with Juno,
a flight of fancy, really, that turned into earnest debate:

Resolved: that the pleasure women take from the sexual act   320
is greater than that of men. Not so, his wife insisted.
And how would one know? To whom could one look for such
    expertise?
There was, of course, Tiresias—impartial, or one who had taken
both parts, as it were. Once, with a blow of his staff,
he had interfered with a pair of copulating serpents
he'd found on the road—in an act of such impious rashness
that he had been changed at once from man into woman, and lived
for seven years in that form. In the eighth, she encountered again
that same pair of serpents, to whom she addressed herself
with awe: "Since you have this magical power, to change the
    gender   330
of one who strikes you, I do so again." With a ritualistic
tap she struck them again, and was changed at once to a male,
as he had been before. To him, who had been a her,
the gods put their dispute. When their judge answered, "Women
have more pleasure, by far," Juno was much displeased,
and blinded him on the spot. Jupiter could not undo
her cruel deed but gave in recompense the rare
gift of second sight, by which one can know the future.
    Quickly, the seer's fame spread through Boeotian towns
and beyond, as people came to consult him. One of the first   340
was Liriope, the nymph, who once had bathed in the river
where Cesiphus, its god, had seized her in his embrace,
held her in his current, and ravished her. In time,
the nymph brought forth a son, an amazingly pretty boy,
whom she named Narcissus. For this, her baby, she came to
    inquire
of the blind seer how he would live, and what fullness of years
he might expect. The prophet replied: "He will live long,
if he does not know himself." Absurd? Or a mystery? No one
could understand or explain what his answer meant. But the truth
came out in its own good time, in his life and peculiar death   350
in the sixteenth year of his age. No longer a boy, not yet
a man, he was truly gorgeous. He had a perfection that stopped
the hearts of tender maidens and handsome young men, but none
who yearned for him was favored, or even noticed. His pride
was icy; his heart, cold. His obliviousness was complete
until, one day, when he was out in the woods hunting deer,
calling out to scare them and drive them into his nets,
and Echo heard him. A nymph, she was singular in her habits,
could not initiate speech, but could not refrain from an answer

when someone else addressed her. Up to that time, she lived   360
not as a disembodied voice, but her conversation
was limited to repeating the last words she had heard.
This was a punishment Juno had visited on her because
of what the nymph had done on several occasions when Juno
had come in search of her errant husband, and Echo waylaid her,
detained her in clever banter, and gave the other nymphs
the time to get away clean. Jupiter, always alone,
would express his delight in this visit from Juno—who soon
          caught on
and said to the garrulous vixen, " Your tongue has tricked me
          enough.
Your powers of speech will diminish to the repetition of short   370
phrases." And from that moment, Echo could merely echo
the tail end of what she'd heard. Now having seen Narcissus,
she was struck by his beauty, enamored, followed along
          behind him,
going from bush to bush, eager for yet a closer
look at this marvelous creature. The closer she came, the more
ardently she burned, as a torch with its coating of sulfur
will burst into flame from another torch that is held nearby.
She longs to come closer, to speak, to accost him with winning
          words,
but what can she say? Her curse prevents her from speaking first.
Her tongue is meat in her mouth, until the charm of his own   380
voice can break the spell. And now that he's separated
from his friends and companions, he calls into the underbrush,
"Is anyone here?" and she answers in joy and with passion,
          "Here."
He looks around but sees no one. "Come!" he calls, and she
          answers,
in the height of rapture, "Come!" Once more he looks and
          calls out,
"Why do you hide?" and she chides him, or teases, and answers,
          " You hide."
He thinks it's a game and invites, "Now let us meet," and she
          answers
with the words she has yearned to pronounce: "Let us meet." She
          appears,
approaches, and tries to embrace him, throwing her arms
          around his
neck, but he flees as he always has. "Keep away! I'd sooner   390
die than have you touch me." Stricken, what can she say

but, "Touch me, touch me!" before she retreats into the woods
she has lived in all her life, to hide her shame in the shadows
of leafy dells and dark caves? She pines, dwindles away,
grows gaunt in her grief, and her body wastes away to nothing.
Only bare bones and her voice are left, until, after a time,
those delicate bones become stone, and there's nothing but pure
   plaint
that hangs ashamed in the air of the woods and mountainsides.
  All unaware, Narcissus went his blithe way, behaving
in just this manner to all, nymphs of the woods and water,   400
and of mountains, too, not to mention the human females and
   males,
who longed for his impossible beauty. One such rejected
gallant protested and prayed to the heavens to grant Narcissus
the pains of his unrequited ardor. Let him know how it feels
to yearn without hope. And one of the serious goddesses heard
   him,
Nemesis, the righteous, who granted this just supplication.
There was a pond, a small but perfect body of water
way off in a distant part of the wood, where no shepherds came,
nor goatherds with their flocks. Its surface was burnished silver,
and grass and waving reeds framed it and kept the winds   410
from touching its pristine surface. To this unearthly spot
Narcissus came one day, hot from the chase and tired,
and with an enormous thirst, which he knelt down to slake . . .
   but another
thirst is born, an impossible longing for what he sees
reflected in the water's surface. That face, that body,
he adores, loves, yearns for with all his heart. He is smitten
utterly, and he feels what the goddess has in her justice
visited on him to feel. He knows it is hopeless, knows
it is only his own reflection, his own face looking down,
but there it is, looking up, handsome beyond belief,   420
with a negligent saucy look that invites as it also repels
and fascinates. He is lost, as motionless now as a marble
statue. But is there a statue as perfect in form and proportion,
as precise in its execution, as subtle in how it is colored,
the way that blush of the cheek gives way to the whiter flesh tone
of jaw and neck? He is sunk in the pond, in the rapture, adores
himself, is adored to be so adored. He lowers his head
and tries to kiss the face, reaches his hands to embrace
the elusive other, the self, the object to which he is subject
forever. It shimmers away, coy, elusive, mocking . . .   430

as he has mocked so many, so often. He cannot desist,
cannot resist. He is crazed, knows it, and tells himself:
"Get up, turn away, forget it. What you seek, you have. It's
          merely
an image, nothing. The face you see in the pond will be gone
the moment you leave. . . ." But that thought is unendurable,
          awful,
as if he had contemplated a murder. He tries again,
reasoning with himself that he can come back any time,
look in the pond, and find that face looking up from the water.
It will be waiting for him—but the thought of its faithful patience
melts his heart. He is ruined and cannot order his muscles   440
to lug his body away. He lies there stretched out in the grass
and gazes down with eyes that are hungry for what they feed on,
thirsty for what they drink. They cannot get their fill,
hating even to yield to the need to blink. He looks up
at the trees that surround the pond and calls out to them to witness.
"Of all the lovers who come here, and there must have been
          many, has ever
a passion appeared before you as desperate as this, as forlorn?
I am deluded and know it, but what love is not delusion?
And ought not love to be judged by its distance from dreary
          reason,
the height of its flight, the depth of its madness? Beside myself,   450
I love what I see and yearn for this face so defiantly close,
so tantalizing. The plane of the pond's surface is hardly
as thick as a wall, or a city gate, but it keeps me away
from the face I love, that upturned and yearning face that
          adores me
as much as I long for him. Our hearts are one, but our bodies
reach out across a chasm as wide and as deep as the world
can offer anywhere." "O my darling, my love, come!
I see you smile when I smile, and weep when I weep, and I see
your invitation, your humor, your grief, your innate
          understanding
of every idle thought that crosses my mind, your immediate   460
sympathy and affection. . . . And in my own heart I can feel
that same quick apperception of your slightest mercurial mood.
I am ashamed of my folly but also proud, defiant,
having found my love despite the laws of man and Nature.
My life is worthless to me, for only in death may I hope
to be rid of this unendurable agony of desire.
I hate the idea that he should perish but know he is willing
as I am to undergo that wonderful *Liebestod*

by which we may be at last united forever. There's no
other or easier way. We'll die with the same last breath."   470
He turned again to the face, the adored, that beloved face
that beckoned and tantalized from beneath the water's surface.
They wept, his tears falling downward, and the other's falling
          upward
to meet and ruffle that cruel plane, and the mirror image
rippled and blurred. Narcissus cried out in torment: "Come back!
Do not desert me. Stay! If I cannot touch, I can look,
as you can gaze up at me in an exquisite consolation.
O my adorable one!" And he crooned and groaned as lovers
have done, and do, and he beat his breast, and tugged at the hem
of his tunic in his distraction. . . . And looked, alas, even better,   480
that flush of emotion providing a special glow to his cheek,
just as an apple has at its moment of perfect ripeness
that ideal tinge of red, or a cluster of grapes beaded
with morning dew seems to pose for a painter's representation.
But he glances down to see how the face has subtly changed,
implausibly but exquisitely improved, and his heart is shattered
anew. He melts, collapses as wax in a candle melts,
or frost on a windowpane as the rays of the Sun assuage
the night's chill. He languishes, pines. . . . He is like a pine
log in the fire that burns and consumes itself. His flush   490
fades to a woeful pallor, and he wastes away to a gaunt
caricature of himself, which Echo might have delighted
to see—except for the pity she felt and the love. "Alas!"
the stricken boy calls out, and Echo gives back his word,
"Alas!" with her own grief descanting on his. He beats
his grieving breast, and the sound repeats in the empty air.
And then, as he weakens further, he calls out a last "Farewell,"
to which she replies with her own heartbreaking, heartbroken
          "Farewell."
His head drooped like a flower, and death at last sealed those eyes
that had undone him or been undone by their owner's beauty.   500
Down in the underworld, where all of us have to go,
he gazed once more at his image in the still pool of the Styx,
and felt the same sweet pangs, while on earth his naiad sisters
wailed and beat their breasts and tore their hair in mourning,
and the dryads joined in the keening and lamentation, and Echo,
faithful and loving, resounded each of their moans and cries.
They prepared his funeral pyre and came to the shore of the pond
to fetch the body . . . but it was gone, replaced by a flower,
with a handsome yellow center surrounded by petals of white.

     This sad story was told and retold and spread the fame   510

of the powers of Tiresias. Everywhere, men and women
did him reverence—all but Echion's cynical son,
Pentheus, who scoffed at the gods and all religion.
He laughed at the old man's predictions and even made fun of his
       blindness,
but the seer seemed almost indifferent as he shook his head and
       warned:
"You may come to envy my blindness, and wish you had
       never seen
those forbidden religious rites that you will one day behold.
I see it plainly, plainer than you, for the day is near
when you shall confront the libertine god, Semele's son,
Bacchus, and you shall refuse to do him his proper honor.   520
Then shall you learn that awe you ought to have known as
       your body
is torn into pieces, scattered, defiling the leaves of the woods
with gouts of your blood. And then will your mother bitterly
       grieve,
and you, in your last moments, curse your intractable blindness,
which refused to see the truth even when someone warned you."
He had not quite concluded, but Pentheus shoved him aside,
yet the words he'd pronounced were true and not so easy to
       sidestep.
       The god comes, and the field resounds with the mad cries
of his devoteés, the men and women, both young and old,
noble and common, mixed together to celebrate   530
the new rites and renew themselves in their Bacchic frenzy.
Pentheus disapproves, is dismayed, even disgusted,
and he calls out, "What is this? Come to your senses, people!
What foolishness is this, you sons of the serpent's teeth!
Have all of you lost your wits? Has reason taken its leave
of every Boeotian mind? Crashing cymbals and skirling
pipes are easy enough to arrange, but it's meaningless, empty,
pointless, and altogether vulgar. Banging those drums
and drinking yourselves to a stupor are not religious acts,
but self-indulgence trying to pass as holiness.   540
What has become of us, a race of warriors, sailors,
and statesmen? We braved the weapons of enemies; we dared
the perils of the seas and came here from Tyre with honored
household gods. Are we now to abandon that and give in
to superstition and excess, enthusiasm? Are we
eager to exchange for the soldier's spear the magic
thyrsus of this *soi-disant* god? Or helmets for flower

power and these absurd garlands? 'Love, not war,'
is an empty and ridiculous slogan; that easy choice
is never on the menu. We are sprung from the brave serpent   550
who died to protect his cave, his home! Will we do less?
Should we go out to meet our enemies holding bouquets?
Thebes is a great city, or used to be. . . . It will fall
more surely from this corruption than any outside attack!
It's a terrible end. Should we not prefer to go down in honor,
in fire and blood, than by this effeminacy and madness?
Are we to yield our city to an unarmed youth, a boy
who claims to be a god and comes with his drums and flowers,
gussied up in cloth of purple and gold and reeking
of eau de cologne? It is nonsense, an insult. I defy him,   560
and say his claims are false—his father is not a god,
and all these decadent rites are a practical joke he's thought up
to see who would go along. Acrisius, King of Argos,
shut his gates in the face of this mountebank. We, too,
can find it in ourselves to defy him and send him away."
Having said this, the king of Thebes gave orders to his
palace guard at once to arrest Bacchus and bring him
in chains to the throne and judgment. His close advisers are
        worried
that this may be a precipitate and dangerous thing to do,
but Pentheus is more determined than ever. A river   570
that flows smooth in its bed, when blocked by some obstruction,
will boil, foam, and roar—and thus it was with the king
of Thebes, all the more insistent in the face of this advice.

      His men return exhausted and covered with blood. The
        master
asks for Bacchus. The guards have not been able to find him
and have taken instead a companion, a priest of his sacred rites,
whom they now deliver up with his hands bound behind him
to Pentheus, who stares in rage at the captive and says:
"You, who are doomed to die an exemplary death, which may
        warn
or at least discourage the others, speak, tell me your name,   580
your lineage, and your country, and explain—if you can—how
        it is
that you came to devote yourself to this strange new cult." The
        other
replies, with his head held high, "I am Acoetes. I come
from Lydia in Asia Minor. My parents were simple
country people, poor—my father fished a little.

There was no farm for him to leave me, only his skills
and the wide and empty sea. To those I was his heir.
I could handle boats and learned to navigate by the stars.
I knew about sails and oars and the winds and the tides. I learned,
as men of the sea are likely to do, the harbors and coves   590
I'd found in the lee of some of the islands. Once on the way
toward Delos I hit some heavy weather and made for Chios.
My men were rowing hard and well in choppy seas.
We landed, beached the boat, and spent the night on shore.
At dawn, I sent some men inland to look for a spring
and fresh water. Meanwhile, I climbed a bluff to see which
way the winds were blowing and how the waves were running.
At length, I called them back to the boat. Opheltes, my mate,
excited, showed me the wonderful thing he'd found in an empty
field—a little boy, a good-looking fellow, who staggered   600
as if he were drunk or sleepy or both. I looked at him hard,
to see if he was healthy. He obviously wasn't normal,
but then I realized what made him special wasn't disease.
He had command, a power you couldn't deny, a presence,
whatever you call it. I knew—was certain of it at once—
that this was a god, a divine being who'd put on a mortal
body for whatever reason. I fell to my knees and begged
his pardon, and also his blessing. 'Allow us to go in peace,'
I asked him. But Dictys, one of my able-bodied seamen,
piped up and interrupted. 'Speak for yourself,' he said.   610
'I'm not praying to him.' Another, Libys, I think,
seconded that, and Melanthus, the lookout, and then Alcimedon,
and Epopeus, who called the time for the rowers, joined in,
jeered, made jokes, and insisted that there might be a ransom
          for him.
I shut them up at once and apologized to the youth.
'I am the captain here! And this is my call, and my order,'
I said, as I stood on the deck. The men might have listened to me,
but Lycabas, a wild man, an exile, a Tuscan killer
I'd taken on for his strength, turned the whole thing around,
rushed me, and knocked me down. I'd have gone overboard   620
if I hadn't been holding a line that saved me. When they applauded
it wasn't for me but for him. Just then the young god roused
from his slumber or drunken stupor, blinked, and asked where
          he was
and who we were, and where we were taking him. This was
          Bacchus
the god, whom Proreus answered—he was my second mate—

that we were a fishing boat crew and would take him wherever he
    liked.
'Naxos,' the god said. 'That's where I live, a pleasant
and friendly place.' And they promised, swore we'd go straight
    there.
It wasn't far, was off to the starboard. I set the mainsail
and helm, but the crew was possessed, and let me know they
    wanted   630
a port tack. They had their own scheme and plan, which did not
include stopping at Naxos. Kidnapping, ransom, wealth,
and mutiny, too, if that was the precondition. I wouldn't
have any part of their scheme and told them that somebody else
would have to take command if they were intent on this crime.
They didn't hesitate for a moment but wrested the helm
out of my hands, adjusted the sails, and veered off to leeward.
After a while, the god looked out over the transom
and, either in fear or to mock the crew with his show of it,
    shouted,
'This isn't what you promised you'd do. I think that Naxos   640
is over there, and we're heading away from it. Why? Sailors!
Where are you going? Why do you all betray me so?
I am a small and defenseless boy! I am your guest.
Where is your sense of decency? Where is your honor?' I knew—
I had known from the very start—that this was a god speaking
and wept at what my men were doing and how they would surely
repent as soon as they understood. I did not consider
what they might suffer for having so gravely insulted a god.
But the tears I shed for them, they mocked, and they laughed
    and joked
as they rowed together as hard as they could in the wrong
    direction.   650
The boat was tearing along, and then—by the god himself,
I swear this is true—it suddenly stopped, stock-still, frozen
as if it were up in dry dock. The men make sail, and they row
as hard as they can, but it does no good, and the boat
    doesn't move.
Sails catching the wind and oars beating the water,
and it doesn't mean a thing. We are fixed there now, and ivy
appears and commences to twine up the oars, and coils to embrace
the spars and the lines of the rigging, and blossoms, and bears
    great clusters
of purple grapes that hang down. The god has similar vines
and bunches of grapes on his head in a sporty wreath. And beasts   660

surround him, tigers, lynxes, panthers, and all kinds of savage
creatures, or not even actual beasts but their forms, their wraiths—
which are even more terrifying. The men begin to wonder
whether their minds have snapped, and some leap overboard
while others—Medon, for instance—notice their bodies
        transforming.
Lycabas looks at Medon and suggests he looks peculiar,
having turned suddenly darker, and having his back hump out
in a weird way, but Medon is staring back at his friend
in dismay as he notes how his friend's jaws are distorted, his nose
hooked, and his skin scaly. Close by, at the oars still, Libys   670
looks down to see that his hands have shrunk, are becoming fins.
This one is growing a tail that ends in a crescent, and that one
is frightened to feel his arms begin to resorb. They leap
in agony over the gunwales and into the water to send up
showers of spray. They dive into the depths and surface,
dive again, and sport like a troupe of dancers or rather
the dolphins they have become, spouting out of their blowholes.
Twenty men were on board, and now only I remained,
cold, alone, afraid, and not knowing what would happen
next, to the boat or to me. The god spoke to me, saying,   680
'There's nothing to fear, my man. Set the course now for Naxos,'
which is what I did, and there I joined in the rites, a believer,
having seen what I had seen, and owing my life to the god."
        Having remained silent all this time, the king
at last addressed the captive: "This is a lovely story,
but only a story, and long and not, after all, persuasive.
You try my patience perhaps to see if my anger may lessen,
but nothing like that has happened. Soldiers, take him away
and stretch him out on the rack as he has stretched out this tall
and fanciful tale. His end should be entertaining enough   690
to make up for these *longeurs* to which we have been subjected."
Hearing this, his men dragged Acoetes down to the dungeon,
and as specialists were preparing their instruments, pincers
        and tongs
and all that bizarre equipment, the doors flew abruptly open.
The heavy fetters that bound the prisoner shattered and fell
from his arms and legs. A marvel and also, clearly, an omen,
but Pentheus wouldn't accept it, refused to believe, and continued
on the road he was sure was right. He himself went to Cithaeron,
that handsome mountain beneath which the cult members
        assembled
to perform their enthusiastic rites and sing their songs.   700

An old war-horse will perk up when it hears the tumult of battle,
flaring its nostrils and rearing in eagerness—so, the king
was roused and his blood was flowing to hear the sounds of
     the cult,
drums and exotic chanting. His fingers tensed and his heart
raced in his righteous anger as he made his way up the slope.
     About halfway up, there's a level place, an open meadow
that's a natural amphitheater surrounded by woods but with clear
vistas that show the mountain's peaks. To this holy place
Pentheus came, the first unbeliever ever to witness
the secret rites. He looked down with a certain curious interest,   710
to which there was added his strong distaste, for he understood
what it would mean to the country if this kind of thing caught on.
This was a challenge to civilization and reason itself.
His own mother was there among the worshipers. She
was the first to notice her son and rush at him in outrage.
She hurled the thyrsus she carried, that staff covered with ivy,
as if it were a spear. She struck him and shouted, "Come,
sisters, a beast has appeared in our field. He must be hunted
down!" They swarmed, a maddened crowd, from every side.
The king is astonished, appalled, and frightened now, and hurt,   720
and he tries to appeal to reason, speaking as if to children
in calm and reassuring tones. But it does no good.
"I am *not* Actaeon," he says to Autonoë, his aunt,
but she hasn't the vaguest idea who Actaeon is, and the sight
of her nephew's trunk—his arms have been pulled now from their
     sockets—
only enrages her further. His mother, Agave, howls
and tosses her streaming hair as she breaks his neck and tears off
his head. She holds it up as a trophy and screams in triumph.
As leaves from a tree in a fall gale are stripped and strewn
in a single night, the bits of his body are scattered about,   730
and Thebes learns to accept the power and truth of the god.
The rites thereafter are thronged as the people come to bow down
in prayer and burn their fragrant incense at Bacchus' shrines.

◫ BOOK IV

Except Alcithoë. She, the daughter of Minyas, refused
to have any truck with these squalid revels, and said that Bacchus
was a fraud, an impostor, and not the son of Jove. Her sisters
shared her distaste for the rites and agreed with her. When the
      priest
called the people to worship, proclaimed that all women servants
should be excused from duty, and prescribed that their mistresses'
      breasts
be covered in furs, that their hair be worn loose and with
      garlands,
and that all must carry a thyrsus, and he threatened the wrath of
      the god
for those who dared disobey, everyone else complied.
All weaving and sewing stopped, incense burned, and women   10
from every quarter invoked the Boisterous God, the Savior,
the Son of the Thunderer, Him Who Was Born Again, and
      the Child
of the Two Mothers. They hailed him as God of Nysa, Heir
of Her Whom the Gods Bore Up, the Shaggy Deity, God
of the Wine Press, Lord of the Vine, the Master of Night Revels,
Chief of Howlers, and other such titles and appellations,
secret and pet names, nicknames, and various periphrases
by which you are known, o Bacchus, all over Greece and
      throughout
the world, loved and adored for your endless youth, the sky's
loveliest being, who rules to the banks of the distant Ganges.   20
Pentheus, you ruined, and Lycurgus, too, the king
of Thrace, where they fight in battles with their double-headed
      axes.
So, you turned those impious sailors to fish and made them
leap into the sea. Your elegant chariot, lynxes
draw with their intricate harness, and frenzied Bacchantes and
      satyrs

follow wherever you go, and Silenus, that aged sot
who totters behind on his walking stick or leans on a mule.
Young men's shouts and women's shrieks echo as drums
beat and cymbals clash and flutes trill to your glory.

"Show us mercy, o god," the women of Thebes implore,   30
all performing the sacred rites as the priest has instructed.
The daughters of Minyas, however, are absent, remain at home,
spinning, weaving, and keeping their servants to all their
     accustomed
household labors. The sisters disapprove of the cult
and its modish, impromptu excess, but are not without their own
traditional pious feelings. One of the mistresses, busy
at her needlepoint frame, suggests they may think of themselves
     at work
in the service of Pallas, a true and familiar goddess. It's nothing
attractive they're missing outside in those rites of the so-called
     god—
but she makes it up to the servants by inviting an entertainment.   40
Why not beguile the time and take turns telling stories?
The sisters agree and suggest that she who proposed it begin.
This she is willing to do, but with what old tale? She considers
which of the many she knows would suit such an occasion,
fantastic, impressive, diverting, and yet with a moral truth
that yields itself in time to the right kind of contemplation—
Dercetis of Babylon, who the Syrians say was changed
into a great fish covered with scales, while her daughter,
Semiramis, became a white dove who ascended
to a perch at the height of the city's battlements? Or better,   50
what was the name of that nymph whose incantations and herbs
changed her admirers into fish and became, herself,
a fish? Or didn't some tale offer an explanation
of how it came to pass that the mulberry tree, which once
bore fruit as white as snow, now has berries as red
as blood because of the stain of its guilt? That's the one they want
to hear, and she's willing to spin it along with the wool on her
     wheel:

"There once was a handsome youth named Pyramus, and next
door lived the loveliest girl in the East, whose parents had called
     her
Thisbe. These two became acquaintances, friends, and, in time,   60
there was love that ought to have led to marriage, but the parents
of both, displeased, wanted something better or richer. . . . Who
     knows?

There were quarrels, scenes, ultimata. The boy and girl were
	forbidden
to see each other, but love is not so easily ordered,
and they burned, both, with a passion they tried to conceal but
	could not.
By occasional looks and nods and other signs, one could let
the other know that the fire, covered over and banked,
was still hot and alive. In the wall between their houses
was a tiny chink in the plasterwork. Nobody knew about it,
but love, they say, will always find a way, and it did—				70
through this aperture, they could whisper words of devotion
and ardor, one on this side of the wall and the other on that,
which kept them apart even though its hole allowed them to
	speak.
They cursed the wall or, worse, implored it, begged it to open
wider to let them kiss, but then, in chagrin, they thanked it
for letting them have at least this gift of conversation.
Each of them kissed the wall, the one on this side and the other
on that, as if its timbers and plaster were bone and flesh.
Morning came. They had parted only some hours before,
but they met again to continue or, no, now to conspire,				80
for there had to be a plan, a way to elude their parents,
the servants, guards, the lot of them, go outside, meet
	somewhere,
and run away together. Where could they meet? At the tomb
of Ninus, a king whom that region worshiped now as a god.
There, in the shade of a large tree, they would find each other.
Agreed, for they knew it well, that tall mulberry tree
growing beside a spring with its snow-white berries. Tonight
they would meet beneath that tree. Of course the hours oozed
like pitch as the Sun dawdled across the enormous sky
in an agonizing extrusion of the indolent afternoon.				90
But even time has its mercy. The Sun went down in the West
as night covered the world. Thisbe opens the door,
looks about, escapes, ventures into darkness,
veiled and not too fast so as not to attract attention.
She reaches the tomb and finds the tree, their rendezvous,
and waits there for her lover. Just then, a lioness comes,
her jaws dripping with gore from a calf she has killed and eaten,
to slake her thirst at that spring. In the moonlight, Thisbe can see
the eyes glowing, the shape of the head and body. . . . She flees,
leaving her cloak behind her. She runs as fast as she can				100
and finds a cave to hide in where she can be safe for a while.

The lioness drinks her fill and starts back to the woods
from which she had come, but she finds that garment still on the
        ground
where it was left and wipes her bloody face on the cloth.
Cats like to be neat. She ambles off to her lair,
and Pyramus comes along, sees the tracks and the cloak
smeared with blood and torn, and knows at once she is dead,
and it's all his fault. On his head is her terrible death. He is crazed
with grief, shock, and self-loathing. He looks around for a lion
to do him the same service, punish him, or relieve him   110
of the awful burden he carries of consciousness and life
without his beloved. But lions are now deplorably absent.
Pyramus picks up the cloak and, weeping the bitterest tears,
kisses the cloth as he recently kissed their friend the wall.
He draws his sword and plunges the blade into his side.
His blood spurts high, like water that sprays from a ruptured pipe,
to dance in the air and mix with what he supposes is hers,
and he dies horribly, blood everywhere now. It has gushed
all over the tree, and its fruit is crimson and running to purple.
        "Now comes Thisbe returning from that cave where she was
        hiding,   120
nervous lest the lion still be around, lest her lover
have come and gone, and she looks, peers, yearning to see
        him. . . .
She wants to tell him of what she saw and how she escaped
the ferocious beast. And there is the tree, but its fruit is different,
somehow darker now. She is mystified. Then she finds
his twitching form. The expiring youth is still in his death throes.
First she is frightened, and then, recognizing him, is appalled,
wails in grief, tears her hair, and beats at her breast
with delicate fists. She kneels. Her tears flow down and into
his huge wound to mix with his blood. She kisses his mouth.   130
She holds him in her arms and asks, in her grief and horror,
'Pyramus, what has happened? How did it happen? Answer
your Thisbe! My dearest, speak!' Hearing her name, he lifts
an all but lifeless head, opens his eyes, and looks
on her beautiful face, then closes them, but this time forever.
        "And now she looks around as people thus distracted
often do, in search of something to which to fasten
her anguished attention, to focus her ache from the universal
down to one particular object. She sees the cloak,
the scabbard of the sword, and understands what happened,   140
what must have taken place—how Pyramus had inferred

from persuasive evidence her violent death and taken
his own precious life. And she is at once transformed
into the noble heroine of the story she is composing,
seeing how it has to go for symmetrical reasons.
He had been brave, and she, who loved him so, could do nothing
less herself than answer his wonderful terrible gesture
with one of her own. She would follow in death, defying
     its power
to keep them apart. Their parents, life, and the world itself
she would dismiss in a single painful action and triumph—   150
at least in the beautiful story she reads in her mind's text.
She can even hear them talking, catch their sobs of chagrin
as they recognize how wrong they have been, and agree at last
to bury the two together, who wanted no more than that
in their short and piteous lives. And looking up, she prays
to the tree that has been the witness of the suicide of her lover
and is now to watch her follow his lead, 'O fateful tree,
in whose shade we both shall have met our ends, grant me
that you will always bear your fruit in the color I see
in sign of perpetual mourning for this double suicide.'   160
Having said this, she has to go on to the next and last
step, seize the sword still warm with her lover's blood,
place its point beneath her breast, and then fall on it.
She felt the stabbing pain, and answering pain of the gods
who granted her modest request. The mulberry fruit is red,
blood-red when ripe. And the parents, touched with guilt and
     shame,
let their children's ashes rest in a single urn.''

     Her tale was done, and, after a moment, Leuconoë started
with a story she had heard and wanted to tell her sisters:
"Even the Sun has felt the power of love. That god   170
whose light guides the stars has, himself, been guided
by passion's yearnings. Consider how he was the first to spy out
the secret of Mars and Venus. His great eye in the sky
is likely to see what others cannot or will not. He brought
the bad news to Vulcan, the goddess's husband, Juno's
son, and told him where and when, and how, and how often.
Vulcan, quite unhinged, dropped the work in his hands
and turned instead to the making of a snare of threads so fine
that, to the naked eye, there was nothing there in the air.
A single strand of wool or a spiderweb's cross hairs   180
are crude cables compared to these insubstantial strands.

And light? It would yield at once to the slightest touch, the least
languid motion. This net he spread on the couch where they liked
to loll and play. When the goddess of love and the god of war
came to each other, ardent and eager, he sprang this net,
and there they were caught, held fast, still in each other's arms,
whereupon the god of smithing threw open the doors
of the hall and invited his fellow gods inside to witness
this *tableau vivant* of shame with its figures of fun and derision—
although some of the jokes were barbed: one god was heard
     to quip   190
that he wouldn't mind changing places with Mars, at least for a
     while.
And they all laughed, louder perhaps than its humor required.
    "This story they remembered for years, and Venus also
kept it in mind—and held a grudge against the Sun,
that spy she took to be the cause of what had happened.
He had betrayed her in love and therefore would be betrayed
himself. What good does it do, in the face of that kind of spite,
to be Hyperion's child, whose radiant beauty lights up
the whole world? He's doomed, will be himself inflamed
with a new and tormenting fire, as the great eye in the heaven   200
focuses down to a single impossible object, his gaze
narrowed now to Leucothoë, lovely, the one and only,
the perfect. . . . Eager to see her, the Sun rises early, dawdles
across the sky, and sets later and later, and time
drags for the whole world as it seems to do for lovers.
Or else, in Apollo's darker moods, when his heart's anguish
dimmed his effulgence, the world's days would be dim and
     ghostly.
Often his sister, the Moon, would come between him and earth
in erratic eclipse, although love itself was the true cause
of these random umbrageous lapses. None of Apollo's other   210
loves compared or even existed. Clymene, Phaëthon's
mother? Forgotten now, as were Rhode the nymph, and Perseis,
Circe's mother, and Clytie, daughter of Oceànus
and Tethys—who still adored Apollo and, jealous, was hurt
to be put by this way. Like a slate wiped clean of its writing,
his memory now was blank. These others might never have
     happened.
It was Leucothoë now, his white goddess, his only
dream and passion, the daughter Eurynome bore to Orchamus,
who ruled the cities of Persia, the seventh of Belus' line.

"Way to the West beyond the water, they say, is a pasture   220
where the Sun's horses graze in the evenings after their daily
task is done. The food is special there, not grass
at all but fields of ambrosia they wander over and nibble,
refreshing themselves and restoring their incredible strength. The
     steeds
amble and stretch while Night is on watch with her tour of duty.
Apollo is also taking his ease, having come to visit—
assuming for this occasion the face and form of the mother.
Eurynome's Doppelgänger, he comes into Leucothoë's
rooms and, of course, is welcomed. There are her maids-in-
     waiting
spinning, chatting. These Apollo dismisses, saying   230
that there are mother-and-daughter secrets they have to discuss.
The attendants excuse themselves and disappear, and the god
announces himself to the girl: 'I am the god Apollo.
I am the Sun, the measure of time, and witness to all
earthly things. And you have pleased me, your beauty dazzles,
entrances me.' The nymph was thoroughly terrified.
The distaff falls from her numb fingers and onto the floor,
making the only noise in a long and dreamy silence.
She stares in disbelief as his features blur and change
from those of her mother to new and grander proportions—it is   240
indeed Apollo who stands there, splendid and awesome! The girl,
meek, is in shock as he comes to enfold her in his strong arms.
     "Clytie, jealous, is snooping. She sees what is going on
and hurries at once to the girl's father, the king, to report
that the daughter's been making hay with the shining Sun.
     Enraged
by what he does not quite grasp, he trots to the daughter's
     chamber
to punish her for her shame. He ignores her complaints and
     truthful
explanation: 'He stunned me. His will was stronger than mine.
He was far stronger than I.' The father renders a judgment,
and she forthwith is buried alive. There is nothing the Sun   250
can do except glare down in the heat of his anger as if
to melt the mound of earth that is piled up over her head.
Nothing does any good. She is lifeless, suffocated
or crushed to death, whichever is worse. The poor dear thing!
Not since his own son's pathetic demise has the god
seen such a thing. He tries to warm the lifelessness back,
to revive, to retrieve the girl, the time, the world. . . . He cannot.

All he can do is sprinkle fragrant nectar and draw
her spirit out of the earth, a wraith to float in the air
as a rare and delicate fragrance. A shrub of frankincense   260
grew up in that place, its roots down in the grave,
and its crown out in the light of the Sun and gracing the air.
     "But Clytie, for all her loving, grieving, and bearing
of tales, was no better off, for the Sun despised her now.
She pined, her passion corrupting into a form of madness.
Out in the rain and wind, by night and day, she sat
on bare ground, rocking a little, but naked and mute,
a pathetic and desiccating shell of what she had been.
She ate nothing and drank nothing but tears and dewdrops,
but only sat and stared with blind eyes at the Sun   270
as it moved across the sky, ignoring her. Her limbs
took root in the earth, and her face acquired color, became
a flower, and she turned into one of those heliotropes
that follows the Sun in rapt and impossible adoration."
The speaker was done. Quiet obtained for a moment or two
as the world of fiction faded, gave way to a sewing room
in which sisters might discuss whether such things could happen.
Some said no, while others maintained that gods could do
whatever they liked—if they were real gods, that is, not this
impostor, Bacchus, whose festival they were refusing to honor.   280
     Alcithoë spoke next, at the loom she continued to work
with dexterous hands throwing the shuttle from side to side.
"We all know about Daphnis, that shepherd boy on Ida,
and how the nymph in her jealous rage changed him to stone.
I won't do that one. Or the story of Sithon, the king of Thrace,
and how he was now a woman and now a man. That's not
right for a time like this. Or the story of Celmis, Jove's
boyhood attendant whom the god turned at last into stone. . . .
That's no good, either. Wait, there's the Curetes' story, those
          people
from Crete who sprang up from rain. No that won't do. There's
          Crocus   290
and Smilax and how they changed into little flowers. But you
know that as well as I do. Better, a new one. Listen:
     "There is a fountain, Salmacis, near Halicarnassus that causes
effeminacy in those men who come to bathe in its waters,
turning them soft and weak. You know how that came about?
It started when Hermes and Venus produced a child, which
          they gave
the naiads to nurse in the caves of Ida. A striking child,

he looked like his beautiful mother, but also was clearly his
       father's
son, and he was given both of their names to carry.
In time he grew up and set out, as young men will do, to wander   300
and have adventures in strange lands. He came to the cities
of Lycia, in Asia Minor, and then to the South, to Caria,
where he found a pool of water so clear that one could see
all the way to the bottom. No reeds grew there, no lilies
or swamp grass in the crystal water. The pool was framed
by a green lawn. In its depths lived a nymph—a delicate sort
who disdained to hunt and shoot and race with her hoydenish
       sisters.
Only she of the naiads refused to join with Diana's
sportsy crowd. For this she was teased and chided. They told her:
'Get off your delicate butt, grab a spear or a quiver,   310
and see what you can bag. Leisure is all the sweeter
after some exercise and exertion.' She pays no mind
but keeps to her pretty pool to bathe her shapely limbs
and comb her glorious hair. She looks down in the water
to judge whether her coiffure might be improved, or she lies
on the grassy edge in a gauzy peignoir you can see through,
and rests from the minimal effort of gathering nearby flowers.
She'd been out on such a decorous errand once when she noticed
that boy, that amazingly handsome creature, and longed to have
       him.
       "She adjusted her little nothing of a robe so that it draped   320
just so, and smoothed and arranged her hair before she
addressed him: 'Young man, if that's what you are? Or are you
       a god
who has chosen to take on human form for the afternoon?
I believe you could be either one: Cupid perhaps;
or else a mortal but special, rare, your family's darling.
Are you perhaps married? If you are, do you fool around?
Or if you are still, by some peculiar and wonderful chance,
a bachelor, let me suggest that you think about matrimony—
with me, for instance. I mean it. You could do worse, you know.'
She winked, and he blushed crimson. He had only the vaguest idea 330
what she was talking about, but the blush made him look
       delicious,
his cheeks, a perfect pair of pippins she drooled to bite into.
Oh, he was something, a dish—the Moon, in eclipse, with its red
tinge almost hidden away. She begged, or rather demanded,
a kiss, nothing heavy, but what he might give his sister.

worshiped throughout Thebes. Everyone spoke of his powers.
Ino—remember her? Cadmus' daughter, the god's
aunt, Semele's sister, whom Jove had given the infant
to tend? She was so full of pride in how her young charge
had turned out in the end, she could not keep from boasting,
referring whenever she could to all his wonders and marvels.   420
She was the only one of Cadmus' daughters who hadn't
suffered: her only grief was what she had felt for her sisters.
Her own children, her husband, Athamas, and of course
her brilliant foster child had all done well—and Juno
couldn't bear it, considered this woman's happy condition
an affront to herself. Each parlor trick that Bacchus had played,
turning those sailors to fish, or arranging it so that a son
might be torn in bits by his mother, or transforming Minyas'
        daughters
into a flock of bats. . . . It was showy, a little bit vulgar,
and she, the queen of heaven, was yet unavenged, her honor   430
not yet redeemed by some cataclysm beyond all reason
and taste. That Bacchus adored Ino, his aunt, was enough
to channel Juno's fury into some practical scheming.
She would contrive some splendid wretchedness for this woman,
who ought not have been excluded till now from the sufferers'
        ranks.
       There is a path somewhere, a gently sloping trail
that turns abruptly steeper to lead, under the shade
of yew trees, down to the gates of hell, where the Styx exhales
its noxious vapors. Here come the newly dead, some sad,
or full of rage, or merely stunned, for whom the solemn   440
rites have prepared the way: It debouches into a cold
wasteland, where the black palace of Dis looms up.
Its thousand gates gape wide to welcome the bloodless shadows.
Just as the earth's ocean swallows the waters of rivers
everywhere but never seems to be filled, so here
there's a limitless appetite for the myriad souls that throng
the bleak fora and ghastly boulevards of the dead.
       From heaven, Juno descended even hither: the threshold
of hell creaked beneath the weight of her sacred and living
body. A nasty business, but hate will drive us to such   450
extremes. Cerberus reared his triple head and bayed
with his baleful voices, which harmonize in a minor key.
The goddess called out to the Furies, those three terrible sisters,
implacable and deadly, the spawn of Mother Night.
They hunker down at the gates of Hades, combing their tresses,

not of hair but serpents that coil in a herpetological
pompadour. Great Juno approaches. They rise in her honor.
This is the home of the damned, where Tityus lies stretched out,
huge and sad, as vultures circle, settle, and tear
at his bleeding guts. Close by, Tantalus strains up   460
for fruit from the branch just out of his reach, or tries to scoop
water for his parched lips from the river, which always recoils
and is quicker than he. Sisyphus pushes his monstrous boulder
endlessly up the hill, and Ixion whirls on his wheel,
and the daughters of Belus race by carrying water in sieves.
      Juno looks around her, or rather, say, she glares,
and her gaze rests for a moment on Ixion—who had made,
in his limitless brazenness, advances to her in heaven.
But it's Sisyphus she addresses, to ask why he should be here
suffering as he does, while his brother Athamas lives   470
easy, proud, and rich. She recounts how he and Ino
have neglected to do her honor, and lists their many offenses.
What she wants is ruin, disaster for all of Cadmus'
house. The Furies must hound that man to the brink of madness
and then beyond. She turns to the trio and asks, begs,
orders, pleads, cajoles, and bargains to get what she craves.
Tisiphone tosses the viperous locks from her wrinkled face
and answers the queen of heaven: "We know what you want,
          and why.
Consider it done, madam. Go back from this pest hole
to your proper and sweeter seat in the realm of the sky." Juno,   480
delighted and gratified, returns to heaven, where Iris,
the daughter of Thaumus, asperses and purifies her with water.
      Meanwhile, Tisiphone seized her guttering, gory torch,
put on the bloody robes she held in place with a viper
instead of a belt, and set out on her fell errand with Grief,
Terror, Fear, and Madness attending in her train.
When she appeared at the gate of Aeolus' house—he was
          Athamas'
father—the very doorposts shrank. The sky was grim,
for the Sun had hidden his face. Ino was stricken with fear,
and she and Athamas both would have fled if they could, but
          the Fury   490
stood in their way and kept them from moving. She held out
          her arms
and shook her head, and the vipers hissed and writhed and spat
deadly venom. The couple stared in fascinated
loathing to see a hooded serpent's head appear

from her bosom's cleavage, hiss and spit, flicker its tongue,
and retreat into that unimaginable valley.
She laughs and grabs a couple of kraits from the back of her head
and hurls them with unerring aim at her stunned victims. They
      do not
feel a bite, but only the breath of these pestilential
creatures, as if their exhalations went straight to the brain.   500
Meanwhile, from the slobber and froth that flecks the jaws
of Cerberus and numbs the mind of all recollection
and even recognition of joys, sorrows, pleasures,
pains, loves, and hatreds, the Fury had made a concoction
mixed with blood and stirred with the green twig of a hemlock.
With this she sprinkled the couple, poured it on their breasts,
and let it eat through their skin and marrow and into their souls.
Then she made a couple of passes with her flaming
torch to improve the spell, and she went back to the bowels
of the earth, having fulfilled her promise and done her job.   510
    Crazed, Athamas runs through the halls of the palace
      shouting,
"Beasts are loose on the grounds. A lion and her two cubs.
Nets! Spears! I saw them! Help me, men!" He pursues
Ino as if she were not his wife but a lioness.
He grabs his son Learchus from his mother's arms and whirls him
around in the air, lets go, and smashes his skull like an egg
one hurls against a rock. The mother howls, enraged,
if not from the Fury's potion, at least from this latest outrage.
With wordless shrieks, she rushes this way and that, her hair
streaming behind her. She bears in her arms Melicerta, her other   520
son, and thinks to pray to her favorite god, to Bacchus. . . .
Now Juno chuckles in scorn: "So may he always bless you!"
    There is a huge cliff overlooking the sea, a giddy
place, its bottom hollowed out by the work of the waves,
so its top juts out like a prow. To this spot Ino climbed,
her strength and courage enhanced as they were by her mad-
      ness, up
and out to the very edge, and then, with her child in her arms,
beyond, and over, and down, leaping into the churning
foam of the terrible sea far, far below. . . .
    Venus pitied the poor distracted woman, her child's   530
child, and in her grief addressed Neptune, her uncle:
"Hear me, god of the waters, whose power is second only
to that of Jove, for I ask enormous favors. I beg
pity for these, my friends, my grandchild and great-grandchild.

Receive them into your comforting bosom and give them
      welcome
as deities of the sea. From that foam did I once
emerge myself—my name in the Greek tongue, Aphrodite,
celebrates this. As your kin, I beg you to grant my prayer."
The god of the sea heard, consented, and gave them new
names and forms: the baby became Palaemon; his mother   540
was from that moment the goddess we worship as Leucothoë.
      The women of Thebes, who had been Ino's intimates and
            attendants,
followed however they could over the rough track
to the edge of the precipice, where they looked out in dismay,
certain of what had happened and that they had both been killed.
They beat their breasts in mourning, wailed, and tore their hair
in grief for the house of Cadmus. To Juno these women
      complained
that this was unjust, that the goddess had been too cruel, too
      harsh. . . .
Juno was not at all pleased and told them that, if they wanted,
they could themselves serve as mementos of her displeasure.   550
One of Ino's friends, in despair or defiance, prepared
to throw herself into the sea as her mistress had done, but couldn't
move, and a second, still beating her breasts, was likewise frozen.
Several more of them stiffened and stuck in their random poses,
becoming the oddly contorted boulders one still may find there.
Meanwhile, other women close to the edge of the cliff
leapt but never landed, turning instead into birds
that swoop and skim and cry out over the turbulent water
of that bleak, awesome, and sacred spot even today.
      Cadmus, the son of Agenor, hadn't the vaguest notion   560
that his daughter and little grandson had turned into gods. In
      sorrow,
overcome by the deepest grief for what the Fates
had brought his accursèd house, he fled the city he'd founded,
left it behind, as if it, rather than he himself,
were the cause of the trouble, preferring in any event the chances
of the wilderness to Thebes and what he had known there. He
      journeyed
far, he and his wife, and came at last to the border
of distant Illyria, where, weary with travel and age
and the bitterest woe, they collapsed by the side of the road.
      There Cadmus
murmured aloud, half crazed: "I remember how once I sowed   570

dragon's teeth on the earth to harvest a crop of men.
I envy that serpent now, would be one myself, would stretch out
to writhe on the ground, hiss, and spit venom. . . ." At once
it was so. His skin turned scaly. He fell on his belly. His legs
disappeared or were welded into a snaky tail.
His arms, which were shrinking fast, he held out toward his wife,
as tears flowed down his still recognizably human face.
"O my darling," he called to Harmonia, "while there is
        something
left of me, touch me, reach out your hand to my own. My
        love. . . ."
He would have said more but his tongue bifurcated and flicked   580
in eerie silence. His voice was a hiss now. His poor wife
moaned and beat her breast. She cried out, "Cadmus, Cadmus,
how can such things happen? Come back to me! Don't leave!
Take me with you, I beg. . . ." With his serpent's tongue he licked
her adored face and glided into her tunic to coil
about those breasts he had tussled with such delight for years
and embrace her one last time. Their attendants were horrified
to see this bizarre business, for she did not quail or recoil
but stroked the scales of the serpent with fondness, pity, and love.
And then she became a serpent, too, and the pair wriggled off   590
into the woods together to hide in the bosom of earth
and maybe remind each other of what they once had been.
        Perhaps in their new incarnations, they took a degree of
            comfort
from what they heard of their grandson Bacchus, whose fame
            and sway
were spreading, had reached as far as India, while in Greece
his temples were filled with adoring crowds of enthusiasts.
Only in Argos there still remained some resistance from one
who, bizarrely enough, was one of Bacchus' own kinsmen—Abas'
son Acrisius. He was opposed to such worship, denied
that Bacchus was any kind of divinity or the son   600
of Jove. He had several such notions and was disinclined to believe
that Danaë had conceived Perseus from that shower
of gold. But the truth has its own eventual power, and he
came at last to regret that he had denied and defied it.
        By Acrisius' leave or not, the heavens had welcomed Bacchus
as one of their own, and the other, Perseus, bearing the head
of the Gorgon he'd vanquished, flew through the air, his grisly
            trophy
dripping blood on the ground, where the droplets sizzled to life

and then wiggled away as snakes of various species,
which is why, they say, that Libya is so full of deadly serpents.   610
     From that quarter of sky, Perseus half-drifted
and half-flew, buffeted here and there by the currents
of air like a cloud that floats where the winds take it. From his
great height, he looked down at tiny trees and buildings
and soared over valleys and mountain ranges and whole countries,
passing the major constellations several times,
the Bear, and the Crab, and again. . . . And again! He was
          breathless, giddy,
and apprehensive, for now the light was beginning to fade.
How could he fly at night and know where he was? In prudence,
he managed to make a descent and alit somewhere in the West,   620
far away in that realm where Atlas lives and rules.
There he would rest a while and wait for the morning star
to signal the dawn's return and Phoebus' fiery car.
Atlas, Iapetus' son, famous for size and strength,
was the lord of the earth and the waters here, where the Sun's
          horses
come each evening to feed and take their hard-earned ease.
As rich as he was strong, he boasted a thousand flocks
and a thousand herds, which roamed and grazed his grassy plains,
all but borderless—no one else lived anywhere near him
to constrain or threaten. A perfect existence, one might imagine,   630
especially with that famous tree he had whose leaves
were all of precious gold and whose fruit was also of gold,
one of the world's rarest and most admirable wonders.
To him, in a quite respectful manner, Perseus spoke:
"Sir, I come to beg your hospitality. I
am a son of Jove, or, if noble birth means nothing to you,
then I can claim great deeds that ought to merit respect.
I ask for a night's lodging." But as Atlas listened, he thought
and could not help but remember what Themis once had
          told him,
that oracle of Parnassus who had warned him how the time   640
would come when "That precious tree will be stripped of its
          gorgeousness
by a son of Jove. The gold and the glory he will take,
wresting them both from you." To prevent such an occurrence,
Atlas had built a massive wall around his tree
and installed a mighty dragon to keep watch and protect it.
To Perseus, then, he answered forbiddingly, "Go away.
I disbelieve your claims of glorious deeds and doubt

your boast about your father, who at any rate is distant
and cannot help you here and now." He had not stopped talking
but was bearing down upon Perseus, looming hugely, shoving   650
and pushing his guest away. Who could resist such size
and strength? With soothing words, Perseus tried to restate
his case, insisting he meant no harm and was only asking
shelter for one night. . . . But the other, unpersuaded,
a huge mountain of flesh, bore down on the hero.
At last, Perseus gave up and resorted to other and more
effective tactics. "Refuse? But let me do you a favor
you richly deserve." Having said this, he drew from the depths of
      its pouch
Medusa's head, which he held behind him. Atlas at once
was turned from man to mountain. His beard and hair became
      trees,   660
his arms and shoulders were ridges, and his head was the
      mountaintop.
His bones were stones, and he grew larger and ever larger
until the sky and its stars were resting upon his head,
as the gods in their dark wisdom had willed they ought to do.

      The morning star was shining, and Aeolus shut the winds
into their pen under Aetna. Perseus put on his shoes,
those special wingèd sandals he wore, and picked up his sword
to cleave the air in flight. Below was that same panorama
of topographical features, a map of themselves. As he flew,
he skirted the Ethiopian lands of Cepheus' kingdom,   670
where Jupiter Ammon had taken that ruler's daughter hostage—
Andromeda, guiltless but nevertheless punished for what
her mother, Cassiopea, had boasted, that she was more lovely
than any of Nereus' daughters. Offended, those nymphs had
      appealed
to Neptune, demanding some drastic exemplary retaliation.
He sent a terrifying monster from out of the depths
to ravage the countryside. The maiden's sacrifice
was the only way to appease it and limit its ruin, so she,
tied down with chains on her arms and legs, was exposed on a
      cliff,
where the sea winds toyed with her hair in a menacing kind of
      foreplay   680
while tears spilled from her eyes to run down her perfect cheeks
in shining irregular courses. . . . Perseus saw her, was stricken,
smitten, undone. He forgot to keep his wings beating
and fell hundreds of feet before righting himself and landing.

"Why are you fettered this way?" he asked of the girl. "The chains
that bind you should not be those of iron, but lighter and stronger
bonds that join two lovers' hearts together as one.
What is your name? Why are you chained here this way?" The
         captive,
modest and silent at first, would have concealed her face,
except that she could not move her arms. She closed her eyes,   690
although tears continued to brim and spill, and she told her sad
story, explaining how she had come to this sorry pass.
Even as she was speaking, the earth trembled, and loud
roaring came from the sea as the monster's head and shoulders
broke through the surface and neared the beach below. The girl
cried out in terror. Her mother and father, both in attendance,
moaned in their grief. But the stranger demanded that he be
         heard:
"I am Perseus, son of Jove. I am the hero
of whose deeds you've no doubt heard—the triumph over the
         Gorgon,
the knack of flying in air. To be brief, I'm a plausible suitor.   700
More to the point, I can save her. For which I ask her hand.
Agreed?" What could they say? Of course they agreed,
         looking out
at that inconceivable creature who lurched ever closer to land
with every passing breath, this humongous beast, as big
as a fair-sized ship with one of those sharpened prows. It comes
with the waves of a wake appearing on either side of its sternum
as if there were hundreds of rowers slaving away below.
It is getting closer now, near enough so a rock
from a catapult could reach it, if there were a catapult. . . .
The hero takes to the air, rising abruptly up   710
almost as far as the puffs of clouds. His shadow flits
across the water's surface, and the monster notices, swats
with a huge claw at the shadow. These monsters are not too
         bright.
Perseus takes advantage of the creature's feint. Off-balance,
it is vulnerable for an instant. Quick as an eagle that swoops
down on its prey, he dives and strikes at the back of its neck
as hard as he can with his sword, deep, clear to the hilt.
It smarts, that does, and the creature rears up high in the air
and makes a kind of whinny as if a hundred boars
squealed in pain together when the hunters and hounds attacked.   720
Again Perseus comes in for a quick blow, and again,
at the back, at the sides, where the tail fans out into fins, he
         strikes.

It roars and belches water and blood. In the spray, the hero's
wings are waterlogged and can hardly keep him aloft.
He sees a rock that's submerged at high tide or in rough
weather, but otherwise stands clear. He alights on that platform
and strikes again with his weapon into the monster's vitals.
On shore, relieved, applauding, the king and queen, Cepheus
and Cassiopea, could have been watching a bullfight. They stand
and cheer him. He nears, and they greet him as son-in-law and
      savior.   730
Andromeda now comes forward, released from her chains and
      terror,
his cause and his prize. He washes his hands in the waves of
      the sea.
To protect it, he sets his Gorgon's head on a bed of seaweed
a little way down the beach, where a very strange thing
      happens—
Medusa's head has its power still, and the seaweed turns
from supple twigs to stone. The sea nymphs laugh, entertained
to see what has happened. They take this new phenomenon down
into their realm in the water, where it thrives and reproduces—
an animal that behaves like a plant and aspires to stone?
This is the birth of coral. Meanwhile, Perseus builds   740
a series of turf altars to propitiate the gods
and offer thanks for their help in his triumph. The one on the left
is Mercury's; the one on the right belongs to Minerva;
the central altar is Jove's. He performs the sacrifices
in the proper manner—a cow for the warrior goddess, a calf
for the wingèd messenger god, and a bull for the lord of heaven.
The ritual having been thus observed in all its details,
he claims his reward, Princess Andromeda. He will ask
no dower for her. The parents grant him his prize, and the couple,
with Cupid and Hymen brandishing ceremonial torches,   750
marries with fires burning and incense coiling in rich
exotic aromas. Flowers? Everywhere flowers! And music
from lyre and flute and the chanting of voices, human and godly,
the outward signs of inward peace and joy. The servants
throw wide the double doors of the palace to show the world
the banquet hall with its tables piled with dapatical fare.
The courtiers take their places to honor Cepheus' house
and offer their thanks and praise to him who delivered them all,
the brave youth who has won Andromeda, the fair.

      Along with the food, there is wine, rich cuvées that Bacchus   760
himself has supplied from his private reserve. The company
      drinks

toasts to the bride and groom, the bride's parents, the gods,
and one another. They drink and laugh, and then it comes time
for stories. Perseus asks them to tell him their history, customs,
and views about life and the world. They, however, insist
that he tell them of the wonders that he has seen and done.
How did he learn to fly? How did he conquer the Gorgon?
By what strength or what wiles did he manage this awesome feat,
cut off that snaky head, and survive? Perseus nods,
clears his throat with a drink of wine, and commences to tell   770
how it was, away in the West, beneath the steeps of Atlas,
in an overhang, a declivity more than a cave. There lived
the two daughters of Phorcys, sisters weird and wild,
who shared between them a single eye they passed back and forth.
This, Perseus stole, sticking his hand between them
and snatching it as they passed it, both of them blind just then.
The guests at the banquet want more details. He is willing to
      tell them
how, as he made his way through the wild and trackless country,
climbing up hills and descending through sudden chasms, he
      noticed
the forms of men and beasts in stone. . . . A sculpture garden?   780
Nothing like that, for each had been changed by a glimpse of
      Medusa's
face to a lithic likeness. A monstrous business! He studied
this difficult situation, saw it as one more problem
intelligence might conquer, and then resolved to try
to use his bright bronze shield as a mirror and see with that.
Might not this indirection of vision protect him? "Suspense
is difficult to maintain, for here I am. And the head
is in that bag." He explains how he came up at night with his
      shield
in his left hand and sword in his right, to cut the head
clean from the neck. Her blood gushed forth, and its flow
      produced   790
Pegasus and his brother Chrysaor. The hero,
having begun to talk, now tells of his other adventures,
the places he's been and what he has seen. There's a pause as
      he takes
a sip of the excellent wine, and somebody asks the question,
"How did it come about that Medusa had snakes for hair?"
"She was the pretty sister," Perseus answers, "with beautiful
tresses, and, once, in Minerva's temple, Neptune took her.
Minerva turned away in shame and anger, and then

it is said that she transformed the victim's attractive locks
to a tangle of vipers—a curse or blessing? It's hard to say. 800
A protection surely, for further rape was now most unlikely.
And the goddess herself now carries that tangle of snakes on her
    shield
to strike fear in the hearts of her enemies everywhere.

BOOK V

He's rambling on. He's having a wonderful time, expansive,
basking in all these Ethiopian chieftains' attention
and admiration, and there is a noise, some sort of commotion
they all try to ignore for a moment or two. But they cannot.
Just as a calm ocean can turn abruptly violent
with howling winds and malevolent waves, so this occasion
is suddenly violent. Phineus, the king's brother, has come
with his brazen spear in hand, as he says, "to avenge this insult."
"She had been promised to me," he declares, and his baleful
    glance
is focused upon Andromeda, Perseus' bride. But now   10
Phineus turns to the hero to challenge, insult, and defy him:
"Your flying boots won't save you this time, you son of a golden
shower, the piss-pot get of a drunken god!" His arm
draws back. He's about to hurl that spear at the guest of honor,
but Cepheus stops him, cries out: "Brother? What are you doing?
Is this how you thank our guest for saving the nation? Is this
a way to woo my daughter? Collect your thoughts! Consider,
Perseus didn't steal her from you. That was Jove's doing.
He sent the monster to threaten all of us, and demand
Andromeda's sacrifice. It was this that cost you your bride!   20
Would you rather have seen her dead? When she was chained to
    the cliff,
where were your spear and bluster? What help were you offering
    then,
as uncle and fiancé? If you were so eager to have her,
what kept you from that beach, that cliff, those chains, the
    monster?
Perseus saved the girl and kept me from having to face
a childless old age. He gave me my daughter back, and will
    give me
grandchildren, too, I trust, for I have given my word.
Your rival is not in this room. Death itself was the rival

to whom you ought to have offered this misdirected challenge."

    Furious, Phineus looked from the king to his son-in-law   30
and back, not sure which one he'd prefer to see suffer and die
first. He hurled his weapon at Perseus and, enraged,
threw it hard but missed. Its point sank into the chair,
and the shaft quivered a moment. Perseus grabbed it, yanked it
out of the wood, and threw it back toward his assailant,
who had taken shelter meanwhile and was crouching behind the
      altar.
But the spearpoint found another target in Rhoetus' face,
and it took him down. Someone close by pulled it out from
      the bone
in which it had been embedded. Rhoetus writhed, and his blood
gushed up in spurts, which splashed the food set out on the table.   40
This was enough to trigger a general riot. The guests,
metamorphosed into a mob, attacked one another, pell-mell,
some calling that Cepheus now deserved to die
with his son-in-law. But they had already got away, calling
Justice to witness, and Faith, and the gods of Guests and Hosts
that this wasn't what they'd wanted, that he had forbidden
      fighting.
Pallas came to protect her half brother with her shield
and give Perseus courage and strength. A handsome youth,
Athis, whose mother was Limaeë, nymph of the far-off Ganges,
was present, a fellow just then at the peak of his manhood, dressed   50
in a robe of expensive purple and fringed with gold, and he wore
heavy golden chains around his neck, and a gold
comb held his perfumed coiffure in place. He was famous
for accuracy with a javelin but picked up his bow, was bending
the weapon to get the bowstring attached, when Perseus grabbed
one of the burning brands from a torchère up on the wall
and, using it as a club, hit the young man in the face,
mashing his cheekbones and turning that profile into a pudding.
Lycabas, his friend, companion, and lover, was there
and saw Athis gasping his last on the floor, and wept,   60
snatched that bow from the nearly lifeless hand, and, fitting
an arrow onto the string, called out in hatred and rage:
"This death will cost you your life. Not glory but my contempt
is what you earn for that deed." He let the arrow go.
It almost found its mark, but Perseus, warned, had turned
his body away from Lycabas, so the arrow passed through a fold
of his tunic, not even grazing the skin. Perseus grabbed
the curved sword that had done such service in recent days

and hacked into the breast of that poor young man, who gasped
as he felt the blackness lapping at the gunwales of his eyes.   70
Before it overwhelmed his vision, he saw his dear
Athis beside him and died with this last image for comfort,
that and the knowledge they'd both go down to the shadows
      together.
      Then Phorbas, Metion's son, and Amphimedon, from Libya,
came out of the hall ready to fight, but they slipped in the gore
that made the paving stones a skating rink. They fell
and were trying to get up when they met that sword coming down
like a sickle cutting weeds: the one felt it slash his ribs;
the other, whose throat it cut, felt nothing much at all.
      Now Eurytus, son of Actor, came at Perseus, hefting   80
a double-headed axe, and him the hero killed
not with the sword but grabbing a huge bronze mixing bowl
to fling at the fellow. It struck and shattered his skull, and blood
was everywhere now, a lake, and the head was twitching and
      twisting
and beating the wet floor, and then was still. Now came
others Perseus killed: Polydegmon, who traced
his lineage back to the great Queen Semiramis; Abaris,
from out in the Caucasus somewhere; Lycetus; Helices, hairy
and wild; and Phlegyas and his companion, Clytus—their feet
never so much as touched the tiles of the floor, for they walked   90
on corpses, who themselves were about to become more corpses.
      Phineus all this time had been hiding behind that altar,
and now, with his blood warmed by this panorama of slaughter
to something approaching tepid, he thought he'd join in the fun,
not in close combat perhaps but doing what damage he could,
and he hurled his javelin, missing his target again. He hit
Idas, of all people, who'd kept aloof from the fighting
and had joined with neither side. Him, the javelin wounded,
and, hurt and angry, he called out his challenge: "Fool! Wretch!
I had no part in this, but now you have made me a foe,   100
and I shall give back as good or bad as I get." He raised
his arm with his own javelin, was about to hurl it, but, weak
from the loss of blood and in shock, he collapsed into a faint.
      Carnage then. It was mayhem. Clymenus hacked to death
Hodites, the Ethiopian minister to the king.
Hypseus killed Prothoënor; Lyncides killed Hypseus
in a demolition derby. One very pious old man,
Emathion, a sage who preached and practiced reverence
for all the gods, called out that this was wrong, that the killing

was evil, had to stop, that the men should come to their senses.   110
He clung to the altar horns with his old clawlike hands
and was calling out in this way when Chromis beheaded him
with a single swipe of his sword. The head rolled onto the altar,
and there are those who swear that the lips continued to move in
        silent
protest and imprecation. But nobody paid attention.
        The twin brothers, Ammon and Broteas, Phineus killed,
and Ampicus, the priest of Ceres, his temples adorned
with the holy ribbons. Off in a distant corner, the minstrel
Lampetides cowered. He'd come to play the lute and sing
appropriate odes, and he watched in utter horror. Pedasus   120
thought it was somehow funny, called out, "Go, sing in hell,"
and drove the point of his sword into the tenor's temple.
As he fell, the lyre in his hand hit with a dissonant chord
he'd never have wanted. Lycormas thought it grotesque and sad.
He grabbed a doorpost, ripped it out of its frame, and swung it
with a mighty blow, which broke Pedasus' neck. He fell,
collapsed like a slaughtered bull. Pelates saw this happen
and, taking his cue from Lycormas, grabbed at the other doorpost
to use as a weapon. Before he was able to wrench it free,
Corythus' flung spear pierced his hand and pinned him   130
to the wood of the post. As he hung there, Abas gave him a jab
with a sword in his side, and he died but couldn't fall. He hung
        there
still, like a piece of meat. On Perseus' side, Melaneus
fell, mortally wounded. And Dorylas, rich in land
and a trader in rare spices, took a spear in the groin
and, looking like some primitive ithyphallic statue,
died in terrible agony. It was Halcyoneus' spear,
and, looking down at his victim lying there, he said:
"All your extensive real estate shrinks down to what you'll cover
when you lie in the earth." Dorylas probably never heard him,   140
but Perseus did, and he pulled the spear from the body and
        threw it
true, striking the braggart's nose, passing into the head,
and sticking out from the nape of his neck. Perseus had
no time for satisfaction, but went on a rampage, taking
Clytius with a spear that skewered his thighs, and Clanis,
his brother, throwing another spear that shattered his jaw.
Celadon died, and Astreus (he had a Syrian mother,
but there were all kinds of guesses about who his father had been);
and Aethion, the prophet, who this time failed to read

the omens that ought to have warned him to decline this
    invitation. 150
Thoactes, the armor bearer, perished, as did Agyrtes,
who had slain his father. Perseus killed them all, but they came,
and kept on coming, more of them than any one man could
    handle.
Never mind that he was the king's guest, was the nation's
savior. Reason had long ago flown out the window, leaving
mad Bellona to spur on every baser instinct,
but mostly blood lust, inflamed by the cries of the dying, the
    sweet
smell of blood and gore, and the clang of metal on metal.
The king, the queen, and their daughter are huddled now near
    the hero,
loyal but useless, and needing to be protected. Alone 160
he faces the crazed mob of Phineus' friends and minions.
The air is full of spears, thick as a winter hailstorm,
making their sinister hiss as they fly by his ears. He stands
with his back to a great stone pillar. But they come at him from
    the front;
on the left there's Chaonian Molpeus; on the right, the Arab
Ethemon. Both are advancing, step by step. Perseus
can't give any ground. He is like a hungry tiger
that can't decide which of two equidistant herds to attack.
He glares and waits. Molpeus feints, but Perseus flings
a spear that pierces his leg. He limps off. Ethemon rushes 170
to try to take him off-balance. He goes for Perseus' neck
but misses and breaks his blade on the stone column. It shatters,
and one of the fragments flies back to lodge in its owner's throat.
It isn't a lethal wound, but he stands there, stunned. His hands
reach for the metal shard, as Perseus gives him plenty
of metal, hacking and thrusting him through with his own
    hooked sword.
    But there were uncountable fighters still coming on, and,
    exhausted,
Perseus had to face it. There was no way he could take them
all, or no human way. He called out a warning: "Friends,
if there are any friends in the hall, turn your faces away!" 180
And he reached in his pouch, pulled out and raised up the
    Gorgon's head.
Thescelus wasn't worried. "Find someone else to frighten
with these magic tricks," he called out. He cocked his arm back
    to throw

a javelin but then froze, turned to marble, became
a statue, part of a sculptural group, for Ampyx, also,
beside him, with his sword stretched forward at Perseus' body,
became an off-balance and therefore rather baroque piece.
Nileus, too, who claimed to be a child of the river
whose name he bore, and who'd come to believe his story and
        thought
he just might be immortal, put his conceit to the test,   190
defied the Gorgon's head, proclaimed his divinity, froze
in midsentence, and turned truthful and silent as stone.
Eryx ought to have taken the hint, but blamed his comrades
for a simple want of courage and spirit. "We can take him!"
he called out, rushed, stopped, and became his own monument.

        Most of them deserved what they got, but there was one,
Aconteus, a soldier who'd fought on Perseus' side,
was still fighting, turned to check his flank, and saw
the Gorgon's head, which changed him at once into stone. His foe,
Astyages, brought a sword down on the shoulder, which didn't   200
give way as flesh does, but rang out as marble. Astonished,
Astyages turned around to see what was happening, looked,
and turned to stone, that startled expression still on his face.

        It's only now that Phineus rethinks his original plan,
understands he was not only wrong but is going to lose.
Having as much as lost, what can he do but assume
the suppliant's posture—completing the hideous diorama
Perseus and his magic have brought into being. Around him
are friends and comrades. He calls each one by name, but their
        only
response is a baleful silence, which is his fault. And he turns   210
at last to face his adversary, "Pereus, you win!"
he declares. "Put that monstrous head back in its bag, I beg you.
Our fight was for the girl to whom I had been betrothed.
There was nothing personal in it, no rancor. And now that you
        have her,
you can afford to show some generosity. Grant me
only my life. The rest, the glory, the girl . . . they're yours."
He kept his eyes downcast, in prudence as much as shame,
and heard the answer, "Coward. I put up my sword. You can
        live—
forever as art, as trophy. I'll keep you, I think, in the hall
of Cepheus' house, but not for his sake or mine. You'll be   220
Andromeda's keepsake." He brandished the dreadful head this
        way

and that. Phineus tried to avert his face but could not
avoid an instant's glance, enough to do the trick:
his neck grew stiff, his cheeks were set, his expression stony,
and that look of his at the end, that cringing suppliant's pleading,
semi-crouching posture was his for the rest of time.

    Now with his bride, Andromeda, Perseus goes back
to Argos, his native city, where there's more strife, his Great-uncle
Proetus having usurped the throne of his grandsire Acrisius.
The head in the bag worked wonders, its baleful gaze producing   230
a sudden end to whatever subversive movement there was.
A satisfying business, this restoration of order,
the righting of wrongs, the correction of error, the fight against
      evil. . . .
One can develop a taste for it and think of oneself as the world's
policeman. But as it happened, one Polydectes, who once
had been Perseus' friend and protector, turned odd, made absurd
advances to Danaë—who, remember, was Perseus' mother.
The hero came to the island kingdom of Seriphos
in the nick of time, and told him to cease and desist. This king,
Polydectes, refused to give credit to all those improbable stories,   240
did not believe there had ever been a Medusa, that this
young man had killed any monster. It was all a ridiculous tale—
Perseus warned the assembled company not to look,
and pulled the head from its holder, no longer a simple bag
but a grandly bejeweled case now, and held it up. And the king
became a life-sized statue: Polydectes, the Doubter.

    That head was indeed a handy gadget, but that wasn't all
Perseus had in the way of divine aid. His half sister
the goddess Minerva had also been looking out for him. Now
that his work was done and his safety assured, she could turn
      elsewhere,   250
and did, heading for Thebes and Helicon, home of the Muses.
Here she descended, assembled the talented sisters, and spoke:
"Word has reached me of something new and strange. It is said
a horse has been born, or somehow sprung to life from the
      droplets
of blood of its mother, Medusa. This horse, I am told, is named
Pegasus, and, where its hoof last touched the ground before
it sprang into the air, a spring has gushed up. Is this true?"
In answer, Urania spoke, "You are welcome, my lady, and, yes,
the story you've heard is the truth. Pegasus' hoofprint produced
a spring. Come, let us show you." She led the way and displayed,   260

in their ancient woods and grottoes where flowers bloom, the
        sacred
waters of Hippocrene. Minerva looked about her
and remarked how lovely it was, the place and the life of the
        sisters,
these daughters of Mnemosyne, happy in where they lived
and what they did with their time. They acknowledged her
        kind words
and said how she might, were it not for her greater rank, join
        them
in their pleasant pursuits and attractive, almost ideal situation.
Then, with some hesitation, one made bold to suggest
that all was not always *calme* and *luxe* and *volupté*. . . .
"We were terrified," she said, "and our virgin souls have not yet   270
recovered from what Pyreneus did, that bad and brazen
king of Thrace. He had fought some battle, captured Daulis,
and ruled the meadows of Phocis. This happened while we were
        en route
to the temple at Parnassus. He saw us, greeted us, showed us
the honor that is our due, and looked to the darkening sky.
'A storm is coming,' he said. 'Take shelter here with me.'
The winds were indeed rising, and a storm was impending. With
        thanks
we accepted his invitation, entered his house, and waited
for the weather to clear. It did, and we wanted to leave, but then
he barred the doors and kept us captive, as prizes, slaves.   280
We put on our wings and ascended through the courtyard to
        fly away,
but he climbed the walls and called out wherever we went he
        would follow,
and however we would travel, he would also try.
And he leapt into thin air and fell on the rocks below
to become at once a nightmarish mess of bloody pulp."
        The Muse had not yet finished speaking, but whirring wings
and disembodied words from the tree limbs above intruded.
Minerva looked up and around, puzzled to find there were birds
chatting away overhead so oddly, nine of them, magpies.
"Who or what are they?" she asked, and a Muse replied   290
that these had only lately appeared in the sacred precincts
of Helicon, and she told their story. "Piërus, their father,
was lord of Pella. Euippe, his wife, was their mother. These nine
sisters, pretty enough, and not without talent, were proud.

They kept to themselves as princesses often do, and assured
one another how they were the best of all possible sisters, believed
the polite comments they heard, and decided to try their skill
in a contest—with us. They appeared here, and invited, or say
            they dared us,
to compete with them, our nine against their nine. That number
was what perhaps had suggested this nonsense. The winners
            would yield   300
not only honor but also lands and titles—our grove
and spring, against the plains and mountains that were their
            birthright.
What could we do? An awkward business no matter how
we responded. Decline? Yield them our home and the spring? Or
            accept
and participate in a contest we could not lose? We had to
take them on, and did, with nymphs as the referees.
They took their oaths to be fair, each swearing by her stream
to render an honest verdict, and they took their seats on the rocks
that surround us here. The boldest sister, the one who had spoken
their challenge, commenced at once without the drawing of lots   310
or any such civil, sportsmanlike gesture. She sang of the war
of the gods and giants—to whom she ascribed disproportionate
            virtue
and gave them credit for courage. The gods, meanwhile, she
            belittled.
She sang of Typhoeus, who sprang from the depths of the earth to
            frighten
the gods of the sky, who fled to the seven-mouthed Nile and hid
in the reeds of its marshes, assuming animal shapes. Thus, Jove
appeared in the guise of a ram, for which reason Libyans still
show him with curving horns. Apollo, she said, was a crow;
Bacchus became a goat; Juno, a milk-white cow;
Venus, a fish; and Mercury transformed himself to an ibis.   320
        "Then it was our turn to perform. But have you the time?
We shouldn't wish to impose. I'd be happy to summarize." "No,
there's nothing I'd like better," Minerva replied. "Go ahead!"
She shifted into a comfortable posture and gave her attention
as the Muse recounted how Calliope then got up, smiled,
adjusted her hair, and proceeded to strum on her lyre and sing
a hymn in honor of Ceres, the bountiful goddess to whom
we owe so much for the gift of the cultivation of fields.
To her we give thanks for the grains we eat, for our daily
            bread. . . .

What better goddess is there to whom we should sing our praises?   330
   "'Sicily,' she began, 'is a huge island. It all
is heaped up on Typhoeus, who dared assault the heaven's
gods in their lofty fastness. He struggles and tries to rise,
but Pelorus' headland has pinned his right hand, and Pachynus'
promontory, his left; Lilybaeum is holding
his legs; and Aetna's whole weight is on his head. He writhes,
nevertheless, and tries with his awesome strength to push free,
to thrust the heavy earth from his body and toss the cities
high in the air. He spouts ashes and vomits forth
sulfurous flames. He braces and strains, and the earth cracks.   340
The king of the dead, afraid lest the roof of his realm be shattered
and sunlight dazzle the timorous shades of his kingdom, hitched
his team of black stallions, mounted his car, and rode
to inspect the island and check for damage. Nothing was broken,
but, as he was making his rounds, Venus caught sight of him,
      roused
her son, and instructed Cupid to see what an arrow could do
to the lord of the underworld. The other gods were subject
to Cupid's powers, the lord of the air and lord of the sea.
Why not see what one of those darts might do to the third
of the great and reverend powers? Cupid's honor and even   350
her own were at stake. Diana resists, and Minerva, and Ceres,
who keeps her beautiful daughter a virgin, cool and aloof.
Two birds we can get with the single shot, she suggested,
and Cupid, willing as ever to do her bidding, agreed,
approved of her mischievous plan, and produced, from out of his
      quiver
of arrows, the sharpest and deadliest, smiled as he bent the bow
and affixed the bowstring, fitted the arrow, aimed, and let fly.
The unerring shaft flew with a sinister whisper through
the barely ruffled air and struck Dis in the heart.
   "'In the island's center—one might say, at its heart—near
      Enna's   360
imposing walls, is a lake that the swans have always liked.
Pergus, it's called. There are woods on all sides. Leaves dapple
      the water
with shade, so the birds can paddle in stately comfort or take
their ease on grassy banks that bloom in an endless springtime.
To this remarkable spot, Proserpina would come
to gather bouquets of lilies or violets, or merely to stroll,
taking the simple pleasures that natural beauty offers,
with its soothing hints of the peace and order everyone dreams of.

She had bunches of flowers, baskets, and more were stuck in
    her hair
and the neck of her blouse. . . . And Pluto saw her and at that
    instant   370
loved her, was stricken, taken, and took her forthwith away,
leaning out of his chariot, seizing the girl, and then lashing
those powerful steeds, while she called out in the terror of
    helplessness
to her friends back at the lake and her mother, the goddess Ceres.
Abducted, innocent, dazed, she saw how the flowers fell
from the baskets, her hair, the blouse, and wept for their loss as
    though
those blossoms were her life, her very soul. The demon
lord of the underworld whipped his horses, called out their names,
and the chariot bounced and rattled through the rugged
    countryside,
past dank caverns and sulfurous pools, where fumes from the guts 380
of the earth seep out in a steady noxiousness. The hints
were not at all subtle and much less pleasant than those of the
    lake,
where Prosperpina's innocent flowers and swans had presided.
These bizarre and menacing landscapes suggested excess,
the pitiless struggle of creature with creature, of man with god,
of greeds and lusts on an unfair field. The maiden blanched
not so much at this savage idea of existence but rather
to see how her innocent notions of life and the world were
    betrayed
and ravished, even as she was being abducted and ravished.
    "'There is a bay near Arethusa, where Cyane lives,   390
that famous Sicilian nymph. To this place Pluto's hurtling
cart had come, but she stopped him, emerged waist-high from the
    water,
held out her arm, and defied him: "This far and no farther! You
cannot do this. This girl is Ceres' daughter, deserving
gentler treatment than this. She wants to be wooed and courted,
as I was, once, by Anapis. Give thought to how you behave!"
She positioned herself before him so as to block the horses'
path, but the son of Saturn, enraged, refused to listen
and would not take this advice he had not asked for. He lashed
the backs of his horses as if to run the nymph down and struck 400
with his royal scepter the water's surface and opened a chasm,
a deep abyss, a dizzying road that led down and down
to Tartarus and that dark kingdom from which he had come.

"'Cyane, mortified at how her spring was defiled,
dishonored, and desecrated by this rape of the goddess' daughter,
dissolved into tears. It was not at that time a mere expression,
some rhetorical turn or poetic and hyperbolic trope
but the fresh, simple, and unadorned terrible truth—she melted,
shimmered into the waters over which she had ruled, the lines
demarcating her body blurring, her limbs less distinct,   410
her hands and feet disappearing, her toenails and fingernails softer
and then no longer there. Her hair, the flesh of her buttocks
and breasts, her bones, all resolved into the soup of the water.
Her blood flowed less and less red, was water flowing in water.
And then she was gone. Meanwhile, Proserpina's mother, Ceres,
uneasy, concerned, then alarmed and frantic, looked for her child,
hurrying this way and that, from one town to the next,
in country after country, and then, when there were no more lands
in which to look, she went from sea to sea to plead
for news of the missing girl, a hint, some secondhand rumor,   420
but nothing of Prosperpina—or Persephone. Aurora sees
the mother rushing and seeking, and Hesperus, in the evening,
finds her still asking, "Where is my daughter? What has become
of that poor girl?" She is tireless, she is obsessed. She takes
pine torches and sticks them in Aetna's crater. They burst
at once into flame, and she holds them high at night to force back
the shadows that might conceal some trace of her lost child.
She is tireless, one might say, but even a goddess has limits.
At length, faint with hunger and thirst, she feels a fatigue
that saps her hopes. In a mood close to despair, she encounters   430
a simple hut with a roof of thatch and knocks on the door
to ask for a drink, for her lips are parched and her spirits,
        flagging.
An elderly woman answers, sees the goddess, and fetches
in decency and kindness a cup of barley water.
To Ceres, it's mead or ambrosia. She takes a tentative sip
and another, a deep draught. . . . And a local lout nearby
laughs at her distress and eagerness as she drinks.
He makes a joke of it, calling her greedy. She flings the rest
of the barley water at him. It splashes over his face.
Each grain of the barley seems to stick there, or leaves a spot,   440
and his arms begin to change into legs, and he sprouts a tail,
which grows as he is shrinking smaller and smaller. Astonished,
he would have been, if he realized what was happening, knew
he was turning into a newt, ugly but perfectly harmless.
The woman who lived in the hut was stricken to see this, wept

as she reached out to touch with a mother's hand this thing
that had been her son—but she could not catch him. He
　　　skittered away
to hide under a bush in his fear and shame, with those spots
of barley forever proclaiming his rudeness and its result.
　　　"'The entire earth she searched, the distant mountains, the
　　　　plains　　　　　　　　　　　　　　　　　　　　　　　　　　450
of Asia, the African jungle, the deserts of Asia Minor,
the seas and their islands, caves, and wherever there was to look,
in the numb belief that somewhere her daughter might yet be
　　　alive.
There was nowhere left to try, but she would not give up. Instead,
she resolved to do it again, start all over, go back
to Sicily, which she did, and scoured the island. At last
she came to Cyane's pool. If that nymph had not dissolved
she would have been able to tell what she'd seen. But however
　　　much
she wished to speak, there were no lips to form the words
and no voice to give them sound and life. But even the mute　　450
can speak if they have a mind. She contrived to let the water's
surface show Persephone's sash. Ceres saw this
and wept as if, for the first time, the truth of her daughter's
　　　disaster
was real. She tore her hair, wailed, and beat her breast
in grief and impotent rage, for she knew her child had been
　　　taken—
but not where or by whom. And therefore the whole world
was hateful and guilty. How could such a thing happen? And how
could it happen to her, the bountiful goddess, the giver of plenty
who deserved better? Honor, love, protection, and thanks
were surely her due, not this. . . . And to show the world,
　　　to reply　　　　　　　　　　　　　　　　　　　　　　　　　470
in unkind kind, she turned off all her blessings and broke
those sharp plowshares that had broken the earth to bring
　　　forth crops.
Instead, she allowed the fields to rebel and teach those ingrates
respect, appreciation, and their absolute dependence
on her good will. No seeds would sprout, no shoots would grow,
no heads of grain would nod in abundance and affirmation.
Drought, she would give them, or rain in torrents to wash away
the wealth of the farmer, his seed corn, the very topsoil he
　　　lived on.

Gaunt birds devoured whatever there was, and hunger
showed in the eyes of men and women and children, as weeds   480
grew on their ruined acres, where golden wheat had waved.
    "'Out of this desolation, there came the plaintive voice
of Arethusa, daughter of Alpheus, who appeared
from the lake in which she lived, water still streaming down
from her lovely hair. She brushed it back and addressed the
        goddess:
"Mother of earth, mother of crops, and the sorry mother
of that poor girl, I implore you, mollify your anger.
The revenge you take is wrong, for the land you punish is
        guiltless.
The earth of Sicily did not purloin your daughter, did not
conspire, and could not prevent what happened against its will.   490
I am a stranger here, an impartial witness who speaks
only the truth. I come from Pisa, lived in Elis,
and now I am here on the island I love and have made my home.
This is hardly the moment to rehearse my story. Another
time, when you are composed and less in pain, we may speak
of how it came that my currents dove down under the sea
to emerge here. What's important is that I've passed through the
        depths
of the world's deepest waters and have come up here to see stars
shining again as I'd all but forgotten they can. And I saw,
at the nadir of my passage, at the shores of the Styx itself,   500
your daughter. Yes, I have seen her with my own eyes. She reigns
as queen of that dismal world, and consort of its grim ruler.
Despondent, she was, forlorn and frightened, but nevertheless
the queen there, and alive." Ceres was mute as a stone.
Who can say what she was thinking, or whether? The mind
        goes numb
and just shuts down when it must. But then, the pain returns
and one must do something, act, move. She leapt in her car
and set forth to the realms of heaven to voice her complaint
to Jove himself. Her hair was wild. She was wild. She declared:
"Jupiter, I have come on behalf of my child and yours.   510
Whatever you once felt or feel now for me counts less
than what you must feel for your daughter. How can you not
        be moved
to hear what I have just heard? Having searched far and wide,
I find her and know she is lost. Stolen? Abducted? Married
to such a brute? Outrageous! He must bring her back! I beg you,

hear my grief! Answer my fervent prayer!" Jove heard
and was moved. He declared Prosperpina was their daughter,
      the fruit
of their love and their joint care. "And yet," he said, "and yet,
we must put the right names to events and things. Reason
      demands
such precision. Was this a crime, an abduction? Or was it   520
an act of love? The suitor, the husband, if we may so
define him, is worthy indeed, my own brother the lord
of the underworld. Had the drawing of lots produced results
only a little different, he'd have been lord of heaven.
This is a son-in-law not easy for us to despise.
Still, if you are determined, so set against this union
that you would have her back, I grant you what you desire,
on the one condition—that there, in the underworld, no morsel
has passed her lips. The Fates, I fear, have decreed it so."
      "'Having said this, he was silent. Ceres indeed was resolved   530
to have her daughter returned to the realm of light and air,
but the Fates were opposed. The girl had already taken that fatal
taste, an innocuous nibble, an all but unconscious gesture,
for walking in the garden—Pluto's château can claim
extensive if rather gloomy grounds with elaborate plantings—
she'd noticed a pomegranate hanging in easy reach,
ripe, attractive. . . . Its purple color had caught her eye.
She had plucked it, peeled the rind, and eaten seven seeds.
Worse, she'd been seen to do this. The mischievous Ascalaphus,
son of Orphne, a nymph of Avernus, had watched and tattled,   540
and the deed was known. For this reason, Proserpina splashed
his face with Phlegethon's water and turned him into an ugly
bird. He feels himself decomposing, reforming, becoming
a large, ungainly thing with somber feathers and baleful
cry. He is the lazy screech owl, that bird of dismal
omen. But birdishness is not a bad outcome always.
Such transformations can carry a number of different meanings.
Consider the not altogether different fate of the daughters
of Acheloüs, who had been Prosperpina's companions
there at Pergus' banks. These girls were turned into birds—   550
or their bodies at least were those of birds. Their shoulders
      and heads
were human still, and their voices, amazing, wonderful voices,
with the gift of astonishing songs, were more than human,
      for these
are the Sirens. How did their transformation come about?

These were the same young ladies who fretted, mourned, and
    searched
high and low for their missing friend. They roamed the earth
in charity and distress, thinking not of themselves
but living only for her, looking for her, and wishing,
having exhausted the length and breadth of the lands of the earth,
to consider the sea's expanses. They prayed, therefore, for wings   560
on which they could soar and glide, the better to search for their
    friend.
These prayers the celestial powers heard and granted forthwith,
and the faithful girls became the gorgeous creatures they are
even now, with their melodies, dirges, and melismas,
the croonings and plaints that pierce the hearts of the gruffest
    men,
entrancing them with the eerie beauty of music's promise.
    "'But Jove now had to decide this question between the two
irreconcilable gods Pluto and Ceres: Which
should have the girl, Prosperpina? Which one would he please,
and which would he risk displeasing? Both, he decided, sadly,   570
as he rendered his solemn judgment, saying he would divide—
not the girl, but the year! A six-month term she would spend
in the realm of light with her mother, and six months down in
    the dark
with her husband, lord of the shades. Ceres is satisfied,
and her countenance now resumes its former pleasant aspect,
as the Sun coming out from behind the banks of clouds reveals
his former face and restores the world to a better mood.
    "'Happy now that her daughter has been returned to her,
    Ceres
goes back to that lovely pool to ask of the helpful nymph,
Arethusa, the missing details of her story—how   580
she fled, and why, and how she became a sacred spring.
As the pleasant babble of water fades away to a hush,
a scintillant silence, the nymph emerges from out of her spring,
wrings her hair dry, and speaks of what happened so long
ago. Her tale is hardly novel, but sad and true.
She recites it, as if it had happened to someone else, explaining
how in Elis, "I was another happy nymph,
doing what nymphs have always done, hunting, trapping,
and cavorting with my sisters. I was a tomboy, really,
and when someone praised my looks—which happened
    rather often—   590
I didn't believe them. I suppose I didn't want to admit it.

What had my looks to do with me, after all? But I learned.
Oh, yes, I learned. I was coming back from the hunt one day,
tired, sweaty, exhausted, and I arrived at a pleasant stream. . . .
It looked harmless enough, with its water clear, its surface
smooth, its banks grassy with willows providing shade.
It was hardly a menacing place. I dipped my feet in the water
and waded a little farther, up to my knees. It was cool,
refreshing. . . . I took off my tunic and hung my clothes on a
    branch
of one of those trees, and plunged into the water. Naked,   600
but not thinking about it, I was a child, a fish,
swimming and plunging, floating, enjoying myself. I heard
a rumbling noise, a murmur that came from the water's depths.
Frightened, I scrambled out, but I heard a voice that was calling,
'Come back, Arethusa. Come back!' It was Alpheus, the river,
the god of the river, calling. I ran away, still naked,
leaving my clothes behind on that willow branch. He followed,
came out of the water, and chased me. I fled. He pursued,
relentless as any hawk that follows a helpless dove,
faster, on stronger wings, its terrible talons closer   610
with each maneuver. I ran in a blind panic, crossing
woods and fields and passing town after town. I remember
Orchomenus and Psophis, and Erymanthus. . . . I crossed
mountains and other rivers, but he kept on, was gaining.
The Sun was setting behind me, and I could see his shadow
stretching out, to pass my feet, and mix with my own.
I heard his breath and even thought I could feel it, hot
on the nape of my neck, fanning my hair. Desperate, I cried,
'Help me, Diana. Save me! I am your creature, your servant.
Protect me now with those weapons I've carried for you so often.' 620
I didn't expect help, not really, but she had heard me,
and answered my prayer. A cloud surrounded me, hid me,
    kept me
safe. He groped and prodded but could not find me. He called
my name, and I shrank as a lamb might do when a wolf calls out
as it circles the fold, or a rabbit, hearing the pack of dogs
baying its secret name, freezes and tries to be tiny.
He didn't see any footprints leading away and stayed
right where he was, waiting and watching, ready to pounce.
I could feel my sweat pouring down. It mixed with the mist,
and, wherever I put my foot, there was a puddle, a pool.   630
My hair was dripping, my hands, and I turned then into a stream,
was running water—and he knew it, could tell it was me,

and, putting aside the guise of a man, he resumed his true
form and became a river to mingle with mine. My goddess
did not abandon me even then, but struck the earth,
and I plunged down deep to arise here in distant Ortygia,
and even now, it is said, whatever one throws in that distant
Greek current will sink and surface in Sicily here.'"
    "'Her tale was done, and Ceres returned to her chariot,
       flicked
the reins of her dragon team, and soared away toward Athens,   640
where she gave her car to Triptolemus, the young man she had
       once nursed
to health and taught the secrets of agriculture. She gave him
seeds to scatter on earth wherever he would, in fallow
fields and untilled meadows, and this he did, on a journey
that brought him even to Scythia, where Lyncus sat on the
       throne.
He bowed to the king and said: "Triptolemus is my name,
and I come here flying through air to bring you the gifts of Ceres:
fertility, cultivation, and civilization itself."
The king, ungrateful, envied the giver. A brute, a lout,
he welcomed the guest and then, in the night, came to his
       chamber   650
with drawn sword to attack him. But Ceres saw and protected
her emissary. She turned the king to a lynx and recalled
Triptolemus and her sacred team home again to Athens.'
    "Here, Calliope ended. When the nymphs agreed her
       performance
had won the day, those upstart sisters complained of the verdict,
protested it wasn't fair. It was fixed, was rigged. Our patience,
already worn thin, was now at an end. It was cheeky
and rude enough of these nine sisters to challenge the nine
of us to this contest. We had indulged them and fairly played
their ridiculous game. . . . But now, to be bad sports when
       they'd lost?   660
Ludicrous! We reminded them who they were, but they would not
listen. They babbled, chattered, squabbled, and waved their hands
in vulgar gesticulation we watched with increasing interest,
for we had had agreed to punish their invincible tastelessness.
We observed those hands and arms sprouting feathers. They
       turned
to wings. We noticed the signs of their nanocephaly, marked
how their faces were more and more beaked. None could see
       herself,

but each noticed the others, and all were frightened or angry
or both, and they babbled more and more loudly, complaining,
      warning.
Or mourning. Birds of a feather they were—and no one
      could now   670
doubt it, seeing them—magpies, whose foolish chatter disturbs
the serene woods even now as they flit hither and thither,
twitter, scold, and complain, their voices exercised
but never truly expressive or making sense. They go on
and endlessly on, devoid of talent, reason, or charm
so other birds are distressed by the dreadful noise of these anti-
Muses, which is what they were and will be forever."

BOOK VI

Having heard this story, and having approved, Minerva
admitted she felt much the same—that praise is all very well,
but what one really wants is speechless awe. That mortals
should even think of matching their powers with those of the gods
is laughable, pathetic, and requires prompt correction.
She remembered how Arachne had vied with her, had considered
the goddess to be her peer—if that—in the art of spinning.
And who was this person? No one! A nothing, from out of
      nowhere.
Her father, Idmon, had worked in Colophon as a dyer,
turning the cloth in his vats purple. Her mother? Dead!   10
Her husband? A common laborer. Yet she presumed to suppose
that her skill, which everyone praised, might be what they said,
      in fact
might be the best in the world. She wasn't by any means bad,
and they say that nymphs would come to her hamlet to watch her
      work—
Hypaepa, I think it was named. They admired her finished pieces
and stood behind her wheel, admiring what she did,
winding the rough yarn into a new ball, shaping the wool
with her fingers, or reaching back to the distaff to grab more.
She could take a cloudy clump of the fleecy stuff and spin it
fine into a slender but nevertheless strong   20
thread with a dexterous thumb she could lay onto the spindle.
The needlework she did at the hoop, sewing the intricate
figures. . . . They said it was just like mine! And she came to
      believe them,
even persuading herself her work was as good as my own.
"I invite the goddess—I dare her—to compete with me," she said,
in jest perhaps, but these jokes are a way of disguising the truth.
"I'd bet whatever I have—my life itself," she said.
"What kind of joke is that?" the goddess asked, who assumed
for this occasion the guise of a bent and gray-haired woman

who tottered along the road, supporting herself with a stick.   30
She encountered the rash Arachne and gave her a little advice:
"Listen to me, young lady, and heed the wisdom of age,
for the old have seen a lot and have learned at least a little.
I think you're a fine and clever young woman. Your work is good,
and you are proud, and should be. And yet do not presume.
Never annoy the gods and goddesses. Nothing good
can come of it. You should think and pray, and apologize,
and all will be well. I say this for your own good, my dear!"
Arachne ought to have listened. Instead, she glared at the woman,
looked as if she might slap her, and, hissing in anger, replied: 40
"What senile drivel is this that your toothless mouth is spewing?
Who asked for your advice? Do you have a daughter-in-law?
If you're set on tormenting someone, why don't you bother her?
The goddess doesn't need you to protect her. Let her come!
I'm ready any time." Hearing this, Minerva,
throwing aside the cloak and gray hair of her imposture,
revealed herself and announced, "She has come. And I am here!"
Straightaway, the nymphs fell down to adore the numinous
          goddess.
In awe, the Mygdonian women prayed she might show them
          mercy.
Only Arachne refused to back down. She knew she'd been tricked   50
and, doubting that she could retrieve herself or take back her
          boast,
pressed on—although with a blush that reddened her cheeks as
          the Sun
will color the sky in the morning but then leave it sickly pale.
If all was lost, what more could she risk? She stared at the
          goddess,
and, stupid or brave or merely resigned, she set up her loom,
as did Minerva. They stretched their warps, threaded their
          shuttles,
and commenced to throw them back and forth to build up
          the wefts
in a show of skill and focused attention that would have been
splendid at any other time or place. The contest
turned everything dreadful and desperate. Their fingers flew   60
back and forth, as they tamped the threads down. One could see
gorgeousness emerging on both of the looms, the purple
threads bright from the dye pot snaking across to give depth
to the brighter colors. Sometimes, after a storm, rainbows
festoon the sky, and children look up to see how the colors

change from one to another in endless subtle gradations,
so the eyes are utterly dazzled, and the mind is unable to give
the right name to the hue of any particular place
in the variegated wonder. That awe, that wonder, these two
contrived on their looms before them in the rich sheen of their
      fabrics.   70
      On Pallas' frame is a vivid representation of Athens:
the Acropolis looming high, and twelve gods on their thrones
deciding what to call this place. You can pick them out.
Jove is, of course, in the middle, noble and royal. To one side,
his brother Neptune is holding a trident, with which he has
      smitten
the cliff behind him. Water is pouring forth from the sea
as if to take the city and claim it for him. She has woven
herself into the picture as well—the one with the shield
held up to her breast, and the spear (you can see its point!) and
      helmet.
The earth has produced a tree in the place where she has touched it,   80
an olive, thick with its fruit, which the other gods admire
as they do her accomplishment. The figure of Victory smiles
on what she has done in a message that surely is clear enough,
but, to drive home the point with even more force, she puts in the
      corners
insets that tell the stories of mortals competing with gods,
always with dreadful results. In one, you see Rhodope, wife
of Haemus, the King of Thrace, who considered herself an equal
in beauty to Juno herself. That couple was turned into grim
and barren mountains. A second inset depicts Gerana,
the Queen of the Pygmies, another overreacher, whom Juno   90
reproved and turned into a crane. The stork in the third panel
is not just another bird, but the sorry transmogrification
Antigone underwent—she was Laomedon's lovely
daughter, who wears a marabou boa morning to night
and croaks and clacks her beak. The last corner displays
Cinyras on the marble steps of the temple, weeping
and hugging those paving stones that were once his living
      daughters.
Around the entire work, the goddess has worked a wreath
of trompe l'oeil leaves of the olive, her tree and emblem, so fine
it is hard to believe they are woven of thread. Her work is done.   100
      On the other loom, Arachne has made an impressive
      tableau—
Europa, deceived by the bull. You look at the bull's muscles

and gleaming wet hide, and are fooled just as she was. She
smiles,
waves to her friends on shore you are sure must be just behind you,
and wavelets that break at her feet are like pearl and diamond
anklets.
She puts in others, Asterie, whom Jupiter wooed as an eagle
and then betrayed; and Leda, struggling with that swan.
Other seductions, betrayals, low tricks, and high jinks she weaves:
Antiope, to whom Jupiter came as a satyr; Alcmena,
whom he tricked into bed by imposture, taking the guise of
her true   110
husband, Amphitryon. And there is Danaë, wet in his golden
shower, and there, Aegina, warm with his dancing flame.
He's a shepherd for Mnemosyne, a snake for Ceres' daughter. . . .
And Neptune's adventures she shows with the same uncomfortable
candor:
here he is as a bull, a ram, a horse, a bird,
or a dolphin, coming on to one poor girl or another,
persuading, deceiving, shocking, or overpowering each
as the mood or occasion suggests, but always unfairly. And
Phoebus
is up to the same low tricks, as a hawk, a lion, or simple
shepherd lad. And other gods—Bacchus, for instance,   120
or even ancient Saturn—pretend, deceive, have their way,
and are gone—but not forgotten. The whole sorry tradition
is here, and she also works a border of flowers and clinging
ivy, perhaps representing those maidens and their affections.
Flawless, really. Amazing! Envy himself can't find
a fault in the work. Minerva inspects the piece and is livid.
Something less, she'd have laughed at and could have dismissed,
but this
is serious *lèse-majesté,* in intention and execution,
subversive in what it proclaims. She rips it in shreds and tatters,
seizes the boxwood shuttle, and with it beans Arachne   130
again and again. Arachne cannot endure it, is pained
as she realizes she has won but that this will do her no good.
If life is unfair this way, then how and why should she stand it?
She stands instead on a chair, puts a noose round her neck,
and kicks the chair away. Minerva, in pity, or shame,
lifts her up and saves her, commanding the girl, "Live!
Continue to hang, but live!" A puzzling doom perhaps,
but she sprinkles the girl with drops of Hecate's magic potion,

which causes her hair to fall out, her head to shrink, and her body,
rounder and smaller. Her fingers—those skillful fingers—
            turn into   140
legs, and she spins and weaves with them still, and continues
            to hang
in the webs she contrives every night, she and her spider kind.

        This news, strange and terrible, travels of course. The world
is speaking of nothing else. It had to have reached as far
as Thebes, surely, where Niobe would have heard the details
of what had befallen her childhood playmate, her friend Arachne.
And she ought to have learned its lesson of reverence before the
            gods,
or at least a modest demeanor, discretion. . . . What do they cost?
But no, she was full of herself, her wealth, her position, her
            husband,
Amphion, his wonderful talent—to strum the lyre and watch
            stones   150
dance into place to become a wall. But these were all trifles
compared to her basic boast, that she had the best of all children,
that she had been blessed in motherhood better than any woman
who ever lived. This claim, had anyone else proposed it,
might have passed itself off as sentiment. But from her?
It was malapropos, as was her rejection of the command
of Manto, Tiresias' daughter, that all should attend in Latona's
temple to thank and praise, and do the goddess reverence.
"This the goddess requires, in words she forms with my mouth,"
the seer's daughter declares, and the women of Thebes obey her,   160
go to the temple, pray, and burn incense on her altar.

        But Niobe's not there. Where can she be? She comes
with her own procession, her friends and attendants, and she's
            decked out
in Phrygian robes with gold embroidered figures. She's angry,
flushed perhaps, but handsome, and knows it, and tosses her hair
in front of the temple, pauses, and then addresses the people,
asking them what they think they're doing. "A goddess? Latona?
But who has seen her, and why should we worship before her
            altar?
What is she to me? My father, Tantalus, dined
at the gods' table. My sisters, the Pleiades, are immortal.   170
My grandsire Atlas holds up the skies. On the other side,
the father of my father was almighty Jove himself,
who is also my father-in-law. Where, then, is my cult,

my temple, my redolent altar? I am queen of the house
of Cadmus, whose wealth and beauty are merely the outward
    signs
of my inner grace. But my children, my seven daughters and seven
sons . . . for these, I am worthy of praise and envy of men
and women everywhere—as much as Latona, surely!
Who is she? The daughter of Coeus? (And who was he?)
What majesty can she claim who fled the wrath of Juno,   180
could not find in the whole wide world a place to lie down
and whelp? In the end, Delos, which then was a wandering island,
was moved to pity a fellow vagrant and settled down
so that she could have a place to bear her children—two!
A seventh of what I've borne! What is there then to worship?
Happiness, we pray for, and wealth, and safety . . . and I
have all these things. They are mine and I, therefore, am they!
Even if Fortune were set against me, knowing what mothers
most deeply fear, and took a child of mine, or several,
I should have more remain with me than Latona bore!   190
Your hopes are banal, your fears are dreary, the goddess you
    worship
is no goddess at all and cannot protect or reward you.
Take off those garlands of laurel you wear in your hair. Take off
those wreaths and fillets! That nonsense of burning incense
    must stop
at once. Rely instead on yourselves and know that mortals
are no mere toys of the gods but masters of our own fates."
A persuasive woman, she is, and powerful, as she says,
so the people put off their wreaths and scatter back to their
    houses,
muttering under their breaths the prayers they have not
    completed.
    Atop Mount Cynthus, Latona, angry to see and hear   200
this offensive business, went to report and complain to the god
Apollo and goddess Diana—for these were her son and daughter:
"You must help me, children. This insult cannot be ignored.
If it is, no one will pray at my altars ever again.
I am, as you know, a goddess second to none but Juno,
authentic, immortal, divine. But this proud woman defies me,
as if those creatures down there had voted us in or could somehow
impeach or recall those gods and goddesses they didn't care for.
What kind of cosmos is that? We are all insulted, but I
in particular am the object of the insolence she shows us.   210
And you, my children, also, for she has preferred her own

enormous brood to you. She jeers that I'm nearly childless!
Let her have some idea of what childlessness is! Correct
the impudence she has displayed in this badgering of those people
who came to do me reverence. . . ." She might have gone on
            with this,
but her children had caught the drift. Phoebus waited a moment
and then, with a smile, interrupted. "No need to go on," he
            exclaimed.
"It would only delay further the punishment she deserves."
Phoebe, his sister, the Moon, laughed and agreed with her
            brother.
They bade their mother good-by and flew through the air to
            alight   220
or materialize in a cloud on the citadel of Athens.
There is at the base of that hill, around its high walls, a road
where the tread of horses has beaten a track and chariot wheels
have made a double path of their ruts. On that day, it happened
that all seven of Amphion's sons were out together,
riding along on their mounts, and sitting tall in their saddles,
gorgeous in robes of white and purple and in their rein hands
holding gold-encrusted bridles. Ismenus, the eldest,
cried out as much in surprise as pain when the arrow struck him,
fixed in his chest, and took him down. He sagged in the saddle,   230
slowly fell to one side, and hit the ground. His brother
Sipylus tried to flee, or fight, or ride for help. . . .
It was hard to tell, for he started to goad his horse to run
but almost at that instant felt the shaft of another arrow,
which hit the back of his neck and quivered there. The point
protruded in the front, and the wounded youth pitched forward,
gushing blood on his horse's mane and legs and hoofprints.
Two others, who had dismounted, were having a wrestling
            match,
Phaedimus and their grandfather's namesake, Tantalus. Straining,
toe to toe, grappling, hugging, each trying to throw   240
the other, they felt an arrow that passed through both their
            bodies,
a single skewer through two quails. Together they groaned,
fell to the ground, and, holding each other, breathed their last.
Alphenor saw them stricken, ran to them to help them,
picked up their bodies, but knew it was too late for them, and
            now
for him as well—for he felt the hot pain of the point
of Apollo's arrow low in his ribs. He pulled the shaft

out and looked in horror to see that a mess of lung
had come out with it. He saw, for a moment or two, his blood
gush forth dark on the ground. Damasichthon then,   250
hit just behind the ankle, fell, and was trying to draw
the arrow out when another hit, this time in his throat,
all the way up to the feathers. Blood spurted forth in a high
crimson geyser, as if from some ornamental fountain.
Ilioneus, last of the brothers, looked around him
at this nightmare of gore and carnage, knelt down onto the
        ground,
and raised his hands in prayer: "You gods, hear me! Have mercy!"
He needn't have used the plural. Apollo, however, had heard him,
was moved to pity and might have relented, had not the arrow
already left the bow, was on its way through the air,   260
and now was about to strike. It only nicked his heart.
        News of this disaster reached the palace at once,
and Niobe heard it, refused at first to believe it, but then
it began to sink in, and her shock and amazement turned to
        pain—
to anguish and rage, for how could a thing like this have
        happened?
How could it happen to her? How had the gods dared treat her
with such rough hands! After all the troubles that she had
        endured:
Amphion, her husband, killed himself with a dagger thrust,
ending his grief and his life at the same instant, and leaving
Niobe widowed, and all their daughters fatherless, grieving.   270
How could she ever have said those things to the temple women?
That question may have presented itself in the back of her mind,
but she had no time now for such rational thoughts. Her spirit
was full of the ache that arose from her heart. She had them
        laid out
and kissed her sons' bodies, still warm—the blood was still
        sticky—
and wept and knelt on the ground, raising distracted eyes
to heaven, and shouted in pain, "Are you satisfied now? Are you
        pleased
by this disgusting scene? Is my agony sweet, Latona?
Do the deaths of my seven sons delight you? A monster, a beast,
would have shrunk from so vile an act. You, a goddess, enjoyed it!   280
These are your triumphs. Count them! What I have left is more
than you ever had. Bereft, I am yet better blessed than you.
Diminished and battered thus, I can claim victory still!"

It was bad enough to think this, but rash to have said it aloud.
She heard on the instant the twang of a bowstring. The crowd
    drew back
in fear and dismay. Her daughters were standing there at their
    brothers'
biers, their hair flowing loose, and their faces veiled in black.
One of the sisters was touching an arrow still in a brother's
corpse, perhaps to assure herself this was real, or perhaps
to draw it out to preserve as a grisly souvenir.   290
She collapsed, it seemed in a faint, her body across her brother's.
A second sister, consoling their mother, then doubled over
as if with some unseen wound. She closed her lips tight and died.
Panic spread through the five remaining sisters. One tried
to flee, took a few steps, and fell. And another tripped,
or seemed to have tripped, on her body and also fell. Both dead?
Indeed, and the mother looked around now, and counted—six!
Only the youngest remained, whom the mother, in awe and
    terror,
draped with her cloak and hid with her body, praying aloud
in keening sobs: "Oh, spare her! Leave me, I beg, this last,   300
this innocent baby, my darling. . . . For pity's sake, I implore. . . .
Spare her!" But all in vain, for the girl shuddered and died
there in her arms. No response or breath or pulse. Gone!
All gone! And the childless mother looks around her, smitten
and longing herself for death, all her sons and her daughters
and her husband are dead, and her poor body, obstreperous,
    stupid,
is living and breathing still. In stony silence she stares
at the bodies she'd held and nursed and bathed, all cold as stones,
as still as stones. No breeze would dare to ruffle her hair.
Her face is pale and unmoving, her eyes are as fixed as a statue's,   310
and her tongue is a stone in her mouth. Her veins, muscles, and
    organs
all are stone, but she weeps as no stone can. She weeps
a rain of tears. A whirlwind catches her up, transports her
back to her native soil, and there, on a mountain peak,
sets her down where she stands, today, a pillar of marble,
and the water that trickles in twin rivulets are her tears.
        A frightful business, and yet from then on men and women
have known to fear the wrath of the goddess. They come to
    worship,
with a zeal that is born of terror, this mother of twin gods.
Leaving one of her temples after the ritual, people   320

will chat and gossip, or else tell stories to one another.
This is one story that someone told on such an occasion:
"When I was a child, I heard what happened once to the farmers
who failed to pay their respects and offer thanks to our goddess.
I saw the lake where they say the marvel happened. My father,
ill at the time, had put me in charge of a herd of cattle.
I'd hired a local fellow as guide and helper. We'd driven
the cows along a path in the countryside and were passing
an unimpressive pond when he stopped and whispered a prayer,
'Goddess, grant me mercy!' He signaled to me to do   330
as he had done, and I echoed his 'Goddess, grant me mercy!'
I could see at the water's edge an altar, old and black
from many sacrificial fires. I asked him to tell me
what naiad or faun or god presided here and invited
whatever explanation he cared to give of his odd
behavior. He told me the tale: 'It is here that Latona came.
She had wandered far and found a sanctuary in Delos,
had made her bed of the fronds of palm trees and olive branches,
and given birth to the twin divinities, but the wrath
of Juno was still to be feared, and she fled from the queen of
          heaven,   340
now with her babes in her arms. Here at the Chimaera's home,
in Lycia, she arrived, tired, hungry, thirsty,
and faint from her long journey and the hot Sun. Her children
were suffering even more, for her breasts had long since gone dry.
She came, they say, to this very pond at which we are standing.
A few of the locals were gathering reeds here to make baskets.
When Latona came to the water's edge and knelt down to drink,
to quench her terrible thirst, they told her to go away!
They would not let her drink. "Will you deny me water?
Would you deny me air to breathe? How can you claim   350
to own what Nature has given freely to all for our common
use?" she asked. But they did not answer, would not relent.
She went on, allowed their absurd claim, but asked, as a favor,
a drink. She wasn't intending to bathe in the water, but just
to quench her thirst and her children's. "My mouth," she
          complained, "is dry.
I can barely speak these words. I ask you to spare my life,
for that is what it amounts to. I'll owe you my thanks forever."
Still, nothing. She holds the infants up, the helpless
babes who reach out their hands as if to touch the water,
or, in an imploring gesture, to the hard hearts of these peasants.   360
But still nothing, except their jeers and insults. They roil

the water with sticks to cloud it with mud from the bottom
        and spite
the suppliant and her thirst—which now gives way to anger.
She raises her arms to the heavens and cries to the gods: "So be it!
Let them have forever this pool they claim for themselves.
Let it be their world!" And it was and is. They plunge
deep into the water, surface, stick out their heads,
or sit on the bank and gribbitz and croak in an endless quarrel,
blaming one another for what has befallen them all.
Their throats puff out in an ugly display of their self-importance.   370
They are hideous now and shameless, with their backs a dull
        green and bellies
a sickly white, and they live in that mud they once so cruelly
stirred up, and, in their shame, they dive deep in the water
they refused to share with a stranger. They are the frogs you see
        here.' "
        The company nodded their heads, approving the tale and its
            warning,
and after a pause another spoke up, for one story invites
another, for all these tales have a life of their own, collect
as birds will into flocks, and they wheel and soar in their lovely
formations no single bird could possibly comprehend.
Another in this company told of the satyr Marsyas,   380
whom Latona's son Apollo vanquished once in a contest.
The satyr presumed to challenge that god as to which could play
a better song on the flute. Apollo, to no one's surprise,
won, and punished the satyr, flayed him alive in fact,
peeling his skin from his body inch by inch to leave
an enormous wound, which looked like a medical illustration.
One jokes, for the mind recoils from a certain degree of horror,
but there he was, howling in pain, his sinews bare,
his vital organs all on display, the blood spilling down,
terrifying, disgusting. . . . He cried out in his torment,   390
but the god had won the contest, and only that was real.
The suffering of his victim was irrelevant, abstract,
although fauns, satyrs, and gods wept to see his anguish,
as the country people wept at his monstrous torture. Their tears
soaked into the earth, which drank them and spilled them forth,
purified, to form a rivulet that swelled
to the stream we call by his name, the Marsyas—with the purest,
clearest, and sweetest water of any of Phrygia's rivers.
        There is quiet, at least, for a while, and then talk turns, as
            it will,

to recent events, the gossip, the joys and griefs of friends,   400
and the larger griefs of the noble and great: they refer to
     Amphion,
dead now, and all his children, Niobe's children,
dead. The mother's fault, they agree, but Pelops, her brother,
shook his head and wept, and beat his breast in mourning,
which made a surprising sound. He explained it by showing how,
under his garment, his chest had been patched with an ivory inlay.
It wasn't always like that. He had been a normal baby,
but Tantalus, his father, had hacked him in bits, and the gods
had intervened and repaired him, putting the pieces together,
or those they could find. One fragment, where the neck and
     upper arm   410
met, had disappeared, so they juryrigged it with this
elegant ivory plate to make him whole again.
     To be made whole! What a dream this is, what a lovely
     vision,
we dare not speak of it even when we come together in
     mourning—
as they did, in those days, to condole with Thebes in its loss.
From Argos, Sparta, Mycenae, the princes came with their trains,
and from Calydon, where Diana's boar had not yet run wild,
from Orchomenos and Corinth, from Patra, Pylos, . . . all over,
they came, as family members will come together to grieve.
Only Athens was missing, occupied with a war   420
against barbaric invaders surrounding its walls. That siege
was lifted only when Tereus, King of Thrace, arrived
to put the attackers to flight. A noble, a wonderful deed!
Athens, of course, was grateful, and Pandion, its king,
chose to reward this savior by making a match between him
and Procne, the princess royal, uniting the two great houses.
But this was a wedding Juno somehow failed to attend.
Hymen also was absent, as the Graces were. Instead,
the Furies appeared with torches plucked from a funeral pyre,
and over the wedding chamber a screech owl called its baleful   430
epithalamion. Omens, in short, were distressing for Procne,
for Tereus, her bridegroom, and the child they then conceived,
but Athens rejoiced at the wedding of Pandion's daughter, and
     Thrace
likewise rejoiced at the birth of Itys, their son. There was feasting,
as if this, too, were a happy occasion. (But how can we ever
even begin to guess?)
     Five long years had passed,

and Procne said to her husband, "I miss my sister. Allow me,
if I have at all pleased you, to visit her or invite her
to come for a visit here. My father will surely allow her   440
to travel for such a purpose." Her husband agreed and, launching
his vessels, worked with sail and oar to arrive at Piraeus'
harbor. He went ashore and greeted his father-in-law.
They clasped hands, and they wished each other well. He
        conveyed
Procne's love and request that her sister, Philomela,
come to visit. He'd hardly finished speaking when she
appeared, her clothing resplendent, and as beautiful in her person
as the naiads are said to be, or the dryads deep in the woods'
secret places. This king, Tereus, saw her, was stunned
as if he'd been struck. Her beauty possessed him entirely,
        crazed him.   450
Was this his sister-in-law? Did it matter? Was this his fault,
or something that fell from the sky too grand for him to resist?
Resistance, however, was far from his mind. He was calculating
how to get her aboard his ship, to his city, his house. . . .
A passionate man, the king of a passionate people, he knew
the not quite believable stories of other men's rapture, and now
found they fell short of the truth. Possessed, so that life until now
seemed to be somebody else's, a sham, a dream, he considered
how he would now be willing to use any force or guile
to possess that delicious creature! Tempt her with riches? Seduce
        her?   460
Rape her? Whatever it took, he would not so much stoop to
        as own
that this was his nature, his fate, and, if he felt some small twinges
of pity or sorrow for what he knew was about to happen,
they were for her and himself together, their destinies joined
inextricably, as their bodies would soon join in embrace.
    As if he read from a script, he recited his speech about
        Procne's
desire to see her sister, her loneliness there in the palace,
her wish for a face and voice she had known and loved from
        girlhood,
and, acting in her behalf, he even produced some tears
to show how deep was the love of her whom he loved. Amazed,   470
the people of Athens decided that this was a fellow of feeling,
of kindness, compassion, virtue. . . . A plausible supposition,
but what do we ever know of the inner heart of a man
when wickedness can appear in whatever form it chooses?

Philomela believed him and begged her father, the king,
to allow her to go. She embraced her father, her slender arms
about his neck, and their guest, Tereus, now reached out
to embrace them both—and touch her delicate arm, its golden
down, its exquisite smoothness, its warmth, a bliss and a torment.
He orders himself to stay calm, to continue his kindly pretense.   480
He thinks of throwing her down on the ground right there. . . .
      He smiles
and lets himself look foolish. Pandion nods and agrees
to let her go. The girl squeals with delight (and he cannot
help but think of the squeals of love he will wring from her later).
She says how happy she is, and Tereus, nodding and grinning,
appears as happy as she—and he is the one with reason.
      The long day draws to a close, as Phoebus' weary horses
hurry home. A feast is spread for the great occasion
with many meats, sweet dainties, and wine in cups of gold.
The court, happy and sated, yields to the soporific   490
effect of their grand gorge, and they all slumber and snore—
except for the king of Thrace, whose mind is a dazzle of pictures
of what he has seen, those lips, those eyes, those delicate arms,
the hair, the fingernails, and the way she holds her head.
More, his imagination is all too ready to offer,
even more vivid images of what he has not yet beheld
but yearns to. He doesn't lie on his bed that night as much
as he seethes in visions he cannot get rid of and his own sweat,
which pours down from his body as if he were stricken with
      fever.
In the morning, looking haggard, he smiles as his father-in-law   500
bids him farewell and consigns to his care a second daughter.
"Your plea, and Procne's, has won my heart. I commend this girl
to your protection. I pray you may keep her safe, and send her
home to her father's love." Turning then to his daughter,
he says, "Philomela, know you go with my love and care.
Visit your sister, but then return to your lonely father,
who cannot long endure to be parted from both his daughters.
Convey to Procne my love." He cannot go on, but hugs her,
kisses her hard, and then forces himself to let her loose,
as his tears spill out with the meaning his voice and tongue intend.   510
      The ribbon of black water widened between the ship
and shore, which began to recede. The hull picked up the swell
of the sea as the sails bellied out. They were underway, and
      the cruel
king could barely maintain the discipline of his face

before his crew, as his soul exulted in triumph, for nothing
could stand in his way now. It was going to happen! Only
a matter of distance and time, and he could wait, could savor
this exercise of patience, knowing what joys to expect.

    They arrived at Thrace, disembarked, and Tereus led the girl,
innocent, unsuspecting, into the woods to a hut   520
he sometimes used when hunting. Puzzled at first, then worried,
Philomela wanted to know where her sister was
and why they were here in the woods in this hut, which was
        clearly not
a palace. He told her then, not gloating but rather in sadness,
of the lot that fate had cast for both of them, of his passion.
Horrified, she fought him—in vain. He was strong, and lust
lent him an even greater strength. He took her, raped her,
there in the hut. And again, and then he cast her aside.
Like a lamb a wolf has mauled and then dropped, she trembled in
        terror.
A dove that an eagle had snatched with its claws and then allowed   530
to escape, she lay on the dirt floor, smeared with her own blood,
quivering in her fear and shock, barely able to breathe.
After a time her breath returned, and she came to her senses
enough to be able to speak: "What have you done? You promised
my father. . . . You promised my sister. . . . Your oaths mean
        nothing at all!
I was a virgin! And now? My life is surely over!
Am I to live as my sister's rival, your concubine?
Or is it a part of your plan to kill me, now that you've had me?
That would be kinder and better. Best would have been to kill me
before you did this unspeakable thing. My ghost would have been 540
untainted then. You have changed my universe, defiled it.
The gods, if they exist, must avenge this crime. Or I
myself shall become a Fury and proclaim the shameful truth
to the whole world, which will then despise your name forever."

    This caught the king's attention. He realized she could make
        good
on this threat to do him harm. Afraid, angry, he grabbed her,
twisted her arms behind her, and tied her up. He drew
his sword from its sheath and held her hair. She offered her throat
gladly for him to cut it and end her pain and shame. . . .
But he didn't. Instead he seized her tongue with a pair of pincers, 550
pulled it out of her mouth, and hacked it off with the sword.
Her mouth is full of blood from the mangled root. The tongue,
he throws onto the floor, where it lies and twitches, a wounded

pink snake at its former owner's feet in this nightmare
she must be having. Or else it's the gods' own nightmare, for now
he puts the bloodied sword back in its sheath and puts
his tool back into her, raping her yet again.
     Perhaps what is most amazing is how, with such bloody
       crimes
on his conscience, he then could return to Procne and, with sang-
      froid,
invent some story to tell her about how her sister had died.   560
He thus could allow himself to show that he was upset—
he even contrived to produce a tear or two. His wife,
absorbed in her own grief, was not paying close attention.
She tore off her rich garments, put on her mourner's weeds,
and ordered a cenotaph built in her sister's honor. There
she went to grieve, lay flowers, and recite the prayers for the dead.
     Time passes, a round of months and seasons. A year
has come and gone. In the woods, in that hunter's hut, the girl,
Philomela, is captive. A wall has been built around her,
and the king has posted guards, both day and night. In mute   570
misery there she dwells, and from time to time he visits.
Her mind, elsewhere, is busy devising a way to carry
the meaning of all those words that teem in her brain, though
     her mouth
can no longer frame one. How to carry that message?
At last, she constructs a loom and appears to content herself
with weaving. The guards and keepers inquire. The king
     makes no
objection. Nobody looks at the cloth she is weaving, or sees
its series of horrible panels—the story of what has happened.
She rolls it up and then with a series of gestures entreats
one of the serving women to deliver this gift to the queen.   580
This, in her pity, the woman is willing to do, and Procne
receives the cloth. At once she divines the fate of her sister.
It's all there—the father, the daughters, the husband's rape,
the extraction of the tongue. She bites her own tongue and,
     in rage,
keeps her feelings hidden. This is no time for tears,
but action, terrible vengeance. Her soul can be satisfied
with nothing less than the righting of these most grievous
     wrongs.
     This was the time for the women of Thrace to observe the
     rites
that come every two years of Bacchus' festival. Shrill

pipes were skirling, and cymbals clashed in the night. The lower   590
slopes of Mount Rhodope echoed. The queen went forth to
        join them
in all the proper regalia—vines on the head, a deerskin
over the shoulder, a spear on the arm, but above all, wildness,
the wildness of grief that could pass here for the god's frenzy.
Her attendants took no particular notice, but followed along
wherever she led—through the woods to those stone walls and,
        inside,
to that hunter's hut. Procne cries aloud, as any
Bacchic celebrant would, the word of divine rapture,
"Evohe!" as she pounds on the door, breaking it down.
There is her sister! She holds her, then makes her don the raiment   600
Bacchantes wear. The vine leaves hide Philomela's face
as she follows along in amazement where Procne leads—her home.
        His home? She is frightened, pale, and cannot help making
        plaintive,
inarticulate noises. Procne holds her close,
as the sisters weep together. Philomela hides her eyes,
convinced she has wronged her sister. Like a hurt kitten,
        she mews
and signs with her hands that what happened wasn't her fault. He
        was strong
and forced himself upon her. Procne says, "I believe you.
I do. And we must not weep, but think of revenge. The sword,
or something even worse, whatever is worst of all   610
the vengeances men or women or gods have ever extracted.
We must stop at nothing now, as he was willing to stop
at nothing. A torch, to set the house on fire, the entire
city? Cut out his tongue? Or his eyes that first beheld you!
And cut off—of course—his dick. And then just keep on cutting
the thousand nicks to allow his soul to filter forth,
polluting the air of the world, which his breath has already fouled.
Whatever we do, its horror and fame should live in the minds
of men and boys forever, to warn them of women's rage. . . ."
        She was still casting about in her mind for some retribution   620
of suitable pain, when her son—by Tereus—appeared,
Itys, that comely child. "How like your father you seem,"
she said in her idle way, and suddenly there it was,
the whole scheme at once—how men were an alien species,
and this child of hers, this son, would one day grow up to become
another man, a beast, like his father. The bond of sisters
is better, truer, and holds forever. But males betray.

And this was a way to pay that monster back. The child,
unaware of these thoughts, ran up to his mother and threw
        his arms
about her neck. Her heart, for a moment, was touched, as anger   630
drained out of her body, and tears poured from her eyes,
but she looked away from the boy, saw her ruined sister,
and thought how strange it was that one could say loving words,
while the other was mute. The one was able to call out,
        "Mother,"
but Philomela as long as she lived would never be able
to enunciate, "Sister." It was therefore her clear duty to speak
in her sister's behalf, and she knew too well what that sister
        would say—
as a daughter of Pandion, she was now disgraced. To remain
faithful to such a culprit would be to inculpate herself
in his evil deeds. Forthwith she dragged the young boy away   640
as a tigress drags a fawn through the faraway Indian jungles.
Way off in the servants' quarters, where no one could hear,
        she drew
a butcher knife from the rack. The boy, terrified, cried,
wept, called out to the mother who'd always protected him,
        "Spare me,"
but she would not spare herself or him or the world. She struck
deep in his breast, to the side where the heart was, never flinching,
not even changing the look on her face. He was changed to meat,
which now she proceeded to butcher, cutting the body up
into chops and steaks. The sister, with eager nutation, helped;
together they flung appropriate portions into the stewpots   650
or skewered them onto the spits of the grill to prepare, in the
        bloody
shambles the kitchen turned into, their banquet of retribution.
        The wife invites the husband that night to a special dinner.
He is delighted, accepts with pleasure, and wonders what
the occasion might be. It isn't his birthday. He sits alone
at the head of the table, and Procne explains it's an ancient custom
her people observe, a sacred feast that's for husbands only—
nobody else may partake. She dismisses the servants and slaves
and says she herself will serve. Alone in the banquet hall,
he feasts, gorges himself on the tasty flesh of his own   660
flesh. At length, he is sated and, happy, he calls for his son.
Procne, delighted to hear him improving thus on her plan,
can barely hide her elation in this moment of triumph,
        announcing,

"The one you seek is here already." And he asks, "Where?"
"Within you," his wife insists, but he still doesn't get it, cannot
possibly comprehend . . . until Philomela, the mute,
bursts into the hall to explain. She is smeared with blood,
and her hair is wild, and her eyes. . . . She looks as she did
        that day,
that first day in the hut. But now she holds in the air
the head of his son she's hacked from the stump of his neck. She
        throws   670
the face in his face, the lifeless head at his head, and shrieks
a wordless cry that requires no explication whatever.
The king rages, retches, and weeps. He is, himself,
the tomb of his son. He draws his sword and chases those cursèd
sisters around the table. They fly from him as if wingèd—
or not as if. They are! And they take flight, soar to the roof,
and one remains there, a swallow. The other hastens away,
returns to the woods and lives there, the nightingale. Their
        feathers
are still stained with the gore of their deed. Tereus, chasing
the sisters, is also a bird, a hoopoe with martial crest   680
and the long curved bill that might well have been his sword.
        Back in Athens, this news staggered Pandion. Never
would he recover. He pined and died very soon thereafter.
The throne of Athens then passed to Erechtheus, famed
equally for his valor and the justice of his reign.
He had four sons and also two daughters. One of these, Procris,
married Cephalus, Aeolus' grandson. The other, Orithyia,
Boreas courted, but she refused him, several times.
After the dreadful business in Thrace, Tereus' country,
she would have nothing to do with anyone from the North.   690
He tried kind words, sent candy and flowers, but, after a time,
reaching the end of his patience, reverted to what he knew
and trusted—force and rage and bluster, which send the clouds
and hail and thunderclaps and terrible gales to shake
the mightiest oaks and cover the ground with a waste of
        snowdrifts.
He can appall the ghosts themselves and freeze the hearts
and marrows of living men and women. "What is this nonsense?"
he asked himself. "I am not one to beg, with my hat in hand,
for favors. It is wrong for me to plead and entreat
Erechtheus to allow me to become his son-in-law.   700
It's I who am favoring them. Enough of this wooing business!
What I should do is take what I want, as I've always done."

He beat his mighty wings, which produced an algid blast
that chilled the earth and rumpled the ocean's even blanket.
He trailed the hem of his hoary cloak along the land,
and snow and darkness fell down together and drifted over
the eyes of men. That darkness is friend to lovers and thieves,
and, wrapped in it, Boreas came to embrace, in his huge wings,
the terrified girl. He enfolded Orithyia and soared
into the air, higher and faster. She quaked with fear,   710
and her tremors and quivers delighted him, made an erotic
       suggestion
he could not resist. It inflamed him all the way to the land
in which the Cicones live. There, she became his bride,
and a mother, too, for the girl of Athens in time bore twins
to the stern lord of the North Wind, little ones who looked
like her at first but later came to resemble their father.
Calaïs and Zetes, she called them. A lovely pair of boys!
As adolescents, they grew, with their facial and axillary
hair, large pairs of wings like their father's. Then, when they
       reached
manhood, they shipped on the *Argo,* as members of Jason's crew,   720
in search of adventure, glory, and that fabulous Golden Fleece.

BOOK VII

Cut to: the *Argo,* of course. The ship is on its way
to Colchis, having already undergone many trials
and achieved numerous triumphs—for instance, over the Harpies.
When we pick them up, they have bidden farewell to the blind king,
Phineus, who is an uncle to Calaïs and Zetes;
they have entered the mouth of the mighty Phasis, with all those
    shore birds;
they have come to demand from Aeëtes the fleece that Phrixus
    gave him
and have heard his impossible terms, the tasks and exploits he
    orders—
or rather, say, he dares—them to undertake. We angle
on: the daughter, the beautiful princess, off to one side, who is
    watching   10
the hero. She hears her father's terms and is worried sick
lest this fine fellow perish trying those long-odds feats.
It makes no sense, this passion. She has never felt it before,
doesn't even know for sure what to call this emotion.
Is this what they mean by "love"? There are other words for
    it also,
but, even while she hates herself for feeling this way,
she cannot help herself. She is possessed, or rather
feels that she now possesses a new, more powerful self.
Her father, whom she has always adored, now seems a monster.
The stranger, whose face she has never before beheld, now
    matters   20
more to her than her life itself. She knows it's crazy,
but that doesn't make it go away. Her desire fights
against her reason and triumphs. Her mind itself is undone
and can only watch from a distance and offer useless advice.
Marriage is what she wants, and to be with this man forever,
going wherever he goes. His noble birth and his youth
speak for him, but his beauty alone is all he needs

as advocate in her heart, which has melted like wax and hardened
to bear his seal forever. What can she do to help him
perform that impossible task her father had set—to tame
those fire-breathing bulls with their hoofs and horns of brass
and with them plow and sow the sacred field of Mars?
She knows—far better than he—what this involves: the bulls
will almost certainly kill him, but if, by some luck or strength
or craft, he gets them yoked and hitched to a plow, the crop
he plants will flourish, arise from the earth as murderous men,
armed, and in multitudes. . . . Her father is grinning, but she
is horrified to think of that lovely body mangled.
Someone must help him. The gods? Or have they already
        done so,
directing her with this passion to come to his aid, to protect,
instruct, and cherish this stranger, who may not be grateful,
        may not
love her for what she has done, or even thank her, but sail
away at once to some distant shore and another woman's
arms and bed? She is jealous, furious at this thought,
and ready to see him die. But no, she is not. She cannot
bear the idea. She will trust him. She will ask him first, and
        he'll swear
to join their lives together forever. The gods will witness
this solemn oath. She is utterly mad, knows it, and takes
a curious pleasure in it. The sense of strangeness that always
dogged her is gone. No longer an awkward young girl waiting
for her life to start, she's a woman, a force of Nature, and knows
that this is the man who will owe her his life, and whom she will
        marry. . . .
Anything else is grotesque, absurd, and implausibly foreign.
She will sail away with him, leave her sister, brother, father,
her gods, and the native land that is hers no longer. She gasps,
catches herself, and wonders, can she bear such multiple losses?
Amazed, she hears her spirit's advocacy in the case:
that her country is barbarous, rude; her father is cruel; her brother
is yet a child; and her sister . . . would desire that she be happy,
whatever the price. Besides, for what she leaves, she will be
rewarded in great abundance, with honor, riches, culture,
and the love—most of all the love, worth all the rest—of this
        man,
this wonderful son of Aeson. She sees herself in his arms,
nestled safe as the huge waves crash on all sides, as his ship
pitches and yaws in a way that would terrify anyone else,

but she is secure in his strength and care. The wandering
    mountains
snap at their vessel; Charybdis' whirlpool sucks at the surface;
the dogs of Scylla bay and bell, but she hardly hears them,
and he is moved to see how her love for him and her trust
have no limits or bounds. She is even frightened herself   70
by what that could mean: some subtle prompting from deep
    within
tries to caution her not to pursue this man and this marriage. . . .
But it is already too late for such counsels of caution and
    prudence.
She can see before her the figures she has long been taught to
    revere,
of girlish modesty, filial love, and, behind them, the dimmer,
grander spirit of general righteousness. They glare
at the elfin sprite of love, now about to take flight.
      She feels both lost and saved, and goes to an ancient altar
of Hecate to consult the spirits of that dark goddess,
in the hope that she might confirm her new resolution and give   80
whatever divine assistance a suppliant might deserve.
That was her purpose, but there, on the forest path to that altar,
she met him again, and her cheeks reddened and then blanched
    ashen.
Sometimes a tiny ember of an all but extinguished fire
will, at a random breeze, revive, fan into flame
and rage hotter than ever, and so it was with her.
His face was a god's, and she was stricken, could not speak,
could not even move—to approach closer or back away.
Then, as if he were some dream version of himself,
he took her hand, looked into her eyes, and, in barely audible   90
tones, asked her to help him. "Without your aid, I can never
accomplish those difficult tasks your father has set me. With you,
I have some hope, may live—and will owe you all. We'll
    marry. . . ."
There may have been more, but she could not hear it, could barely
    breathe,
could barely see for the brimming tears of joy in her eyes.
At last she managed to give him a "Yes," both to his question
and also to his proposal. But to make sure, she said, "Yes,"
a second time. And explained that what she was going to do
would cost her dearly. For love, she would give up her life here,
her family, her position. Would he swear to love her always?   100
Forever and ever? He swore by every god and goddess,

by the triple goddess, by the patroness of the shrine at hand, by
     the Sun—
the father of Aeëtes, his father-in-law to be.
Up and down, he swore, and she heard him, believed, and
     gave him
a packet of magic herbs, the use of which she explained.
He thanked her and then returned to his lodging. Alone, she
     wondered
what she had done, what marvel had moved her, and what would
     happen
in this altogether different universe into which
she felt herself emerging, a new-fledged butterfly.

    After the stars had fled the brightening sky, the crowds   110
of people began to gather to watch the performance—debacle?
That was their expectation, surely, a grand disaster,
and, with spirits high, they cheered as the king took his seat in
     the royal
box, nodding and waving with one hand. The other was holding
the ivory scepter with which he gave the signal to start.
There's a hush, and the bulls appear, flames coming out of their
     nostrils
to shrivel the grass at their brazen feet. There are rumbling noises
of the kind one might hear in a lime works, when water is poured
     on hot
stones, and they crack and sizzle. So, the throats of these beasts
produce the most ominous noises. And, give him credit, Jason   120
doesn't flee. The royal guards do not have to drag him
out onto the field. He walks toward them on his own,
and they turn and face him, paw the earth, lower their horns,
which are tipped with iron, and bellow, snorting puffs of fire.
The Argonauts, in their box, are suitably terrified watching
what looks like the end of their leader, but such is the herbs'
     power
that he is able to walk right up to the bulls, to pet them,
stroking their hanging dewlaps, and put the great yoke on their
     necks.
Amazing! He hitches the plow and sets them to work, as a farmer
might do with the team he has followed day in and day out, for
     years.   130
The Argonauts shout in relief and then in delight, in triumph
at what their captain has managed. Now Jason takes the helmet
and broadcasts the dragon's teeth in the furrows he has just
     plowed.

The spectators in the stands are hushed now to see how
    these seeds
sprout up as men, fully armed, formed into ranks and files—
and turn on Jason, their sharp spears leveled and pointing at him.
Medea now is frightened, ashen. What will he do?
How can one man survive an attack of a host of troops?
She doubts those herbs and begins to chant, under her breath,
a spell to give him strength, to keep him safe, to help him. . . .   140
But he doesn't appear to need any supernatural aid.
He throws a stone that hits a few of the troops in the middle
ranks, whereupon they commence to quarrel among themselves
and fight in increasingly deadly earnest. Jason draws back
to watch them destroy one another, hack one another to bits.
At last, he is the lone figure remaining upright.
The Greeks cheer, and the locals cannot help now but join them.
Medea cheers. . . . She would sooner have raced to his side to
    embrace him,
but modesty prevented, and fear of what people would say.
All she could do was gaze in wonder and love, and thank   150
the gods that had blessed her charm that had worked to keep
    him safe.
    What had the hero earned? The right to approach the dragon
that guarded the Golden Fleece—and the charm worked yet again.
He approached the fearsome beast with its huge crest, its triple-
forked tongue, and its set of gleaming fangs, and aspersed it
with the essence of sacred herbs, reciting a spell Medea
had told him could calm the seas and raging rivers. The dragon
closed his eyes, curled up, and dozed off, so Jason could snatch
the treasure he sought. With it and Medea, he sailed away
to reach, after more adventures, Iolchos' protected harbor.   160
    The aged mothers and fathers of the Argonauts bring gifts
to the gods to rejoice in their sons' return. They heap incense
high on the altars, and slay the sacred bull with the gilded
horns. But Jason's father, Aeson, is absent, old,
sick, with the weight of his years now dragging him down. The
    hero,
strong until now, is undone, and in grief he turns to Medea,
his wife, whose lore from the East includes such skills in magic
that he has not dared to guess her limits. Of her he asks
in his desperation to do what she can, "even to take
years from my life and add them to my reverend father's span."   170
Unashamed tears of love spill down on Jason's cheeks.
Medea, moved by his grief, thinks now of her own father,

whom she betrayed and abandoned. She does not allude to this
sore wound in her heart, but only tells her husband,
"What you suggest is wicked, defying the will of the Fates.
Hecate would never permit such a thing. And yet
there may be a way to extend your father's life—not by transfer
of years from you to him, but purely by my own skill,
if the triple goddess will come to my aid and hear my prayers."
    On the night of the full Moon, then, Medea went out to
      perform   180
her mysterious rites. She was dressed in long white robes, but
      barefoot,
and her hair was undone and streaming over her shoulders. Alone,
she wandered into the darkness of midnight. Birds and beasts
were all asleep. It was silent. Even the leaves hung still,
as if they'd been painted there. Only the stars were moving,
revolving in their slow courses and twinkling high in the sky.
To these she lifted her arms and turned three times. She sprinkled
on her head the running water she'd drawn from a nearby brook,
and three times she gave voice to a piercing ululation
one's blood would have frozen to hear. She then knelt down on
      the ground   190
to intone her prayer: "O night, o stars, o goddess, mistress
of sorcery, hear my plea. And you, o Earth, who provide
your powerful herbs, attend me. And you, the several spirits
of winds, of mountains, of streams and lakes, and of groves and
      trees,
be gracious to one who seeks your aid in this dark hour.
I thank you for the marvels we have worked together before,
the calming of turbulent seas, or the stirring up of calm,
the bringing on of clouds in times of drought, or the opposite,
driving them from the sky when flood threatened my people. . . .
What wonders have we not contrived together? The serpent   200
flees at our incantation, and boulders and rooted trees
dance to our songs and move wherever we will. Whole forests
march like armies, and mountains shake, and the earth itself
trembles as ghosts issue forth from their graves to dance in the
      moonlight.
At times of eclipse, when the earth lies helpless before the assault
of evil spirits, I clang the cymbals that keep them at bay.
My grandfather's fiery car, which crosses the sky, has paled
to hear my spells, as Aurora has quaked in fear and delayed
her dazzling entrance. Those bulls that exhale fire and death

you tamed for me—they allowed my beloved to yoke them
      together   210
to plow the earth. That rabble the earth then produced, you
      destroyed,
saving Jason's life and my love. The guardian dragon
you put to sleep at my bidding. I thank you for all these favors
and ask yet another and greater boon. I have need of a potion
by which old age may return to the vigor and bloom of youth.
The signs are propitious. The stars are gleaming. My car awaits,
and the wingèd dragons are ready. Goddesses, help me now."
    Into the chariot then she mounted and shook the reins
that signaled the dragon team to spring into flight. Looking down,
she could see the Tempe Valley stretching out like a map of itself.   220
She knew which way to go, and headed her dragons toward Ossa,
and Pelion, and Othrys, and Pindus, and Mount Olympus,
for various roots and grasses and succulents. Now and again,
reining in her team, she would stop, dismount, and collect,
with her pruning hook, some specimen her curved bronze blade
      would cut.
She traveled also to rivers for the special plants that grow
only in bogs and wetlands that flood from time to time—
to the Apadanus, Amphrysus, Enipeus, Peneus,
Spercheus, the broad Boebe, and, in Euboea, the swift
Anthedon, where on the banks a grass grows that can give   230
long life (but it wasn't famous then because Glaucus had not
yet seen the fish he had caught revive when he laid them on it,
or experimented to try its effect on humans—himself).
    Nine days and nights she traveled, visiting distant lands,
mountaintops and obscure valleys, and then she returned,
knowing the herbs she had garnered were strong indeed, for her
      dragons,
who had only inhaled their fragrances, proved their marvelous
      power,
sloughing their old skins and looking much younger and stronger.
With confidence then, and reverence, she came to Aeson's
      threshold,
and, resisting Jason's embrace of welcome, continued her solemn   240
business—building the two turf altars, one on the right
for Hecate, and one on the left for the spirit of Youth.
The rites she then performed, with boughs from the forest to deck
the altars, the prayers, the digging of circular ditches, and, then,
the sacrifice of the black ram. She plunged the knife

in his neck, and his blood flowed forth to fill those ditches
     she'd dug.
She poured in honey and bowls of milk still warm from the
     udders,
and uttered her incantations, calling on chthonic gods
who dwell in the earth and preside over lives of men and women.
She invoked the dismal king of the shades, begging his kindness   250
and patience, that he forgo for a time the old man's corpse
and allow him a further measure of life in the light and air.
    At this point in the ritual, she ordered the servants to carry
Aeson's decrepit body out of the house and place him
between the altars under the stars, where she laid him out
on a pallet of all those herbs she had gathered. She then sent Jason
away, and all the attendants and servants, and warned them not
to look back or try to overhear what she did in this secret
business. When she was alone with the old man, she let down
     her hair
in the manner of a Bacchante and moved around the blazing   260
altars, almost dancing, with forked sticks, which she waved
this way and that and dipped in the blood in the ditch and lit
in the altar fires. These she waved at the aged man
in a pattern of careful gestures to purify him thrice
with fire, thrice with water, and then three times with sulfur.
    On a fire between the altars, a large bronze cauldron is
     boiling,
seething, frothing, emitting peculiarly pungent odors.
Into this pot she tosses roots from Thessaly, seeds,
flowers, and other juices and saps from here and there
and elsewhere, black sand from the East, and hoarfrost gathered   270
under a full Moon. . . . God knows what else she puts in.
The wings of a screech owl, its flesh, and some say a werewolf's
     entrails,
which can turn beasts to men and vice versa. Some swear
she puts in the skin of an African asp, an old stag's liver,
the eggs of a crow that had lived for nine of our generations,
and also its head. The list is lively and most inventive,
and still falls short of the strange and repulsive truth of her praxis.
The odd things barbarians know, she knew and was ready to use,
and her test at the end was to stir the mess in that pot with a stick
of olive wood, old and dried out, dead as its parent tree   280
was dead. But the mixture worked on the wood, and it greened
     again,
put forth buds and then leaves, and bore thick clusters of fruit.

And wherever the hot liquid spattered onto the barren
ground, the earth was suddenly green with grass and bright
with anthologies of blossoms. This was perhaps auspicious,
and Medea would almost surely have needed whatever assurance
there was, for now she took an enormous butchering knife
and slit the old man's throat. That would have taken courage,
but even more to stand there and watch him exsanguinate.
As all the old blood flowed out, she replaced it, filling his veins   290
with the soup she had brewed in that kettle, pouring it into
        his mouth
and also into the wound when it no longer gushed old blood.
An amazing transformation then began to make itself clear,
for his hair, which had long ago turned white, was now dark
        again,
more pepper than salt, and then black as when he was in his
        prime.
His lean old frame filled out with the musculature he'd forgotten
he ever had, and his wrinkled and pale skin now was smooth
and tanned. He looked like a young man now, was young and
        strong.
        In heaven, looking down, Bacchus, the god, was impressed
and came down to consult this crafty woman, who gave him all   300
her secret recipes, formulae, and her rituals and chants,
so that he could contrive the same favor for his old nurses.
        Medea's reputation, not surprisingly, spread
far and wide, and she put this to her own advantage in ways
no one could have predicted. She let it be known she had
        quarreled
with Jason and then she fled to his uncle's house, to take refuge
with Peleas—who had usurped Aeson's throne. His daughters
gave her a royal welcome, and Medea seemed sad but grateful,
not at all the imposing sorceress they had expected,
but a warm and friendly woman, open and ready to speak   310
of all her adventures—even the rejuvenation of Aeson.
The daughters of Peleas asked her whether they might arrange
the same wonderful transformation of their old father.
Would she make him young again? Or tell them how to achieve
        that
miraculous change? They offered to pay her whatever she asked.
She hesitated, or seemed to, and then at last consented
to do this great thing for them. And to put their minds at ease,
she would demonstrate her technique. She called for the oldest
        ram

in the royal flocks, and, when it was brought, a feeble thing
with huge horns it could barely carry, she took it away,   320
cut its throat with her knife, and dumped it into the cauldron
she had prepared with the proper herbs and elements. Horns
boiled away, and the carcass's years, and a bleating was heard
from inside that kettle. . . . The sisters were sure it was some kind
        of trick,
but there it was, a young and frisky lamb she drew
from the seething liquid and set on the ground. It scampered away
to find a ewe that might nurse it. Witchcraft, perhaps, but it
        worked.
        The daughters of Peleas now were more insistent than ever,
eager to have their guest undertake without delay
their father's rejuvenation treatment—but she insisted   330
on a little rest before the great undertaking. Three times
the horses of Phoebus descended westward into the Ebro's
valley, and then, on the fourth evening, Medea set out
a cauldron, as before, but this time she put in the brew
petals of local flowers, meaningless roots and random
leaves from bushes and trees. Peleas' daughters suspected
nothing, and, as she had bidden, they waited until the old man
was asleep. (They had drugged his guards with a sleeping powder
        Medea
had supplied beforehand.) Now they entered the royal
        bedchamber
and . . . hesitated. Medea asked them why they had lost their
        faith,   340
and how they expected to help their father live, if their courage
fled at this critical moment. "It is up to you," she instructed,
"a test of filial love. If you fail, he must pay
the penalty death will exact. Be brave and do your duty.
It isn't your father, but age you will stab with the sharp sword
        points,
and age that your wounds will bleed from his feeble body.
        Strike!"
And they did. Each one, in love, aped the acts of hatred,
in virtue, mimicked the deeds of evil, stabbing again
and again the old man in his bed, although each looked away
to hide from herself the sight of the deed her hand had performed. 350
        The old man, awakened in pain and bleeding profusely,
        called out,
"What are you doing, my daughters? What madness is this?" In
        terror,

they dropped their bloodied blades, but Medea struck at his
   throat,
carving there a crimson meniscus, which overflowed
in gore. She picked up the mangled body and plunged it into
that boiling cauldron she had prepared with its potpourri.
Nothing happened, of course, except for the *pot-au-feu*
into which he was changed. She departed at once with her
   dragon-drawn car,
and hardly a moment too soon—the horrified daughters already
had realized something was wrong. High over Pelion's top   360
Medea flew, where Chiron lived (you're supposed to remember
his story) and over Othrys, where aged Cerambus had such
adventures (What adventures? What's going on here? Medea
is supposed to go back to Corinth, to Jason, where she will
   discover
that he is engaged to Creusa, Creon's daughter, . . . and kill
her two children with Jason. That's the story, the dreadful
nadir of spite and despair into which she will fall—for love?
as a punishment from the gods for her meddling thus with life
and death? Who knows? But the point is that Ovid avoids it,
   gives us
instead a bizarre catalogue in the effete Alexandrian style   370
of references we're supposed to get and respond to, pointless
except for the way they obscure what is uppermost in his mind
and ours, too. In dreams, we find ourselves sometimes engaged
in this kind of repression, distortion, transmogrification,
the weight of the thing we dread turning the normal, neutral,
and homely details of our lives unendurable, monstrous,
and yet somehow correct in the punishments they offer.
Footnotes without a text, a quiz, or a gazetteer
of distractions, its only sense is in what it refuses to say,
perhaps so as not to invite a comparison with the Greek   380
tragedian's model. . . . But other, less crafty considerations
are not therefore to be dismissed. And he's just done Procne,
whose murder of Itys suggested to anyone properly schooled
other infanticide mothers: Medea, for instance. And she
loved her husband, was crazed by her love, and no sane man,
or prudent one, has never worried where love can lead.
It's flattering first, and convenient, but these women never know
where to draw the line. And this is precisely what
we are refusing to think of, as Ovid goes on with his elegant
patter—Corythus, Maera, the women of Cos, the evil   390
eye of the Telchines, the transformation of Cygnus

into a swan. It's blather, desperate and slightly mad,
and we are required to think of what madness is, and Medea's
madness that isn't so foreign as we should prefer it to be).

 After forty lines of travels, she alights in Corinth, and Ovid,
still refusing to speak of what is on all our minds,
tells us instead how men here sprang from mushrooms (why
 not?).
Only then does he deign to allude to the bloody business,
the marriage to Creusa, the fire, the double murder, and then
Medea's escape in that car to Athens, where King Aegeus   400
receives her. Indeed, he marries the woman, and this, as the poet
makes clear, is risky, but its ill wind blows us into the next
set of stories—of King Aegeus and also his son
by Aethra, that child he hadn't acknowledged—Theseus, come
at last to Athens to make himself known to his father and claim
his birthright. Medea, displeased at the prospect of sharing her
 husband's
love (and wealth and power) with this young man who might
or might not be her stepson, mixed up a batch of poison
from Cerberus' drool that had spattered on earth when Hercules
 dragged
that hound of hell to the surface. The maddened mastiff howled   410
and flecked the earth with his slobber—which the country
 people call
rock flower, or aconite. This poison Medea brewed up
and gave to Aegeus unwittingly for him to hand on
to his own son. The younger man had taken the cup,
was raising it to his lips to drink from it, when Aegeus
saw on the hilt of Theseus' sword the family crest . . .
and realized (What? That the stranger was his own son, and
 the cup
might therefore be poisoned? What sense does this make? The
 background
story is not impossible, but any sensible poet
would lay it out somehow, give us a hint here and there.   420
He had to have known that the cup was poisoned, but why would
 he kill
a stranger? What far-fetched story had Medea devised?). A cloud
she whistles up with her witchcraft covers her now and
 protects her
from Aegeus' wrath and Ovid from our frustrated annoyance.

 But Theseus now is home safe, and Aegeus is happy
to see him. There are sacrifices, prayers, and, of course, a party

at which the guests in chorus sing their somewhat stagey
and bibulous song of praise, an inset poem-within-
the-poem, a *Thesiad*, one might call it. Imagine a fanfare
and maybe a drum roll as well. (Gentlemen, if you please!):   430
"O hero, how all the lands of Greece join in the paean
your deeds have earned. They speak in Marathon of the blood
of the Cretan bull you caught there and sacrificed to the gods.
All Attica marvels at how in Cromyon's fields you hunted
the enormous wild sow that was killing the farmers' sons
and ruining all their crops. In Epidaurus they chant
hymns to memorialize your combat with Periphètes,
Vulcan's criminal son, who robbed and then clubbed his victims—
until you put an abrupt end to his sinful life.
At the banks of Cephisus, where Procrustes used to beset   440
unwary travelers, you have made the roads safe now,
and the songs that passers-by whistle are no longer of fear
but of gratitude to you. At Eleusis, Cercyon wrestled
strangers and put to death all those he defeated, but you
didn't lose, and you put him to death. You triumphed
over burly Sinis, who liked to pull down the treetops,
catapult men's bodies into the air, and then laugh
at the thuds of their fatal falls, but by your hand he fell.
Sciron, too, is dead, and the earth refused his bones,
as did the sea, each tossing them back until they became   450
the impressive cliff formation that even now bears his name.
Your deeds have given rise to many songs and stories,
the resonance of which will no doubt outlast your lifetime.
But let us salute you with wine, as our thanks and praises
        ring out."
There are cheers and applause, as the rafters resound with the
        people's joy.
    But in this life, it would seem, no joy is unalloyed,
not even this, for Aegeus, happy to have his son
returned and basking in glory, was not yet free from care.
Minos, the King of Crete, was threatening Athens with war
with a mighty army and navy and, worst to be feared, a grudge— 460
Minos was full of grief and rage at the death of his son
the wrestler Androgeus, whom Aegeus is said to have killed.
Minos had formed a league with various islands and towns,
wheedling here and threatening there, as the case demanded,
but combining their strength in a force greater than that of
        Athens:
Anaphe; Astyphalea; Mikonos; chalky Cimolus;

Syros, covered with thyme; flat Seriphos; Paros
with its marble cliffs; and Siphnos, which Arne betrayed for gold
(and was punished for this, was turned into a jackdaw, black-
        footed,
black-hearted, too, and still with its passion for glittering gold).   470
        Some held out: Oliaros, Didyme, Tenos, Andros,
Gyaros, and olive-rich Peparethos refused to sign up
with Crete and King Minos, who ventured to Oenopia
(or whatever you choose to call the place where King Aeacus
        ruled.
He'd changed the country's name to Aegina, after his mother).
Minos approached the palace, and a crowd rushed forth to behold
this personage, this star. The princes Telamon, Peleus,
and Phocus greeted their guest, and their father, Aeacus, tottered
down the steps to greet his august visitor, asking
what was the cause of his coming. Minos replied in a formal   480
manner, which hid the greater part of his private grief,
"I seek repose for the dead, and revenge. And I ask your help
in a pious war against those in Athens who killed my son."
Aeacus answered, "You ask what we cannot give. Our treaties
bind us close to Athens, as our interests always have done."
The other replied, "Your interest ought to be in your people's
survival," and turned away, leaving his threat to echo
behind him. But this was not the time for a war. King Minos
had other, more pressing business. And then, with the Cretan
        fleet
at anchor down in the harbor, an Athenian ship appeared,   490
Cephalus' ship. (You remember him? You remember, in Athens,
when Pandion died, the throne passed to Erechtheus, father
or those two beautiful daughters, Orithyia and Procris?
Procris married Cephalus, of Thessaly's royal house.)
He now disembarked, bringing friendly Athenian greetings
to Aeacus' house and people. Welcomed, invited inside,
and, bearing the olive branch of Athens, he strode toward the
        throne
flanked by Clytos and Butes, two young Athenian nobles.
        They exchanged official and formal expressions of welcome
        and thanks,
and Cephalus then delivered his message from Athens' king,   500
referring of course to their treaty, but giving the further reason
that Minos now posed a threat to not only Athens but all
Greece, the islands and mainland, which he looked to conquer
        and claim

as a part of his own kingdom. Aeacus heard him out
and then, with his left hand resting easily on his scepter,
delivered his answer: "Our friend, you have no need to request.
Our help is yours to command. Our ships and army are yours,
and the time is right and ripe. We are with you. Let us commence
in this great work together." Cephalus bowed his head
in thanks to the king before him and the gods above. "So be it,"   510
he intoned, but then, in a more informal manner, asked
the question that weighed on his mind. Where were those many
        young men
he had known on his earlier visits, a number of them his friends?
Aeacus groaned aloud, and with sadness explained what had
        happened:
"These are good days we are having. The days before were such
that I wish I could speak of the present only. Those friends you
        miss
I also miss, for they all are dead. Dust unto dust,
returned as most of the kingdom did, in a terrible plague
that came—some say—from the wrath of Juno, because our name
was that of her hated rival. We did what we could, but science   520
has its limits. The gods can invent their new diseases,
mystifying and lethal, as this was. The weather was bad,
as a cause perhaps or merely an omen—hot and muggy,
a spell that lasted four full months, and South Wind blew
a pestilential breath. Springs and ponds dried up,
and good-sized lakes. There were serpents in huge numbers. Some
        thought
they were part of the trouble, while others refused to believe it.
Animals sickened first, dogs, then birds, then sheep
and cattle, and then wild game in the woods. Strong bulls fell
        down
in the furrows they had just plowed, and stupid sheep in their pens 530
bleated in their distress, and their wool fell out, revealing
scrawny bodies, which soon thereafter collapsed. Proud horses
forgot their spirit and pride as they groaned in their stalls,
        awaiting
a swift and messy death. In the forests, the boar and the bear
appeared to have traded their old ferocity for some new
modus vivendi—a slothlike lethargy into which all
creatures sank. The face of the world was changed, disfigured
by carcasses everywhere, on the roads, in the fields, in the woods,
and the air was full of that stench of rotting meat. The dogs
and wolves and the carrion birds turned up their noses, refusing   540

this untoward feast. The contagion spread, and the landscape was
    blasted.
      "It comes, in course, to the houses of peasants first and the
    nobles
who live out on their holdings. The symptoms are always the
    same,
a burning feeling inside, and a flush on the face from the fever.
The tongue is rough and swollen, the lips are parched, and the
    breathing
is stertorous and labored. Those who are stricken protest
that they cannot bear the weight or even the touch of their
    bedclothes.
The bodies they took for granted have turned against them.
    They flee
from their sickbeds to lie on the ground, naked, but that also
    burns,
as if the earth were a griddle. Physicians sicken and die   550
from attending the sick, and the best doctors die the soonest.
The luckiest, too, for the plague, bad as it is, gets worse
as hope deserts the people, who begin to misbehave,
for what have they left to hope for or fear? There is theft and
    pillage,
rape, and every kind of disorder. Reason is flown,
and, from desperation, shamelessness blossoms in garish scenes
that illustrate what foulness lies beneath the veneer
of civilization. The thirst that comes toward the end is awful,
and nothing will quench it. The victims drink until they are
    bloated
and cannot stand, and still continue to drink, and they die   560
with their heads in the public fountains and riversides and lakes.
And as new sufferers come to slake their impossible thirsts,
they barely bother to nudge the corpses away to make room
however they can for themselves to drink the polluted water.
Crazy? Indeed, but madness was part of it. Men were convinced
their homes were the cause of their illness. They'd drag
    themselves from bed
and stagger out on the public thoroughfares to lurch
this way and that until they fell in some ditch and died there.
You'd pass the dead in the streets or, worse, the dying, who
    stretched
their arms to heaven to send them release if not relief.   570
One learned not to look, for fear of recognizing one's friends,
for whom there was nothing to do, no help or comfort to offer.

The entire island lay under the sky's dark pall,
and, as in a charnel house, wherever one looked there were
    corpses.
    "As we waited to die, we became impatient, hating the
        pointless
drawing out of our lives. We envied the feckless dead,
who at least were past all caring. In the autumn an apple tree,
when you shake its boughs, will drop its fruit to litter the grass,
or an oak in a high wind will shower acorns below.
In such profusion, human bodies littered our ground.   580
It was enough to drive one mad. Some of us thought to pray.
You see that temple, high on the hill at the top of those steps?
It is Jupiter's temple. That stairway was crowded with suppliant
        husbands
offering prayers for their wives, or fathers praying for children.
One of those fathers knelt down before the august altar
to pray for his son, and I watched as he sickened abruptly and died
there in the temple—his incense yet unburnt in his hand.
One grew accustomed to horror. They'd bring bulls into the
        temple
for sacrifice, and the priest would race through the prayers and
        hurry
to pour the libation of wine between the horns, and the bull   590
would not wait for the fatal blow of the axe but fell
untouched to its unclean death. This happened often. At first,
they tried to continue the rite, but the knife would come away dry
from the neck of the dead beast. And the liver was blackened, its
        omens
ruined—or ruinous. Men hated the gods, defied them,
came to the temple doors at night to leave their loved ones'
corpses, or else broke in and left them about the altar.
There was no such thing as health, but only people not yet
afflicted—and many of them, unable to wait for the certain
onset of mortal symptoms, took their fates in hand   600
and chose to end it all, preferring to hang themselves.
Nobody bothered with funerals. We just made piles of corpses
and set them on fire. Where was the wood for a pyre for each
individual body? Or space for its grave? What mourners
were left to recite the prayers? The only mobs now were souls
that wandered the earth, not having been properly laid to rest,
a further part of the dreadful curse—for that's what it was,
and we cried to the gods to end it, or at least explain its purpose.
    "I prayed, myself, to Jove . . . in other words, to my father:

'Lord, hear me! Your son implores, if I am your son,   610
if you were indeed Aegina's lover, and if you acknowledge
me as your child, grant me a single desperate prayer.
Either restore my kingdom, returning my people to life,
or let me go down to a tomb and join with them in death.'
Just then, a flash of lightning and a peal of rolling thunder
signaled that he had heard and assented. 'I take this sign
as your will,' I said, 'and I pray that the omen may be a good one.'
I looked about where I stood and saw there a mighty oak,
sacred to Jove, a seedling brought from Dodona's grove.
And I saw on the tree a column of army ants, with their burden   620
of grain, hundreds, thousands, swarming along the bark.
In joy, I prayed, 'O father, grant me a like number
of human subjects. Refill these empty walls of my city.'
The air was calm, but the oak limbs waved as if in a gale.
The hairs on the back of my neck stood on end, and my knees
trembled. I fell to the earth to kiss the ground and the tree,
afraid that my prayer might be answered, and afraid that it might
        not be. . . .
This business of miracle-working is terrifying. It means
that you've given up on the world of cause and effect you trusted.
The power you exercise is a guise of a helplessness   630
you wouldn't care to admit to yourself or anyone else.
I slept that night and, in dreams, saw that oak tree again,
shaking its limbs, and the ants fell from the tree to the ground
and lost their middle legs. The front pair became arms,
and the hind pair turned to human legs, as that army of ants
became a real army. I woke in fear and confusion,
and outside heard the confusion continue, shouts and the noises
of crowds of men, which was strange, in our hushed, plague-
        stricken city.
I thought I might still be sleeping, but Telamon came rushing in
to announce that the men in my dream were now outside in the
        city,   640
walking around awake in the light and air. I went out
to hear them greet me as king. I offered thanks to my father,
Olympian Jove, and I welcomed my new subjects and gave them
houses and fields forsaken by those the plague had taken.
I gave these people the name of Myrmidons, from the Greek
myrmex, the word for 'ant.' There is something antlike about
        them
even still, for they all are thrifty, brave, and hard-working,
undismayed by toil and unafraid of danger,

and, if they are sometimes a little too earnest or dull,
there are many more grievous faults a king can find with his
       people."   650
     Long into the night, they talked, drinking, feasting,
and nodding in agreement and then, toward the end, in fatigue.
They went off to bed to sleep. In the morning, fresh and clear,
they looked about them, checked the weather outside, and saw
the winds, still from the East, would keep the ships from
       returning
to Athens. Cephalus' crew assembled there in his room,
and together they went to greet the king, but, old and frail,
Aeacus slept in that morning. Instead, his son Phocus
received the Athenian guests. They went to an antechamber
to breakfast together, and there Phocus noticed the weapon   660
Cephalus carried, a javelin with a gold-tipped head and a shaft
of some strange wood he'd never seen before. He asked,
"Sir, if you will permit me, what is that weapon made of?
I am an experienced hunter and thought I knew about arms,
but I've never seen its like before. Not ash or dogwood,
but a truly marvelous piece." Before Cephalus could answer,
one of his companions volunteered, "More than its beauty,
there's a secret to that javelin—it strikes whatever it's aimed at,
never misses, but flies true to the heart of the target,
and then comes back on its own, bloodied now, to the hand   670
of him who threw it." Phocus, now all ears, demanded
more: How did it do this? Where did it come from? Who
gave such a thing to Cephalus? His eyes were wide with wonder
as he asked to be told the story. Cephalus hesitated,
was silent, even gloomy. And tears spilled from his eyes
as he thought of the wife he had lost. He answered, nevertheless:
"It is a fine weapon, I grant, but it makes me weep, and will
as long as I live. This elegant instrument of destruction
ruined my life. . . . I wish I had never laid eyes upon it.
My wife was Procris. You've heard of her sister, I should
       expect—   680
Orithyia, whom Boreas ravished and married. Procris
was the more attractive one, really. And when King Erechtheus
gave her to me to wed, I was the happiest man
in Athens or all of Greece. And had not the gods decreed
a harsh fate, I still should be happy. . . . But life is uncertain,
and no one can know his future. Two months we had together,
and I went out to Hymettus to hunt deer with my nets,
and I happened to catch the eye of Aurora, the goddess of dawn.

There was nothing I did or intended or that even crossed my
     mind,
but against my will she took me, carried me off with her   690
as goddesses can. I swear, it was none of my doing, and Procris
was ever in my mind, and heart, and her name on my lips
annoyed the goddess, who told me to hold my peace about
     Procris,
and warned me I'd wish I had never met her or heard her name.
Then, in a snit, she dismissed me and sent me back to my wife.
I departed at once, of course, but on my way home, I wondered
what her threat could have meant. How could I wish I had never
heard her name? And the best, or worst, I could think of was
     tawdry
and quite banal, I'm afraid. I supposed she had been
     unfaithful. . . .
That question, not wholly removed from my own behavior,
     attached   700
to her whom I'd never had reason to worry about or suspect.
But lovers, defying reason itself, will invent their reasons,
as I am afraid I did in her beauty, innocence, youth,
kindness, and sweetness. . . . And I had been gone a very
     long time.
I struggled against my baser emotions and lost. I decided
the only way to resolve my doubt was to test her, to make
a judgment that would assure the lunatic or the fool
I knew I was. With Aurora's help, I changed my appearance
and approached my city and house as a handsome stranger
     with gifts
I knew she would like and sweet words I'd whispered before in
     her ear.   710
Self and not-self, I was mad. If my body was changed,
my mind was surely affected. . . . The household was all in good
     order,
with nothing amiss but the master's absence. No parties, no
     riotous
orgies, nothing arousing suspicion, and yet I persisted,
a captive of my own scheme—its victim as much as she was.
I wangled an introduction to Erechtheus' daughter, was ushered
into her presence . . . and all but gave it up then and there.
My heart melted. My soul reproached me. What was I doing?
This was the woman I loved! Why was I playing such games?
She seemed demure and sad, and was all the more lovely for that 720
dejection she showed she felt. I began nonetheless to make love

in all the conventional ways, and despite all her protestations
that she was married and loved her husband. She swore she was
        faithful
to him alone. And I heard her and ought to have trusted her oath.
I could have stopped right there, and lived happily ever after,
as children's stories have it. But that simplicity leaves us,
and I pressed on with my plan, intent on my own undoing.
If not for myself then for her whom I loved, I should have
        shown pity,
but what did I know? In a trance, perhaps in the goddess's spell,
I offered her jewelry, money, enormous wealth, for one night   730
of dalliance, one little adventure that no one would ever
        suspect. . . .
I brandished larger amounts, a king's ransom, a national
treasure. She hesitated. She didn't accept but paused
to consider this offer, perhaps to toy with it just for a moment
before she refused it, too. But I pounced on that instant's pause
and, having proved I was right, revealed myself as her husband!
In shame—I thought at the time it was shame, but realized later
it could have been in reproach for my having thus betrayed her—
she went away. Like that, without a word. She left
the house, the city, the entire race of men, to wander   740
over the mountains and into the valleys in search of Diana's
band and their celibate life of the woods. Left behind, I was
        lonely,
understood that I had been wrong, stupid in fact. I missed her
in every way. I repented of what I had done. Unfaithful
myself, I had turned things around and blamed her for my
        own sin!
In chagrin, I set out to find her, to confess and beg her pardon,
which she granted. Together, we lived in love and delight
for several years. She gave me the greatest gift any woman
can give—herself, her forgiveness and love. But also, to mark
our reunion, she gave me two presents, a most remarkable hound   750
Diana had given her, and the javelin you see here,
this one in my hand. And each comes with its own story.

        "Oedipus, son of Laius, answered the Sphinx's riddle,
and, in a rage, she threw herself over the cliff where those
who'd guessed wrong had gone to their deaths. The people,
        delivered,
rejoiced, but a new terror appeared in the countryside,
an enormous fox that came to raid pens, folds, and meadows
far and wide, and attack several human travelers also.

The wonderful sense of relief and release was gone, and we all
felt betrayed and abandoned. How could the gods let monsters,   760
in such relentless succession, loose upon our land?
All the able-bodied men of the region united
to hunt this creature down, but it was crafty and strong,
eluding our nets and snares and giving our hounds the slip
over and over again. This is where Laelaps comes in,
for that was the name of my most remarkable dog. He strained
at the leash and then, let loose, disappeared like a shot.
We tracked him, followed his footprints in the soft earth, this way
        and that,
but then, on a patch of rocky ground, lost him. Nearby,
a small hill rises up with a view of that plain we'd been working,   770
and we climbed to the top to look for the fox or the dog that
        chased it,
and. . . . How can one describe this? The eyes behold, and the
        brain
tries its best to make whatever sense it can
of the world we have envisioned. I saw the running fox
and, just behind it, the dog, turning whenever it turned,
doubling back, feinting one way but going another,
the huge fox and the dog as if they were bonded, wedded. . . .
I looked away for a moment, to set my javelin's loop
into my hand to fling it, but then, when I looked back down
at the contest between the two creatures, I saw they had been
        transformed   780
into a kind of trophy to signify that their contest
was a dead heat, a draw, for both had been turned to marble
by a sporting god who disliked the idea that either should lose."
At that, he paused, remembering how it had been that day,
or perhaps reluctant to change to the other, much less pleasant
subject, but Phocus prompted, "You said there was also a story
about that weapon you hold in your hand, the other present."
Cephalus hesitated, and then, with a melancholy
nod of his head, he began with the second and sadder tale:
        "I speak of the griefs of marriage, which blossom out of
            their joys,   790
the vision some couples achieve at least for a while of the perfect
bliss of united souls and bodies, a model for every
reconciliation of difference to turn the world
into an earthly heaven. I would not have exchanged
that time I had with her for eternity with a goddess,
not even Venus herself. And she, I am sure, was happy

as I was, would not have preferred Jupiter's love to mine.
Our delight in each other and in those days haunts me now and
        has turned
to a torment of self-reproach and mourning for what I have lost.
I used to wake up at dawn or before, to go out to the woods   800
while she was still sleeping to hunt birds and small game. I would
        go
alone. With this magical weapon, I had no need of attendants,
servants, or beaters. I wandered wherever the spirit moved me,
enjoying the solitude of the woods. It was pleasant to hunt,
and then, when my bag was filled, it was fine to stroll back home,
with the cool breeze on my face in the warmth of the
        midmorning.
That breeze was my reward, my companion, and I would call out
sometimes to invite it to join me, 'Aura, come.' And it would.
A childish indulgence, a nonsense, but, when we're alone, we
        revert
to childishness. Why not? Who will know? What harm   810
can come from such innocent play? But *aura,* the Latin word
for 'breeze,' is also a girl's name, and there could well have been
        some
confusion, if someone heard me—which happened of course,
        some person
of mean and suspicious nature, and also a bearer of tales.
Straight back to the palace and into my wife's ear
this poisonous gossip delivered his or her cargo of venom.
And this is where I'm obliged to assume some share of the blame,
for, happy as we had been, there was still that not quite forgotten
business of my old fling with Aurora, and then my doubts
of Procris. They say some broken limbs heal stronger than ever.   820
That may be true, but it happens sometimes the other way,
when there is a kind of weakness you learn to ignore, but with
        stress
the old wound will reopen. Something like that must have
        happened,
and, much as she wanted to trust me and to disbelieve these lies,
there was still that annoying shadow of doubt she could not get
        rid of.
She rejected the story, dismissed the bearer of spiteful gossip,
and yet she could not quite put it out of her mind. She wanted
to trust me for love's sake—or in spite of it: love, as we know,
is selfish as much as giving. She had to settle the question
one way or another and prove that I had not again   830

been unfaithful. She wouldn't believe it unless she saw
with her own eyes my behavior. Next morning, then, pretending
to sleep, she watched from her bed as I went out to the hunt.
When I was gone, she arose and followed, just out of sight
but close enough for a glimpse from time to time. You can guess
what happened next. At the end of my hunt, I called out to the
                breeze
as was my wont, 'Aura, come, my sweet, to soothe
my brow.' And that was enough. She groaned in dismay. Again,
I called out to the breeze, and I heard a rustle of leaves
behind me. I thought, a deer! and flung this weapon, aiming   840
at what I'd heard. It struck, as it always does, its target—
Procris. I found her, bloody, dying, her hands on the shaft
of the cursed weapon she'd given the man she loved. I tore
her garment away from the wound and tried, with a piece of its
                fabric,
to bandage the hurt and staunch the gush of blood, but couldn't.
The pity of it, the shock that I had done this dreadful
deed, that I had thrown the weapon. . . . It made no sense
until, as she lay in my arms, she managed to whisper to me
with her dying breath, 'I loved you, and love you still. Do not
replace me with this Aura, whoever she is.' I told her   850
there wasn't any such person, that Aura was only a fancy,
my name for the wind, a joke, a game I'd been playing, a dreadful
mistake. . . . 'The wind, only the wind!' I insisted. She may
have believed me. How can I ever know? And which way is
                worse?
She fell back in my arms and smiled at me. In forgiveness?
In pity for all the pain she knew I would have to live with
for the rest of my life? In love? She groaned, and I called to her
not to leave me, please, not to go, but already she
was dead." The hero, remembering how it had been, groaned
and then fell silent, though tears were streaming down both
                cheeks.   860
        And now the aged King Aeacus made his appearance
with his other two sons in train, and an honor guard of those
                troops
he was offering to his tear-stained guest and comrade in arms
against the Cretan horde. Acknowledging these, and the king's
valor, Cephalus offered Athens' thanks and his own.

BOOK VIII

Next morning, the sky was bright and the wind fair from the
    South,
so Cephalus could return with Aeacus' troops to Athens.
They hastened homeward, for Minos already was raiding the coast
of Megara, where Nisus, one of Pandion's sons,
reigned. He had that peculiar lock of purple hair
on an otherwise graying head, and the oracles had told him
that from that curious growth of hair the city's safety
hung—as long as those strands were there, no one could conquer
Megara. Bizarre, but after six months of siege
and skirmish, Minos had neither triumphed nor been repelled   10
from the beachhead where his troops were still encamped on the
    shingle.
On the magical walls of the city, Nisus' daughter would come
to her favorite place, a tower from which she could drop small
    stones
that would hit the wall at the place where the god Apollo was said
once to have had laid his lyre—and ever since, the stones
of that place would resound and sing with a lovely musical note
Princess Scylla had loved to produce as a little girl.
Now, as a young woman, she would not allow the war
to end her innocent pastime. Besides, from here she could see
the army down in the field, the Cretans in bivouac,   20
and, after a time, she even learned to pick out their chieftains,
distinguish the different shields, the crested helmets, the horses,
even their faces. Of those, one especially struck her—
of Minos, their king, handsome, severe, even cruel, but somehow
all the more attractive for that to the girl who watched him
from her perch up on the walls, could not take her eyes away,
was drawn, as a moth is drawn to a lamp's dangerous dazzle.
She stared as he rode, gaped as he drew back his mighty bow
to let fly a deadly arrow, or watched how the muscles rippled
along his broad shoulders and upper arms as he tensed   30

for a javelin throw. But best of all was to see him ride
back to camp with his helmet off and his hair unkempt,
and his face—that remarkable face—gentled by his exhaustion.
Then she no longer was Nisus' daughter, but someone else,
utterly foreign, and not entirely sane. . . . She knew this,
admitted it, even took some pride in the new rapture
she felt in her heart. She imagined herself walking out alone
from the walls of her city to join him, the enemy's leader, her
      father's
foe. . . . She invented several stories, but all with the same
ending, in which she and Minos could be thrown together in love.   40
Sometimes she thought of herself as opening up the city's
strong gates, and the conquest was dreadful, dreadful. . . . But he
was grateful and loved her beyond all measure. She stared from
      the wall
down to his gleaming tent, and whispered as one might
to a lover in bed: "I hate this war with its killing and waste.
And yet I am thankful for how it brought us two together."
She imagined herself his hostage. A lovely idea, for that ended
the war, and she was a pledge of peace, her country's savior,
and utterly at his mercy—which is just what she wanted to be.
She thought of how his father and mother had met in their
      passion,   50
the god and the huge bull who had burned for the beautiful
      maiden.
She felt that burning herself, and concluded that he might also,
as product and heir of such lust, reciprocate her ardor.
Sometimes the stories were utterly strange—she could fly through
      the air
like a bird to land at his tent and confess her love and offer
whatever dower he named. And he would not require
her city's capitulation but only her naked self.
She stared out in love, inventing excuses—elaborate stories—
that he surely supposed this war to avenge his murdered son
a just undertaking. But was that true? And would justice prevail,   60
as it always does in tales? If the doom of her city was sealed,
why should its fall be owing to weapons that maim and kill?
Would it not be better to accomplish the same result
by love's machination or her own miraculous intervention?
That would be safer for all concerned, including, of course,
Minos, who she worried might somehow be killed or, worse,
maimed and disfigured, which could happen, even if Crete
were fated to win. And then, as if it were only another

story she told herself, a plan formed in her mind
of how she might deliver the city over to Minos,   70
bringing peace as her dower. Prayers and a young girl's fancies
are useless and foolish unless one nudges the world a little,
seizing the helm of events and making oneself a god—
or rather, say, dedicating oneself to the gods' control
with total abandon. To love, she therefore offered herself
as only heroines do, but that's how they get to be
heroines, after all. Her father, the king, whom she feared,
held the keys to the city gates, and he was protected
as long as that lock of hair remained on his head. Very well,
if that was the only way, she would do what had to be done.   80
She had no need of a sword, or armor, but only a little
scissors to cut that lock—and the daring to undertake it.
       Night, the healer of care, settled over the city.
For her it brought a time of testing—how would her story
come out, she wondered. As if she read of her own adventure,
she held her breath and listened and watched as she made her way
along the darkened hallways from her room to her father's
chamber, where, as if she followed a script, she cut
the sacred purple lock of hair from his head. She left
the room, the palace, opened the city gates with the key   90
she had taken, and strode, fearless, across the no man's land
to the enemy camp and Minos' tent to present herself:
"I am Scylla, daughter of Nisus, the king, and love
has brought me here to deliver my people, my father's life,
and my devotion. I ask no other reward than love."
So saying, she held out her hand with the lock of hair in the palm
for him to accept as he clasped her in a gentle but firm
              embrace. . . .
But not having read this script, he looked at the girl in horror
that anyone could behave in such an unnatural way.
He didn't love her, couldn't imagine what kind of monster   100
would do such a thing, and said so. "Disgraceful," he cried, and
              "Foul!"
She stared in disbelief to hear him pray that the gods
might banish her from the earth. "May land and sea be denied
              you,"
he exclaimed in shock and disgust. "Crete, at the least, refuses
that you should ever set foot on the island of Jupiter's childhood."
       Now the girl looked on, as if in a nightmare from which
she might yet rouse herself, while Minos took the city.
Then, as the Cretans embarked, cast off the hawsers, and rowed

out from the harbor's shelter, she knelt down on the beach
to pray, but nothing happened. She called out in her despair: 110
"Bastard! Where do you go? How can you leave me here,
who gave you victory? Monster, to whom I gave my love,
my fatherland, and my father. . . . How can you run away?
How could my gift not please you? How can you now betray me,
leaving me here deserted? I can't go back home to my city.
It's ruined, gone. And my people, my own family, hate me,
while everyone else fears me. No one in all the world
will take me in. Not even Crete will open her doors
to someone like me. Europa was not your mother, but Syrtis,
the wild Armenian tigress. Jupiter wasn't your father,   120
but some honest-to-god bull, some slavering beast
covered with shit! O father, punish me now, I beg you.
I repent of my deed and life, and only ask to be slain—
but not by Minos! Let those whom I have so gravely injured
take what satisfaction they can from my death. A fool,
I ought to have known that something was terribly wrong with
        the man,
if Pasiphaë, his wife, preferred to embrace a beast
and from her miscegenation delivered the Minotaur
to amaze and appall the world. . . . Can you hear me out there?
        Does the wind
blow my words away as it fills your sails and drives you   130
back to the home and bed—or let us call it the crib—
of that harridan wife of yours? I watch as his vessel takes him
out of hearing and soon out of sight, as the flashing oars
propel him farther and faster in the hope of escape from me. . . .
But he won't escape, he'll never be rid of me. I'll follow
wherever he goes. . . ." And then, taking all leave of her senses,
or at least of the world of sense and reason, she waded in.
She followed him in the water, swimming with rapid strokes
of amazing strength, for her passion was mighty and made her
        strong.
She caught up to the swift boat and clung tight to its transom   140
in an act of desperation, which Minos and all his crew
hated to see. They rowed as hard as they could, but she held
fast to the stern until, from above, an enormous osprey
swooped down from the sky—her father, Nisus, now changed
to one of those sharp-beaked sea birds eager to tear her flesh.
In panic, she let go, fell free into the wake
of the swift ship, but then, in a magic moment, rose up
to skim just over the water behind the vessel, her hands

feathered now into wings, and her body turned to a bird's.
She is a shearer now, called that from what she did   150
to her father, and still she shears the water, and fears the osprey.
   Returning to Crete, Minos offered his thanks to Jove
with a hundred bulls and hung in the great hall of the palace
the trophies and spoils of Megara, but of these he took little joy
or pride, for that monstrous creature Scylla had mentioned was
      grown,
a skeleton now too large to be hidden away in a closet.
Minos therefore banished this cynosure of disgrace
to the labyrinth Daedalus built for the purpose, a strange
      construction
with turns, twists, and blind alleys. As the Maeander flows in
      Turkey—
wriggling this way and that so randomly through the plain,   160
as if it were not at all eager to empty into the sea—
so Daedalus made his confounded, confounding maze,
in which he himself got lost a number of times (and felt
triumphant more than ashamed, for that was the whole idea).
   In this wonderful structure, Minos shut the half-bull, half-
man creature, and twice he prepared him the special meal,
the triennial table d'hôte of Athenian youths and maidens
the Minotaur devoured live (in the early stages).
At the third of these vile occasions, Ariadne, King Minos'
daughter, fell in love with a gorgeous young man from Athens—   170
Theseus, our old friend. As Scylla had first betrayed
her father for Minos' sake, now his daughter conspired
with the enemy alien, giving him thread to reel out by which
he then could retrace his steps. And what was her payment for
      this?
Theseus, son of Aegeus, having dispatched the monster,
took the young maiden on board his ship and set sail for Naxos
(Dia, it's sometimes called). From there he sailed off and left her,
bereft, pregnant, abandoned, and more than half out of her mind
with grief and rage. But Bacchus brought her comfort and help,
gave her the crown from his head, and watched as she put it on   180
and with it ascended to heaven. The jewels in the diadem burned
like stars, and became stars, as she took her place in the sky's
vitrine—that constellation not far from Hercules.
   Such spectacular flight is what Daedalus, back in Crete,
was thinking about. Though the sea surrounded the island,
      and Minos
controlled all shipping, the air was nonetheless open and free.

Why not soar up in the sky and fly like a bird to escape
this barbarous land? He schemed and planned, made small
        drawings,
and, figuring human minds might be stronger than Nature's laws,
started to build an object of feathers and wax by means   190
of which he might perhaps take wing, leap up in the air,
and glide through it to swoop and swim in the sky like a gull.
Icarus, his son, watching close by, would play
with the feathers, flinging them up into the air to see
how they swirled as they fell, or else he would fool with the
        warm wax
that was fun to mold—like clay. Often his father would scold him
and caution him never to touch his worktable, his tools,
or the objects on which he was working. "Only be patient,
        my son,
and we shall have fun soon enough." At last, with two pairs
        of wings
completed, he told the boy how he had planned their escape   200
and what to do and what to avoid. "Do not fly too low,
where the sea spray can soak your wings and make the feathers
        soggy
and heavy. But don't go high, where the heat of the Sun's fire
can melt the wax. Keep to a middle range if you can,
and don't try to show off—it isn't a game but a matter
of life and death. Do you understand what I'm trying to tell you?"
The young man nods his head and promises he'll be good,
will take no foolish chances but do what he's told and follow
his father's lead. The parent wants to believe the child,
hopes for once to rely on the promise the son has made.   210
His hands nevertheless tremble some as he straps
the wings onto his son. He hugs the boy, and his eyes
fill with tears as he kisses his cheek and wishes him luck.
Daedalus then takes off, ascends into the air,
and, like a huge bird that leads his uncertain fledgling, wheels,
makes a few turns and maneuvers to show how these feats are
        managed.
The son flaps his wings and rises up to follow his father.
Far below, on the ground, a farmer looks up from his plow
at these figures high in the sky and supposes gods have come
on a visit. Out in the country, a shepherd glances up from his
        flock,   220
sees these creatures, and wonders if they are about to attack
his sheep. Or out at sea beyond the mole of the harbor,

a fisherman out in his boat stares up at the flying
people but doesn't believe it, rubs his eyes and rejects it
as nonsense. The father and son are passing Samos, Delos,
Paros, and now Lebinthos, and honey-rich Calymne. . . .
But here the youngster's initial fears have been mostly calmed.
His confidence now has developed. He wonders what he can do
with this splendid toy, what limits there are to his father's
          invention.
He flaps his wings and rises higher—but nothing bad   230
happens. He figures he still has plenty of margin and rises
higher still. It's exciting, wonderful fun, as he soars
and wheels, but he doesn't notice the wax of his wings is melting
and feathers are falling out. And then, it's too late, and he's
          flapping
naked arms, which do nothing to hold him up. He is losing
altitude. . . . He is falling. He cries out. His father hears him,
and watches in horror the plummeting body splash into the sea
that takes its name from its victim. He calls down to his son,
"Icarus! Where are you?" but he sees only melted blobs
that had been the wings, and the larger blob of the body he grabs   240
and buries then in a tomb on the beach of the small island
nearby—that people now call Icaria, in his honor.
          So, there he was at the tomb on the beach, when he heard
          a bird,
a small partridge appearing from out of a ditch, flapping
its wings, and making that chirring sound partridges do
when they're pleased, as this one was, delighted by Daedalus'
          grievous
bereavement. Why? The bird had recently been transformed
to its avian incarnation. Once, it had been a person,
Daedalus' nephew, in fact, his sister's son. She had sent
Perdix, her clever youngster, to serve an apprenticeship   250
with the master builder and engineer, and the lad had proved
an apt pupil—indeed, too good, for the master was troubled
to see a young fellow who matched and sometimes even outshone
his own abundant gifts. This youngster looked at a fish bone
and cut a set of teeth in that pattern to make of a metal
blade the world's first saw. He also invented the compass,
with one foot stable and one foot swinging around it to draw
a perfect circle—brilliant, obvious, and outrageous.
Daedalus couldn't endure it, threw the boy over the wall
of Athens' lofty fortress, planning to tell the world   260
his apprentice had accidentally lost his footing and fallen.

But Pallas, who likes bright youngsters, caught the boy in midair,
saved his life, and turned him into a partridge—the *perdix*
he remains to this day. His quickness of wit is now literal
            quickness,
and the bird, having once fallen, still fears and avoids
heights but scurries along the ground and nests in hedgerows.
        The king of Sicily, Cocalus, received the dejected and weary
Daedalus and gave him refuge. In Athens, where Theseus
returned with his good news that the years of dreadful tribute
were over at last, the people came out to give thanks to the gods,   270
filling the temples with flowers and calling upon Minerva,
Jove, and the other gods to protect them from further harm.
They offered burning incense and the streaming blood of beasts.
Theseus now was famous through all the cities of Greece—
even to Aetolia, where the people of Calydon called him
to come to their aid in their hour of need. They had their hero
in Meleager, but now they needed what help they could get,
all the valiant men of Greece, to kill the enormous
boar Diana had loosed on their land, to avenge what she thought
was an insult no serious goddess ought to permit.   280
At the time of the harvest, their king, Oeneus, had offered his
            thanks
to the gods of the fields and the vines, giving first fruits of
            the grain
to Ceres, and pouring the wine fresh from the barrels to Bacchus.
There were offerings, too, to Minerva, of oil from her sacred
            olive,
and they thanked and praised the local deities of their valleys
and hills, as was their custom. All the gods had their due. . . .
Except Diana! Her altar alone was empty, deserted.
Why should this be? she wondered. And why should she
            tolerate it?
It made no sense. She had nothing to do with crops and harvests,
but gods have their frailties, too, their moods and even
            depressions,   290
and, looking around at the altars of other gods, she declared,
"I may be without honor, but not without power and vengeance,"
and, to teach those churls a lesson, she loosed on the country
            a boar,
huge, as big as a bull, with red eyes shining like coals
in a hearth, and with bristling neck. . . . Its bristles were like spear
            shafts.

As he grunted and oinked, hot foam flecked from his lips, and his
     tusks,
like elephant tusks or those of a saber-toothed tiger, gleamed
in deadly menace. His breath could kill what vegetation
his trotters had not destroyed. He left a swath behind him
of devastation tornadoes or hurricanes leave, whole fields   300
of wheat reduced to useless pulp. Threshing floors got nothing,
and granaries lay empty. He ruined vineyards as well,
and even attacked the olive groves and the herds of cattle
grazing out in the meadows. Not even people were safe,
unless they huddled within their fortified town walls,
from behind which they could peer out to watch for more
     depredation
on the part of this pig from hell. At last, Meleager assembled
a kind of posse to ride out and deal with this menace, a band
of tough young men who were brave and eager for glory. Castor
and Pollux were there, the twin sons of Tyndarus' wife,   310
Leda (their father, however, was Jove himself). Great Jason,
the Argo's captain, was there, and Theseus, with his faithful
friend Pirithoüs. Also Thestius' sons, Plexippus
and Toxeus, the uncles of Meleager, joined in,
as did Lynceus and Idas, Aphareus' boys. Caeneus,
who once as a girl ravished by Neptune, had got him to grant her
the power to change her sex and now was a burly young man
who wanted to hunt with the other men. Leucippus came, and
     Acastus,
and Hippothoüs, and Dryas, and Phoenix, son of Amyntor.
Actor's sons, Eurytus and Cleatus, came, and Phyleus   320
from Elis came, and Telamon, and mighty Achilles' father,
Peleus, showed up. Admetus, the son of Pheres,
and Iolaüs appeared from Boeotia, along with quick
Eurytion and fast Echion. Lelex of Locri
was there, and Penopeus, too, and Hyleus, and Hippasus,
and Nestor—not that gerontological wonder Homer
is always trotting out, but a young and coltish Nestor,
barely old enough to take part, but he was there.
Laërtes, Ulysses' father, joined in, and Mopsus the prophet
and seer, and Ancaeus showed up, and Amphiaraüs, too. . . .   330
And Atalanta, the girl from Tegea, the famous huntress,
appeared at the last moment—and Meleager was smitten
at once by her curious beauty. Her face, on a boy, would
     have been

girlish, but there, on a girl, seemed boyish and even tough.
One look, and he was done for. The flames of love in his heart
raged, and he thought any man she ever found worthy of love
would surely be happy and blessed. But he kept this thought to
    himself,
for this was a time for more earnest action and bloodier business.

    Off to the deep woods then, with nets, weapons, and dogs
barking, excited, eager to slip their leashes and follow   340
the all too obvious track of their quarry. Down in a vale
rainwater had turned to a marsh and covered with swamp grass,
rushes, reeds, and ferns, the beast lay in wait, then charged
the disorderly swarm of dogs and hunters. Shouts of excitement
(which sound very much like shouts of terror, but never mind)
resound, and various men throw spears with iron points
as the boar comes rushing to scatter the dogs, slashing, wounding,
or killing those who are nearest. Echion's throw is first
but misses and grazes the bark of a maple tree. The second
spear is Jason's, and it flies true but goes too far,   350
passing over the boar's bristly back to land
in the muck beyond. Mopsus, the seer, now prays for Apollo
to guide his hand aright and let his spear find its mark.
This prayer the gods are amused to grant in most literal terms,
for Mopsus' spear flies true to the boar and bounces off
its hide, for Diana has interfered, and the spearhead has fallen
in midair. The boar could have been hit in the side with a
    broomstick
for all the damage the pointless weapon is able to do.
In fact, what it does is annoy the boar, which now seems to
    breathe
fire and smoke as though in porcine disguise a dragon   360
were roused to fight. It charges—a missile flung through the air
has the same lethal force as this wild beast, which gores
Hippalmus and Pelagon, way out on the far right
of the line of hunters. Their friends run to their sides, among
    them
Enaesimus, who, on the way, gets caught, feels the boar behind him
slash at the back of his legs. It cuts his hamstring; his leg
gives way; and he falls and is gored and trampled to death.
    Nestor,
just behind him, almost bought it then—he'd have missed the
    entire
Trojan War!—but he used the shaft of his spear as a vault pole
and bounded up to a fairly high branch of a nearby tree,   370

from which he looked down as the beast charged its trunk and
    sharpened
his razor-tusks on the bark. He then turned away to attack
Hippasus and, with one sweeping cut, ripped his upper thigh
open. Castor and Pollux came riding up with their weapons
ready, but now the boar ran into the heart of a thicket
too dense for a horse or even a man to try to follow—
as Telamon found out, for he went in after the pig
only to trip on a root he couldn't see. His friend
Peleus came to help him up—he'd sprained his ankle
and couldn't walk unaided. Atalanta fitted an arrow   380
onto the string of her longbow and let it fly. It grazed
the boar's spine and lodged in its head, just behind the ear,
where a trickle of blood appeared, staining the stiff bristles.
Atalanta was pleased. Meleager, even more pleased and proud,
announced that her brave and skillful deed would receive all honor
from those in the hunt. The men, goaded on by his words
and perhaps a little ashamed to have been outdone by a woman,
hurled their spears into the midst of that thicket—and missed,
every single one. At this point Ancaeus, wielding
a double-headed axe, announced that he would go forward   390
to do what he called "a man's job." "It's pig-killing time," he
    declared,
and defied Diana herself to protect this beast from the blade
he brandished over his head. With her help or without it,
the boar lay in wait and then charged when Ancaeus came into
    range,
and managed to drive a tusk into his groin as if
it were a lover and he were a woman. His guts poured out
as if, in a kind of childbirth, he brought forth his own death.
The dirt around him was soaked with his gore. Then Ixion's son
Pirithoüs advanced with a hunting spear in his hand to make
his attempt on the creature, but Theseus called out, "Careful,
    careful,   400
you don't want to get too close, old pal. After what's just
    happened,
there's no disgrace in a long-range throw. As a favor to me,
watch yourself, dear friend." And here Theseus threw
his javelin, but the branch of an oak tree got in the way,
and the missile missed. Then Jason took a quick shot and hit . . .
not the boar, but a dog that had got in the way, and killed it
instantly. Meleager tried, and his first throw missed
and stuck in the earth, but the second hit the boar in the back

and penetrated. The beast whirled around in its pain,
sprinkling blood and foam and trying to free itself,   410
and Meleager moved in with his spear and pricked and annoyed
the wounded boar until the opportunity opened
and he could strike at the shoulder and plunge the spear in deep
for the kill. There were shouts and applause, and the hunters
    shook his hand
and gazed in awe at the huge carcass stretched out on the ground.
In a complicated gesture of triumph and reverence, each
dipped the point of his spear into the animal's blood.
    Meleager, planting his foot on the boar's head, announced:
"This prize is Atalanta's. Take it, fair lady, and share
the glory with me. The skin, the head, the enormous tusks   420
are yours!" Delighted, she thanked him, accepting his generous
    gesture,
but some of the others murmured in disapproval or muttered,
and a few were moved to speak out in anger, among them
    Plexippus
and Toxeus, Thestius' sons, who were Meleager's young uncles.
"Do not presume to these honors, young woman," one said; his
    brother
was more to the point, "This lovesick man is perhaps your victim,
but not that boar on the ground." And he seized the trophies
    from her,
which act of disrespect to her and himself Meleager
could not allow to remain unpunished. "Braggarts! Cowards!
You're nothing but hot air," he cried, and pricked their balloons   430
with a thrust of still bloody steel into Plexippus' heart.
Toxeus couldn't decide whether to fight or run,
froze for a moment, and then was frozen for all time, pierced
with the spear Meleager had just pulled out of his brother's
    corpse.
    Back at the gods' temple, Meleager's mother, Althaea,
was offering prayers of thanksgiving for what the runners
    reported
as triumph: the boar was dead, the countryside was delivered
from death and loss, and the hunters were mostly alive and well.
But then the party returned from the hunt, and they brought the
    bodies
of both her beloved brothers. She beat her breast in woe   440
at this double bereavement. Both of them dead? It was hard to
    believe,
but then harder, hardest, was what they told her, the story

of how they had died. Been killed. And by her own son, their
 nephew. . . .
Grief at a certain pitch transforms itself into rage,
and, as if the heart in her chest had turned to a stone or a weapon,
she turned her thoughts to vengeance for these despicable
 murders.
 Her son! She cursed the day of his birth, which she now
 remembered,
and how, when she'd lain in childbirth, the three mysterious
 sisters,
spinning between their fingers and thumbs the threads of life,
had decreed as a kind of whimsy that the length of the newborn
 baby's   450
life should be the same as . . . that log over there, in the hearth.
The sisters then had vanished, and the mother had dragged herself
from her bed to the fireplace to snatch up the log and keep it
safe from harm, for her child's sake. She'd kept it hidden away,
guarding it with her life. Now she fetched it forth
and ordered her servants to gather tinder and kindling, light it,
and leave her alone with the fire. Four times she picked up the log
and made as if to throw it on top of the hungry tongues
of flame, but every time her mother's love held back
the sister's furious passion for retribution. Her cheeks   460
now blazed with rage, now paled at the thought of what she
 intended.
In the same way, tears for her son would spill forth, then dry up
as her anger at her brothers' killer would heat her passion,
and then the crying resumed, and then the rage. A ship
driven one way by the wind and the opposite way by the strong
tide, she bobbed and yawed, making no clear headway,
until at the end she gave up all human feelings. The gods
demanded justice, she thought. The family honor required
a blind capitulation to piety's clear dictate.
She stared into the flames and then looked down at her hands,   470
which would lift the sacred log. "This, be the funeral pyre
for the flesh of my own flesh. Eumenides, behold,
by a wicked deed, I avenge a wicked deed. Forgive me!
I cannot leave it alone. My father's sons are destroyed,
and so must my husband's son die to unite in grief
a family otherwise doomed to blood guilt and hatred forever.
Thus may my brothers' ghosts lie easy, accepting the heavy
tribute of my womb." And she waited, but could not throw
the log onto the fire. Her body, paralyzed, useless,

refused to obey the orders that issued from her distracted   480
mind as another voice within her spoke out to protest:
"Admitting that he deserves to die, must these be the hands
that execute this dire sentence? I cannot bear it,
no more than I can bear that he should go scot-free,
enjoying his success against his own house and blood
and lording it over the town. . . ." A welter, a babble then,
of wisps of half-framed thoughts of her months of pregnancy,
     pangs
of birth, and that surrealistic moment when she first heard
the prophecy of the Fates. She remembered how she had reached
for this very log and held it over her head—a mistake?   490
Would the world and her life have been better if she had not
     touched it then?
"You lived by my gift," she said aloud to the wood in her hands,
"but die by your own evil-doing." And the red of the dancing
     flames
was the red of her brothers' blood, which ran as wet as her tears
in their unendurable blur. Their wounds cry out for an answer,
call out for her to join them. She hates her life, all life,
can even imagine she does her son a kindness by freeing
him of the fetter that binds his soul to this sty of a world. . . .
Her hands tremble with life, and she turns away to avoid
seeing the log fall in its arc to land in the fire,   500
where it seems to give out a human groan as it catches and burns.
    Elsewhere—it doesn't much matter where—Meleager
     feels odd,
hot with a sudden fever. He's burning up, and he's weak.
He falls to the ground in pain, knows he is dying, and hates it—
not death itself, but the manner of dying, the coward's bloodless
demise. He remembers with envy Ancaeus' spectacular end.
A better way to go than this handing over of strength
and breath, as if life were a plate of cookies one were refusing.
He thinks of his father, his loving wife, his brothers and sisters,
and thinks, too, of his mother. Has she told him the strange story   510
about the log and the length of his life? Does he guess that his end
has something to do with a fire at home in the hearth his mother
even now stares into? The pain prevents his thinking
deeply or even in sequence. Images flash and flicker
as if his mind were in flames, as it is, and he writhes on a spit
until the fire dies down and his spirit, like smoke, curls up
to float away into thin air, leaving white ashes behind.

Now Calydon is in mourning, for the death of its hero. The
    young
and old look to each other for comfort and reassurance
that they may survive this loss. The women, too, are bereft   520
and, down at Euenus' banks, they cry, tear their hair,
and beat their breasts in grief. Oeneus, father, king,
lies on the ground moaning, and dirt and ashes befoul
his long white hair as he laments he has lived too long.
But the grief of the mother, Althaea, is worse, worst, for she
    knows
that she was the cause of the death, that her mind framed the deed
her hands performed—and she watches them seize the dagger and
    turn
the point to her own bosom, and then, in a sudden spasm
of rage, pain, and the wish to be done with it all, drive home
the blade into her heart. Oh, pity, pity! Had gods   530
granted me what Homer prayed for—those hundred mouths,
each with its own tongue, and his genius and inspiration—
still, I could not describe the grief of the weeping sisters
Meleager left behind. They surround the corpse, caress it,
kiss the cold and rubbery skin, and carry on
as no decent people do. They gather his ashes up
and press his urn to their breasts, or they fling themselves on
    his tomb
and cling to the stone of his marker, while their rivers of tears
    flow on. . . .
Unbearable and unseemly—even Diana is moved
to bring to an end the grief of Oeneus' unfortunate house.   540
She transforms the girls, and their limbs and bodies are covered
    with feathers
as the sisters become guinea hens (or, to give this gallinaceous
bird the scientific name ornithologists use,
the *Numida meleagris*). This change affects all but two
of the sisters—Gorge had her destiny yet to fulfill
in a marriage to Andremon and the birth of their son, Oxilus.
The other was Deianara, who would later become Alcmena's
daughter-in-law. (We shall soon be occupied with her story.)
    As they flew up and into the air, Theseus, too, took off
for home and Athens, but on his way he paused at the river   550
of Acheloüs. He gauged the banks of the swollen stream
and considered whether to cross. The god of the river counseled,
"Hero of Athens, take care. This current is treacherous, carries

trees and boulders that crash and resound. Horses, cattle,
entire stables that stood by my banks have been swept away,
and all the strength of those beasts has been nothing compared to
        the eddies
and swirls of my current you see before you. Be prudent, wait,
and accept my invitation. Stay as my guest. When the water
subsides to its accustomed level, you'll be on your way
in safety, I warrant." Aegeus' son accepted the god's   560
suggestion and invitation and entered his gloomy abode.
The floor was damp and clammy, and the walls were of porous
        pumice
and rough calcareous tufa. The chambers were thick with moss,
and their ceilings were decorated with conch and purple murex.
It was late in the day, and the travelers fell upon the large couches
in the grand audience chamber, Theseus, Pirithoüs,
Lelex, and all the others. The river god entertained them,
and barefoot water nymphs brought trenchers of food and wine
in elegant jeweled beakers. With gusto the guests partook,
ate, drank, and relaxed. When the meal was over, the hero   570
pointed out at the water and, on the horizon, an island.
"What is the name of that place over there?" he asked. "Or places?
Is it one island or several?" The river god answered, "Five
islands, but close together. They're hard to see from this distance.
They have an interesting story, for they were once water nymphs
who slaughtered two bullocks each, and invited the rural gods
to come to their feast—all the gods, that is, but me. Ignored,
forgotten, I raged in anger, swelled, tore at the forests
and fields, and swept the nymphs and the spit of ground they
        stood on
into the sea. They remembered me well enough, then. And I
        chipped   580
away at their plot of ground until, with the help of the sea,
I formed those Hedgehog Islands you see out there. Beyond them
is another island I love, which sailors call Perimele.
She was a girl I loved—lusted after, but loved.
Her father was Hippodamas, who disapproved of our union
and thought I had wounded his honor as much as her own, for
        which
ridiculous reason he hurled her down from a cliff to drown
in the sea. . . . I caught her, held her up as she swam, and cried
        out
to Neptune, 'Show her mercy. Grant her a place of safety.
Or let her become a place and live on forever.' He heard   590

this rather baroque request and granted it. New land appeared
and embraced her floating body; an island grew where you see it,
a transformation of anger and love, despair and faith."
　　The river god fell silent, and the men in the room considered
his words, which echoed yet in their minds of the marvel of
　　　　things.
But Pirithoüs, perhaps to be entertaining or merely
in the wrong mood for such yarns, argued, "Those things don't
　　　　happen.
You are telling us children's stories. The gods do not perform
　　　　tricks
as if in a side-show world, turning this into that, transforming
one shape to another, to dazzle the simple-minded."　　　　　　600
This was a shocking thing to think, let alone to say,
and the company, stunned, was silent as if they hoped the words
they had heard might go away. Then Lelex, Troezen's hero,
whose temples were gray and whose eyes had seen much, spoke
　　　　up in gentle
reproof: "The powers of gods are great indeed. No man
can even imagine their limits. They do what they like. A story
comes to mind of an oak and a linden tree that stand
intertwined in the Phrygian hills. I've seen them myself,
these trees with a low wall that surrounds them. King Pittheus
　　　　sent me
thither. Around that place is marshland now, where birds　　　　610
paddle, dive, and fly. Two travelers once, it is said,
appeared in modest disguises that hid their glory, for Jove
and Mercury were the two. They knocked on door after door
seeking a bed for the night, but over and over again
were turned away. In the end, in one house they found a
　　　　welcome—
or a hut really. Its roof was thatched with reeds from the marsh.
The couple who lived there were Baucis and Philemon, old and
　　　　poor,
and yet content with their lot. They were decent people, simple
country folks, one might say. And when strangers came to their
　　　　door
and stooped a little to enter without bumping their heads,　　　620
the old man fetched a bench for the travelers to sit on—
there were no servants or masters here, but just these two—
the man and his wife. Baucis fetched a piece of cloth
to pad the rude bench so that the strangers might rest
easy. She stirred the coals in the hearth and fanned the fire

to cook them a meal. She had one of those country kettles
of copper lined with tin, in which she fixed them a dinner
of cabbage from out of the garden, and a little smoked pork for
        flavor—
this was the best they could do, but unstintingly they did it.
Philemon cut a generous rasher off the cured pork butt,   630
which hung from a hook in the blackened ceiling beam, and his wife
put it into the kettle. Then, to be sure that their guests
might dine in comfort and even a show of style, she brought out
a bolster filled with sedge grass to put on their wickerwork couch.
Over this she arranged the embroidered throw they saved for
        feast days
and special occasions—a bit worn here and there, and frayed
at one of its ends, but still a nice piece of work, which looked
good on the wicker couch. She invited the gods to recline
as quality people do when they eat and, with trembling hands,
set the bowls on the tripod table—one of its legs   640
was a bit short and had to be propped with the shard of a pot.
But leveled, steadied, and wiped clean, it would have to serve,
        and did.
She set out a plate of olives, green ones and black, and a saucer
of cherry plums she had pickled, and an endive and radish salad.
She had cheese and some roasted eggs, all in the earthenware
        dishes
that remained of their set—handsome, embossed pieces, with only
a few chips here and there. The wine beakers were carved
of beech wood and lined with beeswax on the insides. Philemon
        poured
wine—no special vintage or old cuvée, but a hearty
honest wine he'd made himself. And Baucis served   650
her cabbage and pork stew. For dessert there were nuts, figs,
dates, and plums, and baskets of ripe apples and grapes,
in the center of which they produced, with a show of modest
        pride,
a honeycomb for sweetness. They beamed with their sweet smiles,
taking pleasure themselves in what they'd given their guests.
        "Philemon then was about to refill the empty wine bowl.
He picked it up but felt that it wasn't empty. Instead,
as much as they drank, the wine had replenished itself, and the
        bowl
was as full as before. Bizarre! Frightening even. He caught
his wife's attention and gestured. She looked herself at the wine
        bowl,   .   660

watched as one of the gods refilled his glass—and the wine
in the bowl didn't diminish. They stared at the ceiling and prayed
for mercy, mercy. They thought of the simple meal they had
     offered
their supernatural guests and felt dismay. They had done
far too little, had failed to recognize these strangers
or give them enough. In the yard, they had a goose, a pet,
a kind of watch-goose, but now Philemon went out to kill it
to serve their divine guests. The gods watched as the goose
ran this way and that and the old man tried to catch it.
The wife went out to help, but the goose was too fast for her also,   670
and it ran inside to the gods themselves, who laughed and
     commanded:
'Let it live. We are gods, and we thank you. You've done enough,
more than your nasty neighbors thought to do. Follow us
up to the foothills and watch from the mountainside as the gods
chastise the sins of men with the punishment they have earned.
You alone shall be spared. Come with us now.' In awe,
the couple put on their mantles, took up their walking sticks,
and followed after the gods, struggling higher and higher
up the slopes of the nearby hills. Not far from the top,
perhaps a bowshot away, the gods stopped, turned, and pointed,   680
and the aged couple turned to look back down at the region,
all covered now with water. Only their house remained.
An astonishing thing! A marvel. But they did not rejoice. They
     wept
at the ruin of all their neighbors, and quaked with fear at the
     power
that could, in an instant, transform an earth they had taken for
     granted
and make it strange. Or worse, that the strangeness is always
     lurking,
always there but seldom visible. Poor little house,
but it was changing, too, their simple cottage becoming
larger and grander, a glittering marble-columned temple.
The straw and reeds of the thatch roof metamorphosed into gold,   690
and gates with elaborate carvings sprang up, as ground gave way
to marble paving stones, which were fit for a king's courtyard.
Wonder on wonders! In shock, they listened as Saturn's son
spoke in a reassuring voice: 'Old man, old woman,
ask of us what you will. We shall grant whatever request
you make of us.' The husband whispered into the ear
of his wife, and then turned to listen as she whispered into his.

'We ask only to serve as your priest and priestess to guard
your temple. And having spent all our lives together, we pray
to die at the same time,' he said. 'I'd hate to see   700
my wife's grave, or have her weep at mine.' And Jove
nodded. As long as they lived, the couple took care of the gods'
temple that had been their house. Their lives had become
a dream, a story, the ending of which was more strange than all
that had gone before. Arrived at a very old age together,
they stood at what had been their modest doorway and now
was a grandiose façade, and Baucis noticed her husband
was beginning to put forth leaves from his head and shoulders. He
saw that she, too, was producing leaves and bark. They were
        turning
into trees, and they stood there, held each other, and called,   710
before the bark closed over their mouths, a last 'Farewell.'
And then there was only silence, or the whisper among their
        leaves
of the intimate secrets trees confide in each other. Today,
in that part of the world, the peasants will point out the two trees
that seem to be growing out of the single trunk, the oak
and linden tree together. Their wise men swear it happened,
and people come from miles around to hang in the boughs
of that double tree their wreaths and gifts of woven flowers.
I myself was there and touched my hand to the tree
and recited the prayer they say: 'Let those whom the gods have
        loved
                                                                        720
be gods. Let those who have worshiped well, be worshiped
        themselves.' "

        Here, Lelex fell silent. The tale and the teller had moved
everyone in the room, but Theseus most of all.
He wanted more stories of wonders the gods have done and
        can do.
The river god, their host, lolled on his couch with his head
cupped in his chin and his arm leaning upon his elbow.
"There are some," he said, "whom the gods change, and they stay
        that way
forever. To others they give a remarkable power to take
one form after another, whenever they will. So it happened
to Proteus, who dwelt in the depths of the blue sea. He   730
could appear as a young man, or a lion, or boar, or perhaps
an adder that men might fear, or a bull with a great pair of horns,
or even a stone, or a rooted tree, or flowing water,
or tongues of dancing flame, which water hates and fears.

'So it happened with Mestra, Erysichthon's daughter
and Autolycus' wife. This man, Erysichthon, scorned the gods
and declined to sacrifice on their altars or do them honor.
One day he went to a grove sacred to Ceres to cut
firewood and defile those trees with his axe head's steel.
A mighty oak in that stand of centuries-old trees   740
was hung with votive tablets, twists of wool, and wreaths
that postulants had left in the hope their prayers might be granted.
Dryads would often dance around this tree, holding hands
and forming a huge circle—for the trunk was a good fifteen
yards around. It towered over other trees, as they towered
over the grasses and shrubs below them. Erysichthon,
nevertheless, instructed his servants to cut it down,
which they were afraid to do. This only made him angry,
and he grabbed an axe from the nearest man and announced to all:
'It's only a tree the goddess likes, but assume instead   750
it's the goddess herself, I'd cut it just the same. Its top
shall touch the ground this day.' As he said this, the tree shivered
and groaned, and its branches shook. Its acorns grew ashen and
        pale.
Anyone else would have been deterred, but he swung his axe
and struck the tree, and blood came gushing forth from its bark
as if he had plunged that axe into the neck of a bull
at an altar. Astonished, appalled, his attendants protested that any
sane man would desist from further assaults on the tree.
One fellow close by attempted to take the axe from his hand,
but Erysichthon glared in fury, called out, 'You pious   760
son of a bitch, take that!' and, with one swipe of the weapon,
beheaded the man. Forthwith, he returned to the tree and hacked
again and again, deep cuts. From within the tree, a voice
called out, 'I am a tree nymph Ceres loves, and my pains
of death are eased by my knowledge that you shall be punished
        for this
terrible deed. I prophesy doom!' But he would not listen
and continued to chop, to weaken the trunk, and he tied strong
        ropes
his men could tug at to fell the enormous tree. It leaned
farther and groaned and crashed at last to the earth, and leveled
a wide swath of destruction among all the smaller trees.   770
    "The dryad sisters, stunned at this loss, put on black
        mourning
and went to Ceres to plead that the malefactor be punished
grandly, as he had offended grandly. The bountiful goddess

nodded her head in consent, and wheat fields nodded with her
as if a wind had passed to ruffle their ears. Her mind
moved upon torments that people would pity had not their victim
severed all human connection and claims by his evil deed.
Hunger, she thought, would be right—the worst thing she could
    think of.
But it is forbidden for Ceres and Hunger ever to meet.
She summoned, therefore, a sprite of the mountains, an oread,
    saying,   780
'There is a distant place, in far-off Scythia, icy,
gloomy, and barren. No trees grow there, no wheat. The soil
is barren stones. Go there, where Cold, Fear, and gaunt Hunger
huddle together, and summon Hunger. Say I command her
to visit this brute and establish a home for herself in his belly,
which nothing may satisfy. Tell her I yield my powers
to fill that void, to feed him. I give him to her as a toy.
It's a long journey, young lady. Take my wingèd dragons
and magic car and let them carry you there in an instant.'
She gave the reins into the oread's hands, and the nymph   790
flew off at once to the place in the mountains that people call
the Caucasus, a bleak and nightmarish region, in which
she arrived at Hunger's home. There, in a stony field,
that creature gleaned with her filthy fingernails and her teeth
among the stones for their bits of moss. Her hair hung down
in lank and matted locks. Her eyes were sunken and circled,
and were all the more marked in her pallid invalid's face.
Her lips were slack and cracked, and her skin was crazed with
    chilblains.
Beneath her eczematous throat, her breasts hung down like purses
emptied and long forgotten. The vaults of her ribs stuck out,   800
as did every bone in her body. One could count the knobs of her
    spine.
Only her legs and feet were swollen and waterlogged.
    "The oread saw all this from hailing distance. She dared not
approach closer but shouted the commands of the goddess,
    frightened
to be in sight of the dreadful creature. She felt, at this distance,
a terrible pang of hunger, not merely appetite,
but a deeper sense that comes from long deprivation, a need
for nourishment with her body's organs crying in want.
Her message delivered, she turned, remounted the car, and was
    gone.
    "Hunger did as the goddess had ordered or, say, permitted.   810

On wings of surprising strength, she flew through the air to the
		house
of her victim, the wicked king. She entered his room and saw him
in the dark, in bed, asleep. She wrapped her cadaverous arms
about him in an embrace, and covered him with her greedy
kisses. She breathed her spirit into his spirit. His veins
were burning, on fire with longings that seethed in his blood. She
		left him
and the fertile world to return to those bleak, exiguous haunts
she knew and had learned to love, her world of woe and want.
	Erysichthon, asleep, is dreaming of food, banquets,
grand buffets, of all-you-can-eat, belly-burster specials.   820
His jaws move as his teeth masticate thin air.
His molars grind on nothing, and his throat muscles work to
		swallow
oneiric steaks and chops. He awakes, ravenous, famished,
an insane craving to eat mastering all his other
instincts. He calls for food, for the bounties of land and sea
and air, beef and fish and fowl on which he gorges,
but, even while he is eating, he is planning other menus,
and complaining of his hunger. He cannot be satisfied
but gobbles whatever he sees, enough for an army, a city,
a whole nation. He swallows more and more into that maw.   830
As the ocean ingests the water that rivers pour into its craw
but is never filled and remains thirsty and guzzles more
and more forever, so he calls out for more. As fires
consume whatever they touch and burn the hotter in greedy
appetite for destruction, so he demands ever larger
and larger portions of more and more, as his hunger grows
with every orectic bite, an unfillable black hole.
	"His ravening empties the palace larder and royal storerooms,
the warehouses and barns of the city. His treasury melts
as purchasing agents rove in widening circles to buy   840
provender for their master. His hunger is unabated;
his fortune is swallowed up in gorging, but still his wolfish
hunger gnaws at him as he gnaws bare bones. What is left
to sell? He looks around his ruined house for an asset,
some bauble he might swap for a couple of loaves of bread,
and he sees—his daughter! He'll sell her, as a prostitute and slave.
Why not? His only daughter! He tells himself she deserves
a better father than he and, with this peculiar excuse,
offers her for sale. He finds a buyer at once,
who drags her away. At length the girl rebels, runs off,   850

and stands at the seashore to pray with hands held out to Neptune
to save her from this man who has taken her maidenhead
and now is about to seize the rest of her life. 'Help me,
deliver me from this monster, I beg you!' she prays. The god
hears her entreaty and does not deny her the help she has asked.
He changes her into a man and gives her the garb and gear
of one of the local fishermen. The slave master, pursuing
his runaway, follows close behind, is approaching, and now
accosts the fisherman: 'Sir, I say, you with the rod,
may your hook catch many fish and the sea offer its bounties   860
if you will be kind enough to tell me, Where is that girl
who must have passed her only a moment or two ago?
A slave girl, dressed in rags, and running this way. . . . You see
the footprints she left in the sand! They stop here, but I don't
        see her.
Which way did she go?' Mestra realized at once
that the god had granted her prayer and she was saved. 'What girl?'
she asked. 'I've seen no one here. But I have been staring seaward.
Still, I can swear that no one was here on the beach but me.'
The man believed her and walked back down the shore, assuming
his slave had escaped. As soon as he was gone, the guise   870
of fisherman dissolved, and the girl was as she had been.
Astonishing! The father welcomed her home, for now
he could sell her again and again, and each time she could change
        form
to that of a mare, or bird, or milch cow, or deer, whatever
the occasion or her whim of the moment happened to prompt.
And still, this wasn't enough. He consumed whatever he saw,
and finally ate himself, gnawing at his own body
in a deplorable act of auto-cannibalism, which ended
in the only possible way the punishment Ceres had ordered.

    "But why do I tell the stories of others, when I myself   880
can change my form to a certain extent? I appear sometimes
as what you see, but also as serpent or bull, with my strength
in my horns—or single horn, for I have lost one of these
        weapons."
Thinking of this, he groaned aloud and then fell silent.

BOOK IX

Theseus asked the god to explain why he had groaned.
What was wrong with his forehead? What bull's horn? The river
deity, turning a baleful look at his guest, replied,
"Defeat is never a thing one likes to speak of, and yet
it was no disgrace to have been defeated, but rather an honor
to have striven as I did with such an adversary.
Or that's what I say to myself. And I shall tell you my story,
should you wish to hear it." They all assured him he had their
        complete
attention and fell silent. He spoke then of Deianira.
"You've heard of her, of course—an especially beautiful maiden   10
whom many suitors pursued, I among their number.
I entered the house of Oeneus, her father, to make my offer
of marriage, along with a number of others, including the mighty
Hercules. To us two, all the rest yielded their claims.
So it was he and I. He pointed out that his father
was Olympian Jove and referred to his celebrated labors.
To this I replied that it wasn't right for a god like me
to have to compete with a mere mortal (he hadn't yet
become divine). 'I am,' I proclaimed, 'the lord of the river
that flows in its familiar winding course through your own   20
realm. Should your daughter and I wed, she will not go far
but dwell close by, as a neighbor. I am also happy to say
that Juno doesn't detest me, as she does my rival. No labors
have been imposed upon me. Jove, he says, is his father.
It's a claim anyone can make, and either it isn't true
or else it's disgraceful, and he is a bastard son of a shamed
mother. But either way, it's nothing to recommend him.'
That's what I said in answer, and Hercules glared at me, angry,
which wasn't at all surprising. I wanted to show him up
as a musclebound thug. He answered just as I'd hoped he might,   30
saying, 'My tongue isn't much. My fists can be more persuasive.'
I put up my own to defend myself, and we fought, but a dirty

kind of combat. I mean it literally, for he grabbed
a fistful of dust and threw it into my face to blind me.
He seized my neck, my crotch, whatever he could. I am strong
and heavyset, as you see, and my weight was what saved me. I
    stood
like a cliff that the waves of the sea batter in vain. He pulled back
and rushed me again, and we struggled, hand-to-hand, toe-to-toe,
and forehead straining against the other's forehead. We battled
like two bulls in a field striving for some prize heifer,   40
while at a distance the rest of the herd looks on and wonders
which will win. Three times I almost had him, but every
time Hercules managed somehow to break free of my hold.
On my fourth attempt he hit me a stunning blow with his fist,
which spun me around. He leapt on my back, clung there, and
    it felt
as if a mountain had jumped me. I staggered this way and that
and, with arms slick with my sweat, managed at last to break free,
but he grabbed me again, this time by the neck, and he pulled
    me down
and rubbed my face on the ground. I could taste the dirt in my
    mouth.
I struggled, but I was pinned, and he was as strong as . . . well,   50
it's Hercules I was fighting. What could I do to win?
Where strength isn't enough, one has to resort to cunning,
or whatever skill one has. I turned myself into a snake
and started to wriggle away. Then I turned back, coiled,
hissed, and tried to look fierce. . . . He only laughed aloud
and remarked that, even from his first days in the cradle, serpents
had been his playthings of choice. He told me I wasn't much
in the snake department. 'I've fought the Hydra of Lerna. For
    every
head I cut off, that creature was able to sprout two new ones,'
he boasted, 'and still I managed to kill it. And you? You think   60
you are likely to be impressive in that herpetological getup?
Get serious, my friend. Or better yet, get dead!'
He grabbed my neck and commenced to squeeze my throat. I
    couldn't
breathe or even see. The world began to go black,
and, just before I passed out, I changed again, this time
into the form of a large and powerful bull. I charged
and would have run down any lesser man. But he seized my neck
and wrestled me down as if I were only a newborn calf.
I felt my footing give way, and my head touching the ground

again. And this time he grabbed my horn with his hand and
    twisted,   70
tugged at it, pulled it off. . . . Along with the searing pain,
what I felt was humiliation, in which, of course, he took pleasure,
giving the horn he had taken from me to the naiads to fill
with fruit and flowers. That horn is the horn of abundance now,
the cornu-copia—mine!—that the goddess of plenty carries."
    So spoke the god of the river. As he finished, a nymph
with her hair flowing free appeared to serve dessert—a selection
of autumn fruits and nuts arranged in a horn of plenty.
A joke? Or a modest and rueful claim that he had thus signed
a page of the world's long story? Take it however you will.   80
The dawn was beginning to show in the East, and the Sun's rays
were restoring the world to what it had been, as mountaintops
emerged from the darkness to loom again in their proper places.
The guests now roused themselves and prepared to depart, the
      river's
floodwaters notwithstanding. Acheloüs did not appear
to bid them a proper farewell but hid his face and wretchedly
maimed head beneath the turbid water's surface.
    And yet, his wound was slight, one that was easily hidden
by a not very artful arrangement of willow boughs on his head.
He'd not come off so badly compared with someone like Nessus,   90
the centaur, who also burned with desire for Deianira.
Traveling back to Tyrins with his new bride, Hercules
had reached the banks of Euenus, swollen with rains of that season
and dangerous with its eddies and rapids. The hero looked down,
not at all concerned for himself, but for his young wife's
sake somewhat apprehensive. How to get her to the farther
shore in absolute safety? That was the problem, and Nessus
appeared from out of the woods. He knew the river, was strong,
and, being half-man, half-horse, he offered an easy solution:
"You swim across on your own and let me carry your wife,   100
which I should be only too happy to do." Hercules thanked him,
promised his bride that all would be well, and then flung his club
and mighty bow across to the other side, and plunged in
where he was, not even trying to find the easiest crossing
but taking the shortest route, so much did he trust his own
amazing strength. He bulled his way over, emerged, wet
but unharmed, and was busy retrieving his bow when he heard
frantic calls for help. His wife was screaming, and Nessus
was abducting her, was betraying Hercules' trust. Enraged,
the hero shouted: "Villain! What do you think you're doing?   110

Ixion, your father, who was also a rapist, spins
on his wheel in hell, where you'll see him yourself in very short
      order.
However fast your horse's half may run, you cannot
escape my vengeance. . . ." And fitting an arrow onto the
      bowstring,
he fired. The shaft flew true and struck the back of the centaur,
pierced his body, and then protruded from out of his breast.
Nessus, frantic, tore the arrow out, and his blood
gushed forth in a torrent mixed with the Hydra's terrible poison,
in which Hercules had soaked his arrowheads. The centaur
was dying, knew it, but would not go gently. He took off
      his tunic   120
and dipped it into the poisoned blood. Then, with a wan
smile, he presented the garment to Deianira, a token,
a gift, a dismal memento of fatal passion. "Take it,"
he told the young woman, "and use it—should ever the need
      arise—
to revive a dying love." He handed it to her and died.
     Years pass, and the deeds of Hercules are renowned
all over the world. His labors and triumphs are commonplaces
of the conversations of men. Even the gods respect him.
Juno herself, her fury spent, is resigned and accepts him
as a stepson. He is returning home from the fight in Oechalia,   130
where he has destroyed the entire city to punish its king,
Eurytus. It has been another glorious triumph
to add to the list and keep bards busy. But Rumor also
has come as his unwelcome companion, implying, suggesting,
hinting of this and that, and mixing in snippets of truth
with large swaths of fabrication, prompted by envy
or mischievousness. The story, this time, is that the hero
has loved Iole, daughter of Eurytus. She was the reason
he pressed that ridiculous quarrel and razed the town to the
      ground.
Did Deianira believe these nasty stories? Of course,   140
and was overcome and gave way to groans and rivers of tears.
These, however, she checked and said to herself, "Weeping
will do me no good, and only please my rival. For such
reasons, I must control my emotions. What can I do
more to the point? I am not yet out of the game, and may play
a hand or two with the cards left to me—grief and noble
silence? Or rage and fury? Or would it be better to leave,

return to my home in distant Calydon? No! I must stay
and fight for what's mine. The sister of Meleager, and noble,
let me prove what a woman's anger can do. . . ." She considers   150
one far-fetched scheme and another, some of them bloody and
          dreadful,
and some ending up with a happy reunion of husband and wife.
At last, she remembers the shirt the centaur had given her,
          finds it,
and hands it to Lichas, her husband's servant, to give him—a
          present
to celebrate his return. The centaur had said it was charmed
and would serve to restore and revive a guttering love like her
          husband's.
Lichas delivered the gift, to Mount Oeta, where Hercules
          draped it
across his enormous shoulders—the deadly cloak with the poison
from the blood of the Hydra he'd put on the arrowhead, himself.

          He was on his way to the altar to give his thanks to the gods,   160
offer the incense and prayers at the flames, and pour libations
of wine into the marble bowls. The heat of the fire
triggered the poison to act and the blood to work its evil.
Hercules felt the shirt turning unbearably hot.
His skin was burning. The pain was more than a man could
          endure
without crying aloud. In agony, he attempted
to rip the corrosive garment from off his back, but it would not
separate. Where the cloth came away, it took his skin,
laid bare muscle and bone, which seethed now with the venom's
dire effects. His blood hissed like a blacksmith's bucket   170
into which glowing iron is plunged to cool. Dark sweat,
plasma, and blood poured down from his suppurating tissues.
His sinews pop and give way, and his bones crack as his marrow
sizzles and burns in the ghastly chemical fire. He knows
he is dying and stretches forth his enormous arms to heaven
to pray, complain, and plead for an end to his trials and torments:
"Mighty Juno, behold me, and take what pleasure you may
in my ruin and pain. Does it please you to see me thus? You
          have won!
Can you not show pity, even to me, whom you've hated
all my life? That life is over now, with its hateful   180
labors, battles, and pains. Death will give me that ease
I've longed for. O cruel goddess, stepmother, adversary,

acknowledge me now in my anguish! Was it for this I killed
Busiris, who fouled his temples with the blood of strangers, or
        fought
Antaeus, whose mother restored his strength every time he fell?
Geryon I battled, and Cerberus, hound of hell,
and the Cretan bull. The stables of King Augeas I cleansed.
I caught Diana's deer with the golden horns, and rid
Stymphalus of its birds. On the banks of the wild Thermodon,
I faced the Amazons and won Hippolyta's golden belt.   190
Hesperides' apples that Atlas guarded, I managed to steal.
Against me, centaurs could not prevail, or the wild Arcadian
boar, or even the Hydra, which kept on sprouting new heads.
In Thrace, I managed to kill Diomedes' man-eating horses,
whose mangers were full of mangled corpses and human blood.
With these arms I hold out in supplication to you, I wrestled
the Nemean lion. This neck held up the sky of the cosmos!
I was not yet exhausted, although you had run out of tasks—
battles, snares, and dangers. And what does it come to at last?
This agony? This deadly poison I cannot fight,   200
or outwit or evade? Each breath I am forced to take
is fire. And still, Eurystheus, who was once my cruel master,
is alive and well. . . . How can anyone believe in the justice
        of gods
who hears of what happened to me?" Then he was past all words,
and only the raw bellows of his uninflected pain
rang out on the mountainside, as if some wounded beast
were running in its mortal hurt, with the weapon's shaft
a torture at every step. In pity and terror, see him
as he roars in his agony, groans, uproots great trunks of towering
trees, and plucks and tears at his garment of burning flesh.   210

        He is rushing this way and that, blindly . . . but then he sees
Lichas, hiding in fear underneath some rock overhang,
and in rage Hercules cries out: "What have you done to me? Why
did you bring me this fatal gift? You've killed me, Lichas!" The
        servant
cowers in terror and tries to explain he had no idea
there was anything wrong with the present. He'd done what
        Hercules' wife
had told him to do. . . . But the words would not come. He
        knelt down
to clasp Hercules' knees and mutely to beg forgiveness,
but the hero caught him up, raised him high in the air,
whirled him around and around his head, and then let fly   220

a human missile that soared into the sky and over
the waves of the sea of Euboea. The young man sailed through
        the air
for a long time and stiffened in terror. As drops of rain
congeal in the cold of the sky to snowflakes or sleet and,
        condensed,
fall like stones to the earth, so Lichas was changed
from a warm and living body to the object fear had made.
His terror turned him bloodless, solid, and icy. His humors
dried, and he landed as solid stone. In the sea off Euboea
you can see the rock that the waves eddy against. It appears
not unlike the form of a person. Sailors today   230
call this the rock of Lichas and will not set foot upon it.
        And Hercules then? He cuts down enormous trees and
        stacks them
on the top of Oeta, constructing his own funeral pyre.
His companion, Philoctetes, the Argonaut, he orders
to touch a torch to the kindling. His friend is horrified, mute,
as Hercules hands him his bow and huge quiver of arrows.
(These he will take to Troy.) Tears spill from the eyes
of the Argonaut as he watches the hero set the pelt
of the Nemean lion atop his pyre and then lie down,
with his club as pillow, as if he reclined on a banquet couch   240
at ease and decked with garlands. He nods. Philoctetes touches
the flame of the brand he holds to the kindling, sees the fire
blossom and climb like a fierce flower to lick the indifferent
limbs of Hercules. Even the gods are in awe,
and Jove, knowing their thoughts and feelings, addresses his
        colleagues,
speaking to them with these consoling words: " Your care
is a comfort to me, and I thank you, brothers and sisters. My
        heart
is full to overflowing, as I watch my suffering son.
But I know that what is divine in him will survive, immortal
as we are immortal. As gold is refined in the fire, so he   250
will be refined, and his earthly parts will be gone, to leave him
a better and even more noble creature. The victor of many
battles, he will triumph also in this, his last
ordeal, and the dross will melt, leaving the precious metal
death cannot touch and corruption can never rust or tarnish.
Then can we recognize him and welcome him here in the heavens
as one of our own. . . . I assume that this will be pleasing to you,
that no one begrudges this last reward, or objects to my son's

elevation to godhead?" The lord of heaven looks
from side to side as if to invite—or dare—complaint,   260
but not even Juno can bat an eyelash. Indeed, she appears
distressed that her husband might think she'd refuse, at a time
       like this,
to give him her full support and love. Meanwhile, on earth,
the fire had done its work, and Hercules had been changed.
Whatever was human and mortal from his human mother was
       gone;
now, like a serpent that's shed its old skin, a new creature,
brighter, stronger, more splendid, appeared, even more heroic
than ever before in its new and awesome guise as a god.
Jove looked down and dispatched his wingèd car to fetch
his son up to his rightful place among the stars,   270
and Atlas groaned as he shouldered this added weight of the sky.
     Eurystheus meanwhile was still full of rage at his lifelong
rival. Having from childhood wronged and abused the hero,
he could not forgive his victim but extended the grudge to include
Hercules' children and house. Alcmena, Hercules' mother,
consoled herself in long talks of her son's many misfortunes,
confiding in Iole—she had married Hercules' son
Hyllus and now was pregnant, about to deliver the hero's
grandchild. Alcmena offered advice and recalled the troubles
of her lying-in, as if telling her pains might serve to diminish   280
the younger woman's fears. "The gods, I pray, will be kind
and give you an easy birthing," Alcmena said, as she patted
Iole's hand, "when the time comes for you to call on the midwife
goddess, whom Juno had turned against me. My time was near,
and the baby, huge—no doubt that Jove had been the child's
       father.
My pains were dreadful—to speak of them even now makes me
       weak—
and went on for seven days and nights, each hour an eon
of anguish. I wailed and moaned and cried out to the heavens
to let it end—even to let me die if that
was the only way. But Lucina had pledged to Juno to keep me   290
in pain as long as she could before she released me to death's
cold comfort. She sat there inside my doorway, deaf
to my howls of pain, my prayers and curses, her right knee
       crossing
her left, and her fingers entwined to stay the enormous fetus
from coming forth. She muttered magical charms as well
to the same purpose. I bore down, breathed correctly, pushed,

and squealed like a wounded beast. My suffering would have
        made stones
weep. The matrons about me cried out in pity and awe,
but only Galanthis could help, one of my servants, a peasant
who'd been in the household for years. A big, tow-headed
        woman,   300
she was shrewder than one might have guessed and knew this was
        Juno's doing.
She figured out that the woman crossing her legs in the doorway
had to be Lucina—and thought of a way to deceive her.
She went out to announce, 'The mistress has given birth to a son.
Our prayers are answered. The baby is born. Will you send good
        wishes?'
Astonished, the goddess of childbirth leapt up, unclenched her
        hands,
and held them out to the heavens as if to ask for instructions—
and this was enough. In that instant, the obstacles disappeared
and the baby was born. Galanthis laughed, and Lucina caught her
by that straw-colored hair, dragged her down to the ground, and
        held her,   310
pinned her down as her arms shrank to an animal's forelegs
and her shape was changed to that of a weasel, whose hair remains
the shade of flax that Galanthis' hair used to be. And because
she had used her mouth to fool the goddess, she bears her young
through her mouth. It's true! I've seen this. She lives here still,
        near the house,
and sometimes comes in to visit, as a pet might, or a friend."
She thought of the woman, sighed at the sacrifice she had made,
and shook her head in grief. Iole tried to cheer her
mother-in-law. "It's sad, but it's not as if she were blood
kin, as my sister was, whose misfortune I weep to remember.   320
I can scarcely speak of it even now. She was her mother's
only child—we two were half sisters. A beauty,
Dryope was assaulted: Apollo saw her and took her.
Andraemon nevertheless made her a marriage proposal,
which she accepted. The couple lived together in peace
and comfort a year or two. No, not so much as two. . . .
There is a pond in the woods, an attractive place with a gentle
slope that rims the water, over which myrtle branches
offer shade and protection, and to this inviting spot
Dryope came with her babe in arms, Amphissos, who then   330
was almost a year old. She had come there to gather flowers
for garlands to please the nymphs of the wood. A pretty picture?

Happiness, contentment, innocence? Most of all,
the innocence hurts the worst! She hadn't the vaguest idea
what fate had in store for her there at this tranquil pond. I was
        with her
and watched as she picked a flower, a water-lotus blossom
to give the baby to play with. I reached down for another
and saw that the place she had picked was bleeding drops of
        crimson
blood, and the broken branch was quivering as if in pain!
The country people believe that plant, before, had been Lotis,   340
that nymph who fled Priapus, who pursued her through the forest
with an evil leer on his face. When she asked the gods for
        protection,
they changed her into the shape of the flower that keeps her name.
        "My sister had never heard this story and didn't suspect
the flower she'd picked was anything other than what it seemed.
I showed her what had happened, and she looked down in sorrow
and fear and prayed and tried to retreat, to hide or run
from this terrible thing, but she could not move. Her feet were
        clinging
rootlike to the ground. Her legs were hardened. Her upper
body still could twist and turn, and she held her baby   350
safe in her arms, but she felt the bark creeping up her thighs
and loins. . . . She reached with a hand to feel the hair on her
        head,
but the hair had turned to leaves. The child at her breast sucked
at a useless wooden breast that produced neither milk nor sap.
I stood there and watched in horror, and tried to help her but
        couldn't.
There was nothing to do but hug her and try to hold off the
        change,
keeping her what she was. Or perhaps I thought I might join her,
share in her fate, and become a tree myself. But in vain.
        "Eurytus, our father, came, and with him Andraemon,
her husband, looking for her, and I showed them their
        disappearing   360
daughter and wife. They held the tree, caressed it, fell
to the ground, and in grief they touched its roots, while still
        human tears
rained down from the upper branches. The face was visible
still, and the voice could speak. She said, 'If the oaths of a dying
woman have meaning, I swear that I have done nothing wrong
        here.

I have lived an innocent life and die having broken no law,
having violated no sacred custom. If I lie, let
axes cut me down and fire devour my limbs.
But take my baby and keep him safe. Find him a nurse
who will feed him, hold him, love him, and bring him here
     to play   370
under my tree. When he learns to speak, let him know this tree
is his mother. But warn him about this treacherous pool and
     teach him
never to touch the blossoms of any plants, lest he hurt
or somehow offend the goddesses they may disguise. Farewell,
father. Farewell, my beloved husband. Protect me from
     thoughtless
people who carve initials in tree bark, and keep the sheep
from nibbling at my branches. I cannot bend down, so kiss me
one last time, and take the boy. I can feel how the bark
covers my neck and grows toward my mouth and eyes. My death
will not require the touch of your hands to close my lids. . . .'   380
There she fell silent and turned entirely tree, but one still
could feel the warmth of her branches, which moments before had
     been flesh.' "
    Iole had ended her poignant story, and both the women
were drying their tears and offering comfort to each other
when a strange thing occurred, a marvel that knocked at the door.
It was Iolaüs, the son of Iphicles and Alcmena,
Hercules' half brother and charioteer—but restored
to the prime of his youth! The hero in heaven who now was a god
had married Juno's daughter Hebe, the goddess of youth.
She had granted as a nuptial gift that Iolaüs' clock   390
of life be reset and years be restored to him. Making clear
that this was a one-time favor, she had been on the point of
     swearing
that never again would it happen that an old person be made
young again, but Themis, the Hours' mother and Mistress
of Seasons and Years, prevented this ill-considered gesture.
And now we get Themis' list of myths in which time stands still,
moves around, plays tricks . . . not stories but only allusions,
some of them clear, and others oblique or coy. Our attention
wanes, as the voice—of Themis? Ovid?—falters and drones.
Tired perhaps? We strain to follow its murmur and feel   400
frustration, even annoyance. Why has he thus betrayed us?
Is this a place he'd have fixed had the gods not sent him away
(or, to keep to the pattern, turned him from darling to exile,

the victim of Caesar Augustus' whim)? But there is a way
to read this passage and turn time back. We are children again,
hide in the hall at the top of the stairs and strain to hear
the phrases that float up from our parents' conversations.
Greedy for what we can catch, we hold our breath to listen
and to comprehend their words and the world's unpleasant secrets
from which they have tried to protect us as long and as well as
     they could.   410
The question is one of trust, which Ovid invites or tests.
Have we learned in these pages to yield to his moods and moves,
     to read
with that mixture of love and awe we felt many years ago
in the upstairs hall? The subject, at any rate, is the business
of youth and age, how the gods can turn back the clocks—not
     often,
but every now and again. We get Amphiarius' story,
and Callirhoë's, who prayed that her young sons might be made
mature to avenge their father's death. There are others who ask
Hebe's interference: Aurora, for instance, would like
her old and enfeebled husband, Tithonus, hale again.   420
A number of other gods appear with their several requests
that this one or that be restored to beauty, vigor, and youth.
But Jupiter puts a stop to this business before it gets started,
explaining that here and there the Fates have decreed departures
from the rule, but the one-way flow of time is beyond the control
of the gods. Were it in his power, he'd have made Aeacus young,
and Rhadamanthus and Minos. This seemed to settle the question,
for the gods looked down to see those three men, bent with years.
Of Minos, in his prime, great nations had quaked in fear,
but now he was old, infirm, and worried himself that Miletus,   430
Deïone's son by Apollo, was planning an insurrection.
At another, earlier time, he'd have banished Miletus, or dared him
to come out and fight, but now lacked the strength and the will.
Miletus, however, packed up, embarked, and sailed away
of his own accord to Asia Minor, and there he founded
another city that even now bears his name, near the banks
of the winding Maeander River, which snakes its way to the sea.
That river god's daughter was Cyanee. She and Miletus married,
and their union produced the twins Byblis and Caunus, she
a beautiful girl, and he a remarkably handsome boy.   440
     We're back on track now. This story, a somewhat mannered
     performance,
is one of those nice rhetorical set pieces Ovid loved

to dazzle with. He could put his lawyer's training to use
as he made up elaborate speeches for his characters to declaim.
We're all ears now, or they are sharper for having been jangled
a while, as if, in a concert hall, a composer had scored
a tune-up, white noise to get us into the proper expectant
mood. There's even a warning, a moral (not quite on target,
but, if it were, the story would be otiose and redundant).
Byblis, he says, is a warning that girls should be careful to keep   450
their passions in check and direct them only to lawful and licit
persons—and this is a rule it's difficult not to agree with.
Byblis, you see, was smitten with unnatural love for her brother.
Or say that she loved as a sister should not love a brother. At first
she tried to conceal her secret even from her own self.
Denial, they call it now. But more than most sisters do,
she found occasions to kiss her brother, or hug or touch him,
or at least to be with him. For this, she found herself scheming
        and plotting,
and always she took pains with her wardrobe, her maquillage,
coiffure, and jewelry, too. What troubled her after a while   460
was having to recognize the jealousy she felt
whenever another pretty or clever or funny young woman
seemed to engage in the slightest way her brother's attention.
On the other hand, she could still persuade herself that this
        interest
was normal enough—for a brother and sister who shared their
        special
heritage as Apollo's grandchildren. Who in the world
could understand him as she did, or catch his jokes, or admire
his grace on the playing fields or out on the hunt? As long
as she kept herself from putting a name to the feeling, she had
nothing to worry about. She disliked calling him "brother,"   470
preferring a simpler "dear." And she asked him to use her name
rather than call her "sister." This he was willing to do.
        Well and good, at least in the daytime. At night, though, the
        truth
refused to remain obscured but paraded itself in her dreams—
in which they two were the last people on earth, and human
survival depended upon their reproducing themselves.
Their embraces embarrass her, even in dreams, but they also
        delight her.
She burns with passion, wakes, and blushes, but lies there in bed
remembering those voluptuous visions the night had supplied.
She knows it is wrong, forbidden, and yet, what harm can there be   480

in dreams? One is hardly guilty, if one has no power to fight
what the mind does on its own. It's only through action that sin
can corrupt the soul. The dream is not of the love but rather
that he is somehow not her brother—in which event
their love would be blameless, faultless, and . . . lovely! She thinks
of his handsome
body and feels bereft in knowing it's out of reach
forever—except in dreams, which are free, and truer than truth.
She offers a prayer of thanks to Venus and Cupid in hopes
that they may visit her slumbers often and with such rich
gifts as the sweet and vivid dreams of the night before.   490
        She talks to herself, persuading, cajoling, and reassuring,
and sometimes imagines her speeches to him, teasing, confiding,
even provoking: "How sad, how dreadful that you are my
brother!
If we could somehow evade those silly taboos against incest,
what perfect lives we'd have. There wouldn't be in-law troubles.
I'd love your father and mother as if they were mine (which of
course
they are), and vice versa. I'd be happy to give up my claim
to be Apollo's grandchild, so that you could be better born
than I am—which means that you'd love me only for what I am,
my looks, my charm, my humor. . . . The gods have done this to
tease me,   500
and it isn't fair. It's stupid, considering how those gods
have always behaved. Consider how Saturn married Ops,
his sister. And think of Tethys, who married her brother Ocean.
Jove himself is married to Juno, who was and remains
his sister. And why should the gods have different rules for
themselves?
The answer is, they are gods, and we, who are merely mortal,
must obey the laws and customs that apply to the lives of humans.
I must rid myself of this passion, or pray that I somehow die
before it has mastered me, or betrayed itself, to my shame
and my brother's, too. Dead, I shall lie there upon my bier,   510
and he shall come to mourn and plant a kiss on my cool
and insensate lips. What a lovely idea! My spirit will watch
and imagine how it would feel if blood still flowed through my
veins
and my flesh were warm and responsive. Oh, I am a wicked girl!
But there is a certain degree of safety that I can rely on:
we both would have to agree if the sin I'm thinking about
were a real risk. It's unlikely that he thinks of me in this way.

"Or does he? Why not? It has happened now and again. I
  remember
Aeolus' sons and daughters, who married and lived together
in evident harmony. What am I saying? What am I thinking?   520
It cannot happen, and shouldn't. And won't. He's given no sign
that this is how he feels—unless, of course, he's afraid,
as I am. What would I do if he let me know he loved me?
Would I be shocked? Reject him? Would I dare answer back
that I love him, too, in spite of what people may say. It's mad,
but any love worth the name is a kind of madness, and lovers
willingly trade the world for their monomaniac passion
or else they are mere pretenders, seeking the comfort,
      convenience,
and companionship convention sanctions. I will be bolder
and, for the sake of my love, will dare even its object.   530
I must let him know, must risk extending the first invitation,
which, for all I know, may evoke instant assent.
If shame is all that prevents me from speaking out, I can write
an artfully pleasing letter confessing to him my secret."

     She reaches then for a pen, an empty tablet of wax,
and inspiration, as if the right words may, like a spell
or charm, produce the effect she wants in his mind and heart.
She starts, hesitates, erases, thinks, and begins again,
as if to do this right would correct the more spacious wrong
she contemplates, as if it were only a matter of diction   540
to correct the universe. Shame and daring contend in her spirit
as she starts again to write: "I am mortified. I am bold
enough to confess my love, but too frightened to write
that name you know too well but may perhaps relearn
to whisper to your Byblis that you understand, forgive,
and feel for her as she feels so recklessly for you.
     "Or have you already guessed? Have my pallor and tears
        betrayed
long ago the secret my tongue would not speak, and my mind
could hardly allow itself even to think? My passion
has mastered me, overcome me, as one of those gods overcomes   550
every so often some helpless nymph in the woods or fields.
Only you can save me, as only you can destroy me—
and I cannot say for certain which of the two I wish for.
The choice is better and properly yours. I am in your hands.
Tired old men may babble of right and wrong, but the heart
knows its own necessities. Destiny calls our names,
and we must decide whether to answer or cower and hide.

Are the gods so sinful? Should mortals dare to do as they do?
We need not brave the world, but may keep our passion private,
for brothers and sisters may visit freely, talk, and embrace   560
and even kiss without setting the gossips to bitter buzzing.
What is left to desire? You know as well as I.
And want it? I've no idea. I beg your patience, your pity,
but warn that I would not write thus if I could help it.
It's life or death for me now, beyond all logic and reason.
A harsh answer from you will ruin me absolutely."
  She read it over, amazed that she'd found the nerve to set
   down
these all but unspeakable phrases, and set her seal in the wax.
She calls a servant to deliver the tablets, but even this
simple business is taxing. She blushes, stammers, mumbles,   570
"Take this to my . . . " Pause. Hard swallow. Finally, "brother."
She holds the letter out for the servant to take, but drops it.
It slips and falls to the floor—a terrible omen. Accept it?
It's not too late to change her mind. But she cannot do it.
She sends the servant away. He goes to the brother's apartment
and hands him the message. Caunus reads it, at least the
   beginning,
but as soon as he sees where it's going, he throws it down in rage.
He can barely keep from attacking the servant, from wringing
   his neck.
"Get out of here," he warns. "Pimp! Monster! I'd haul you
before a judge except that I'd only bring disgrace   580
on our house. But if there were justice, you'd hang, as you
   deserve."
The terrified servant runs back to report the brother's answer
to Byblis, who pales, trembles, and feels her body shiver
as if it were suddenly chilled. She is not really surprised,
blames herself for having been stupid and rash, and thinks
how else she might have done it, differently or better.
She shouldn't have written but gone instead to test the waters,
herself, starting out with hints and questions. Sailors proceed
with such discretion, trying the winds close-reefed before
they spread their sails. And she has been rocked by a sudden gust   590
of wind. Her ship is in danger, taken aback. The rocks
to leeward loom and threaten. There's no room to maneuver.
  She thinks of that inauspicious moment she dropped the
   letter.
She ought to have taken the hint, or waited at least for a better
time for this long-odds gamble. The gods were trying to warn her,

and she wouldn't listen. She ought to have gone to him, face to
        face,
and her tears would have spoken for her. Instead of those scratches
        on wax,
she could have thrown her arms around his reluctant shoulders
and neck and embraced him, pleading, or else, on the floor
        before him,
she could have begged for him not to end her reason for living.   600
She cannot accept what has happened, or must find some
        extraneous reason.
"The servant," she says, "was clumsy, chose the wrong moment,
        was brusque,
pushy, intruded on Caunus' other important business. . . .
    "But it does no good to fret over what has already happened.
The question is, Where should I go from here? How to repair
the damage? It would be better if I had never begun, but now
I might as well press forward. . . . Perhaps I can get him to change
his mind, or even to take some interest in what I propose.
He likes me, always has. We get along well. I'm attractive,
I have always thought. Besides, there's no going back. He'll
        remember,   610
no matter how many years may pass, that once I was shameless
and threw myself at him. To give up now would only suggest
I'm a trivial person, fickle, was toying with serious subjects.
Or else that I'm plain crazy. For all I know, I am."
Crazy, perhaps, but hardly stupid. It stands to reason
that she cannot lose any more by further attempts. Having
        plunged,
there's no more fear of falling. Therefore she presses onward,
continues her siege of her brother's affections, tries forays,
skirmishes, diversions, underminings. . . . Relentless,
she will not admit it's hopeless, refuses to think he means   620
his no, and no, and no. It must be some game he's playing,
an ongoing test, or the kind of teasing that brothers will do
to torment sisters whom nevertheless they love and would fight
to protect from anyone else. The brother can stand it no longer
and finally flees his deranged sibling. He goes away
and in Caria founds the city that is known by his name—Caunus.
    Then, bereft, Miletus' daughter broke down completely
and, mad with grief and frustrated passion, tore at her garments,
wept and screamed, or mumbled, or else, in apparently lucid
moments, proclaimed in eloquent periods how she adored   630
her brother, was still determined to join him, to live her life

with him and for him. This was distressing enough, but one day
she was gone, having taken off in the night to find the brother
she loved, to follow wherever he'd gone. . . . Utterly mad,
as Bacchantes are when the thyrsus drives them into their frenzies.
The women of Bubassus watched in dismay as this stranger,
ululating and raving, wandered across their fields.
She crossed and recrossed Caria, where the fierce Leleges saw her.
She climbed the towering Cragus, forded the Limyre, and crossed
the flowing Xanthus. High on the mountain ridge where
      Chimaera   640
terrifies the bold who adventure there, she wandered
careless of that fire-breathing, lion-headed monster.
There, at the end of the world, she fell down, exhausted, her hair
streaming out, and her face buried in windblown leaves,
an altogether woeful creature. The nymphs of the wood
found her there and attempted to lift her up in their arms,
to comfort her, perhaps to cure her of this odd love
that ate at her like a cancer. But Byblis would not be soothed
or comforted; she clutched at the blades of grass with distracted
fingers and watered the ground with endless and copious tears.   650
Endless? You and I have wept till our eyes were dry,
and know how even our worst griefs will subside at last.
But the gift of the naiads to Byblis, whom they could not
      otherwise help,
was that her tears should continue inexhaustibly flowing.
It was what she wanted, the only gift she was willing to take.
As drops of resin ooze from the cut bark of a pine tree,
or as tar will continue to rise and ooze from the earth, or as ice,
when the gentle winds of spring arrive, will melt and flow forth,
so Apollo's granddaughter wept and became her weeping,
became, that is, a fountain, which to this day produces   660
her inconsolable tears under the shade of an ilex
in the distant Carian valley, where they call the fountain Byblis.
    This would have been the important story that year, but
      in Crete
the talk was of something else, a perhaps even stranger event—
the change of Iphis. In cities and towns and around village
      wellheads,
the people would meet to talk of this bizarre business, as if
to reassure one another that such things could actually happen,
or perhaps one might put it the opposite way and say that they
      wanted
to affirm that the normal rules of how things behave would still

apply and the world next morning would be what it was last
 night. 670
There was, not far from Knossos, in a Cretan town called
 Phaestos,
a certain Ligdus, freeborn but poor, and his wife, Telethusa,
great with child and about to deliver. The indigent husband,
considering this change in their lives and what it would mean,
came to speak to his wife and let her know his thoughts:
"I have two prayers," he told her. "One is that you may deliver
with the greatest possible ease. The other is that our baby
may be a boy—for girls are trouble and cost more to raise
and marry off. I'm afraid we cannot afford a daughter.
Bad as it is to consider, we'd have to expose a girl 680
on the mountainside. I am sorry, but, poor as we are, there is no
other or easier way." His cheeks were bathed in tears,
as hers were, too, of course. She pleaded with him to rethink
the question, to reconsider and not impose this awful
judgment upon them all. But he would not or could not.
That night, in a dream, she saw the goddess Io—decked out
as Isis, in her Egyptian guise, standing beside her
bed, and with her was all her train of attendant gods,
gorgeous in their regalia. Isis wore a pair
of gilded horns like crescent Moons and carried a sheaf 690
of golden wheat. With her were Anubis, human in body
but with a dog's head; Bubastis, whose head is a cat's;
great Apis, the dappled bull; and Isis' son Harpocrates,
with his finger at his lips. Osiris was there as well,
the god whose fragments they searched for and then reassembled.
 The snake,
whatever they call him, that writhes and spits its lethal venom
came along as a pet. Telethusa saw and heard it all calmly,
without fear, as the goddess addressed her with comforting
 words:
"My child, I have come to help in your trouble. Do not obey
your husband's orders, but rather, when Lucina brings forth
 your baby, 700
wrap her well and save her. I shall be here to protect you
and keep your daughter alive. You shall never say that your
 prayers
have gone unheeded. Your goddess cares for you and loves you."
Then she was silent, and then she was gone with all her
 procession.
The woman rose from her bed happy and raised her hands

to the skies in thanks and in supplication, hoping the vision
was real, was true, was the goddess speaking the will of heaven.
    The pains came and increased, more frequent and more
       intense,
and the child was born—a girl. The mother swaddled her up
and told her attendants, but only the closest, her plan to keep mum, 710
which they did. The father gave thanks to the gods and named
       the baby
Iphis, after her grandsire. The mother rejoiced in this omen,
for Iphis is one of those names, like Leslie, that suits both sexes.
Once begun, the deception continued for days and weeks,
and the mother began to breathe easy. She dressed the child
       in blue
and then chose the infant rompers a cute little boy might wear.
    Months passed and years. The child was thirteen when the
       father
found a suitable bride, the golden-haired Ianthe,
Telestes' daughter. The two, equals in age and charm,
had been in school together, and they loved each other at once,   720
but not without some complication, as one may expect.
Ianthe was happy and looked to a marriage a girl might dream of.
Iphis knew there were problems but wanted nevertheless
what she understood was hopeless—and loved with all the
       more ardor
because it was absurd. She wept, wept like a girl,
which, of course, she was, and in love with another girl.
Bizarre, as she knew quite well, and said to herself, "The gods
should either have truly saved me, or else destroyed me—this ruin
is more than I can bear. Cows do not love cows,
nor mares, mares, nor ewes, ewes, and the gentle doe   730
mates with a stag and not with another doe. Dumb beasts
are smarter than me. No female animal lusts after females.
Pasiphaë loved a bull, but it was male. In my case,
she'd have wanted to pair with a heifer—and no clever
       machination
Daedalus could have devised would enable that! There's no
operation to make Ianthe or me a male."
    Distracted, despairing, Iphis tells herself to give up
this impossible love. "Admit your biology. Let logic,
order, and decency reassert themselves in a strange
and frightening world. Other lovers have yielded to force
       majeure—   740
a jealous husband perhaps, or a disapproving father.

Or else the girl is herself unwilling. And I must yield
to Nature's stern demurral. The gods have kept me alive,
and my wedding day is at hand. It's a cruel joke. I perish
of thirst, surrounded by sweet water. Juno descends
to bless the nuptials, and Hymen comes to join our hands—
where no man takes these women for lawfully wedded wives.
I shall die of shame, or my father's rage, or Ianthe's chagrin,
or Telestes' fury. It's awful!" She ran out of words and wept.
Meanwhile Ianthe was praying that Hymen would hurry the
    marriage   750
day, although Iphis' mother, Telethusa, contrived
delay upon delay, pretended sickness, or, finding
an inauspicious omen, postponed yet again
the rite. But after a while an inventive woman must reach
the end of these less and less convincing explanations.
The wedding day approached, was upon them, and what could
    they do
now? Neither mother nor daughter could even begin to imagine
a goal, let alone a plan. How could they extricate
themselves from this dreadful fix? The women loosened their hair
and, hand in hand, approached the altar to pray together: 760
"Isis, Queen of the Nile and Mistress of Egypt, help us.
You remember you came to me years ago, and I trusted your
    words.
I saw your torchlight procession, heard your rattles and cymbals,
and I believed. My daughter walks in the world of light
only by your gift. Help us again, we implore you."
The mother and daughter lay down before her holy altar
to weep together. Then one of them thought she noticed a
    movement
there on the altar: the figure seemed to be nodding its head.
Impossible, but, yes, it happened again. The Moon-shaped
horns were glowing, shooting out sparks of eerie light.   770
And holy rattles were sounding, as if an invisible priestess
were shaking them in prayer. What could it mean? Did they dare
trust these peculiar events? Were they signs and blessed portents?
They wanted with all their hearts to believe in the goddess, but
    dared not
presume too far. They stood, and, slowly, the pair retreated
from the altar and back to the secular world, where inanimate
    objects
do not cavort. In any event, their fates were now
out of their own hands and in those of the goddess. Iphis

walked with a jauntier, confident stride Telethusa noticed.
Confident? Yes, or one might even describe it as bold.   780
The set of her jaw was different, and the way she held her head.
Her complexion also was changed, darker now. With resolve?
Her features were sharper, stronger. And her hair was becoming
        shorter.
That was most strange. The daughter was less and less girlish, was
        turning
into a boy, was changing gender, had changed. Could it be?
Can such things happen? Can gods rescue us thus? They feared
to trust their senses and minds. But what other way did they have
to hope or even to think of? "Let us return to the shrine,
my child," Telethusa said, "to offer our thanks to Isis,
who redeems that life she once spared and makes it worth your
        living.   790
They give the gifts with gladness, and set up a tablet to praise
the goddess and also let other suppliants know that even
the farthest fetched prayers can be answered, that miracles happen:
FOR · ANSWERED · PRAYERS · OF · IPHIS · THE · MAIDEN · THE · YOUNG ·
        MAN · GIVES · THANKS.
In the sunlight that broke through the morning haze, the tablet
        glinted.
The day was turning clear and fine for the marriage of Iphis,
the handsome, grateful bridegroom, and Ianthe, his lovely bride.

BOOK X

From these festivities Hymen went to his next appointment
among the Ciconians, there to preside at Orpheus' wedding,
which didn't go well. A bad job all around. The torch
the god held kept smoking and dying out in a most
inauspicious manner. The guests were concerned, alarmed,
and then, in a matter of moments, horrified, for the bride,
on the grass among her attendant naiads, stepped on a viper,
whose sharp and envenomed fangs killed her at once. The
        wedding
abruptly turned to a wake. Orpheus, the bridegroom,
all but out of his mind with grief, went into mourning,   10
carrying his complaint to the ends of the earth and beyond,
even down to the shadows below, where the insubstantial
spirits shimmer. There, he sang out in pain and anger:
"Gods of the dim domain to which we are all consigned
sooner or later, hear me. I do not come as a tourist,
as Hercules did, or for sport to fight the three-headed dog
with snakes on its head. I am here to follow my wife, my bride,
whom a serpent abruptly dispatched in her youth's prime. I have
        tried
to bear it, to come to terms with the world's inherent unfairness,
and master my grief, but I cannot. I cannot go on this way.   20
In the name of love, I am here to throw myself on your mercy—
for love, I believe, extends its power even down here.
If the stories we tell in the light of Pluto and Proserpine
are in any way true, then passion has moved and can still
        persuade you.
Desperate, bereft, I appear to ask, in the name of these fearsome
caverns, towers, and silent expanses, these ghastly voids,
to grant me your dispensation, undo the decree of the Fates,
and restore to me that young woman you took before her time.
We all come in the end to our ultimate home here. You
receive every man and woman. And you shall have her as well,   30

but, until she has lived her allotted years, let her be with me,
either above, alive, or else accept me here
and rejoice in the death of us both. Let me remain with her."
        But it's risky, even for Ovid, to try to do Orpheus' voice.
What poet, what bard or *Dichter*, does not doubt his powers,
know how clumsy and thick-tongued he is? To perform as the
        proto-
poet? The task is daunting, and Ovid turns our attention
from cause to effects—he shows us how in that infernal
landscape Orpheus' lyre drew from the insubstantial
shadows physical tears, droplets of water, which formed   40
on the wraiths of their cheeks. Tantalus, grabbing at water that
        shrank
from his cup, was transfixed, stopped for a moment his greedy
        attempts,
listened, and mourned. Close by, Ixion's wheel came to rest.
The vultures, ignoring Tityus' liver, settled to roost.
The daughters of Belus paused with their urns, and Sisyphus
        stopped
and sat on his huge stone to consider the griefs of the mortal
condition. The Eumenides wept for the first time since creation,
and the queen of darkness granted the suppliant's prayer that
        his wife,
Eurydice, be summoned. From the newly arrived shades,
the attendants called her. She came, still limping from the viper's   50
bite, and the mistress of shades gave her up to the singer-
hero of Thrace with this one proviso only—that he
should not turn to look back until he had left Avernus
and returned to the world of the living. Hesitation or doubt,
and the gift would be nullified. A simple enough condition?
It ought to have been, and the singer led the way, ascending
the sloping path through the murk. A long way they traveled,
        almost
all the way, and, concerned for her, or not quite believing
that it wasn't a cruel delusion, a dream or mirage, he turned
to confirm for himself what he couldn't unreservedly trust,   60
and there she was, but slipping backward, away, and down.
He reached out his empty arms to hold her, touch her, catch
at the hem of her garment, but nothing. Not even words of
        complaint,
for what could she charge him with except that he'd loved her,
        loved her
too much perhaps? She spoke but only one word, "Farewell,"

which he barely heard as he watched her vanish back into
     darkness.
     Grief now, not at all assuaged but redoubled, a bruise
upon a bruise. He was stunned, was catatonic. His heart
was stone, like that nameless man who watched as Hercules
     dragged
the three-headed dog in chains, and, terrified, turned in an instant   70
into a monolith. Or what other stones? There's Olenus,
Vulcan's son, who assumed the guilt of his wife, Lethaea's
presumption, and they became a pair of stones—but together
in eternal embrace on Ida's foothills somewhere. Alone,
bereft, and desperate, Orpheus tried to cross yet again
the Styx, but Charon refused him, despite the fact that he camped
     there
on the riverbank for a week with nothing to eat or drink
but the salt and bitter taste of his own continuous tears
as he cursed the Fates and the gods. At last he picked himself up
and went home to Thrace, to the mountains, Rhodope and
     Haemus,   80
that queen and king who, turned to mountains, stand side by side
forever and ever, enduring together the winds and the rains.
     Time passed, three years in which Orpheus kept himself clear
of women and love and its risks. Women, of course, loved him,
expressed in one way or another their interest, but he refused
     them,
preferring the random spasms of passion with adolescent
boys in whom no one invests sentiment, knowing they'd grow,
change, and in any event forget him as promptly as he
would forget each one of them, longing in vain for her.
     There is a hill, or call it a mesa. Its top is even,   90
grassy, and quite devoid of shade as the Sun beats down
on its open space. Listen as Orpheus plays his lyre,
and look, see how the trees assemble, the oaks and poplars
jostling closer to hear him, the lindens and beeches nodding
their leafy heads in praise as laurel, hazel, and ash
all crowd in. The fir and ilex, plane tree, maple,
the willow tree and the boxwood, and even the tropical pine . . .
They want to hear the exquisite songs he sings, the soothing
lyrics that both induce and assuage the pains of the world
to let us suppose, at least for the moment, that we can bear them.   100
Ivy appears and grapevines, and all the attendant brush
in the green, attentive hush of the earth itself as he strums
his instrument and performs improvisations, inventions,

or entertains himself with impromptus and variations.

    Among these assembled arboreal listeners, one is a cypress,
now a tree but before that a boy whom Apollo loved.
On the Carthaean plain of the Island of Cos, there once was a stag,
a huge beast with antlers that spread out from his head
like the limbs of a large tree. Around his neck was a collar
studded with jewels. On his forehead he sported a silver pendant,   110
and hanging down from his fuzzy ears were matched earrings.
A tame stag, a pet, he had no fear at all of people
but wandered into the homes of those he knew and permitted
strangers to pat his neck and shoulders. But none of his friends
admired him more or cared for him better than this young man
named Cyparissus, who came to him every day to lead him
to fresh pastures and see that the springs were running clear
so that the stag could eat and drink. He would, on occasion,
fashion garlands of flowers to twine in the animal's antlers.
Sometimes he would mount the stag in fun and ride   120
on his strong back as a joke that the boy and the creature shared.

    There are boundaries, and we cross them always at some
      peril.
This wildness tamed was one such crossing, as Cyparissus'
love for the beast was another. A simple mistake was their ruin,
when the youth, out hunting, failed to distinguish his pet from
      the rest,
who were quarry, legitimate targets. His javelin flew and mortally
wounded the one stag he'd have given his life to protect.
And now he hated his deed, his life, and wanted to die
along with the poor sweet beast. . . . Apollo tried to dissuade him,
to tell him that even grief ought to keep itself in proportion.   130
Animals die, and men, and it's bitter, but most of them bear it.
The young man would not listen, wailed, and begged of the god
as the only gift he wanted or ever had asked to mourn
forever, to be excused from the ceaseless changing of moods
of the fickle soul, but to focus and stay at that one fixed point
of sorrow. There was no answer, but he felt his life force ebb
and his limbs began to droop and turn green, as he dissolved
from human to rooted tree, a cypress. The woeful god
sighed and at last pronounced a blessing: "I shall mourn
your loss, and you will mourn for others, for you will attend   140
at the funerals of men to condole with all those who grieve."

    For this and the other trees around him, Orpheus sang,
and to beasts who had come to listen, and birds that lit in the
      branches

to hear him recite what they knew in their hearts—the pity of
    things
and the secret of how to bear it. Orpheus strummed the strings
of his instrument to tune them, to temper them into a concord,
which, if we could only believe it, we might suppose reflected
a cosmic order, a pattern. He raised his voice and intoned:
"Jove, the Lord of the Heavens! All things begin with him,
and I shall begin by celebrating his power and majesty.   150
Let him inspire me now, not to recount his triumphs,
his lightning bolts and his battles, but something gentler,
    sweeter—
diversions, his and ours. Let me celebrate love,
the adversary of death and even sometimes the master
of gods themselves. Their passions for mortals, both boys and
    maidens,
I honor and praise, as the last hope of those who are desperate.
    "Jupiter loved the delectable Phrygian Ganymede
and turned himself into a bird for the sake of this dishy boy,
but not any bird. . . . Oh, no! It had to be one that could carry
the monstrous thunderbolts. An enormous eagle with talons   160
large enough to sustain the Trojan boy, which he did,
catching him up and flying back to the heights of Olympus,
where now, despite the distaste of Juno, he serves at banquets,
filling the nectar cups of his master and all the gods.
    "Another such favored fellow was Hyacinthus. Apollo
would have done much the same for him, plucking him up
and setting him high in the sky, had fate allowed it. But still
a kind of immortal fame attaches to him, each spring
when Aries bounds into the heavens, taking the watch from
    Pisces,
for then Hyacinthus appears and blossoms to deck the tender   170
pale green of new grass. My father, Phoebus, adored him
and abandoned the sacred precincts of Delphi to wander through
    Sparta's
meadows, groves, and hillsides carrying Hyacinthus'
nets and snares, or else holding his pack of dogs on the leash,
putting aside for the time his godhead to serve as adoring
gallant, attendant, servant, and would-be lover and friend.
The more time he spent with this handsome youth, the more
    deeply
his spirit burned with ardor. One day, at noon, they decided
to try an athletic contest, stripped down, oiled their bodies,
and readied themselves to compete with discus throws. The god   180

set himself and hurled with a mighty throw, which sent
the whirling iron platter into the distant clouds.
After a very long time, it fell to earth with a faintest
clang. Hyacinthus ran straightaway to retrieve it. But earth,
having been so assaulted, returned the throw, and the missile
smashed the young man full in the face. The god went pale
as he saw the young man drop. He ran to him, held him, tried
to revive him, to staunch the bleeding, to cure the terrible wound
with herbs and spells, but the soul was already on its way,
leaving the broken body behind in the arms of the god,   190
distraught and dismayed. You have sometimes seen in an ordered
        garden
a violet, lily, or poppy whose stem some thoughtless person
has broken off. It will languish and seem in its drooping to gaze
at the earth about to receive its body. So, this youth
drooped his ruined head from a limp neck, as Apollo
mourned, 'O Hyacinthus, cut down thus in your prime,
I have robbed you of your life. Your death is by my hand.
I am at fault and hate it that, being immortal, I cannot
journey with you, as both my love and my shame prompt,
to the land of the teeming shadows. But as the Fates prevent this,   200
I'll keep your memory with me. One way or another, my lyre's
every tune will resound with my grief at your premature
death. And a new flower shall bloom to bear your name
and fame, and a mighty hero will one day bear as his blazon
this remarkable blossom.' The god pronounced these words,
and the dark blood on the grass was blood no more but a flower,
bright as the purple of Tyre, a lily in shape but this vivid
and almost garish color. Not satisfied yet, great Phoebus
inscribed on every petal the 'Ai' of his deep lament
that the generations of men could read it there forever.   210
Near Sparta, in Amyclae, they celebrate each year
their solemn Hyacinthian rites and do him honor.
        "There are many of these peculiar local rites, some merely
curious, others violent or even obscene. I have heard
in Amathus, where they're rich in metal ores, that city
was shamed by its women, in two entirely different sects
in the one god-ridden, godforsaken Cypriot town.
The Cerastae put horns on their heads and offered sacrifices.
Travelers used to inspect their altars sacred to Jove
and stained with blood they supposed must have come from
        calves or sheep.   220

They discovered—always too late—what the dreadful cult had
        been doing
and was up to again, inviting strangers into their temple
and then, in a cruel frenzy, setting upon these guests
to make of their bleeding bodies offerings to the divine
gods—who, it then turned out, were not at all delighted.
Venus, indeed, was preparing to quit the cities, the plain,
the entire island, and let it return to the brutal existence
of godlessness, but she thought again and decided better.
The cities had not committed offenses; the plains and hillsides
hardly deserved to be punished. Only this group of devout   230
but altogether misguided zealots had been offensive.
These she would punish. She looked down and took her cue from
        their odd
headgear: she left them their horns, but turned them all into cattle.
        "Another odd religious group, the Propoetides, dared
to deny that Venus was sacred, or even a god, and, to prove it,
they resolved to offer themselves as prostitutes in the temple.
They were, at least for a while, famous. Tourists came
from all over. But after a time, as their shame diminished,
they seemed to grow hardened to what they were doing—until
        they became
not even the flesh they were selling, but cold and insensate stones.   240
        "Pygmalion, having seen these women's disgraceful behavior,
resolved to live the bachelor life. He kept to himself
and worked away at his art, carving remarkable pieces,
statues the like of which Nature itself had never quite
achieved. His diminutive women were perfect absolutely,
without blemish or mark. One, especially lovely,
he fashioned out of a piece of snowy ivory flesh
could never have duplicated. No skin was as smooth and clear,
nor had any face or figure that harmony of proportion,
that astonishing beauty that stops the breath and even the heart.   250
He could hardly believe what he'd made, stared at it hour on end,
rapt, delighted—in love, one might say, except that the word
doesn't somehow apply. Nevertheless, this object
was his, what he'd made, what he wanted, admired, desired,
        reached out
to touch once again to persuade himself that it was not real—
or to reassure himself that it was, that he'd turned his dream
into a solid substance. Only too solid and dumb.
But not so dumb as its maker, who knows better but talks

to his ivory figure, chats with it, brings it occasional presents,
flowers, necklaces, rings. He kisses its lips and caresses 260
its elegant limbs, and he feels his fingers sink into yielding
flesh. . . . He's afraid he's bruised it. But no, nothing. A perfect
surface remains, aloof and indifferent. He sues with more ardor,
dresses it up in robes of expensive stuff, or bedecks it
with jewels. Sometimes he stretches it out on a couch to let it
loll like an odalisque on a pillow, as if it were sleeping,
as if it enjoyed his wooing but just now were feeling fatigued.
   "The midsummer eve had arrived with its celebration of
      Venus.
Heifers with gilded horns ambled their way toward the altars
and the fine-honed axe. The smoke of incense curled in the air. 270
Pygmalion went to the temple to make his sacred donation
and ask, as was the custom, for the goddess to grant him a favor.
He could hardly speak, knowing that what he wanted was crazy,
foolish, absurd, and yet there was nothing else he cared for.
He started, 'Gracious goddess, grant me a woman to wed
who is . . .' How could he ask for the statue to quicken with life?
      He settled
on ' . . . *like* my statue.' But Venus knew well what he was
      thinking
and, pleased with his modest prayer, gave him auspicious signs
with the tongues of fire leaping three times high in the air.
The artist was puzzled, afraid she was teasing him, had no way 280
to read the divine response. Eager, anxious, afraid,
he went back home to the image he'd made, and touched it,
      kissed it.
Warm, was it? He couldn't allow himself to believe this.
He kissed her again. He touched with a diffident hand her breast,
the hardness of which he could feel as yielding, like wax that
      softens
whenever you work it and takes what shape you choose to
      impose.
Torn between hope and fear, he touches the statue again,
and cannot believe it is flesh, warm and with arteries pulsing
blood and life. . . . Astounding! He gives his thanks to the
      goddess
and tenderly kisses the lips of the maiden to bring her awake. 290
She blinks, blushes, opens her eyes, and gazes upon him,
her maker, her lover, her man, and behind him the light of
      the sky,
for which she is grateful to him and the goddess. Venus presides

at this marriage she has contrived and enabled. Nine months
    elapse,
and a daughter is born to them, Paphos, for whom that island is
    named.
    "Cinyras was the son of Paphos, and, had he died
without any issue, he might have had reason to offer thanks,
for his daughter was Myrrha, and hers is a truly terrible story
to make every father tremble and every daughter afraid.
Some there will be who would rather disbelieve that such things   300
can ever happen, or else they admit that in backward regions
remote and exotic tribesmen may behave in this way, but it doesn't
count or affect anyone we'd know. Does the human species
vary so much? Is there ever safety anywhere? Distance
doesn't prevent those oddly dressed people from sending us
    spices—
cinnamon, balsam, mace, and frankincense, which their trees
exude, and their odors pervade our houses here. And myrrh . . .
do not forget the myrrh, rare and grievously costly.
That tree was once a young woman, who fell in love. But Cupid
denies that he ever touched her, blaming instead a Fury   310
who came from the depths of the Styx with a torch to singe
    her soul
and drive her to actions of crime or madness to make us shudder.
There have been girls who have hated their fathers, and this is
    wrong,
but how much greater a wrong is the love that Myrrha felt
for her sire? Suitors, noble and rich, appeared at her door,
princes of many neighboring countries and faraway kingdoms.
She spurned them all, though she gave no reason, denying there
    was one,
unable herself to face it, or else she still struggled against it,
for she knew perfectly well that this was forbidden, was wicked.
This was what animals do, and humans ought to behave   320
in a better and different way. A heifer will stand and allow
her own father to mount her. Or a goat will mate with the same
billy that sired her. Horses do this, and birds. . . . But people
have standards, a civilization's pieties, laws, and customs
by which we are meant to govern our passions and our behavior.
On the other hand, any reasoned argument must allow
an answer, a contrary case, which she's hardly loath to
    construct—
that these beasts are fortunate, graced, have not allowed artificial
constraints to veto the promptings of their spontaneous feelings

and natural inclinations. Man, with his civilized rules, 330
departs from the natural order, violates and defiles it.
But not all men, for there surely are primitive tribes somewhere
with bones in their noses, plates in their lips, and elongated necks
stretched out with coils of metal. Who knows how they behave?
Fathers may mate with daughters in the dark of their conical
        huts . . .
with what result? That the bonds of love that already connect
        them
are strengthened, doubled, perfected. Why can she not have
        been born
there in that happy tribe, where there isn't a word for 'sin,'
and they do as they please? Or here, if only she weren't his
        daughter,
then she could come as a stranger to Cinyras and be closer 340
than what was allowed to a daughter, an intimate whose nearness
is only a torment. She thinks of that blessed lack of connection,
which beckons. Yes, she will leave, go far away. It will hurt
less if she does not see him every day. It will keep her
from dwelling upon this madness. The only intelligent course,
it nevertheless would deprive her of what she can now enjoy,
the chance to see him, touch him, talk with him, even kiss him,
as daughters so often may do. And what more does she imagine
is ever likely to happen? Can't she accept this much
and be content? Would she truly think to supplant her own
        mother 350
in Cinyras' bed and heart? Would she bear him a child and be
        mother
and sister at once? She thinks of those other older sisters
with snakes in their horrible hair who confront sinners with
        smoking
torches. She can imagine them turning on her, knowing well
where her sordid thoughts have been tending all this time, in fear
but in fascination, too. Her father, hardly a sinner,
must save them both, must resist her vile and forbidden passion.
    "Thus, in torment and all alone, she considered the question.
Her father, meanwhile, inquired which of her many suitors
she might perhaps prefer. He named them over and watched 360
her averted face for some sign of animation or interest
or even attention. Nothing but silence and brimming tears,
which Cinyras supposed were owing to maidenly fears
all girls go through. He dried her tears and kissed her lips.

Myrrha brightened at once. He asked her what sort of a man
she'd thought of as a husband. 'One just like you,' she replied.
Failing to understand what she meant, he was pleased, delighted,
and kissed her again as she blushed in pleasure, shame, and
    confusion.
   "That night she could not sleep but tossed in her bed,
    consumed
by her passion's flames, despair, renewed desire, and fear,   370
which warred in her heart. A tree that woodsmen have cut with
    their axes
wavers thus at the whims of the winds, leans this way and that,
will fall, but in which direction? Nobody can predict.
She thinks, herself, of the only escape she can even imagine—
death itself, which appears as her least unattractive option.
She rises and walks like a zombie, as if she were only rehearsing
or reenacting her death. She flings her sash round a beam,
ties a knot, and recites, as if from a script, 'Farewell,
my beloved Cinyras. For you, for us both, I die.'
She has fashioned the noose and draped it around her neck, when
    her nurse   380
appears in the nick of time to save her, to keep her darling
from doing this dreadful thing. She screams, grabs at the noose,
and snatches it off the head of the girl she has loved and protected
for so many years. She weeps. They weep together, embrace,
and the nurse asks the poor girl to say what drove her to do this.
Myrrha stares at the ground, sorry that she has been saved,
and the nurse holds her, enfolds her in dear, scrawny old arms,
strokes her hair and rocks her, croons to her, and begs her
in the name of their years of love to confide in her. But the girl
groans and turns away. The frantic old woman clutches   390
a hand to her sagging bosom, which once gave suck to this
    nursling
she still loves and would give what is left of her life to protect.
'What is it you want? I'll help you, whatever it is,' she assures
the silent young woman. 'The old are not altogether helpless
but know the secrets of herbs, philters, and powerful charms.
Has someone bewitched you? Spells may be broken, unsaid,
    undone. . . .
Or have you crossed some god? Still, you may look to appease
by sacrifices and prayers even the heaven's anger.
What else can it be? Your mother and father are well, and the
    household

prospers. . . .' And there the girl, hearing her father mentioned,   400
sighed from the depths of her suffering soul. The old woman
      noticed
and, though she failed to connect the sigh with its object, guessed
that love was somehow the trouble, the source of her darling's
      pain.
Of course, with that train of suitors! She took the girl in her arms
and said, 'I know. It is love. It must be love. And I'll help you.
Whatever it is, whatever you want, I can be of service,
smoothing the way. You must trust me. Your father will never
      know. . . .'
The girl broke away. The nurse's words had touched a nerve
that renewed her exquisite pain. 'Go away,' she said, and sobbed.
'Don't ask questions; just go. What I want is unspeakably evil.   410
You don't want to know.' In horror and grief, the old woman
      kneels
before the young girl and begs her to trust, to confide, to share
her terrible burden. She even threatens to tell what she's seen,
to go to the master with word of this suicide business. The choice
is that or accepting the help and advice of her loving *nounou*.
The girl raises the kneeling woman before her, embraces
and kisses her, weeping copious tears that dampen both
their blouses. She attempts to confess, begins, then halts,
then begins again, but cannot go on. She hides her face
in the sleeve of her robe. Once more she attempts it, stammers,
      'My mother's . . .   420
my father's . . . my father . . .' She gives up, as words give way to
      her groans.
But the nurse, cold with the shock of what she has guessed, is
      certain
of what possesses the girl. Disaster! Is there advice,
except to forget this, deny these awful promptings, suppress
these ruinous thoughts? The girl nods her head in agreement,
for this was her own view, too, and the noose was her way to
      achieve
this otherwise unattainable goal. And her death remains
a way to escape from the other and much worse fate. The nurse
feels the hairs at the nape of her neck prickle in fear
as she tells the girl, 'Live, then, and I shall help you have
      him. . . .'   430
She cannot say his name but swears by all the gods
she will do whatever is needed to satisfy her desire.

"The feast of Ceres, this was, when matrons would offer
      wheat sheaves
to thank the bountiful goddess with the first yield of the harvest.
For this sacred rite, they put on the white robes of the vestals
and lived for nine days and nights as those celibate priestesses do,
keeping themselves from their husbands, among these women,
      Cenchreïs,
Myrrha's mother and Cinyras' pious wife. The king,
therefore, went alone to his bed each night, and the nurse,
shrewd and alert, chose her moment. He had been drinking that
      night,   440
was muddled and feeling lonely, and likely—as any man can be—
to listen to her suggestive report that a pretty girl
adored him, loved him, and wanted to visit his bedroom.
      Could she?
'Attractive?' 'Yes, and young.' 'How young?' 'Your daughter's
      age.'
He smiled at this and nodded assent. The nurse hurried off
to report this triumph to Myrrha, who received it with some
      mixed feelings,
delight and dread that her fate had presented itself. She was ready.
      "In the small hours of night when all was still in the palace,
when the moon had fled from the sky and the stars were
      concealing themselves
in a shroud of cloud, she set out for her father's apartment,
      stumbled,   450
recognized that the omen was baleful, but nevertheless
continued along the hallway, as one does in dreams or nightmares,
unable to turn back now. She froze in her tracks as she heard
the warning cry of a screech owl, which sounded again and
      again—
a treble caution confirming her worst fears. She continued
down the corridor, clutching her nurse's arm for support.
The hall is apparently endless, but then—too soon—they arrive
at the door the nurse pushes open. The girl's knees flutter and
      tremble.
Her body shudders as much in fear as desire. Her breath
is caught in her throat's constriction. Her resolve has abandoned
      her now,   460
and she would turn back if her nurse were not propelling her
      forward
toward the looming hulk of the huge bed in that darkened room.

The woman takes her hand, puts it in Cinyras' hand,
whispers, 'Take her. The girl is yours,' and scuttles away,
leaving the doomed couple in the dark together to do
whatever they would. Unknowing, the father takes the daughter.
His flesh cleaves to his own flesh. To calm her fears
he tells her all will be well and calls her 'Child.' In reply,
she calls him 'Daddy,' as if to confirm their mutual guilt.

    "Full of her father's seed, the girl slips out of the room,   470
guilty but shameless—there's nothing to fear or to hope for now.
The next night, she returns, because twice is no worse than once.
And the third night, she is back yet again, but this time her father,
wondering who she is and what she looks like, lights
a lamp, which reveals the dismaying truth. He is speechless,
     appalled
to see what he's done, what they've done. In grief and anger, he
     grabs
his sword from its sheath, which it hangs on the wall nearby, to
     punish
this unnatural child, but she flees and escapes into the darkness,
out of the room, the house, the city, and into remote
and exotic lands, even as far away as the Arab   480
wilderness, where she rests herself and her womb's great burden.
Exhausted now and indifferent, she doesn't know what to
     pray for,
and cannot even imagine a welcome among the living
or among the dreaded dead. What she has done and been
and what she is now is hateful. 'Gods,' she invokes, defiant,
'I accept my punishment gladly, whatever it is. I offend
the light and defile the darkness. I pray you, therefore, change me,
make me something else, transform me entirely, cleanse me. . . . '
There must have been some god who heard her desperate petition
and granted her prayer, for the earth now covered her feet, and
     her toes   490
were rooting into the soil to support the trunk of her body,
which stiffened as flesh and bone transformed themselves
     into wood,
blood became sap that flowed up and into her branching arms,
and skin became bark. Within her, under the wood, in her womb,
a restless fetus moved, and the tree could feel it and grieve
at the ruin of those fresh hopes that a baby's birth should imply.
Tears flowed from the tree, miraculous fragrant tears
of what we know as myrrh. Her name, surviving, preserves
from age to age her singular story, her singular grief.

"And what of the child within her, that poor and ill-
      conceived   500
half brother and son? He seeks a passage into the light,
a way to be born and live. The tree is swollen, contorted,
and, although it cannot call out, it appears to writhe in its pain.
Lucina pities its tears and the plaintive sound of the wind
in its groaning branches. She touches the wood with gentle hands
while reciting charms that assist mothers in labor. The tree
cracks open, the bark splits, and the baby boy is born.
His cry startles the silent woods, and naiads come
to swaddle the infant in leaves and wash his body in soothing
myrrh. Envy herself would praise his perfection. He looks   510
like one of those putti painters do in their pictures' borders
to suggest the ideals of love, of innocent beauty—whatever
is just out of reach, for which we strive, and of which we dream,
and, much to our shame, we fail to achieve and betray or forget.
      " Years pass, and the baby grows in size and strength
but remains an extraordinarily beautiful child. He looks
like Cupid except for that quiver of arrows the mischievous god
carries. He turns from boy to youth, and is handsome still,
an example of how we all should like to look, if we dared
imagine such perfection. Venus herself looks down   520
and is struck by the young man, utterly stunned. Some suppose
the goddess was wounded and make up a story of how her own
      child
Cupid, whom she once embraced as mothers do,
unwittingly grazed her breast with one of his magic arrows.
She is hardly aware of the superficial abrasion, a mere
scratch, but it has its effect. Her mind's balance is ruined,
and she finds herself indifferent to her old pastimes and haunts.
Cythera is dreary now, and Paphos only another
island out in the sea. And Cnidos? The same old Cnidos
with squid hanging from nets at fishermen's bars near the quay.   530
Amathus with its clever goldsmiths no longer attracts her.
Even the skies are boring. What she wants is Adonis,
that gorgeous young man, that dream turned to delicious flesh.
For him she pretends to outdoorsy interests, gets outfitted
      for them,
finding among those simple tunics that huntresses wear
some that reveal a tempting glimpse of cleavage or thigh.
The colors are earthy, simple, and not at all unbecoming.
She only goes after small game like rabbits, or sometimes deer,
but never the larger beasts that, when they are cornered, turn,

charge, and, with menacing teeth or horns or claws, can do
    damage. . . .   540
What kind of fun is that? She simply can't understand it.
She likes the dogs well enough, thinks the puppies are darling,
but the business of hunting and killing seems to be something to
    leave
to servants, perhaps, as a branch of cuisine. She tells the young
    fellow
please to watch out for himself, to exercise some basic
caution, if not for his sake, then for her own—she'd miss him
dreadfully if he were killed. Or, even worse, disfigured!
She makes a *moue* of distaste he thinks is absurd but adores
nevertheless. She explains why she is anxious and tells him
a story. 'But let us lie down in the shade of that poplar,' she says.   550
'All this walking undoes me. Some shade and a seat in the grass,
and a good story?' She pats the turf, and then she reclines,
using his chest as a pillow, and, stroking his face with her fingers,
tells him the following tale: 'There was a girl once, a beauty
who ran like the wind. She was famous as much for her looks as
    her speed.
You've heard of her, I am certain. Her name was Atalanta.
She went, as girls do, to consult with the woman who speaks for
    the god
and learn from the oracle's mouth what sort of husband to choose.
But the god's answer was dreadful. "Flee from a husband.
    Marriage
will be your utter ruin. Flee, or you'll lose your life."   560
Frightened by this, she returned to the woods determined to live
a celibate life and a safe one. All her insistent suitors
she sent away or refused, explaining she had to be won
in a foot race. Anyone faster could take her to wife, but losers
would be put to death. These terms discouraged the casual
    swains,
but such was her radiant beauty that several said they'd compete.
A barbarous contest, but people come out to watch these events,
and one in the stands that day was Hippomenes, fascinated
and horrified at once. He was clear in his disapproval:
"What kind of madman would do this? Who is so rash, so
    headstrong,   570
as to risk his life in this way? What woman is worth it?" But then
she appeared, stripped down for the race, and the scornful and
    mocking tone
was gone, had changed to awe, to helpless desire. He could not

bear to live without her, which canceled the risk. She was lovely,
my equal I think, or even yours, if you were a woman.
He stretched out his arms like a baby who wants the world, and
      took back
all his ignorant words. "Forgive me. I had not seen her,
could not imagine her worth and beauty, could not have
      believed. . . ."
He was smitten, not only in love but jealous of all the others,
worried that one of these suitors might somehow outrun and
      win her.   580
How could he not take part? The gods favor the daring!
Or that's what they say. Just then, Atalanta sped by like a shot.
Hippomenes watched her, impressed with her speed but more
      with her looks
as the wind whipped the hair on her shoulders, and beads of sweat
on her body were diamonds bright in the sunshine. What an
      astonishing
creature! Not to compete for her hand would be worse than death.
She crossed the finish line first, and the judge put the wreath on
      her head
as the other contestants were led to their instant executions.
    "'Ignoring that part of the tableau, Hippomenes now
      addressed
the radiant girl: "I extend my congratulations, but still,   590
it wasn't a challenging field. The times were not so impressive.
Allow me to try my luck. If I win, you shall have the excuse
that I am the child of Megareus, who was grandson of mighty
      Neptune.
There's no disgrace in losing to someone of such a bloodline.
Or, if I lose, the distinction you'll win will be all the greater."
It wasn't only his words that worked with the girl but his smile,
his playful grin that disarmed her. She hardly knew what she
      wanted—
To beat him? To lose and be married? Pleased but confused, she
      replied,
" What naughty god can it be who toys thus with your fate?
Why should you risk your life for me? I know I'm not worth it.   600
Lots of girls would be pleased, would be honored, to marry you.
      Pick one!"
And yet, as she spoke, another voice within her was saying
how young he was, how rash, how delightfully reckless. And
      handsome!
She recognized her desire and admiration and, therefore,

felt a degree of guilt, which turned, at once, to anger.
What of those others? He had seen them go off just now to die.
Had he learned nothing? A stupid and stubborn young man, he
        deserved
whatever he got. . . . And yet that youthful and almost girlish
face of his, and that smile! She wished she had never seen it.
How could she bear to defeat him? Yet it was none of her doing.   610
We each choose for ourselves, find our own way, and assume
the risks of our deeds and desires. What he would do, she could
        not
prevent or change. She warned him of what the god had foretold
for her should she take a husband, but it did no good, and she
        knew,
the moment she framed the words and propelled them into
        the air,
that his ears might have been deaf. She might as well have
        confessed
she liked him, cared for him, even could think of herself as
        in love. . . .
But then, there was hardly a need for such reassurance. He knew.
That smile of his made it clear that he had divined her feeling
and was utterly unpersuaded by all this discouraging talk.   620
She found in herself a forgiveness for whatever foolish thing
he insisted on doing, and therefore could also forgive herself
for loving him, for failing to heed the oracle's warning.
One's fate, after all, is one's fate. Fighting against it is pointless,
and trying to live as if one had choices is vain imposture.
However it went, she knew that her marriage bed would be
        bloodied.
        " 'Around this distracted pair the crowd had gathered, was
        eager
to watch them run, to observe the contest, and see its result,
whichever way it came out. Atalanta's father, King
Schoeneus, announced that the race would now commence.   630
Neptune's descendant prayed, calling on me for my favor
and help in this time of trial. On a kindly breeze, his words
floated upward to heaven. I heard it, was pleased, even moved,
and wanted to do whatever I could in his behalf,
although there wasn't much time. Still, I thought of the sacred
tree that stands in the field of Tamasus in Cyprus,
with leaves and fruit of dazzling gold, which hang from intricate
golden boughs. I had been there not long before, to visit
one of the temples an ancient cult there erected to me,

and I happened to have on hand three of the apples I'd picked 640
from that wonderful tree. With these in hand, I descended,
appeared
to answer Hippomenes' prayer—nobody else could see me—
and handed him these golden apples, which, if he used them
as I instructed, would surely help him win the race.
Trumpets were already sounding their warning. The two
contenders
crouched at the starting blocks, were ready, set, and the signal
sent them speeding away. Flying along the sandy
course, their feet seemed scarcely to touch as they ran like the
wind
that ripples the waves of the sea or the ripening grain in a field.
The crowd in the stands cheered. Some of the fans were
supporting 650
him—they knew what awaited suitors who lost these races—
while others cheered for her, for Schoeneus' daughter, whose
beauty
and speed seemed rare and blessed gifts in which all could rejoice
for the way they enriched and enlarged how we think of the
human condition,
as if all men and women shared in what she had achieved.
But along with the physical race they ran was another contest
in the heart of the girl, who wanted to win and not to win,
who could have passed him several times, could have left him
behind,
his stertorous gaspings loud in his dry and desperate throat.
She could have shown him her dust and a dismal view of the
broken 660
ribbon of his life at the finish line, but she could not
ruin altogether his hopes and pride. She ran
side by side with Hippomenes. And then he surprised her,
throwing
some silly bauble. . . . Gold? Surely, it was. An apple.
She slowed, stopped, snatched it up, and the crowd erupted,
roared in delight. The girl, not at all sure what they meant,
put on a burst of speed that made up the time she had lost
and brought her back to his side. Then she was past him again,
but he threw down the second apple. Again, she slowed, stooped,
stopped to grab it, and then in a furious sprint reclosed 670
the gap. They were now in the stretch, could see the finish line
looming
ahead, and Hippomenes prayed, "Be near me now, sweet goddess.

Make it work one more time!" This third apple, he threw
off to the side, where she had to go out of her way. Did she
    want it?
Or him? Or what? In confusion, she hesitated, then lunged
for the apple I had commanded her spirit to want. With the three
pieces of heavy golden fruit, it wasn't so easy
to run now, and the burden of her ambivalent feelings
also slowed her down. She tried but she could not quite
catch him, let alone pass him. By a couple of steps, he won.   680
    "'A mighty cheer went up—but not for me, I'm afraid.
And was I not the victor as much as Hippomenes? Was I
to have no share in the praise with incense and chanted prayers
of thanks? I ask you, Adonis. Stupid, churlish, he acted
as if he had done this alone and unaided. It made me angry.
I decided to make of him, and of both of them, an example
for all the world, to remind men and women that gods should be
    thanked
for the gifts we deign to bestow. The bride and groom had
    departed,
were on their way to Hippomenes' home, and they happened
    to pass
a shrine Echion had built to Cybele, mother of gods.   690
Tired, they stopped to rest, and there, in a sudden seizure
of lust I visited on the husband, Hippomenes took
his wife in the temple's holy precincts, among the icons.
The sacred figure tried to avert her eyes, but could not.
Cybele, mortified, was ready to take the pair
and plunge them into the world of darkness across the Styx.
But that would have been too easy, as I pointed out. Instead,
I offered my own idea, and they felt their skins become hairy,
and their fingernails grow to claws in their hands and feet that
    were paws.
Tails sprouted out of the ends of their spines to twitch on the
    sandy   700
ground, and their words of love became growls of lions—not
    kings
of beasts, but the tame lions that draw Cybele's car
with bits in their huge mouths and her reins over their tawny
manes—which lions, of course, resent. Therefore, be careful
of large and ferocious beasts, who mean me harm and will do
whatever damage they can to injure someone I love.'
    "This was the goddess's warning, the point of her story. But
    stories

never do any good. People don't listen. They hear,
but won't understand. They insist on learning, themselves, the
   hard way,
which is to say they prefer to be characters in new stories—   710
even assuming the risk of sad or violent endings.
The goddess had to depart for a while on heavenly business,
ascended in her swan-drawn car, leaving the boy
to his own devices—hunting of course, and he paid no mind
to what she had told him. He went with his hounds after some
   wild boar,
pierced its side with a lance, but it wasn't a mortal wound.
Instead, the boar was enraged, worried the lance shaft free,
and then charged, and gored with his huge yellowy tusks
the son who was also the grandson of Cinyras deep in his groin.
And killed him. The boy sank down on the yellow sand his blood   720
was drenching. High in the air in her chariot, Venus heard
his piteous groans and returned to try to staunch the bleeding,
to heal the wound. . . . But too late, too late. As he slipped away,
the distraught goddess tore her tunic, beat those beautiful
breasts that were meant for other and happier business, and cried
out against the implacable Fates: 'You shall not have him
all. I will not allow it. I shall keep some of Adonis.
His memory and his beauty shall live again, and my grief.
Each year this blood shall change and blossom as delicate flowers.
Persephone once changed that woman whom Pluto loved,   730
Minthe, into a sprig of aromatic mint,
and I can do at least as much for my own Adonis.'
Saying this, she sprinkled drops of divine nectar
onto the blood-soaked ground, which seethed, bubbled, and grew
vegetation that sprouted and, within the hour, bloomed
in delicate blood-red flowers, the color of pomegranate.
This flower is short-lived, for the wind tousles its petals
and strips it bare, but the wind also gives it a name—
the anemone, which blossoms and then prematurely dies.' "

BOOK XI

These were the songs that Orpheus sang to the trees and rocks
that had drawn around him to listen to how things go in the
        world,
sad or glad—but their truth was consoling and liberating.
The wild Ciconian women he'd scorned found him out,
        pursued him,
and, swarming down from the crest of a nearby hillside,
        attacked him,
screaming their oaths and imprecations and hurling as weapons
whatever came to hand. One of these hurled her spear
straight at the mouth of the poet—but as it flew in its deadly
arc it heard his singing, was overcome by the poignant
sweetness of what he crooned, and fell at his feet, relenting   10
and asking for his forgiveness for the harm it had tried to
        bring him.
Another woman threw a sizable stone that softened
its hard-heartedness, flinched, and deflected the blow she'd hoped
it might produce. It fell to the ground, tame and harmless
as all their weapons and missiles might have been, but, in rage
or perhaps by calculation, the women banged on their drums,
tootled their flutes, and blew their brassy horns, or screamed
in unearthly ululation, which drowned out the poet's
        performance,
the gentle sounds of the lyre, and his words' music and meaning.
Deafened, thus, or distracted, the stones, no longer charmed,   20
struck again and again. His face and body were bloodied,
but he hardly noticed his own pain as he watched in horror
the women destroying the innocent birds that had perched on the
        ground
to hear him sing, and the beasts and reptiles. In their crazed
        rampage,
the Maenads tore those creatures to bits, and then they turned
on the poet himself. They flocked like enraged fowl that savage

unlucky intruders, as day birds will swarm to attack an owl
that lingers too long. It was brutal, one of those ghastly shows
you see sometimes in arenas when they let a pack of dogs loose
on a single defenseless stag to watch its spectacular end.   30
The thyrsus isn't a weapon, but that was what it became
as they beat him about the head and shoulders. Some used
          branches
of trees, and some hurled stones or clods of earth. Nearby,
a farmer was plowing his field, while some of his field hands were
          working
the earth with mattocks and hoes. These men, of course, ran off,
but the women hurried to seize those tools they could use as
          weapons.
In manic rapture, they first destroyed the poor dumb oxen,
turned them to chopped meat, and then went back up the hill
with the tools to kill the singer, whose pleas they ignored,
          whose words
for the first time were of no effect, were useless phonemes.   40
These women were worse than beasts or trees, and their hearts
          were harder
than solid stones, for they did not listen, they would not hear,
and they struck him down. O gods! What a world is this? His soul
took its leave at last through that mouth and lips and followed
          his words
up and into the air, which was henceforward diminished
and would never resound again to the songs only he could sing.
          Birds and beasts fell silent and mourned; trees shed their
          leaves
as if they had torn their hair like grief-stricken women; and rocks
were full of woe, and their silence was different, heavier now.
Rivers wept, and their banks overflowed with their tears.   50
The naiads and dryads were inconsolable. The poet's
limbs were meat strewn over the ground. But the head? Where
          was
the head? Amazingly, it had fallen into the Hebrus.
The head and lyre floated together, and some say the water
stroked the strings of the instrument, making a faint dirge
to which the lifeless tongue in the dead mouth seemed to croon
in a sweet and eerie descant to which the riverbanks echoed
or even harmonized. This musical progress continued
onward, into the sea, and across to the shore of Lesbos
on a beach not far from Mithymna, where it rolled ashore—still
          singing!   60

A serpent, seeing the helpless head on the beach, coiled
to attack, but Apollo appeared, drove it away, and, in pique,
turned the serpent to stone, its mouth still yawning and ready
to strike at the dead head. Enough, the god thought, is enough.
        The shade, free now to flee to the land of shades below,
could recognize those landscapes it passed through before, as it
            searched
through all those ashen faces for Euridyce's dear face—
which he at last beholds. He takes in his eager and airy
arms her beloved wraith, and side by side they walk
through the blessed fields. He leads a step ahead and looks back   70
again and again to see how each time she follows him still.
        A happy ending, in part. But Bacchus, not at all pleased
at those women whose crime had lost him the songs of his
            sacred bard,
turned those women to trees. They felt their feet catching hold
in the earth, and they writhed and twisted, only to snag the more
            surely,
as a bird, caught in a snare that the clever trapper has set,
flapping, fluttering, helpless, is only entangled tighter.
The bark grew up their calves and thighs. Their bellies were
            wood,
their breasts and shoulders, oak, and their arms were leafy
            branches.
        This was only a start. Bacchus, still angry, disliked   80
being in Thrace and left it, abandoned the place for Tmolus,
whose vineyards he much preferred. With his old coterie, he
            settled
there by the Pactolus' banks, in which gold had not yet been
            found.
But among his satyrs and merry pranksters, where was Silenus,
his jolly tosspot pal? Missing? How could that happen?
It turns out that Phrygian peasants have taken him captive,
            tied him
with vines and wreaths, and brought him into their king's palace.
It isn't at all surprising. He's one of the usual suspects,
whatever the problem may be. That king, however, is Midas,
himself one of Bacchus' train. He'd been brought into the cult   90
by Orpheus himself—and the king recognized his fellow
enthusiast, laughed, freed him at once, and threw a grand party,
which lasted a good ten days. The eleventh, he sent Silenus
back to the court of the god who was also his foster child.
        Bacchus, delighted to see the old reprobate, was disposed

to grant Midas a favor—a minor miracle, something
to do at parties perhaps. He invited the king to choose
something amusing. The king, whose fate it was to misuse
this happy chance, overreached himself in his greed and requested
whatever he touched might turn at once to glittering gold.   100
This wasn't a good idea, as the god understood, but he'd promised ·
and had no choice. In sadness, he nodded his head and granted
this terrible gift. The Phrygian king was delighted and started
home. On the way he played with his wonderful power, testing
to see if it always worked. He touched one thing and another,
broke off the branch of an oak and saw the green twig turn
yellow and gleam like a jeweler's bauble. He picked up a stone,
and it was a nugget of solid gold. Or a clod of earth?
That, too, was instantly gold. A sheaf of wheat, and it changed
to gold in his hand. An apple was gold—you would think it
        had come   110
as a gift of Hesperus' daughters from their magical tree. He
        touched
the wall of a house and it, too, turned gold. A pillar? Even that
was solid gold. It was lovely, elegant fun! He tried pouring
water over his hands, and the cascade turned into precious
metal there in midair. He was rich beyond all dreaming,
could not even think what to hope for, or what to touch next.
He would need a definite plan, a reasoned course of behavior. . . .
But that would all come later. He ordered his servants to serve
a great feast, a banquet to celebrate this momentous
occasion with different kinds of meats, and breads, and wines.   120
But abruptly his mood changed as he reached for a fragrant loaf
and watched it turn from sweet and doughy to unappetizing
gold. A morsel of chicken? It chilled, congealed, turned hard,
and was also gold. And the wine he tried to sip turned metal.
Hungry, thirsty, afraid, he had nothing to eat or drink
but these goldsmiths' simulacra of food, these vitrine victuals,
a nightmare menu of wealth to break one's teeth on, and heart.
He might as well have tried to nibble the golden plates
on which the food turned golden as soon as he touched it. Rich,
he is nonetheless impoverished, starving, hates his power,   130
and no longer wants the blessing that turns out to be a curse.
He lifts his hands to the skies and prays to Bacchus for pity,
for pardon, for some remission from what otherwise will be
his certain death. "I have sinned," he admits. "I am truly sorry.
Save me from myself!" The gods may be hard of hearing,
but they are not stone-deaf. Sometimes they hear contrition,

as Bacchus did, and restored him to what he had been before.
"Go to the stream that flows by the town of Sardis and climb
to the water's source. Plunge yourself into that cleansing flow,
and there you may wash away your greed and the gilt of your
      guilt."   140
This the king did, and the power he'd asked for was taken away.
No more did whatever he touch turn to precious metal,
but the strange gift leeched out into the stream, which still
produces gold from that vein at the source, and nuggets appear
along the watercourse and even in fields alongside it.
     Midas, now a changed man, hated the thought of wealth.
He lived in the woods and the fields, simplifying his life
and worshiping Pan. In wisdom and peace, you might think—
       but no,
stupid is always stupid and never likely to change.
Poor benighted Midas was fated to get into trouble   150
again, for that was his only talent. The mountain Tmolus
looms over the sea, with the slopes of Sardis on one side
and, on the other, the lesser hill that they call Hypaepae,
where Pan liked to come to play his musical pipes to admiring
listeners, mostly the nymphs, who heard and beamed approval.
Delighted, Pan took on airs, assumed his playing was matchless
and that not even Apollo could make better music than his.
A rash and preposterous boast, but, having made it, he could not
back down with any good grace. A contest? someone suggested.
Of course! Why not? And Pan proposed the judge be Tmolus,   160
the ancient lord of the mountain in whose benevolent presence
he'd done so well for so long. Tmolus appeared on his seat
to hear the musicians vie with each other—he shook his ears
clear of trees and bushes. His forehead was decked with oak leaves,
and here and there hung acorns, which jiggled whenever he
      spoke.
"I am prepared," he announced. "You may begin when ready."
Pan performed at his best, his simple songs on the pipes
that quite delighted our Midas, who happened to hear the recital.
When Pan's last number's echoes died away, the judge
turned to the Sun to invite Apollo to do what he could.   170
The golden head of the god was wreathed in Parnassus' laurel,
and his cloak, which swept the ground, was splendid with Tyrian
      purple.
In one hand he held his lyre inlaid with jewels
and ivory panels. The other strummed with an ivory plectrum.
He struck a pose and sang; the contest and day were his,

all his, as Tmolus announced, as he signaled to Pan to put down
the rude pipes and bow his head to the master, his better.
      It wasn't at all a close call, and all agreed with the judge—
all, that is, but our poor misguided Midas, who railed
that the referee was deaf, the contest was fixed, and Pan   180
had been wronged and robbed. Apollo, not at all pleased, decided
that Midas' ears were defective and needed immediate treatment,
whereupon they commenced to grow longer, larger, grotesque
rabbit ears at first, and then they were donkey ears,
shaggy, twitching, and terribly funny. Midas was shamed
and tried however he could to hide these monstrous otic
appendages. He affected a sizable purple turban
to cover his asinine ears. No one would ever suspect!
Only his hairdresser—he, that slave who tended his tonsure,
was sworn to keep the secret. He kept, at least, a straight face,   190
but had to tell someone, unburden himself of this rich
bêtise. He trusted no one, but went deep into the woods,
dug a hole in the ground, and spoke to the mute brown earth,
      imparting
the great god's marvelous joke. Then he filled up the hole
and walked back home. You would think a secret buried that way
would stay buried, but no, the reeds that grew in that spot
at the end of the season whispered into the winds the truth
of what they were so deeply persuaded had happened. And winds
scattered the news to the normal ears of the rest of the world.
      Satisfied now, Apollo ascends into air and flies   200
from Tmolus across the sea to the Hellespont—the strait
of Helle, daughter of Nephele—where he comes to earth in
      the land
Laomedon rules, the son of Ilus. Hard by the sea
on a promontory, an ancient altar stood to Jove,
who thunders throughout the world. There Apollo discerned
Laomedon, who had started building himself the mighty
citadel of Troy. An enormous undertaking.
Apollo approved it and even resolved to help. He and Neptune
together put on the guise of mortals and offered themselves
as masons who, for a price, would build Laomedon's wall.   210
Done and done, and the walls rose up, but the king refused
to pay what he'd promised and owed. Indeed, he swore by
      the gods
that he'd never promised and didn't owe them a thing. The gods
would not suffer such lies, and Neptune decided to give
a fair reward to the king for his deviousness. The sea

rose up in waves that battered the walls, reduced them to rubble,
flooded the farmers' fields with water, and salted the plains
and meadows in a disaster that turned the whole region to
      wasteland.
What could the people do, or the king? The price for relief
was steep—a virgin, the king's own beloved daughter, Hesione,   220
must be bound to the rocks by the shore and offered up to a
      monster
in sacrifice to assuage the hurt her father had done.
Catastrophe! But the hero Hercules then appeared
with Peleus, his companion. They and their friends undertook
to save the daughter—for payment in so and so many horses
of Laomedon's famous herd. Again, it was done, and done.
The daughter was saved and the monster killed—and again,
      the king
reneged. So Hercules conquered Troy and slew its twice-perjured
king. To his friends he offered the daughter—whom
      Telamon took
for Peleus had been promised a goddess to take to wife,   230
and he, Aeacus' son and the grandson of Jove, would be wed
to Nereus' daughter, immortal, eternally lovely Thetis.
      Proteus once had foretold to Thetis—as warning? as
      promise?—
that she should conceive and bear a son to outshine his father,
which news, to Jove, who had lusted after the beautiful goddess,
was grim indeed. Should he risk that the earth might produce a
      rival,
one greater than even himself? He sent in his stead the son
of Aeacus, his grandson, to woo the aquatic maiden.
      There is an almost too pretty cove in Thessaly, forming
a regular arc like a sickle's. Myrtle hangs there with clusters   240
of berries to brighten the leaves. To this place, Thetis would come
on the back of a bridled dolphin, her bare breasts dazzles of spray.
There Peleus found her asleep on the beach, where he seized her
and tried to wrest by his strength what she had refused to grant
his importunate pleas and cajolings. He grabbed her around
      the neck
and tried to hold her, but she transformed herself into a bird.
He didn't let go of the bird, and she turned to a tree to whose
      trunk
he still held on, but the tree became in an instant a tiger,
and he wasn't ready for that and, in his shock, let go.
What to do now? He performed at the water's edge the proper   250

rituals, poured the wine, and burnt the entrails of sheep,
into the smoke of which he added savors of incense
to summon from out of the depths the god of changes. He came,
and Proteus spoke these words to Aeacus' son: "Try again,
waiting until she's asleep, but this time carry a net
and, no matter how many forms she assumes, hold on until
she is herself again." He was under the water and gone.

Night falls—but imagine the splendor of it, the fiery
Sun as it sizzles down into the water to westward
in a grand display that more than hints of miracles, glories,   260
or, at the very least, some meaning to things. The gorgeous
daughter of Nereus comes to her resting place in the cove,
and Peleus, waiting with snares and strong nets, springs out to
        grab her
fast in those knots and coils. She turns straightaway into creatures,
objects, frightening monsters, boulders. . . . But nothing works.
The nets hold, and at last Thetis resumes her original
shape and complains with a plaintive sigh that such an assailant
is either divine or must have had some godly assistance.
Cheerful, Peleus admits this, taking her into his arms
for the tender embrace he has longed for and to which she now
        submits,   270
recognizing as fate. And there they beget the mighty Achilles.

A fortunate man—one would say of one who married a
        goddess,
blessed in his son, his wife, and the course of his life—except
for that dreadful business back in his youth, when he killed his
        brother,
half brother really, Phocus. For this he was banished, impure
with blood guilt on his hands. He went to the land of Trachis,
where Ceyx, Lucifer's son, ruled with his father's brilliance
and cheerful grace, except that then he was in deep mourning
for the death of his brother Daedalion. To Trachis Peleus came
worn with his grief and guilt, and weary of travel. He landed   280
and left his men on the shore in charge of their flocks and herds
while he betook himself to the city walls and the palace
to beg asylum. Approaching, he held forth an olive branch
hung with the suppliant's wisps of wool and declared himself,
his name, race, and the place of his birth. And he formed
        the words
to tell the rest, the secret, the crime of which he was guilty. . . .
But could not, or dared not. Did not. Instead, he begged
        permission

to settle and live within the city walls or outside them.
The king replied reassuringly, saying, "We welcome strangers,
even without such noble lineage as you claim.   290
There's no need for your pleading. A descendant of Jove is
      welcome
with special warmth and honor. Pick out some land and settle
wherever you like. I only wish we could offer you better
and richer, as you deserve." Here, he broke down and wept.
When Peleus asked the cause of his grief, the king replied:
"See that bird, that raptor. He is no bird but a man,
changed to a feathered creature that flies through the air. My
      brother
was a bloodthirsty man, and he keeps still to his violent ways
and character. We were born to Lucifer, the morning
star. I was the placid and peaceful brother, while he   300
was the braver and more combative. He loved fighting and
      conquered
many kings and nations. Now, as a hawk he harries
birds, all of those gentle doves that flock about Thisbe.
A dismal story this is. He had a lovely daughter,
Chione by name, at fourteen a beauty *en fleur*,
with hundreds and hundreds of suitors. But nothing is safe
      or sure,
and it happened that Phoebus Apollo and Mercury together
saw the attractive girl, and both, smitten with love,
were rivals for her. Apollo bided his time until darkness,
but Mercury wasn't disposed to wait. He touched her eyelids   310
with his magic wand, which put her to sleep, and then he
      took her,
coming to her in a sudden violence she may have dreamed of.
Apollo, not at all put off by this, appeared
that night to enjoy the other's buttered bun. She conceived
and bore to each god a son. Mercury's boy was called
Autolycus, a sly and cunning creature who'd twist
your words in the air and make you agree that black was white.
Apollo's son was Philammon, famous for song and lyre.
So far, so good—or not, at any rate, too bad,
but Chione started to boast of how attractive she was,   320
how she had polyandrously borne two sons to two different
gods. Who else had done this? She was a goddess, she claimed,
the equal of any—Diana, for instance. This was an error
Diana proposed to correct. She let fly an arrow that silenced
the blathering woman, transfixing her tongue, her voice, and
      her life.

It was in my arms she died, this niece of mine whom I mourned
as if I had been her father. I went to my brother to tell him
what had befallen the girl, and it drove him mad, I'm afraid.
He was the cliff that the waves break on, roaring and sighing
in elemental despair. We bore her corpse to the pyre   330
and had to restrain Daedalion, who kept on trying to join her,
to fling himself on the burning wood in a last embrace
of his lost darling. Deranged, he was a bullock whose neck
is stung by hornets and rages over the trackless hills,
goaded by insupportable pain. We tried to follow,
but his was the strength and speed of a madman as he raced up
Parnassus' slopes to the top, where Apollo—his son-in-law—
took pity at last upon him. My brother hurled himself over
the topmost precipice hoping to smash on the rocks below,
but the god caught him and turned him there in midair to a bird   340
with claws and a great hooked beak, a hawk who glides over
       the land,
strong as ever and brave as he ever had been as a man,
looking for what to tear into bloody pieces and eat.

    As the son of the morning star was telling this story, Onetor,
one of Peleus' wranglers, came running in with disastrous
news of the herd. Great Ceyx fell silent at once as they all
heard the report: "I had driven the cattle down by the shore,
where some of them knelt down to rest in the midday Sun,
and others were wandering, browsing the marsh grass, or wading
       in cool
water up to their withers. It was near some simple old temple,   350
one of those fairly primitive timbered structures. This place,
a fisherman told me, is sacred to Nereus and to his daughters.
Near that temple, a little way back of it, there is a salt marsh
that's not quite dry at low tide. From this place we heard a
       roaring,
and then we beheld a huge beast, a slavering wolf with his jaws
caked with drool and blood, and eyes that were flaming with rage
more than simple hunger. Or maybe we thought that later,
after we saw him attacking one beast after another.
He wasn't apparently hungry but eager only for killing,
for blood and death. We ran down to drive him away, but the wolf 360
was hardly fazed. He charged and wounded some of the men.
I ran to get help. You must hurry. If we wait, there won't be a
       single
cow left alive or, for all I know, any herdsmen either.
We must get down there at once with reinforcements and
       weapons."

Ceyx told his men to put on their armor and grab
spears and lances and hurry down to the shore. He was dressing,
preparing to lead the party, when his wife came in, the queen,
Alcyone, who was troubled by terrible premonitions
and wanted him not to go, begged him with prayers and tears
to send the men willing to go but not to go there himself.   370
Ceyx looked displeased to be shamed so before his guest,
but Peleus spoke up and said to the queen, "Your fears
are groundless. Nothing will happen. No men need go. This
          is not
a mere wolf but a monster sent by the gods to torment me.
I must go myself to pray for remission of sin
and ask of the nereid Psamathe pardon for what I have done."
          There was, on a bluff near the shore, a lighthouse tower.
          To this
Peleus made his way and climbed up to get some idea
of how bad it was. The beach was a shambles, with bloodied and
          mauled
carcasses strewn about in a tableau of the violence the wolf   380
had done. And there he was, still prowling, a sinister beast,
worrying what was left of a dying heifer whose blood
had turned them both gory, a garnet horror that shone
in the late afternoon glare. Peleus held out his hands
and prayed to the sea nymph to ask forgiveness. He had not meant
to kill his half brother, her son. Accidents happen, and grief
must somehow be borne. And the guilt. But her bitter rage was
          more
than he, contrite, deserved. Could she believe and accept
his deep regrets, and relent? No, she refused him. But then
Thetis, Peleus' wife, added her prayers to her husband's,   390
and the grief-stricken nymph at last granted Peleus' prayer
and forgave him. That wolf on the beach, that dreadful
          representation
of wolfishness, froze and turned into marble. The heifer also
froze and hardened. And both turned from their red to an eerie
white, which inspired a different and greater degree of terror.
The Fates are sometimes hard—as they were in this instance,
          decreeing
that Peleus could not stay in Trachis but had to move on,
wandering even farther before he could find at last
an eventual haven somewhere. He moved on into Magnesia,
where in the end, in a fight with Acastus, that headstrong king,   400
he redeemed himself and regained the blessing of almighty Jove.

As one might imagine, Ceyx was much impressed by these strange
and disturbing events—his brother's fate had perhaps unsettled
his mind, and this business with wolves that turn into statues was
     scary.
He resorted, as some men do, to gods, and decided to ask
advice from the oracles. Surely, the power of heaven was such
as to force any prudent and sensible man to take care not to give
offense to these unruly powers. He planned to travel
to Claros, which, after Delphi, was Phoebus' favorite haunt—
but Delphi was under attack at this moment, for Phlegyas
     resented   410
Apollo's rape of his daughter, Coronis. To punish the wanton
god and show that mortals are not always inconsequential,
he raised an army to march on Delphi and burn it to ashes,
if it was the last thing he ever did . . . which it was.
But second only to Delphi was Claros, which Manto, the
     daughter
Teiresias left, had founded. Hard by the lake of her tears
in a small temple, a woman announced the words of the god.
She was the one whom Ceyx wished to consult. He proclaimed
his purpose to all—but the queen again had her premonitions
and begged him to change his mind. Frightened, chilled to her
     marrow,   420
and ashen, she begged her beloved husband to stay home.
     Her sobs
and tears made it hard to follow the words she gasped and
     choked on.
Her meaning, however, was perfectly clear. "How can you
     leave me
alone? I'll pine at your absence. Overland, it's a long
and arduous trip, but one I'd prefer to a voyage by sea,
which I fear, for my father's winds are wild and savage. You
     think
as his son-in-law you may get some special treatment. Not so!
Once they've escaped from Aeolus' cave, those winds are wild
and beyond anyone's control as they menace the clouds of heaven
itself. As a girl I watched them come home exhausted and spent,   430
and I learned to fear them then. Now I am petrified, surely,
for if you die my life is over and I shall be cursed
with every reluctant breath I draw as I wait to rejoin you.
Take me with you at least, so that storms may keep us together
in life or death, which I fear much less than to be left a widow."

How could he not have been moved by these plaintive words?
        The son
of the morning star adored his wife, but he hated choosing
between his journey and her. How could he live that way,
domesticated, diminished, unmanned, a kind of a lap dog?
He spoke whatever comforting words he could think of, but
        nothing   440
he said could assuage her griefs and fears—until he devised
a promise that he would return within two months. For that short
time, she could surely be brave and endure the trial of waiting.
She was hardly enthusiastic but could not hold out any longer
in the face of his resolve. She allowed herself to be soothed
and consented at last to his going. He ordered his ship to be
        readied
and manned for sailing. She watched the sailors set to their tasks,
and collapsed and gave way again to her terrors. They made no
        more sense
than did his voyage, but then they made no less. She was sure
she'd never see him alive again, and she wept and held him   450
in a desperate embrace, from which he broke away at the last
to board his vessel. There were no more details left to be checked,
no last-minute changes to make, and the men, arranged on their
        benches,
were ready to row and go. He boarded and gave the sign,
and the oarsmen pulled with a will, sweeping the long bright oars,
which flashed in the Sun and churned the sea in their rhythmic
        strokes.
Alcyone lifted her face and, with glistening eyes, stared out
at the man she loved, who was posed on the high-curved poop
        abaft
the mast, where he waved his hand. She waved back a last
        farewell,
and stared at the vessel, which dwindled into the middle distance   460
until the face was no longer distinguishable, or the figure.
Still she could see the ship and follow as it receded
to a smaller and smaller object. And then the whole hull was
        gone,
and only the sails remained as a tiny dab in the sky,
and that, too, disappeared. She gazed still at the empty
and desolate blue and then went to her empty bedroom to lie
on the huge and vacant bed and give herself over to weeping.
A piece of her body was gone, her life was gone, and this husk
remained, a derelict thing she scarcely could recognize.

The vessel had cleared the harbor and caught the freshening
    wind,
which set the rigging to singing and slapping against the spars.
The captain ordered the rowers to ship their oars and the sailors
to set the yards and make sail. The ship ran before the wind,
and behind it a churning wake fanned out on the sea's blue
    surface.
They made satisfactory progress all that day and had reached
a point of no return, with as much blue water astern
as remained ahead, when the wind picked up further. The water,
everywhere blue until now, was flecked with the whitecapped
    waves
sailors dislike. The Sun was low in the West, and the weather
turning worse every moment. The captain ordered the sails   480
reefed, but the wind in his face tore the words from his lips,
and the roar of the sea was louder than any human could shout.
The sailors nevertheless are doing what needs to be done,
some of them bailing the water washed in over the gunwales,
some of them closing the oar holes, and some of them reefing
    sheets,
while others secure the spars. Meanwhile the winds are raging
as if with evil intent, and the waves appear to be angry
and meaning the vessel harm. The captain is terrified now,
won't admit it, but cannot think what to do, what to order
or what to forbid. He prays to be spared but knows his belief   490
is minimal and his chances therefore bad, for the storm
is stronger than all his skill or the strength of the craft he sails.
The men are shouting and working as the waves crash over
    the bow,
enormous bilious green catastrophes. They are mountains
come to life that have turned spiteful as they hammer
an insignificant boat. The spray they churn up is topless
and seems to extend to the skies, to mix with the lowering clouds
that pile on the defenseless crew as bullies will do
in a free-for-all fight. In the day's last light, the dejected captain
looks out at the water, which churns in a dismal array of colors,   500
now a sickly tawny with the sands it has roiled from the bottom,
now the dismal black of the even deeper Styx,
or now a funereal white as the spume spreads out on the surface,
which hisses its derision. It's all a matter of luck,
always was, but the captain knows that his luck has run out,
and this is the end of the world, which is turning, pitching,
    yawing,

as the ship is heaved and plunged, tossing this way and that,
so there is neither an up nor a down, let alone a course
set on a two-dimensional chart. The ship lurches,
careens suddenly downward as if to fall into Acheron's   510
pit, but time after time it rights itself, and the water
punishes it each time for its impudence in surviving.
The timbers creak and shudder under the battering blows
of the crazed sea, and the captain feels each shock in his soul,
thinks of the ship as some desperate besieged town that a horde
of madmen is attacking, and each blow of the ram
against the gate is a warning of what the flesh will endure
of every man under arms, and every woman and child
after the strength of the beams of that gate has given out
to the rhythmic onslaught whose cadence is their own funeral
     march.   520
He looks out at the water the winds have lashed to a fury
and thinks in an oddly abstracted way that the waves are lions
that the wounds of hunters' spears have made more dangerous,
     charging
in single-minded rage. He hears the pegs of the hull
pop from a strain they were never built to withstand. He sees
the pitch that caulks the strakes washing away in the maelstrom
that rushes in to mix with the rain water that seethes
in the bilge. It's only a matter of time, he is sure, looking up
to check on the way the torrents of rain continue to fall
in opaque sheets. One would think the heavens were crazed with
     lust   530
to join the turbulent sea, which returned their bizarre passion
and tried to rise up and embrace the air as their waters mingled.
The sky is utterly black except when a bolt of lightning
throws a dreadful and livid glare on the skulls of the men,
whose flesh is still somehow—it is hard to believe—alive.
The waves continue to beat at the hull, each one a soldier
determined to scale the walls of that poor beleaguered fortress
and be the one to open the gates for the rest of the horde.
Nine waves try and fall back, but the tenth, with a mightier heave,
inundates the vessel and almost sinks it. The men   540
have lost their belief in their captain, their courage, their nautical
     skill,
and even their will to live as they wait for the end. One weeps
and groans aloud. Another, no braver, is silent, dumbstruck.
One calls on the gods for mercy. Another curses his fate.
One thinks of his wife and children. One envies landlubbers dying

warm and safe in their beds, with their families huddled about
them.
Ceyx thinks of his wife, who begged him not to attempt
this pointless journey, who saw that this would be how it would
end.
Alcyone's love was a treasure he'd been crazy to let slip away—
for surely that would now happen. It isn't death he dreads   550
but leaving her. He remembers she wanted to come, and rejoices
that she is not here in the boat. . . . But to see that face once
again,
what wouldn't he give? He opens his eyes and the water of sky
and sea is all but blinding. The mast shudders and cracks,
breaks away, and is washed overboard. They are lost, all lost.
The rudder is also gone, and the helpless hull is a toy
the waves can play with and torment, taking delight in their
triumph.
Then comes at last the monster wave, a mountain of water
or, worse, a flood that could wash whole mountains out of their
sockets
and into the sea—it towers and falls, overwhelming the tiny   560
broken vessel, and plunges it down to the bottom. Sailors
drown, sucked down with the ship. A few splash around in the
eddies,
clinging to broken spars and other such fragments of flotsam
as tumble by. One of these is Ceyx, whose hand once held
a jeweled scepter and now is clutching a length of timber,
calling now on his father-in-law, the lord of the winds,
and now on his father, the morning star, but none of it helps.
He calls on the name he loves best in the world, on Alcyone,
with a modest prayer—that his corpse may wash ashore at
her feet,
where she may with gentle hands prepare it to be entombed.   570
Again and again he calls her name, which the howling winds
shred to a garble. And then in the water it turns to a glug
and then to silence. That dawn, Lucifer hides his face
in thickest clouds of mourning for the loss of his precious son.
At home, meanwhile, the queen, counting the days and
nights,
works at her loom to fashion his homecoming present, a robe,
and one for herself to match. The incense she burns and the
prayers
she recites at the altar of Juno are useless, irrelevant now,
but she has no idea, and fervently asks of the gods

that they bring him back to her, keeping him safe and sound and
    faithful   580
(all too late, except for that last part of her plea).
    Juno, deeply troubled by these piteous hopeless prayers,
sent her messenger, Iris, to the house of Sleep to arrange
a nighttime visitation that might show her the sorry truth.
Iris put on her rainbow cloak and glittered across
the skies to the misty palace where the lord of dreams presides.
    Far off in remotest Campania, beyond where Cimmerians
    live
in their gloomy caves, is a deeper and even darker grotto,
the home of Sleep, where the Sun can never, even at midday,
penetrate with his faintest beams. In that cloudy twilight   590
no rooster dares disturb the silence with his rude crowing,
no dog or nervous goose gives voice to challenge the passing
stranger. No cattle low, nor do humans chatter and prate.
Not even branches sigh in occasional passing breezes,
but an almost total silence fills the air, in which one
may detect the barely audible murmur of Lethe's snore
from below in its gravelly bed, inviting an endless sleep.
At the mouth of this cavern, red-headed poppies nod soporific
blossoms, which radiate sweet and narcoleptic odors
into oppressive air. No doors are allowed in this singular   600
palace—lest their hinges should creak or their locks squeak
to disturb the night. At the heart of an almost painted stillness,
in a huge, darkened chamber, on a towering couch draped
in the thickest black duvets, the god himself relaxes,
drifting in languor. Around him the fragments of ill-assorted
dreams hover over the floor in grand profusion like leaves
the trees have let go to float through the currents of air and fall
in their gorgeous billows below, making impromptu pillows.
    Into this strange and breathless place, Iris intruded,
brushing aside the phantoms, wishes, and fears that blocked   610
the path she trod, which her brilliant garments lit as she moved.
The gloom of the room retreated, and in the big bed the sleeper
stirred, fluttered his heavy eyelids, which then in an instant
closed, but he had seen and recognized his guest.
He dozed as he gathered his energy and focused his attention
until, at last, he was able to speak in a kind of groggy
mutter words of welcome to his remote, obfuscate
abode. He rested a moment and then remembered to ask her
why she had come so far. "O somnolent one," she said,
"mildest of all the gods, soother of souls, and healer   620

of wearied and pain-wracked bodies and minds, I bring
    instructions.
Devise, if you can, some form to resemble King Ceyx,
the Lord of Trachis, and send in that guise to his wife, the queen.
Let her know the news of the wreck of his ship and the death
of the husband she loved so well. Juno has bidden you do this."
Then, with a hand to her mouth to conceal a yawn—for the place
had begun to affect her, too—Iris withdrew, retracing
her path to the shining heights of the sky from which she had
    come.
    Now the father calls out to one of his thousand sons.
It's Morpheus he summons, who knows the secrets of human   630
forms and can put on the look and gait and the habits of speech
of any man in the most uncanny way, as his brother
Icelos can put on disguises of birds or beasts
or serpents that creep on the ground. (Phantasos, another
brother, is said to be able to look like a rock or a tree
or even a puddle of water—any inert thing.
These three sons of Sleep present themselves at night
to the minds of chieftains and kings, while their younger brothers
    appear
to the common folks to enact their dreams as well as they can.)
Sleep rehearses Iris' message, and, waving a languid   640
good-by with a hand that falls in midgesture exhausted
back to the cushion, he sends Morpheus off to deal
with this business while he resumes his now well-deserved rest.
    On noiseless wings, his son darts through the gloom to arrive
at Trachis, where, taking off the wings, he assumes the look
of Ceyx, not as he was when he sailed, but Ceyx now—
his drowned face a puffy caricature, his eyes
dead and sad, and his beard and the hair on his head streaming
water more bitter than tears that pour from his eyes as he leans
over his sleeping wife to chide her: "Do you not know me?   650
Has death undone me so? Look at me, I charge you,
and know your husband's ghost. Your prayers have done no good,
for I am gone, beyond all help or hope forever.
I am not some bearer of tales, but the man himself
to whom it happened. Get up from your bed and put on the
    garments
of mourning. Weep for my death. Do not allow my shadow
to go down unlamented to the land of uncaring shadows."
He spoke these words in the way that Ceyx used to speak,
the tones and timbres his, and all the gestures and pauses

those of the husband she'd loved. He even wept real tears,   660
which poured onto her skin and burned like liquid fire.
He seemed so real, she reached out her arms to try to hold him,
to embrace him one last time, but her arms enfolded only
agonizingly empty air, and she cried aloud:
"Wait for me! Come back. Where are you going? Wait,
and I will go with you, as wives are supposed to go with their
          husbands."
The sound of her own voice woke her out of her dream,
and she looked around the darkened room, but he was gone.
One of her female attendants, hearing her cries, brought in
a lamp, and they held its flickering light in all the corners,   670
but nothing, nothing. . . . She wailed again, louder and longer,
and tore her sleeping garment and beat her breasts as she cried
for the worst thing in the world she could think of. It had
          happened,
and living now was a pointless burden, an imposition
of her stupid body. She pulled at her hair to inflict some pain
to match the pain of her soul. Her old nurse tried to console her,
but Alcyone would take no comfort from her. "He's gone.
And I am gone. We have died together. I saw him myself.
The poor waterlogged hulk of his corpse was here in this room.
I reached out my hands to hold him, but he was already air,   680
a shadow's shadow—but his. I knew him, pale and naked
and dripping from all that water. . . ." She knelt in the place he
          had stood
to search for the wet footprints he'd left, but they, too, were gone.
She thought she was going crazy. The world from moment to
          moment
was not to be trusted. She rocked on the floor, and each breath
          was a sob
or groan as she keened for her loss. "I told you. I knew it would
          happen
and begged you not to go. I felt it was wrong, was risky—
that a terrible thing would happen. I knew the day you sailed
I had lost you forever. The ship, my hopes, and my life grew
          smaller
all at the same time. You should have allowed me to come,   690
for then we would be together in death. This is no good,
no good—that I should be living and you be elsewhere or
          nowhere.
I drown now in the air, am wrecked here on the land,

where the currents are just as cold and cruel, and the pain is as
        great
as waves of unbearable grief wash over me in dreadful
storms no soul can expect to survive. I see my end
and will not struggle against it. Instead, I shall cleave to your spirit
and dwindle away. Our ashes may not be inurned together,
but a single gravestone's letters shall spell out both our
        names. . . ."
And here her words dissolved to the pure vowel sounds of
        keening   700
from the depths of her hurt heart, which continued all night long.
    Morning came, and the grieving woman walked forth from
        the palace
and down to the strand where she'd stood to watch his boat
        disappear,
dwindling into the offing. The iodine tang in the air
was reassuringly real. She remembered how on that other
terrible day she had stood there and kept her moans to herself,
which she felt welling up from her vitals. Now she could let
        them loose
to the empty sea and the sky, where they did neither harm nor
        good.
She remembered his last kiss, the way he turned to the ship,
walked a few steps, looked back, could not quite bear it,
        continued   710
into the vessel and out to sea. . . . Again her eyes brimmed
with tears she rubbed away with instinctive fists. And she saw
something afloat out there in the harbor. A creature swimming?
Or no, it seemed not to move except as the waves and the current
tossed its indifferent bulk. An animal then? Some fish?
It drifted in toward shore, and she startled. A human corpse?
A shipwrecked sailor! The omen struck her, but what did it mean?
"Poor man, whoever you are," she started to say, "alas
for your wife and your children. . . ." But then her breath caught
        in her chest
as it drifted closer still, and she saw it was he whom she mourned.   720
She shrieked with a birdlike cry into the seaside air,
and her fingernails raked her cheeks, and she tore her widow's
        garments.
She waded into the surf and reached out her hands to the dreadful
hulk, calling out, "Ceyx, o dearest, o poor, poor Ceyx!
Is this how you return?" There was, at the harbor, a mole

of large stones men had built to shelter the cove. To these
rocks she hurried and clambered out to the end, from which
she leapt into the wash of the sea, or over it, skimming
the tops of the waves, still crying that same mournful birdcry,
long and drawn out, and her mouth drew out and hardened
      to beak.   730
She was, by the time she reached his floating corpse, a sea bird,
and she settled onto this lifeless body and spread her arms,
which now were wings to embrace and protect him. She tried
      to kiss
the cold flesh with her bill, and, by some trick of the ocean's
heaving, it seemed that his head reached up to hers in response.
He couldn't have felt her kissing. But better ask how the gods
could not have felt it, could not therefore have shown their
      compassion,
for the dead body was changing, restored to life and renewed
as another sea bird, that mate whose loss Alcyone mourned.
Together they still fly just over the water's surface,   740
and mate and rear their young, and for seven days each winter
Alcyone broods on her nest that floats on the gentled water—
for Aeolus, her father, then keeps the winds short-reined
and grants to the sea for that week a respite of peace and safety
for the sake of those helpless nestlings, his grandsons and
      granddaughters.
      Thus, some waterfront geezer will tell you how things are,
and point to the birds and recite their story. Another old salt
will nod and point to another bird, that long-necked diver,
and tell the yarn that explains why this one behaves as he does:
"No ordinary bird you see out there, but a fellow   750
of royal blue blood, he comes from a line that traces back
through Ilus and Assaracus, and Ganymede whom Jove
took up with him to Olympus to serve him there, and old
Laomedon, and Priam, the last of Trojan kings.
King Priam was his father, and Hector his half brother. . . .
If he'd lived, and if fate had been otherwise, he could well
      have been
another Hector, as brave and famous. . . . Who knows how these
      things
happen in this life? On Hecuba Priam begot
Hector, but on the daughter of the two-forked Granicus River,
Alexirhoë, he begot in secret this one, Aesacus,   760
who was born in Ida's foothills. Maybe that's why he hated
palaces, city walls, the jostle of streets and alleys,

preferring the quieter life of the woods and the mountainsides.
He kept to himself mostly but wasn't indifferent to women,
and he took a liking and more than that to Hesperia, daughter
of the River Cebren. He'd seen her drying her hair in the Sun
on the banks of her father's stream. When the nymph saw him,
    she ran
as a doe runs from the wolf or a duck from the circling hawk.
A chase, then, friendly enough, but suddenly she falls.
It's a snake in the grass, a viper, and she has been running
    barefoot.   770
She's hurt by its bite, is killed, in fact. And the lover stops dead
in his tracks and is stricken with grief and terrible guilt. He feels
like the serpent's accomplice and wishes he'd never seen her or
    chased her.
He wants still to run after her, to comfort her or atone
for what he has done. He calls aloud to the trees and rocks,
'I never meant to hurt her. I wish I had never beheld
that lovely creature, whose ruin I seem to have caused. It's my
    own
fault, my blindness, my lust. . . .' And he runs to a high cliff top,
where the waves have chewed a hollow below, and he hurls
    himself
over and into the sea. But Tethys pities the lad,   780
retrieves him as he's falling, sticks feathers on him, and makes him
into a kind of a bird. He isn't pleased, but keeps on
diving into the water, surfacing, soaring again
and plunging, over and over, as if his spirit were still
intent on this precipitous ending. The spirit rebels,
detests the body, the world, and it hurls the desperate creature
down. Its feathers break its fall, and it slices unharmed
into the waves. This only enrages him further. He keeps
at it. Aesacus' frenzy and the exercises have made him
stronger than ever. That bird is the one we call a merganser—   790
the *mergus* part meaning 'diver,' and the *anser* being 'goose.'
It couldn't be any better designed to do what it does,
with its small head, long neck, and slender legs like arrows.
It spots a fish and dives down to the fish's death or its own—
he doesn't seem to care a hell of a lot which one."

BOOK XII

Father Priam had no idea that his son Aesacus
was still living. That bird he may very well have noticed
soaring and diving out there meant nothing to him. He mourned
this lost child. At the empty tomb, his brothers—Hector
and all the others but Paris—offered prayers in his honor.
Paris, off somewhere else on a long trip, returned
soon enough and with trouble: a stolen wife and a train
of a thousand ships full of angry Greeks set upon vengeance.
They would have come more quickly, but the winds had been
    blowing wrong,
and their army was stuck on the coast of Boeotia, at fish-rich
    Aulis,   10
where the Greeks consulted, prayed, and prepared their customary
sacrifices to please or appease the god of the winds.
When the altar was glowing with sacred fire that crackled and
    danced,
there came a giant serpent, which crawled up a nearby plane tree,
where high on a branch was a nest with eight young fledglings the
    mother
was rearing. These, the serpent devoured, gulping all nine
birds in dreadful omen. Of what? Calchas considered
and then explained to the host what he thought the portent meant:
"We shall assuredly conquer. Let us, therefore, rejoice.
But the task will not be easy. It will take us nine long years   20
of bloody and brutal war—one for each of those birds."
As soon as he had stopped speaking, the serpent turned to a stone
monument curling around the tree, which was also stone.
    But North Wind kept on blowing, and the ships were stuck
      in the harbor,
and there couldn't be any war until they put out to sea.
Some supposed it was Neptune protecting the walls of Troy
he'd helped to build, himself. But Calchas, son of Thestor,
wasn't convinced. He was sure Diana was angry, the virgin

goddess to whom the Greeks had to offer a virgin's blood.
A terrible judgment indeed, and Agamemnon the father   30
struggled with Agamemnon the king—whose concern for his
      people
and army and common good and fate outweighed the private
grief he felt. With tears streaming down, he ordered—do it,
take Iphigenia and shed her innocent blood
at the goddess' altar. Diana, moved, however, to pity,
spread a cloud of confusion throughout the camp and changed
the girl at the last minute into a fine young doe,
whose shed blood calmed the waves and shifted the winds to blow
fair for Troy so the thousand land-bound ships could depart,
as they did, forthwith. After many vicissitudes, they reached   40
the distant Phrygian shore, where Priam's citadel loomed.
    There is a far-off place at the center of earth and sea
and sky where those three realms abut. There Rumor lives
in her lofty castle perched on a mountaintop. Her house
has a thousand open windows, and the entranceways are
      countless,
but nowhere is there a door for servants to close. The world's
sights and sounds all come here, words, images, gestures
swirling together by night and day where the corridors' brazen
walls echo and hum in an endless susurration,
a welter of words, a babble of phrases and broken phonemes,   50
which may mean nothing or much. It is never silent here,
and yet no single voice rises from out of the murmur
and seethe of continual whispers. The waves of the sea from a
      distance
sound like that, or the first or the last mutters of thunder
when Jove is making a storm that is far away. In the halls,
crowds of apparently busy people are coming and going
on various urgent errands, but along the way they exchange
rumors, falsehoods and truths jumbled together but all
passed on from one to another. As it travels along, a story
takes on a life of its own, growing, changing, reversing   60
its implication, as Error embellishes here and there,
Credulity simplifies, Generosity touches up
and improves wherever she can, or Panic darkens the palette
to suggest a world more in keeping with what she has always
      believed.
Rumor herself attends to whatever is written or said,
in heaven, at sea, or on land, grist for her mill of stories.
    She was the one who reported the news of the Greek armada

approaching the Phrygian shore. The Trojans, therefore, were
     ready
with shoreline fortifications. The first Greek off the boats,
the first to set foot on the beach, was Protesilaüs, the first   70
to fall bleeding and die—the victim of mighty Hector's
spearpoint. The battle was joined, and the precious blood
     spilled out
as each side tested the other's mettle of valor and strength.
The stony shingle turned to an abattoir's gory floor,
and Greeks and Trojans hacked, stabbed, and clubbed one
     another.
Cycnus, the son of Neptune, had chalked up his tenth and
     hundredth
and thousandth kill. Achilles, on the other side, was riding
back and forth in his chariot, a farmer harvesting corpses,
killing whole ranks with that famous ashen spear from the tree
that had grown on Pelion's flank. But his eye was on grander
     prey—   80
Hector he wanted, or else, if fate should deny him this prize
so early in these proceedings, then Cycnus would do as well.
He lashed his horses, whose snowy necks strained at the harness,
and pointed his chariot straight at the enemy's line as he shook
his spear above his head and shouted, "Whoever you are,
you strong or lucky fellow, prepare to die. Be proud
to be dispatched by the hand of Achilles of Thessaly—me!"
He hurled first these words and then his great ashen spear,
which flew through the air and bounced, harmless, off Cycnus'
     chest.
The latter called back in reply, "Hear me, o son of Thetis,   90
I am unscathed. A marvel! This armor I wear is merely
for show. I could take off the helmet, breastplate, and greaves,
and ride, as Mars himself could if he chose, stark-naked
into the fray. You are proud to be son of Nereus' daughter,
but I am a son of him who rules over Nereus, lord
of all the wide blue seas!" He punctuated his sentence
with the exclamation point of his spear, which stuck in the shield
Achilles carried, piercing nine layers of hide and stopping
at last at the tenth. The hero shook it free and replied,
flinging another spear at the enemy standing before him.   100
Again, the Trojan survived unhurt, untouched. Achilles
threw yet a third spear that Cycnus defied, not moving
or even trying to dodge this missile—and nothing happened.
Achilles now was enraged, a bull in the sandy arena

that charges the fluttering cape, misses, and charges again,
and the horns never find any solid target of meat or bone,
but only the empty air. He picked up one of the spears
and looked to see that the brazen point had not fallen off.
It was still there on the shaft. How then to explain this business?
"Is my arm, after all, so weak? Has my strength abandoned
　　　me now?　　　　　　　　　　　　　　　　　　　　110
It was more than enough to tear down Lyrnesus' walls, and
　　　to hurt
at Tenedos and at Thebes, awash in their warriors' blood.
The Caïcus also ran red with blood, and Telephus twice
learned to fear my spearpoint and what it could do. At Troy,
I have piled the corpses as high as cordwood that this right arm
has, in its strength, destroyed." Then, because words are easy
and deeds are the only test of the truth, he hurled his spear
at Menoëtes, one of the Lycian soldiers, and skewered
the man through his breastplate. He fell like a chopped tree to the
　　　ground
and twitched his head and died. Achilles pulled out the spear　　120
from the hot wound it had made and held it up. "This spear
is dangerous still and can do to you what it did to him."
Saying this, he hurled the weapon once more at Cycnus.
It struck with a clang on the left shoulder and bounced away
but left a pretty patch of blood on the armor. A wound?
That's what Achilles thought for a moment, but then he saw
it was Menoëtes' blood that had spattered onto Cycnus'
entirely unscathed trunk. The mighty Achilles, enraged,
leapt down from his chariot, drew his sword from its scabbard,
and closed for hand-to-hand fighting, hacking away at his quarry,　130
cleaving his helmet and slicing his shield, but not even scratching
his body. The smooth white skin was like rock and blunted the
　　　sword.
To hell with it then. He turned the sword around and beat him,
using the sword as a club to bludgeon his face and head.
Cycnus gave ground, retreating. The other pressed after him,
　　　raining
blow upon blow. Now Cycnus is frightened, confused.
　　　Giving way,
he backs himself onto a boulder. Achilles grabs him, trips him,
throws him down to the ground, kneels on his chest, pins him,
seizes the knot of his helmet's laces, and chokes off his air,
twisting the rawhide thongs so that Cycnus can't breathe. He
　　　kills him　　　　　　　　　　　　　　　　　　　　140

and then begins to strip the armor, his prize, from the body,
but the armor is empty. The body is gone, changed to a bird,
the beautiful white swan whose name he had always worn.

      After such a battle, both sides agreed on a truce,
a respite from fighting in which they could lay down their arms
      to rest,
recoup, and regroup. The Trojans detailed guards to the walls,
and the Greeks posted sentries along their trenches and
      earthworks.
They declared, meanwhile, a feast day. Achilles offered his thanks
to Pallas for what had happened with a heifer he slew. The entrails
burned on the altars, and wreaths of smoke, which delight the
      gods,   150
ascended through fragrant air to heaven. The portions for mortals
were served in proper form and order to chiefs who reclined
on couches, sipping their wine, while musicians played sweet
      music
on flutes, harps, and bouzoukis. Late into that evening
they talked, exchanging stories of battles, of pains endured,
of perils overcome, and how, in a hard and uncertain
world, men and women survive and even sometimes triumph.
Of what other subjects should warriors speak in Achilles'
      presence?
They talked, of course, of the battle with Cycnus, and how his
      body
was proof against all weapons—a marvel, surely. Its like   160
nobody there could recall—except for Nestor, who told them,
"In your generation, no, there never has been such a thing,
but long ago, I saw another man whose body,
even after a thousand strokes of spear or sword,
was absolutely untouched! I speak of Caeneus, who lived
in Thessaly, high on the wooded slopes below Mount Othrys.
A fellow famous for warlike exploits . . . I'll get to them,
but the really remarkable part of his story is that he was born
as a girl, and only later changed to a man." This detail
fascinated Nestor's audience, who then begged him   170
to continue and tell them more. Achilles himself spoke up,
"Sir, give us the pleasure and benefit of your wisdom.
Tell us who was this Caeneus, and how and why he was changed
from woman to man, and say what battles he fought and with
      whom."
Nestor cleared his throat, took a sip of wine, and commenced
to tell the tale: "A lot that has happened to me, those things

I've seen with my own eyes or heard other men speak of,
time has blurred. But there are some things I'll never forget—like
    this,
a most peculiar business. Nothing in war or peacetime
is clearer now in my mind. I've lived a very long time,   180
for two generations of men, and now am well into the third.
And these events of Caeneus' life could have happened last week.

    "Elatus had a daughter, a delightful girl named Caenis,
who became in time a beauty for whom many suitors yearned.
Throughout the Thessalian towns—even in yours, Achilles—
people spoke of this truly gorgeous creature. Your father
would, no doubt, have heard these reports (which didn't concern
    him,
for the Fates had already arranged the match between him and
    your mother).
Caenis didn't seem pleased by any of these proposals,
and the story is that she strolled alone one day on the seashore,   190
where Neptune saw her, wanted her, emerged from the water,
    and took her—
raped her there on the beach. When it was finished, he asked her
what he might do to please her, as she had so much pleased him.
'Choose whatever you want. Name it and you shall have it.'
And Caenis said, 'What I want is not to be ravished again,
ever. . . . I have a serious prayer that matches the serious
wrong you have just now done me. I want you to make me a man
so that nothing like this can happen again.' As she spoke, her
    voice
began to resonate deeper and fuller. The god of the ocean
had granted her prayer. Her body was turning to that of a male— 200
and, to make it an even better gift, Neptune allowed it
the further favor—that never should swords or weapons wound it.
Caenis, renewed as Caeneus, left the beach rejoicing,
to roam wherever and do whatever he would as a man.

    "Now that it all comes back, I see how what happened then
is like what happened just now with Cycnus. A wedding feast—
I remember that—for the rites to unite our friend Pirithoüs
and Hippodamia. Splendid! A huge crowd was invited,
even the cloud-born centaurs, who were only too eager to come.
All of the chiefs were there, as I was myself. The palace   210
was hung with festoons, and the halls rang with the singing of
    songs.
There were smells of roasting meat. In came the bride and her
    train

of young matrons and wives. We all gasped at her beauty
and said to the proud bridegroom what no one should ever say
aloud—that he was indeed a fortunate man. Unlucky
to say such words, for Eurytus, one of the centaurs, the wildest
and randiest, of course had too much to drink, got sloshed,
forgot where he was, and attacked the bride. He dragged her away
to have her himself. A fight ensued at once, a melee,
a battle royal with tables upset and china and glassware   220
flying about the room, for the rest of the centaurs joined in,
picked out attractive women, and dragged them off or attacked
      them
there in the banquet hall—it looked like a conquered town
that troops were laying waste. Except they'd forgotten the battle,
the lack of which we made good on the instant. Theseus hollered
that Eurytus had to be crazy, giving offense to two men
at the same time. The women were shrieking in fear and disgust
at what those half-men, half-horses—and total brutes—were
      trying
to do to them. We attacked them, flailing, punching, and beating
with our bare hands or whatever there was to grab. On a stand   230
behind the high table, there stood an ancient crater, a giant
cauldron covered with bas-reliefs. This Theseus hefted
over his head and flung it, full as it was of wine,
at Eurytus, hitting him full in the face. There was wine all over
and blood, and mixed in were gobbets of brain, and he fell down
      dying.
His brothers, the other centaurs, were furious now and rallied,
out for revenge and emboldened by wine, shouting their insults,
and altogether crazed. There were bottles and flasks in the air
and basins. It looked like some jugglers' act gone out of control,
funny except for the cries on all sides of the injured and dying.   240
      "Amycus, one of the centaurs, went to the shrine to plunder
the sacred regalia and seize an enormous bronze candelabrum.
He raised it over his head as a priest will raise an axe
over the neck of a sacrificial bull, and he swung it
down upon Celadon's head, crushing the face of the noble
Lapith. The bones of his face were smashed; his eyes popped out
from the ruined orbits; his nose was driven into his brain.
Amycus watched him die and then felt the terrible impact
of Pelates' blow with the leg of a maple table that felled him.
He was down on the ground, dazed, spitting out blood and teeth   250
when Pelates hit him again, and this time the blow was mortal.
      "Another centaur, the wild-eyed Gryneus, close by the altar,

called out his challenge, 'You want trouble? Then here is trouble!'
and picked up the whole altar, fire and all, and hurled it
into a group of the Lapith chiefs not far off, and two—
Broteas, I remember, and Orios also—were crushed
in dreadful deaths. To avenge them, Exadius found a weapon,
a pair of stag's antlers on the wall as a decoration
and votive dedication. These he grabbed and charged
like a crazed beast, and, whether by luck or skill, he hit   260
at Gryneus' eyes. The tines of the antlers gouged the eyeballs
out of his head. One stuck on the point like a cocktail cherry.
The other broke and hung in the centaur's beard, a gobbet
of glistening bloody goo. From the centaur's company, Rhoetus
caught up a burning brand of wood from the altar and whirled it
around and around his head. He smashed Charaxus' temples
and set his hair on fire, so the blood that oozed from the wound
sizzled like grease in a pan. Charaxus, insane with the pain,
reached for whatever was close and huge to throw at the centaur.
In desperation he raised the threshold stone from the doorway,   270
an enormous piece of chiseled rock, and tried to throw it
back in the centaurs' midst. No sane man would have tried
to lift that rock, much less throw it. And he did well
to get it up in the air, but not even he could fling it
across the room. It fell far short and hit Cometes,
his friend and ally, and killed him. And Rhoetus stood there and
        laughed
and called out to the Lapiths his taunt: 'So may you all
be brave and strong, until there are none of you left. We'll watch!'
Having said this, he charged and attacked Charaxus again,
hitting him heavy blows at the back of the head and smashing   280
the bones of the skull, which collapsed to mix with the mess of
        his brains.
      "Now, filled with the power that victory gives one, Rhoetus
turned on another group of likely Lapiths, Euagrus,
Corythus, and Dryas. His blazing brand dispatched
Corythus first, a boy with the first down of manhood
on his cheeks. He fell on that downy face, and Euagrus cried out,
'Where is the honor in killing a mere boy? What glory
can you find in that?' There might have been more, but Rhoetus
        poked
that torch into the open mouth of Euagrus and down
his throat, and the words fried, turned to a shriek of pain,   290
which soon enough died away. Now to the last of the group,
Dryas, the centaur turned to finish the job, but this time

with much less luck, for Dryas picked up a charred stick,
which had spilled onto the floor from the flung altar, and stabbed
the charging centaur right where the neck and the shoulder meet.
Rhoetus cried out in pain and managed to pull the stick
out of his muscle and bone, as blood welled up from the wound.
He fled the room and the battle, at the same time Orneus fled,
and Lycabas and Medon, who'd taken a wound in the shoulder.
Thaumas also ran off, and Pisenor. Mermeros, too. . . .   300
Mermeros was the speedster but now, with that wound in his
        foot,
wasn't anywhere near so fast. The centaur's numbers
were dwindling sharply, for Philus had fled, and Melaneus,
and Abas, the hunter of wild boar, and the augur, Asbolus—
he'd known that something was wrong and had tried to persuade
        his friends
not to come, or stay, or fight, but they hadn't listened.
On the way out, though, he offered some reassuring advice,
as he said to Nessus, his friend, 'You're safe. Nothing can happen
for you to fear today. Your fate awaits in the future,
in the quiver where Hercules keeps his envenomed arrowheads.'   310
But many centaurs died that day: Eurynomous fell,
and Lycidas, and Areos and Imberus, too, all these
slain by the hand of Dryas, who fought them face to face.
Another centaur, Crenseus, seeing this carnage, turned
to run away, but he made the mistake of looking behind him
to see if he was pursued—and a flying javelin hit him,
at the top of the nose where it joins the forehead between the eyes.
    "A peculiar business, this fighting. Aphidas lay on the floor
dead to the world, as we say, having drunk a good deal of wine.
He'd curled up, fast asleep in a bearskin under the table,   320
where he lay snoring softly. Phorbas, one of the centaurs,
saw him there and called out, 'Mix your wine with the stronger
water that flows in the Styx, you sot!' and he threw a spear
at the sleeping man. The iron tip transfixed his neck
and pieced his brain, and the saying was made good, for he was
dead to the world. Blood poured from the wound and into the
        cup
his hands, still clenched, appeared to be holding, as if in a toast.
    Another centaur, Petraeus, I saw hugging an oak tree
out in the courtyard and trying to pull it up by its roots,
or break its trunk so he could use the thing as a weapon.   330
But Pirithoüs also saw him, watched for a moment,

and then hurled a spear that hit him and pinned him fast
to the trunk of the tree, like a butterfly someone has killed and
    mounted.
Pirithoüs also killed Lycus, Chormis, and mighty
Helops. I saw that last terrible death myself,
as the javelin pierced Helops' right temple and then came out
on the other side near the left ear. It was truly awesome.
Dictys turned away and was running from Ixion's son,
who chased him and pressed him hard until Dictys stumbled
    and fell
over a garden wall on the terrace and onto a tree   340
below, which he broke, and the spikes of the splintered wood
    impaled him.
"To even the score, Aphareus tore a sizable boulder
out of the hillside and made to throw it, but Theseus saw him
and gave him a clout with his huge club that smashed the arm
and turned his elbow to mush. Theseus then jumped up
onto Bienor's back and rode him—centaurs detest this!—
and, grabbing his hair in the left hand, used the club in the right
to smash Beinor's skull in that tender place near the temple.
Then with that club he walloped Nedymnus and Lycopes,
killed them and slew long-bearded Hipassos, and Ripheus,   350
tall as a tree. This list of victims continued with Thereus,
who had earned a degree of fame for catching bears in the woods
and bringing them back alive to tame and keep as living
trophies. The centaur Demoleon, watching this series of killings,
decided to interfere, pulled a dead pine from the ground
roots and all, and whirled it and hurled it at Theseus' head. . . .
Either Theseus saw it coming or maybe Minerva
gave him a quick warning. In any event, he ducked,
and the tree sailed harmlessly past him. Nevertheless, it hit
Crantor full in the chest and sheared off his whole left arm.   360
You surely remember Crantor, your father's old armor bearer?
The Dolopian king Amyntor gave him as hostage to Peleus
in pledge of their treaty of peace. Your father, watching him
    bleed,
and knowing he was dying, cried out in his grief and anger,
'At the least you shall have your funeral meats,' and he hurled his
    ashen
spear at Demoleon's ribs. It hit him and quivered there,
for the point was stuck in the bone. The centaur tugged on the
    shaft

and managed to pull it out, but the head remained inside him,
and whenever he moved or breathed it caused him such
      exquisite pain
as to drive him utterly mad. He reared, cried out, and tried   370
to strike at Peleus' head and shoulders with those sharp hoofs
that rang out on the hero's helmet and shield. In his other
hand, Peleus kept his swordpoint poised, and he drove it
into the breast of the centaur where the human and equine parts
come together, and killed him. He had by then killed many:
Phlegraeos and Hyles with spears he had thrown, and then,
in closer combat, Iphinoüs, Clanis, and now odd Dorylas,
who affected a wolf's-hide cap onto which he had fastened horns
he'd bloodied during the fracas. I had myself called out
that his horns would do him no good, as I threw my spear at
      his head.   380
He put up his hand, from instinct I guess, to protect himself.
My spear went right through the hand and pinned it onto his
      forehead.
Peleus then, who was near him, gave him a thrust with his sword
into the side of his belly. The stricken centaur leapt forward
but left behind a trail of guts his hind feet stepped on
as they unraveled. The legs were tangled up in his gleaming
entrails, and then he fell, groaned once or twice, and died.
      "Maybe the handsomest centaur was one called Cyllarus,
        young. . . .
The human part was splendid, with that down of youth on his
      cheeks
and blond hair he wore long so it flowed like a girl's.   390
His neck, shoulders, and chest were those any sculptor or painter
might either have envied or else dismissed as too nearly perfect.
The equine part was also attractive, as horses can be,
with a deep, well-muscled chest, a strong back, and a rump
all jet black but a snow-white tail, and the legs were white.
He was the kind of creature all female centaurs adored,
but his heart belonged to Hylonome, the loveliest centaur
in all the woods. She would comb her long hair and entwine
sprigs of fragrant rosemary or violets into her tresses,
or roses or sometimes lilies. She liked to refresh her face   400
in the brook that babbled along the heights of Pagasa or bathe
in the stream where it widens and deepens. She decked her body
      in hides
she had cleverly sewn together in a kind of oat couture.

But their love was no joking matter. They were always together in
    woods
and fields, and in caves they'd found in which they took shelter
    from storms.
Inseparable, they were, a single four-legged creature,
and they'd come to this wedding feast of the Lapiths, of course
    together.
They fought on the centaur side. A javelin somebody threw—
it was never clear who this was—hit Cyllarus low in the neck,
and he shuddered and fell, and his body quivered and then was
    still.   410
Hylonome embraced him, tried to staunch the bleeding,
and, placing her lips on his lips, attempted to keep him breathing,
or at least to prevent that last breath of the soul from escaping.
But nothing helped. He was cold and dead. And her heart
    was cold
and dead. She said some words no one could catch in that din,
and then she threw herself onto the spear that had killed him
and, holding her love in that fatal embrace, let go of the world.
    "I remember another centaur, the doughty Phaeocomes,
who had tied a half-dozen lion skins together to make
a shield he held in front of his chest in one hand. The other   420
swung around his head an enormous log it would take
a couple of teams of oxen just to drag along on the ground.
Tectaphos, son of Olenus, he hit in the head and crushed
the front of his skull. His face was a horror, with brains and blood
and snot all dripping the way that the curdled milk drips down
through the cloth when you're making cheese. Phaeocomes
    dropped the log,
and started to strip the body and claim the armor, but I
poked the tip of my sword into his groin. Your father
was there, saw it, and cheered, and perhaps has told you the story.
Chthonius, too, I killed, who fought with a huge forked stick,   430
and Teleboas, whose spear gave me this wound. . . . You can see
the scar, here, from that day. A terrible day, I thought then,
but now I am old and long for the strength I had then, and the
    courage.
What could I not do here if I were that young man again?
I would be ready to fight any Trojan—Hector himself.
But he wasn't born back then or else was a babe in arms,
and the days have stolen my strength and tamed that battle,
    turned it

into an old man's hazy story. You nod and approve
as I speak of Periphas killing the centaur Pyraethus. Those names,
what do they mean now? Or Ampyx? He was the Lapith   440
who poked a headless spear into Echeclus' forehead and
          killed him.
I saw it, was there, but it's all remote, or they're separate bits
of odd events. Macareus grabbed a crowbar and hurled it
at Erigdupus' chest, and it hit him just right, and he died.
Nessus, of whom you have heard, threw a spear that impaled
Cymelus—I think in the groin. At any rate, he died.
Details blur, and only the names remain, and when I
am gone they will be gone as well. You all know Mopsus
as prophet and seer, but I remember his fighting prowess.
Hodites, the centaur, was about to speak, to challenge   450
or taunt someone of the Lapiths, when Mopsus threw a spear
that pinned his tongue to his chin and his chin to his throat, and
          the roar
rose in pitch and then gurgled with blood that he spilled and
          drowned in.
          "But what was the point of this story? What got me started?
          The fighting
was brutal, fierce, but . . . oh, yes! I was telling the tale of
          Caeneus
and how he died. He was there that day, and he fought
          alongside us.
Styphelus he killed, and Bromus, Antimachus, Elymus, and also
Pyracmos, who fought, I believe, with a double-edged battle-
          axe, huge,
but it did him no good. I cannot remember how each of
          them died,
but the names and the number, I think, are correct. In any event,   460
Latreus, an enormous centaur, came on, having killed
and stripped the body of Alesus. In his prime he was, this centaur,
at the peak of his vigor. His hair was silver around the temples,
and yet he was fit, all muscle and bone, and he waved his lance,
one of those Macedonian pieces with bits of ribbon
along the shaft, and he pranced around in a circle calling
insults and jeers to Caeneus—or 'Caenis' was what he said,
'for you were a girl and still are the girl the god of the sea
put it to on the beach, as I will do here again,
to show you up! Go home and tend to your knitting basket.   470
Leave the fighting to men.' He whinnied a centaur's laugh,
which stopped abruptly as soon as Caeneus had hurled his spear,

which grazed the centaur's side and left a long welt in his hide.
It must have hurt, for Latreus returned the attack with a throw
of that barbarous lance that sailed through the air and hit his face
but bounced away having done no damage, not even a scratch.
You'd have thought a hailstone or pebble had bounced off a tiled
      roof.
The centaur closed and prepared to strike with his short sword,
      shouting,
'Your luck—and that's all it is—has run out now, little darling.'
He struck with the sword but nothing happened. It would not
      stick in   480
or through the skin. He poked, hacked, beat with the metal
on the flesh of his foe, but he might as well have been trying to
      slice
a marble figure. He hit at the groin, and the blade clanged
like a struck gong and shattered in pieces onto the floor.
The centaur stared down in shock with his mouth hanging open.
      The other,
Caeneus, smiled and asked, 'Giving up so easily? Try!
It isn't so hard to do,' and he took his sword and thrust
deep into the centaur's vitals and twisted the blade,
making Latreus' wound inside a gaping mess.
The centaur keeled over, fell, and the other centaurs swarmed   490
in rage and fear about the man who had done this thing,
hurling lances and spears, which bounced off and fell away
like so many toys. Caeneus stood there unharmed, not moving,
not even trying to dodge their ineffectual blows.
One of the centaurs, Monychus, called to his brothers, 'Shame!
Shall we let a single man, who is scarcely a man, defy us?
What is the good of our strength? What good to be wise as a man
and strong as a horse, if this haughty creature stands there and
      mocks us?
For Ixion's sake—our father who aspired even to Juno's
bed—we must cut him down to size and teach him respect!   500
If we cannot break his skin, that doesn't mean he's immortal.
Let us try another and simpler method: stones
piled upon stones will crush him to death with their weight.' He
      picked up
a huge tree trunk the North Wind had lately blown down and
      flung it
at Caeneus' head. Now the others were heaving boulders and
      trees,
stripping the woods of Othrys and Pelion, too, to cover

this enemy up to his head and over, to bury alive
this foe against whom their weapons were useless. Still
    unwounded,
he was able at first to withstand the weight of these stones and
    trees,
but, as the tumulus grew and the pressure increased, he struggled.   510
He could not breathe. He squirmed and tried to break free but
    could not,
was caught now and barely able to move, and the pile
of scree and timber trembled and heaved. It looked and felt
exactly like an earthquake whose temblors at last subsided.
    "Why am I telling this story? What is the point? The crushing
is like what Achilles did today, but the end . . . oh, yes,
I remember the end. Some say the weight continued to build,
and the body of Caeneus, squeezed down into the earth, fell
    through it
right through the crust of this world, and into the one below,
that yawning pit that awaits us all. But others dispute this.   520
Some there are who insist that from out of that pile of rubble
a bird with golden wings took flight, soared up in the air,
performed a turn or two, and then disappeared—a bird
the like of which we have never seen before or since.
I saw it myself, and Mopsus, staring into the sky
to watch it circle the camp, called out, 'All hail, Caeneus!
The Lapith hero's glory we see again in this form,
an *avis* not only *rara* but *unica.*' I believed him,
seeing with my own eyes that enormous bird with its flapping
wings, and trusting in Mopsus, who could see through to the
    truth.   530
We were amazed, but our grief was not at all diminished.
Instead, we realized how great a loss we had suffered, and, angry,
we set upon the centaurs again with an even greater
determination and spirit. Half the centaurs we killed,
and the rest we put to flight, chasing them into the forest."
    He rested. Was he done? It was sometimes hard to tell
with Nestor's stories. At length, Tlepolemus, Hercules' son,
suggested that this account of Nestor's was not exhaustive.
"Sir," he said, "you seem to have left out the name of one
of those who were there, and not obscure, I think—my father,   540
Hercules, was also fighting the centaurs that day.
Or so he used to tell me when I was a boy on his knee."
Nestor, Lord of Pylos, replied in the sternest tones,
"This is a painful subject to which you force my attention,

an old wound I had rather not reopened. The truth
is sad—for I hated your father and had good cause to do so.
A hero, he was, whose deeds for mankind earned much praise,
but what is that to me? I think of him and I think
of the harm he did my house with fire and sword. To praise
such a one is a burden. I remember those he killed—   550
of the dozen sons of Neleus, I am the lone survivor.
The rest, your father slew. And how can one explain this?
Listen to me. Men die. We bear it somehow, the common
fate of the common man. But what about the uncommon?
The rare and the gifted? The strange? The precious? That
        Periclymenus
should have met that same fate . . . that was unbearably bad.
That was what broke my heart. To him, our grandfather Neptune
had given the special gift of metamorphosis. He
could transform himself as he pleased, put on what forms he
        chose,
and, during this terrible fight, turned himself into an eagle,   560
which carries the thunderbolts of Jove in his curving talons.
He soared, swooped, and attacked Hercules, raking his face
with those sharp claws. The blood poured down from the parallel
        lines,
but the hero from Tiryns aimed his bow at the bird above him
and shot an arrow high in the sky that found its target,
hitting the joint of the wing with the body and cutting the sinew,
so my brother couldn't remain aloft but dropped to earth,
and, as he hit, the weight of his body fell on the arrow.
It impaled his upper chest and came out the other side
at the base of his throat. This happened before my eyes, and the
        world   570
changed, ever since has been darker and uglier. And you ask
that I should sing the praises of Hercules. If it's small
and mean satisfaction I take, passing over his valorous
deeds, it's all I have. But with you, I have no quarrel."

        Nestor, with that fair speech, concluded, took the wine bowl,
had a noisy sip, and passed it on to the next Greek chieftain.
After that round of drinking, they arose from their couches, tired,
and eager for bed and sleep, and the dreams that are also stories.

        The god of the sea, however, was wide awake, was angry,
and filled with a father's grief for the death of his son Cycnus.   580
He hated Achilles and what that man had done, and he watched
for the ten long years of the war, until, in frustration, he turned
to Apollo, his shaggy colleague and also his best-loved nephew,

to say to the younger god, "Together we built these walls
of doomed Troy. It grieves me to see how soon they will fall.
How can you bear to think of the thousands of men who were
        slain
defending what we made? I look at our work and imagine
Hector's pathetic corpse as they dragged it along in the dirt
around those walls. And Achilles, who killed him and then defiled
the body that way, still lives. If only he came near the water   590
I'd make him feel my anger and pain with a blow of my trident.
On land, out of my range, only you can reach him. Do
your bow and arrow's worst. Kill him." The god of Delos
nodded assent and forthwith, wrapped in a cloud, departed.
In the heart of the Trojan lines, he materialized and saw
Paris taking his easy shots at whomever he spotted
in the crowd below. Apollo presented himself, revealing
himself in divine glory, and said to the Trojan prince,
"Why do you waste your arrows on insignificant targets?
Serve your people better. Take revenge on your slaughtered   600
brothers. Kill Achilles!" He pointed down where that hero
was skewering men with his spear. Apollo touched the bow
Paris was holding, aimed it, and even steadied the arrow,
which flew true to that little spot on Achilles' heel
that was not immune to wounds. And Achilles' death was the first
joyous moment Priam had known since the death of the noble
Hector. No man's sword had killed him, nor even an Amazon's
double-headed axe, but the shot of a ladies' man,
coxcomb, kidnapper, rapist . . . just as Apollo had planned.
        Achilles, the greatest Achaean, was dead, and the Greeks
                mourned   610
and burned his body in fire whose flames leapt to the skies,
brothers to those old flames in which Vulcan had forged his
        armor.
They crackled with that rage that had been the hero's life.
Nothing is left but dust to fit in an urn and glory
to fill the world—and which is the true measure of man?
Peleus' son is alive in the minds of men in his fame.
Such a man cannot dwindle down to a feckless shadow
in Tartarus' pit. His shield and his sword are gleaming still
in the Greek camp, and the chieftains discuss, drop hints, make
        threats.
Diomedes wants them but will not risk making a claim.   620
The lesser Ajax keeps quiet, biting his tongue all the while.

Menelaus and Agamemnon consider the cost
and decide, at last, to forgo this prize, as do all the others—
but Telemonian Ajax and Laertes' son, Ulysses,
both of whom stake claims. Agamemnon has to choose
but cannot and calls a meeting of all the chiefs in conclave.
They will talk, decide the question together, and settle the
        quarrel,
avoiding, if they can, another schism, and chaos.

BOOK XIII

The great men took their seats, while the rest, the commons, assembled
in circles around them. Ajax rose up as if to speak,
but only glared at the fleet drawn up on shore. He pointed
and finally said, "By the gods, in the presence of these black ships,
I put my case before you. Or, better, consider his,
Ulysses', case, who ran before Hector's assaults, while I stood
my ground. Indeed, it was I who drove back his arson squad,
which is why those ships are still there. His words will be clever,
        convincing. . . .
He's always better at words than deeds of battle. My gifts
are in these hands, which have done for our cause more than I
        need   10
rehearse. You all have been here, have seen and remember.
        Ulysses
will tell you of feats he performed in the night, unseen and alone.
Maybe he did and maybe he didn't. The prize is great,
worth perhaps even lies to try to claim. It's absurd
that he and I should be weighed in the balance, one and another.
His reward, he already has, in abundance—he's vied
with me, now, with Ajax, in this dispute. It is ample
for him to be able to make, as long as he lives, this boast.
        "But valor is only a part of my claim. There is also birth,
the precedence I can assert as the son of Telamon, friend   20
to Hercules. Together, they razed these walls long ago.
Telamon's father, Aeacus, is a judge in the world below,
weighing the crimes and lives of all those who come before him.
His father—my great-grandfather—was almighty Jove himself.
That glorious descent makes me, you all will acknowledge,
Achilles' cousin, and therefore I claim his arms as a kinsman.
Ulysses can trace his line to Sisyphus, whom my grandsire
condemned to eternal hard labor, pushing that heavy boulder
up the endless hill as penance for his cheap tricks—

of the kind that entire clan resorts to whenever it can.   30

   "But let us confine ourselves to the present business, this war
with Troy—to which I came as a volunteer, while he
pretended to be a loony. Palamedes found him out,
showed him up as a fraud, a malingerer. . . . Or has madness
seized him again to let him suppose he can make a claim
as a patriot now, a valorous fighter, and steadfast comrade
worthy to bear Achilles' arms? Is this not the same
man who abandoned his wounded companion, Philoctetes,
whose curses rang through the woods of that desolate island for
      years—
richly deserved curses, on Ulysses' devious head?   40
He roams those woods in rags or naked by now, and treats
that terrible purulent wound as best he can as he shoots
birds to keep himself fed, using Hercules' arrows we miss
here in our fight with the Trojans. A dreadful business, I say.
But he, at least, is alive, and safe from the vengeful spirit
Ulysses showed with Palamedes. Trumped-up charges of
      spying, . . .
false witness, and planted evidence. Now we know
how Ulysses vilely framed him, contriving a sentence of death.
For this good service, reducing the numbers of Greeks, let Trojans
vote him thanks and honors. Let them give him heroes' weapons.   50
On this side of the line, those courtesies we have shown him
are more from circumspection and fear than respect or love.

   "Whatever he says will be graceful, clever, and even
      persuasive.
He sounds as wise as Nestor himself—but let Nestor's lesson
open our eyes. Remember when Nestor's horse was wounded,
and Nestor called for help on the battlefield? What happened?
Was it brave Ulysses who came to the aid of our elder and dearly
beloved friend? He called to Ulysses by name! And again,
and yet again, and soon he cried out in rage that the coward
refused to come. And the gods, who hear and see all things,   60
elected to teach him a lesson, contriving to turn the tables,
and so it happened Ulysses was left on the field in need,
pale with the fear of a coward who stares death in the face.
Ulysses called out for help, and with little hope, I must say,
for he assumed that others would behave as he had behaved,
and that all men are cowards and villains like him, and that only
fools would risk their precious skins to save their friends.
But somebody came to save his contemptible life—I did!
I held out my huge shield to cover his fallen body.

He has let this slip his mind. But let us return to that spot,   70
let us restore the moment, the wounds, the battle, my shield.
I gave him my arm, on which he could lean as he limped back
to the Greek lines—and his wounds seemed not to impede him.
         ·He ran
as fleet of foot as a healthy deer—or make it a rabbit.
Let him repeat now all those oaths of indebtedness I
remember clearly, although they seem to have blurred in his mind.
Now that the danger has gone, the words have also vanished.
        "Hector attacks, and the gods are with him. Not only
             Ulysses
but even men of courage and honor are frightened, their blood
cold in their veins as if unwilling to spill on the thirsty   80
ground that has drunk so much already—for Hector has killed
many that day, in his strength and skill and his appetite
for death, which are truly awesome. I was the one who flung
the stone that knocked him down. He staggered back to his feet
and challenged us all to name a man who would meet him in
             single
combat, a champion fighting for all. We drew our lots,
and the prayers of much of the camp that the task be mine were
             answered.
I fought with Hector, and here I stand, having survived it,
as I survived again when the Trojans came with their weapons
to burn our ships, but we stood together—and we repelled them.   90
For the sake of those ships I saved, I ask for Achilles' armor.
        "Or put it the other way, and say that Achilles' arms
seek me as their rightful owner, Telamon's son Ajax.
If Achilles' noble spirit inheres in the chased metal
Vulcan fashioned, it surely recoils from being the booty
of this man whose claims of victory all turn out to be tricks,
ambushes, night forays, as when he and Diomedes
stealthily entered the camp of Rhesus, slew him, and rustled
his horses. Or timid Dolon, they killed, who had begged for his
             life
and divulged the Trojan plans. Or Helenus, Priam's son   100
and another captive, these two slew—unarmed or asleep.
And always with Diomedes to do the dirty work. Let them
make their claim together! And let them wrangle together,
in a kind of comedy act, which one is the less deserving.
        "For a night fighter, a sneak, a guerrilla, what is the use
of gleaming armor. The helmet's shine will give him away,
letting the enemy's sentries know that something is out there,

some snake in the grass that slithers. . . . How will his neck
  support
its awesome weight, and how will he lift the ashen spear shaft?
It's far too heavy. He'll drop it, stabbing himself in the foot.   110
That famous shield is also a burden. A man like Ulysses,
who runs rather than fights, will find that it slows him down.
Worse, these arms will attract the greedy Trojans' attention—
they'll come like ants to a picnic, swarming about him to take
these famous arms as loot. It's a sobering prospect, really.
And what does he need a shield for in any event? His own
is quite untouched, while mine is scarred, pierced by a hundred,
a thousand different blows, and I need this to replace it.

     "It's not such a hard question, but I know a way to decide it
without speeches, without your making the awkward choice   120
between us. What I propose is to send the armor into
the Trojan camp. Let heralds deliver it there, and we'll see
whichever Greek can take it. He'll be the one who deserves it.
This is what I propose, if only Ulysses agrees."

     Thus Telamon's son spoke, and the Greek camp cheered,
applauding his brave words and bold proposal. At length,
Ulysses, the son of Laërtes, arose and strode to the circle's
center. He lowered his eyes and stared at the ground a moment,
thinking, or letting the audience anticipate what he would say.
Then he looked up, stared at the kings and noble leaders,   130
and started to speak in words that were—not surprisingly—
  graceful.

     "We can't have what we want. If prayers could work, Achilles
would still be wearing this armor, and we would have him with
  us.
But he is gone. . . ." And here Ulysses paused for a moment,
to rub his hand across his eyes as if he were wiping
tears that were welling up. Clearing his throat, he continued:
"Who has a better right to this armor than he through whom
Achilles joined our party and came here to fight at Troy?
Ajax holds it against me that I have the knack of speaking
persuasively. . . . Sometimes, I do, I suppose. But this gift   140
I have used for the common good and in your behalf. I suggest
you therefore ought not hold it against me, or give him special
credit for blunt and direct speech. Each of us does
the best he can with whatever the gods and fate have given.

     "Genealogical boasting has never made sense to me:
men can't pick their forebears and should take neither credit nor
  blame.

And yet, if we listen to Ajax and think of him as the grandson
of Jove, then I can claim as much—my father, Laërtes,
was the son of Arcesius, who in his turn was the son of Jove.
No criminals, scoundrels, or such black sheep, as far as I know,   150
on my side of the scale. My father wasn't a killer
and never went into exile. Indeed, through my mother's house,
I can claim a noble line of descent to Mercury. Both sides,
therefore, arose from the gods. But what has that got to do
with the present question? Let it be solely a matter of merit
or deeds to decide which one deserves this glittering prize.
The suggestion that great Achilles and Ajax are cousins, though
          clever,
is absolutely irrelevant, immaterial. If relatives'
claims are honored, then send the armor to Phthia, where Peleus,
our hero's father, may have it. Or send it to Scyros, where
          Pyrrhus,   160
his son, may receive it. But cousins? Teucer can claim as much,
and it never crossed his mind to make so absurd a suggestion.
Deeds of valor and honor—these are the only measures
of worth and what a man deserves from men of the world.
A disagreeable business, recounting one's own exploits,
and yet there is no other way. I adduce them, then, in order.
          "When Achilles' mother dressed him in women's clothing to
          hide him,
all of the Greeks were fooled, including Ajax, but I
set out, among the pots and pans and the combs and spindles,
a couple of weapons, a shield and a spear—the things that a man   170
might want to examine. The hero gathered his skirts about him
and went at once to the shield. I greeted him, 'Son of Thetis,
the doomed city of Troy awaits you, as does your glory.
Waste no time. Give up this charade. We'll set forth together.'
I put my hand on his shoulder and led him down to the harbor,
so all of his deeds of valor on our behalf at Troy
are mine, and I stake my claim to them all. Telephus, hurt,
I persuaded Achilles to heal with the rust of his spear, and the son
of Hercules came to fight on our side and thus to fulfill
the oracle's quirky proviso. By this same reasoning, Thebes   180
is mine, and Lesbos, Tenedos, Cryse, Cilla, and Scyros
are mine, and by my hand were the walls of Lyrnesus razed.
Even the death of Hector was therefore mine, and I claim it
and the arms Achilles wore and bore—in exchange for those
I set out so long ago that day in the marketplace
to trick him into revealing who and what he was.

"We are here for the sake of King Menelaus, whose sorrows
we share. Our thousand ships were gathered at Aulis, where
        winds
kept us all from our purpose. The oracle's words were harsh,
and Agamemnon was disinclined to give to the goddess   190
the life of his dear daughter. I was the one who convinced him
what the common good required. A terrible thing to do,
and I look to him still for pardon—but mine was the voice that
        made
the difficult case to a most reluctant judge that his brother's
honor, and ours, demanded no less from our august chief.
I was the one he sent to Mycenae to fetch that princess,
deceiving Clytemnestra. . . . Imagine plain-spoken Ajax
trying to tell the mother how we needed Iphigeneia
for some ceremonial purpose. We'd still be there on the beach,
and those same onshore winds would still be blowing to
        westward.   200
    "I was the emissary you sent to the Trojan council
chamber to plead our case. It was full of warriors, heroes,
but I ventured into their lion's den and told them our cause—
that Paris had done a great wrong, and Helen should be returned,
together with reparations to us who had been aggrieved.
Priam listened, conceding the justice of what I had said,
and Antenor agreed with him, but Paris and all his brothers
and henchmen in the theft of Helen were deaf to my words,
as the guilty are often deaf to voices of right reason.
It was only a matter of luck that we got away with our lives,   210
as Menelaus can swear. And this was but one of the dangers
I faced for the common good and on which I base my claim.
    "The rest is a catalogue, unnecessary to tell you,
for you have all been here through these long and tedious years.
During the siege that continued for most of that time, such
        fighters
as Ajax here did nothing but sit and wait for their moments.
I worked on designing fortifications, on stratagems, plans,
negotiations with allies, supplies, and logistic arrangements
for keeping the troops provisioned, and armed, and in fighting
        order.
It isn't the glamorous part of a military campaign,   220
but somebody's got to do it. And I was the one who did.
    "Remember, then, how the king was deceived by a dream, a
        vision
that Jove had sent to test us all? He was ready to quit,

lay down the burden of war, and withdraw. What did Ajax do?
Insist that the war be brought to a finish and Troy be destroyed?
Did he stand on the beach and argue with those about to embark
for the homeward voyage? Or take up weapons to rally the men
and turn them from a straggling mob back to an army?
Nothing, nothing whatever. That's for irrelevant, clever
manipulators of words—like me. Mine was the voice   230
that kept us here. Indeed, he also was ready to flee,
had boarded his ship and was ready to set his sails and sneak off
like a whipped dog with nothing to show for his ten long years
except disgrace. I stopped him. I argued, jeered, and annoyed,
and made him angry enough that he had to stay here and fight.
Nothing from Telamon's son. Thersites jeered and taunted
the kings of our host with nasty words for which he was
        punished—
by my hand, you recall. And the rest of the war is mine,
mine alone, to claim, as the victory here is mine.

        "Ajax suggests that I've shared my exploits with Diomedes.   240
It's true, I have. I do not admit it but boast in pride
as any man would do, glad he'd been singled out
by such a fighter as chosen companion and trusted partner.
Those ventures to which he makes dismissive reference—the
        killing
of Dolon, for instance—were missions of risk, and we
        volunteered.
We went at night through the enemy lines. And it wasn't a mere
'assassination.' We didn't kill him until we had learned
the Trojans' battle order and all their contingency plans.
The camp was grateful, but did I then rest on those laurels?
I went out again to Rhesus' tents to destroy that chieftain   250
and all his captains, too, and drove their horses back here
in the chariot of that late and most unlamented leader.

        "The list of my conquests runs on and on. Sarpedon and
        many
Lycian soldiers, I killed: Coeranos, Alastor, Chromius,
Alcander, Halius, Noëmon, Prytanis, Thoön, Chersidamas,
Charopes, Ennomos. . . . All these, I killed in the bloody
        fighting,
and others besides whose names I've forgotten or never knew
I turned into meat in the dirt below the walls of that haughty
city. My scars attest to the pains these victories cost me.
Let my body speak." Here, he threw open his tunic   260
to show his livid scars. "The body of Ajax has never

in all these years been touched. His skin has no mark or blemish.

"Ajax says he defended our vessels against the Trojan
assault, and he speaks the truth. It is not my purpose here
to belittle the good he has done us. But he was not quite alone
as he fought on the beach. Beside him, Patroclus, in this very
      armor,
pretending to be Achilles, frightened the Trojans and drove them
back in disorder and then in a rout to their walls and safety.
He stood against Hector? He did, indeed, but he was not the only
Greek to do so. A look at the records of fighting will show   270
that he was the ninth to volunteer to engage that Trojan
in single combat, and did so by drawing of lots. And Hector
retired that day without a wound or even a scratch.

"It is sad to refer to the bitter hour when Achilles fell.
But who can forget it? The grief and, yes, I admit it, the fear
that every man here had to feel was a terrible burden—but I
was the one who bore the body itself, who lifted the corpse
from the ground and on these shoulders carried the limp cadaver
back to our lines. The armor I claim now clanked at each step
of the death march. For that moment's terrible burden, I claim   280
the right to bear again those arms and to wear them myself.
Dismal prizes they are, but also beautiful objects,
works of splendid refinement—which want a discerning eye
and a sensitive, subtle mind to appreciate how they are made
and what they mean. That shield Vulcan made with its map
of the cosmos, the earth and sea, the works of men, and the stars
of the heavens . . . What does our simple, direct, but—let us
      admit it—
crude Ajax know about art? Or craftsmanship?
Or, heaven protect us, beauty? The very idea is an outrage,
a travesty, or a joke. . . . It isn't pleasant to say this,   290
but it's true, painfully true, and has to be said and admitted.

"Let me turn now to the charge that I was laggard in joining
the expedition. Indeed, I was, as Achilles also
was less than enthusiastic. We share what guilt may attach
to our similar and equivalent reluctance. I had a wife
who wanted to keep me home, as he had a loving mother
who wanted to keep him from coming to Troy. But we both did
      come.
In fact, Achilles delayed longer than I, but we both
made up by deeds here later for that first disinclination. . . .
Again, I suggest it was I, not Ajax, who found Achilles   300
and got him to take off that silly dress and strap on his armor.

What Ajax says is impertinent, wrong, and even disloyal;
for if I was wrong to accuse Palamedes of his treason,
does it not follow that all were wrong who voted him guilty—
every one of us here—and then condemned him to death?
I say once again he was guilty and that we were correct in our
      judgment,
and the gold bribe I discovered proved it beyond all doubt.
    "For Philoctetes on Lemnos, I feel the enormous regret
that everyone here who consented in this decision must feel.
What I proposed, I remind you all, was a rest on that island,   310
a stretch of time where he might recuperate and heal,
soothing his dreadful anguish. I made my suggestion in kindness
and good faith. And the patient survives. He is still alive,
which is good for us who need him, as the seers now inform us.
We require his aid and arrows to vanquish Troy, but will Ajax
go with clever words and artful tricks to invite
or persuade or somehow entrap this needful man? Can we hope
that the wit of Ajax may work to provide us with what we need?
Eloquence, shrewdness, guile, and skills in negotiation
are not—to be perfectly blunt—his stronger points. Indeed,   320
Simoïs will change direction and flow uphill,
and Ida will shrug off her trees to stand there barren and rocky,
or Greece will send allies to Troy to fight against us
here on this cursed beach, before we shall see our Ajax
taking my place as an envoy to persuade anybody to do
or give or help or supply what I should have managed to get us.
We need Philoctetes now, and he hates us all. He resents
the king and despises me more than any man alive,
but I shall go and endure his rages and hear him snarl
how he will drink my blood, and I shall bring him back here   330
to fight with us and for us, and share his sacred arrows.
I shall do with him what I did with the Trojan seer, our captive—
with words, I got him to tell us the secret we needed to hear
of the destiny here of the Trojans and how we could win this war.
I was the one who stole Minerva's sacred statue
from the heart of their sanctuary; it no longer keeps them safe.
Ajax asks how I can presume to compare myself
with him, but he puts the question the wrong way around. Ajax
never ventured forth from the lines, or dared the sentries
the Trojans had posted. The brave, the mighty Ajax, the hero,   340
might then have volunteered, but his eloquent voice was quiet.
Perhaps the words had formed in his mind about setting forth
into the heart of their city at the citadel's top, where they keep

their talismanic icon in its shrine, but somehow his voice
failed and couldn't project them into the chill night air.
But I went out, and returned with the statue, and in that exploit
conquered the city and won the war—for, without that idol,
all we have done and suffered these years would have been in vain.
     "Look at him there as he scowls and mutters. What is he
          saying?
That Diomedes was with me? He was, and we shared the credit,   350
as you should have shared with others the praise for defending the
          ships.
Many Greeks were with you, as I was myself, you'll recall,
but fighters, for all their value, are not quite the same as planners.
A strong right hand can do nothing unless a brain directs it.
Diomedes is clever enough to have understood this,
as other fighters have who otherwise now would be claiming
the armor here. I could mention the lesser Ajax, or Thoas,
or brave Eurypylus, or Idomeneus, the Cretan King,
or another from Crete, Meriones. Or King Menelaus. They each
could make a persuasive claim of what their sword hands have
          done.   360
I assert the higher claim of the mind that directs our strength,
which is why these silent others have yielded to me. Your might,
Ajax, is surely great, but you need my mind to apply it
with any useful result. You are the muscular oarsman;
I am the navigator and captain who stands at the helm
and gets the ship to its destination. The body is nothing
without its brain, its mind, its divine and perhaps immortal
part that distinguishes us from the beasts and the flying birds.
Even a life of action begins in prior thought
and ends in the thought that follows, as meaning at last comes
          clear.   370
     "I say to you in conclusion that I have done you some service
over these many years. My calculations and plans
deserve this recognition and prize. We have come to the end
not only of my extended speech but of this whole war—
for the obstacle to our purpose is here, in the form of that statue,
and nothing now prevents us from taking the city, defenseless
and ready to fall at our slightest effort. Give me the armor,
or else you should give it to her, that fateful statue of Pallas."
He made a sweeping gesture and pointed his index finger
at Minerva's figurine and then, abruptly, sat down.   380
The chieftains, moved by his words, gave to the eloquent man
the brave man's arms, while Ajax stood there in disbelief.

He who had stood in the thick of the fighting, had withstood
      Hector,
had struggled with fire and sword and the gods themselves, could
      not
stand this terrible insult. Resentment seized him. He seized
his sword and drew it forth from the scabbard. "This is still
      mine,"
he shouted aloud, "unless you suppose you can take it from me.
The use of it I have retained—even against myself.
It has reeked with Phrygian blood often enough, and now
will drip with its own master's. No man but Ajax can conquer   390
Ajax!" he bellowed and suddenly stabbed himself in the breast,
which, until then, had never suffered a single wound.
He plunged the blade so deep that no man's hand could have
      pulled it
out again, but his heart, powerful, broken, pumped
the blood that popped it forth like a cork from a shaken bottle.
Where that crimson gush hit the ground, the droplets bloomed
      into flowers
like those that appeared in long-ago days from Hyacinth's blood,
with their petals bearing the same inscription of letters, the cry
of grief, "Ai, ai"—which could also be read as the name
of the hero with only a little transformation, as "Aias."   400
     Now Ulysses departed for Queen Hypsipyle's island,
Lemnos, where Philoctetes raged and sulked and moaned,
to fetch the man and the sacred arrows by which high Troy
might be brought low. He did this, and Troy at last collapsed.
Priam, the king, was dead, and Hecuba, widowed now,
changed from her human form to that of a dog, which barked,
howling into the night an eerie inhuman keening.
Behind her, Troy was in flames with red tongues lapping the sky's
irredeemable blackness. At Jove's altar, the blood
of old Priam was still a fresh stain on the floor.   410
Apollo's darling, Cassandra, dragged by the hair, complained
to her captors and the gods in heaven, but all in vain,
as the other Trojan women wept, embracing their household
gods and watching as Greeks looted their palaces, temples,
and modest homes. They stared in horror to see the son
of Hector, Astyanax, thrown from the tower to die
on the stones below. And then it got worse, for the North Wind
      rose,
and the Greeks embarked and took the women aboard as captives.
They saw the hawsers drop and the strip of black water grow

between the hulls and the beach. Behind them the garish glow   420
of their smoldering city was awesome; ahead was the blacker
    future
of exile, concubinage, contempt, and a lonely death.
The last to walk up the gangplank was Hecuba, Queen of Troy,
whom the Greeks found in the graveyard among the tombs of her
    sons.
Ulysses dragged her away and down to the waiting vessel.
She was able to take a handful of Hector's ashes with her
and to leave a lock of her ashen hair at his grave with her tears.
    Directly across from the Phrygian coast is that of Thrace,
where Polymestor ruled the Bistones. To his care Priam
entrusted one of his sons, Polydorus, whom he had sent   430
far from the fighting at Troy for safety, a prudent plan,
except that he also sent a treasure, a fabulous hoard
to tempt any greedy soul—including of course Polymestor's.
This wicked and faithless man cut Polydorus' throat,
and then, as if it were nothing to murder a man, as if corpses
were only garbage, he flung the body over a cliff
and into the maw of the sea, which swallows whatever it's fed.
    A little way down this coast, Agamemnon moored his fleet
to wait for the storm to exhaust itself and the winds to shift.
Here on the beach, from a gaping hole in the earth, Achilles   440
sprang up as large as life with his sword in hand to challenge
all the Achaean host and Agamemnon, its chief:
"Is this how you all go home, you nation of ingrates? Is this
the thanks I get for my deeds and sacrifices at Troy?
My body has been interred, and gratitude, too, it would seem.
I want a prize for myself. My ghost requires what you
have all picked out for yourselves—a woman, or rather a girl.
Polyxena, I shall have. Let her be sacrificed
to appease my neglected spirit." A dreadful request, but the
    Greeks
could not refuse the pitiless ghost. They tore the girl   450
from her mother's arms and took her away, and they sacrificed
    her.
Brave and self-possessed she was, as she stared at Achilles'
son and said, "Neoptolemos, go ahead, then. Kill me.
Plunge your sword in my body and spill my noble blood,"
saying which, she bared her breast. "A daughter of Priam,
I have no wish to live as a slave and am glad to die—
except that it will further burden my already heartsick
mother. And yet it is not my death she ought to regret,

but her life. There is only one request I make, as Priam's
daughter: no man should touch my virgin body, but let   460
the women bring my corpse to my mother. That spirit you here
appease will thank you, as I do. And do not ask for a ransom.
She will pay in tears what she once would have paid in gold.
Give her my corpse to prepare for the tomb with the usual prayers
of the sacred rites." She spoke without any quavers or tears,
although, through the Greek camp, the eyes of strong men were
          weeping.
Even the priest wept as he raised the ritual knife,
and the crowd gasped as he struck with the sharp blade at her
          bared
breast. She shuddered, sank to her knees, and then collapsed.
As she fell, she managed to close the front of her robe to cover   470
her body's fatal wound in modesty, pride, and honor.
          The women take up the body and weep as they count the
          dead
of Priam's house. This youngster, this virgin child, they lament,
but also her mother, Hecuba, burdened anew with grief,
who, only a moment ago, was herself a princess, the queen
of Troy and of all of Asia, the envy of women, who now
was brought so low that other captives, then and forever,
would think of her with pity. Ulysses had chosen her only
because she was Hector's mother—as a conversation piece.
Now she embraces the body of one more child, the last   480
to call to her as "Mother." She kisses the cold lips
and the terrible wound in the breast. She beats her own poor
          breast,
which has taken so many blows. She tears at her silvery hair
caked with the daughter's blood and cries aloud to her baby:
"O my child, my child, my last reason to care,
or feel, or grieve, you are gone. That wound of yours is mine.
I feel it more keenly than you. I have lost my sons to violence,
and hoped that you, as a woman, were safe from the sword's sharp
          kiss.
But the sword is relentless, rapacious, promiscuous. Evil Achilles,
who killed your brothers, has claimed another victim in you.   490
When Apollo steadied the hand of Paris and guided the arrow
that killed Achilles, I thought there'd be no more reason to fear
          him.
What harm could the corpse of that monster threaten us with? I
          was wrong.

His ashes are hot with hate for our house and race. My womb
was fruitful not for Priam and Troy but for him. I detest
his ghost as much as I hated the living person. Troy
is not gone but burns in my heart. My dreams are loud
with the screams of those nightmare nights. I am dragged away as
    a prize
of the worst of the Greeks, into exile, alone, and bereft of those
    tombs
I love and must leave behind. I go to a distant island   500
to sit and spin at my wheel, while Penelope tells her callers,
'This one is Hector's mother, who used to be Priam's queen.'
Having lost so many, I ought to have learned to bear it,
but all my losses and griefs are renewed in this latest death
of my last daughter, the one whose love consoled me, whose need
for my love and attention gave me a reason, or pretext, for living.
Sacrificed to the ghost of an enemy we detested?
How can this be? What kind of world is this? What gods
can bear to look down and consider what they allow to take place
in the foul pit where I live as queen of the earth's wretched?   510
What have I done to deserve these punishments? I linger
in odious, otiose age, presiding at funerals, wakes,
and every breath I draw is expended in dirges and moans.
I wept when Priam died, but I realize now he is happy
and envy him his escape from witnessing such disasters
as poor Polyxena's murder. He left his life and his throne
at the same moment, but we, the relics of Troy, must endure
a demeaning diminution. Our glorious memories chide us.
That city we knew and loved indicts us, moment by moment.
I think of the proper rites for a royal interment, and look   520
at this paltry business here—where your funeral gifts will be only
your mother's bitter tears as we lay you in alien earth
on a foreign shore we are never likely to visit again.
What is there left to live for? I have but the single strand
that binds me yet to this world—my son young Polydorus,
the one we sent here to Thrace and safety. Our line, our hopes,
remain alive with him. Once we have washed these wounds
with water to cleanse the blood from her face, we shall lay her to
    rest.
Then we shall seek my son, whose face I yearn to behold."

    Allowing herself a bitter groan, she arose and tottered   530
down the shingle to fetch some sea water to bathe
her daughter's corpse. She tore her hair and banged the empty

urn on her skinny hip. She knelt to fill the vessel,
but remained kneeling to pray that her eyes were deceiving her
        mind,
or her mind had given way—that the corpse she saw in the sea
washing ashore was not her son's body, her child's,
its gaping wound a disgrace, its face a bloated and ghastly
distortion of that dear face she had yearned to behold. Her prayer
was too late: it was he. It was Polydorus. The women
shrieked, but Hecuba's voice was gone. She was dumb with grief.   540
As still as a rock, she stood there and stared down at the ground
or up at the heavens, defying them both, or back at the body,
its horrid wound and its puffy, cruelly parodied face.
Of this poor meat she was mother? Of this she was queen? Her
        rage
blazed forth from her soul's furnace, and she was transformed,
was queen again, or even a goddess, wholly absorbed,
and altogether resolved on splendid and terrible vengeance.
As a lioness whose cub has been stolen away will rage
and follow with narrowed eyes the predator's tracks, so she
also raged and set forth with implacable regal wrath   550
to Polymestor's palace to confront him as murderer, liar,
and violator of treaties. She spoke, however, of gold.
There was a hoard of gold she had brought to give to her son
and wanted now to entrust to his guardian's care. Would he
accept it? Of course, he was willing to do this further favor
for Polydorus and Troy. He followed where Hecuba led,
to the hiding place of the treasure, taking his solemn oath
that "What you give shall be his, as what you have given before
was solely his." She heard him pronounce this lie and swear it,
as her barely contained wrath exploded. "Villain," she cried,   560
and she and her women attacked him. She reached with her aged
        and bony
fingers into his face, his eye sockets, and plucked
his eyeballs out of his head like a couple of ripe grapes.
She flung them away as useless baubles and reached back in
to gouge at the bloody sockets as if she were feeling for brains,
for the evil thoughts of a mind that could do and say such vile
and hateful things. The Thracians meanwhile appeared, and stared
at their cruelly stricken king and these Trojan women, whose
        hands
were dripping with his gore, and set upon them with stones
and the fallen branches of trees they used as impromptu spears. 570
Hecuba turned to face them and would have spoken or shouted,

but all she could make were the noises a tortured dog might
        produce—
howls, barks, and growls. They call the place where this happened
Cynosema, which means, in our language, the Sign of the Dog,
and the people who live there insist that they still on occasion hear
in the dark of the night the howling of Hecuba's bitter complaint.
Her story touched the hearts of Trojans, Greeks, and the gods,
and Juno, her old foe, admitted that how she'd suffered
and died was more than she—or any woman—deserved.

    For Hecuba, all the gods and goddesses grieved—but Aurora,   580
who was occupied with her own woe for the death of her son
Memnon. Achilles' spear had dispatched him on that windy
plain before Troy. She had seen this dreadful thing, and her rosy
colors had faded to duns and dusks of a clouded sky.
She was unable to watch his corpse on the funeral pyre
char to ash, but she went to Jove to weep and to plead
with the lord of Olympus: "I come before you, a minor goddess
who can claim only a handful of temples mortals attend
to praise or pray or offer sacrifices to me,
and yet I am here, a goddess who does the best she can   590
to keep our ordered cosmos working in its routines.
I do not require thanks, or honors, or any reward,
but only pity, bereft as I am of my child, my son,
who died in his uncle's service fighting for Troy. Grant me
solace, I pray, dear master. Let my son be remembered
in some significant way." Jupiter heard and granted
the mother's prayer. On the pyre, flames were leaping and
        dancing,
as the logs crumbled to earth. The air was black with their smoke,
thicker than any mist or fog that the river nymphs send
to blot the Sun from the skies—but unlike a fog, this rose   600
higher and higher. You'd think it alive, some kind of a bird,
which it was, or then a whole flock of birds, all black,
all sisters, sprung from the single source. Like smoke,
they wheeled and circled three times, making a harsh clamor,
and again, but this time dividing in two separate agglomerations
which commenced to fight with each other, battled with beaks
        and talons,
murdering one another, so their bodies fell back to earth
like cinders of ash from the billowing towers of thick smoke.
These peculiar birds, these ruffs, are black as Memnon, Aurora's
son, the Ethiopian king, was black—or black   610
as ashes and the clothes of mourners are black—and once

each year they appear in skies to wheel, circle, then fight
and kill one another again, reenacting their father's demise.
While the rest of the world, mortals and gods, grieved for
      Hecuba,
Aurora, Memnon's bereaved mother, wept on her own
and continues throughout the ages to do so. Thus, at the dawn,
we find the dew of her tears, which shine in the morning's dazzle.
     But the absolute end of Troy was not what the Fates
       intended.
In those last hours, Aeneas, walked away, escaping,
carrying with him the family gods and, upon his shoulders,   620
Anchises, his frail old father. By the hand, he led his son,
Ascanius. With his band of survivors and refugees,
he put to sea at Antandros, leaving behind them bloody
Thrace and, with fortunate winds and currents, arriving at Delos,
Apollo's city. Its priest-king, Anius, welcomed them warmly.
He gave them the guided tour of the city, the sacred shrines,
and the trees under which Latona was said to have brought forth
     her godly
twins. They burned the incense, poured out the good red wine,
and sacrificed the cattle, whose entrails they burned in the flames
of the holy altar. Then, in the banquet hall of the palace,   630
where they lay on the couches, feasting, breaking bread together
and drinking that same good wine, Anchises addressed his host,
asking the sacerdotal ruler what had become
of the children, "For surely, as I recall, when I was last here,
there were little children, a son and several daughters . . . four?"
The other shook his head and answered in deepest sadness,
"You recall correctly. There were, indeed, five children, but all
are gone, and I am bereft, for such is the nature of men.
Our joys are never secure; our children are pawns of the Fates.
My son now rules in Andros, which takes its name from his.   640
He serves there as priest and soothsayer, Apollo having given
the gift of prophecy. Bacchus, meanwhile, gave to the girls
another and even stranger gift—the power to turn
whatever they touch to food, to grain or wine, or oil.
A useful skill, we thought, and were grateful—until the Greek
king, Agamemnon, heard their story, and came to drag them
away, my unwilling girls, from their father's arms, to provide
for his troops on the Trojan plain, putting their heavenly gifts
to his base use and profit. They ran away when they could,
two to Euboea and two to their brother's protection on Andros,   650
but Agamemnon sent platoons in all directions

to find them, seize them, and bring them back, threatening war
to any who dared to hide them, give them shelter or aid,
or refuse to hand them back. Andros, my son, was frightened
and, much as he hated to do it, ordered his weeping sisters
back to their forced labor—for Hector, who held onto Troy
for years, was nowhere nearby, or Aeneas, either. My daughters
saw the Greeks approaching with chains, hand and leg irons,
and raised their arms to the heavens to beg of Bacchus his aid
yet again, and he gave it—or what one may think of as aid.   660
Their shapes were transformed from human to those of two
          snow-white doves,
the birds that so often attend on divine Venus, your consort."
          With this and similar tales, they talked through the festive
                    evening
and into the night. The banquet at last was done, and they rose
from the emptied plates and bowls that littered their banquet
          tables.
They went to their separate chambers, fell on their beds, and slept.
In the morning they rose up early and went to consult the god
to learn what Apollo might tell them, as caution or else as
          promise.
Phoebus told them to seek their ancient, distant mother.
(What could that mean? Anchises supposed that it might refer   670
to Dardanus' birthplace to westward—on the central Italian
          coast.)
King Anius went to the shore to see them embark and exchange
gifts to mark the occasion: for old Anchises, a scepter;
for his grandson, Ascanius, a robe and a handsome quiver for
          arrows;
for Aeneas, a wonderful goblet Therses had long ago sent,
a piece the Hylean Alcon had made. On its sides were engraved
in several panels a story. The first showed the walls of a city
with seven gates—which was Thebes. Before the gates there were
          pyres,
blazing in funeral rites, and women with hair streaming down
were beating their breasts and wailing. Nymphs were weeping
          and mourning   680
their dried-up springs, and the trees, forlorn, were bare and
          leafless.
In the parched and stony fields, goats nibbled the naked
clods of earth while, within the city, Orion's daughters
were killing themselves, slashing their throats and plunging their
          daggers

into their breasts to save the rest of the city from plague.
We see their pathetic corpses borne aloft in funereal
pomp and honor, and burned to ashes amidst the grateful
but nevertheless grief-stricken mob. And then, in the next
panel upon the goblet, the ashes' children spring up,
whom Fame has named the Coronae; they join in their mothers'
    rites.   690
Such was the ancient tale on the sides of the old bronze vessel,
around which was scrolled in bas-relief an elegant wreath
of acanthus leaves, which framed and connected the panels
    together.
In exchange, the Trojans presented gifts of no lesser value:
an incense casket a priest might use, while conducting prayers;
a libation saucer for rites he might perform; and a crown
of gleaming beaten gold into which jewels had been set.
    They sailed away, debating whether to try the coast
of Italy—or did the god intend them to return
to Teucer's ancient homeland in Crete, which was so much closer?   700
They made for Crete, the island of a hundred cities, but there
they found a mean welcome of troubles that Jove had prepared.
Deciding they had been wrong, they changed their goal to the
    coast
of Italy and set sail again, but the winter seas
were rough, and the winds that raged and howled drove them off
    course.
At the Strophades, the Harpy Aëllo attacked, and they fled
for their lives. They kept on going and passed Dulichium, Samos,
Ithaca, where the crafty Ulysses lived, and Ambracia,
Pyrrhus' city, which now we call Nicopolis (Victory
City) after Augustus' triumph at Actium. There   710
they saw the stone figure that Judge Crageleus became
when he rendered a verdict Apollo didn't like. They passed
Dodona's murmuring oaks and Chaonia's sheltered harbor,
where King Munichus' sons escaped the robbers' flames
by becoming wingèd birds and soaring up into the air.
    They went from there to Corfu, where Phaeacians tend their
    orchards,
and landed next in Epirus at Buthrotos' harbor—there Trojan
Helenus, the prophet and holy man, had erected
a small copy of Troy. He welcomed them grandly but urged
that they push on to their fated reward. To Sicily next   720
they traveled, that odd-shaped island with three promontories
    pointing

south, west, and north. The winds were right, and the currents,
and they reached the sloping beaches of Zancle as darkness fell.
The dangers there are famous, with Scylla off to the right
and Charybdis close on the left. The latter sucks down and spits
    forth
unwary ships, while the other menaces, monstrous, her waist
belted with savage dogs that nip and slash. Her face
is nevertheless that of a shy virgin, and poets
say she once was a virgin whom suitors besieged, but she spurned
    them
and hid out with her sea-nymph friends, among whom she
    giggled   730
and whispered about those ridiculous men and their hopeless
    courtships.
Galatea, a nymph who was combing her auburn hair,
was less than amused. She sighed and reproached the ebullient
    Scylla:
"You're lucky, you know. Those suitors were gentlemen. You
    could refuse,
as a girl cannot always manage to do. I had no such easy
choices—Nereus' daughter, and Doris'! We're safe enough now,
gossiping here together, but dangers are lurking outside
everywhere. I shall never forget how the Cyclops pursued me
and at what cost I refused him. . . ." Here she broke down and
    wept.
Scylla dried the sea nymph's tears and patted her shoulder.   740
"Tell us what happened," she urged her woebegone friend.
    "Confide
in companions eager to share your burden, whatever it is."
The nereid then replied, telling Scylla, Crataeis' daughter,
the whole deplorable story: "I was in love with Acis,
whose father was Faunus, the king, and mother, the nymph
    Symaethis.
A beautiful boy he was, a youth at the threshold of manhood,
with a delicate peach-fuzzed face beginning to hint at the strength
it soon would show. I loved him, but Polyphemus, the Cyclops,
decided that he loved me—and it's hard now for me to decide
which emotion was stronger, my love for the boy or distaste,   750
my intense physical loathing, of that too persistent Cyclops.
Not that we have much say in how Venus governs our hearts,
but what she decrees, we accept, endorse, and claim as our own
personal choices. But Cyclops? The beasts in the woods are afraid
of that savage face, which portends harm to all who behold it.

He hates the Olympian gods and their notions of civil existence,
and lives like a bandit, an outlaw. Ludicrous now in his passion,
he combs the snarls and tangles out of his hair with a rake
and trims his beard with a pruning hook, staring down at a pond's
surface (he doesn't possess a mirror) and scaring the fish.   760
He tries to look like a gallant, a cave-man fashion plate,
and even amends his behavior, so that passing ships are safe
from his depredations. His love of blood and slaughter comes
          second
to the love he's conceived for me. At about this time, I have heard,
Telemus, eminent seer and the gifted reader of omens,
arrived on the island to visit Aetna, and met the Cyclops.
He greeted Polyphemus and ventured to make a prediction:
'Beware of the Greek who will come to pluck out your eye—
          Ulysses
is on his way!' But the Cyclops, unimpressed, only joked,
'My eye is already gone. Both it and my heart belong   770
to the beautiful Galatea.' And he stomped away in a huff
to walk the pebbly beach or else hunker down in his cave
and brood as he muttered or raged, or even—bizarrely—sang.
There is a promontory that juts out into the sea,
a splendid if desolate place, with the waves on both sides boiling,
breaking, and then reappearing in an endless agitation.
To this the Cyclops came, and he clambered out to the point,
and sat on the rocks, where he lay down his walking stick, that
          enormous
pine-tree trunk he used, and played to himself on his syrinx,
which was large and loud—imagine a pipe organ he blew in.   780
The mountains echoed, and rocks on the beach resounded, with
          music.
From far away, where I hid in the woods in my Acis' arms,
we could hear his baleful bellow and even make out the words:

> O ruddier than the cherry,
> O sweeter than the berry,
> O ruddier than the cherry,
> O sweeter than the berry,
> O nymph more bright
> than moonshine night
> like kidlings blithe and merry.   790
>
> Ripe as the melting cluster,
> no lily has such luster;
> yet hard to tame as raging flame
> and fierce as storms that bluster.

O ruddier than the cherry,
O sweeter than the berry,
O ruddier than the cherry,
O sweeter than the berry,
O nymph more bright
than moonshine night   800
like kidlings blithe and merry.

"He went on that way for hours. Who can remember it all?
It was altogether the usual kind of thing, but grotesque
coming from him. I was 'harder than oak, falser than water,
vain as a peacock, deaf as a stone, sharp as a snake,
crueler than fire. . . .' You'd think he'd made this up on the spot.
The same old thing, but performed much louder, I do believe,
than is customary with lovers. There were also the blandishments
I should have found insulting if I hadn't thought they were funny.
He enumerated his assets, his mountainsides and his caves—   810
as if his extensive holdings in Stone Age real estate
might win me over. He boasted, 'Warm in the winter's chill,
and cool in the summer's heat.' It was probably true, but the catch
was that he would be there as well. His orchards were full of
          apples,
and his vineyards were rich with grapes on the vine, both white
          and red.
His strawberry patch was thick with berries; his trees were heavy
with fruit, cherries and plums, both black and the pale greengage.
His flocks were too many to count, and their udders were full, so
          milk
and cheese were never wanting. If romance wouldn't do it,
he figured he might fall back on appeals to a smart consumer.   820
     "Some of what he thought up had a dopey kind of charm.
I remember he talked about presents, pets that he'd caught to give
          me—
a pair of does, or hares, or goats, or a pair of doves
from a nest he'd found on a cliff. There were also a couple of bear
          cubs
he'd found on a mountain slope that he'd trapped, brought home,
          and tamed,
and wanted me to have. How could a girl refuse
a brace of bears, after all? Or that's how he'd worked it out,
and if I was not responsive, then I was ungrateful, perverse,
and wrong-headed. He granted that looks weren't his forte,
although, as he put it, 'For sheer bulk, my body and Jove's   830
are more or less the same. And if I'm a trifle hairy,

with my beard down on my chest, and my body covered with
    mats
of thick and curly hair, trees are much better with leaves;
horses without their manes are ugly; plucked birds are silly;
and shorn sheep are pathetic.' This was the general trend
of the argument he put forward, and I was expected to be
persuaded, although there was still that one eye, which, he
    admitted,
set just above the nose in midforehead, was . . . striking?
A bit off-putting even? Large as a fair-sized shield?
'But the Sun, which is hardly deformed, looks down with its
    single eye   840
from a vantage place in heaven to mark what goes on in the
    world.'
    "These disquisitions went on for days, for weeks, at a time,
and, though I wasn't much moved, their cumulative effect
on him was hard to miss. He seemed to persuade himself
that he was a plausible match, an attractive catch, a decent
mate any sensible girl would welcome with open arms.
He mentioned his family tree, as if the negotiations
were well underway and now confined to such details.
His father, lord of the sea, would soon be my father-in-law,
mighty Neptune himself. This notion seemed to delight him,   850
and, if I was less than pleased, it meant I was being obtuse,
for he knew I wasn't a woman who hates all men. He had heard
that Acis and I were lovers—and this, he thought, was
    outrageous.
I should prefer someone else to him? It was not to be borne,
and he refused to allow it. That's when he changed his tune
from love's melodious plaint to boisterous battle anthem.
He'd teach Acis a lesson, tear out his living organs
and scatter them over the endless waves of his father's realm.
He'd do astonishing things, cruel and amazing. His rage
knew no limits, but burned in his breast like Aetna's lava,   860
which sooner or later would spew forth to destroy whatever it
    touched
and teach me and the world a lesson we'd never forget.
    "Was there ever such a lover? How did he think I'd react?
Or by then, I suppose, he knew his chances were less than good.
He pawed the ground like an angry bull the farmer has left
alone in the field, having taken his charming heifer away.
He ran through the woods, and the earth shook with each footfall.
We could feel him coming closer and tried to hide, but he found
    us

and called out in that bellow of his, 'I see you. I've got you!
And that was the last embrace you will ever have together.   870
However good it was, the last time is always special
and something you'll remember. . . .' And here was a sinister
          laugh
that sounded like Aetna's rumblings just before it erupts.
Terrified, I ran for my life and dove into the sea.
Acis was running the other way, to the deeper woods,
and praying as he ran, to me, his parents, the gods. . . .
He knew the odds against him were long indeed and could feel
that shaking ground as the Cyclops pursued him, relentless,
          gaining.
How long could he hope to survive? He had never run so fast,
but fear helped him along, and he'd started to think there was
          hope,   880
when Polyphemus grabbed a piece of a mountain and hurled it
ahead with a mighty grunt. As it fell, the protruding edge
of a boulder you'd think had barely grazed poor Acis hit him
and killed him there in an instant. Buried him. I could do nothing
but watch the blood come trickling out from the rock and dirt.
It continued to flow, but it lightened in color. I saw it changing
until it was like some stream that's cloudy in early spring
from the runoff of melting snows. And then it was crystal clear.
That piece of the mountainside the Cyclops had thrown split
          open,
and a tall reed grew up in a gushing of waters, a fountain   890
where, waist-deep in the water, with horns that were wreathed in
          rushes,
Acis stood, larger than ever, his face now a startling blue,
the one I loved but changed, remote, inaccessible, lost—
now the god of the river that has borne, ever since, his name."
     When Galatea fell silent, the nereids all dispersed,
swimming away like so many dolphins among the waves
while Scylla, who could not swim as well as the rest, returned
to the shore. She waded out of the gently heaving water
and wandered along the beach, letting the sunshine dry
her dampened hair, or now and then going back to the surf   900
to wade or even to take a cooling plunge—and Glaucus,
a merman, swimming along offshore, espied her, naked,
gorgeous, and he was smitten at once with a passionate yearning.
He called to her, said whatever a man can say to a maiden,
but she was not responsive. Indeed, she was mostly afraid
and ran away, her speed increased by her fear. He followed
as she headed inland and up whatever inclines she could find,

until she reached the top of a bluff that juts into the sea.
There was nowhere further to run. She stopped and turned as
     Glaucus
approached—a monster? a god? She looked at his flowing shaggy   910
hair, his muscular chest and broad shoulders, and, lower,
the place where his manly thighs abruptly merged to a fish's
tail. He stopped and called from a decent distance, "Young
     woman,
I am, I promise, no monster or ogre you ought to fear
but a god of the sea, the equal of Proteus, Triton, Palaemon,
or any of those of whom you have heard, and with powers as
     great.
I was a mortal once who lived on the land, but fate
had plotted its course on my chart. Even then, I would put to sea
to fish from a boat with nets, or from shore with rod and reel.
I knew a special place, with a grassy meadow behind it.   920
From a rock that projected out to the sea, I would cast my line.
That meadow behind me was perfect . . . untouched. No cows
     grazed there,
or goats, or sheep, or even bees making rounds of the blossoms.
No peasants came with sickles to mow the grass. It was land
somehow hidden away, as if my feet were the first
ever to cross that turf. I spread my gear there to dry,
and I put my fish in the shaded grass there to keep them fresh. . . .
Nothing at all peculiar so far, but the fish began
to stir, to wriggle, to nibble the grass, and to flop about
and move on land as they'd moved before in the depths of the sea. 930
I watched as they made their way back toward the beach and
     returned
to the water in which I'd caught them. I'd never seen anything
     like it!
Was a god telling me something? Was it, perhaps, this grass?
My curiosity led me to try, as a kind of test,
that grass to see what its powers might be. . . . I plucked some,
     chewed it,
swallowed its strange juices, and instantly felt my heart
quaking within me. I knew that I'd undergone some basic
and fundamental change. I couldn't imagine resisting
but turned—or felt myself turning—and did what I had to do,
or say that I watched my feet as they walked down to the water   940
and entered the beckoning sea, for which my entire being
suddenly yearned. It invited, and something within me answered.
I called to the world and the life I was leaving behind me,
     'Farewell.

O Earth, farewell,' and I knew in my heart and my bone's marrow
I should never come back to walk on the firm ground. I plunged
cheerfully into the water, which has ever since been my home.
The sea gods welcomed me grandly, and brought me before
       Oceànus
and Tethys to purge my mortal nature and make me pure
in order to give me a place as one of their number. In sacred
rites, they intoned their affecting magical hymns and spells   950
nine times in a row and sent me to bathe my mortal
flesh in the running waters of a hundred different streams.
I remember the start of the deluge of water that poured on my
       head
and sluiced along my limbs . . . but then it's a pleasant blur.
After a time my senses returned, and I was what you see
before you now, with my body changed but also my mind.
My greenish color, my long and flowing hair, my enormous
shoulders, were all new, and these legs that fuse to a tail.
My understanding was also new, richer and truer—
but useless, all of these gifts are useless and even hateful   960
if you don't think them attractive. You are not at all pleased?
You are even perhaps repelled? What good is it then to be
       welcomed
by gods of the sea? What good does it do me to be a god?"
She didn't even reply but darted around him and ran
pell-mell down the slope, and he was alone, dismayed,
and full of grief, which turned, as grief ofteh does, to rage.
At length he found a resolve, a purpose had formed in his mind,
and he set off to visit the court of Apollo's daughter Circe.

BOOK XIV

Aetna was now behind him, that mountain piled on the head
of the buried giant, and the Cyclops' virginal fields, which plows
and harrows had never touched, fell away beyond the receding
horizon as Glaucus progressed past Zancle's protected harbor,
sailed by Rhegium's walls on the mainland, and crossed that strait
where many good ships and crews have come to such sudden grief.
He made it into blue water and, across the Tyrrhenian Sea,
came at last to the flowery hills of Circe's domain,
that beguiling place where the palace of Phoebus' daughter looms
among the band of her victims that snort and grunt as the beasts   10
into which she has turned them all. Glaucus approached her, was
    welcomed,
and thus addressed the goddess: "Lady, I come to beg
a favor. I pray you, help me, a goddess aiding a god.
I require some of your herbs, or spells, or whatever magic
you use to adjust and improve the world, to effect such changes
as I myself can attest. I am in love with Scylla,
who rejects my passionate pleading, my compliments, my
    songs. . . .
Nothing I do seems to work. She remains indifferent, aloof,
not even, I blush to admit it, amused or diverted. Give me
something more to the point, some charm perhaps, or potion—   20
not to assuage my pains or to cool my fiery longing,
but to set her heart ablaze so it matches the heat of my own."
Circe looked at this fellow who'd come on so novel an errand,
was interested both in his plaint and indeed in him. . . . Who
    knows
how these abrupt and irrational transactions begin? In him?
Or in her own heart or eyes? Or his passion for somebody else?
Or was it Venus herself, still angry that Circe's father
had run about heaven beaming and carrying tales? In any
event, and for whatever reason, Circe replied:

"Why should you care about her? Despise whoever despises   30
you, and love who loves you as you deserve to be loved!
Why should you be the one to pursue, who ought to be wooed,
desired, yearned for by day and dreamt of by night? I assure you
these things I say, although you can scarcely believe them, are
          true!
I have those potions and charms you think you require but don't—
your face has the magic; your eyes have the irresistible power.
Believe the report of a woman who feels their effects as she
          speaks."
Glaucus answered the goddess but offering not much hope:
"The sea will burst into flower, and dank seaweed will float
on the peaks of the loftiest mountains, before my affection shall
          change.   40
As long as the lovely Scylla lives, my heart shall be hers."
The face of the goddess abruptly changed from her adoration
to fury. But what could she do? She couldn't cause harm to a god
(especially one whom she loved), so she turned her wrath
          elsewhere,
to the girl, her enemy, rival, a fool who had spurned one god
and now offended another. Circe would give her a lesson
in manners. She put together a mixture of powders and juices,
while singing incantations. Hecate's charms she mixed in,
and she put on her deep blue robe and strode through the gates of
          her villa,
shooing away the fawning beasts that groveled and swarmed   50
to block her path. She arose and flew to Rhegium's coast,
where she hovered low on the water, or walked along on the
          waves
as if they were solid ground. There was a little pool,
a place that the curve of the beach protected, where Scylla would
          come
to take her ease in the heat of the day and bathe in the water.
This pool, the goddess bewitches, pouring into it noxious
substances she has compounded, murmuring sinister charms.
Three times to the third power she casts the syllables' net
over the innocent water, turning it into a cesspool
into which Scylla wades, waist-deep in the water,   60
which changes whatever it touches, infects, deforms. . . . She
          looks down
at her thighs and loins, now monstrous with pustules that bark
          like dogs.

She cannot believe these are growths of her body and tries to
    escape them,
running back out of the water. . . . But who can escape from one's
    self?
Her thighs, her calves, and her feet are lumpy with heads of
    hounds,
which snarl and growl and snap as Cerberus does. Her nether
parts are a horrid pack of wild and ravening beasts.
    Glaucus sees this and weeps. Horrified, he will have nothing
whatever to do with the witch who has punished Scylla so cruelly.
Scylla, fixed in that place, detests all men and destroys   70
whomever she can—her victims include Ulysses' companions.
She would have destroyed Aeneas' party as well, had she not,
before they hove into view, been changed again to a rock,
which stands offshore to this day—and sailors give it wide berth.
    The Trojans had passed this monster and Charybdis as well.
    They had neared
the Italian shore when a storm blew them off course to the South,
where Dido welcomed Aeneas to her hearth, her abundant table,
and even her bed. He departed, driven by destiny, leaving
the woman behind, bereft, to fall on her sword like a man.
Horrified thus by the world, she horrifyingly answered   80
by killing herself. Aeneas returned to the North and landed
on Sicily's sandy shore, where his friend Acastes ruled.
There he performed the sacrificial rites to pay honor
at his father's tomb. It was here that Juno's messenger, Iris,
all but destroyed the ships with the fire she brought, but the
    Trojans
avoided ruin, escaped, set sail once again, and approached
the Aeolian Islands, which smoke with volcanic fumes and hot
    ashes,
where the Sirens, the daughters of Acheloüs, have made their
    home.
Here with his pilot, the brave Palinurus, lost, Aeneas
coasted along the shore, off Inarime, Prochyte,   90
and Pithecusa's barren hillsides, where the Cercopes
pay their wretched penance. . . . They are called that, from the
    Greek
kerkos, which means "tail." The tale is that Jupiter wearied
of all their tricks and lies, turned them from men to beasts,
shortened their limbs, blunted and furrowed their faces, and gave
    them
hair all over their bodies, and tails, and he took away

the powers of speech they had used for perjuries, falsehoods,
    deceptions,
and such breaches of faith. As monkeys now, they complain
in raucous but nonetheless honest jibbers and wordless shrieks.
     This curious place Aeneas left behind as he neared   100
Naples, Parthenope's city, where Misenus, Aeolus' son,
is entombed in one of those ancient mounds. At Cumae, he landed
and entered the Sybil's grotto, to pray that he might adventure
down to Avernus' forbidden realm to visit his father's
ghost. The Sibyl gazed for a long time at the earth
beneath her feet as if she expected it might, at the least
provocation, open. She looked at the hero again,
and spoke the mad and inspired phrases the god had put in
her mind: "Great things do you ask, but you have endured great
    trials
of strength and faith by fire and sword, and you shall succeed.   110
What you have asked shall be granted, and I shall serve as your
    guide,
for virtue's reward is the world, and even its secret places
shall welcome you. We shall visit Elysium's fields in the kingdom
where all men go at the last, and encounter your father's ghost."
Thus she spoke as she led him through Proserpina's dark glades,
where she showed him a tree that gleamed with gold and told him
    to pluck
one of its sacred boughs for its talismanic power.
He did as she had bidden, and ventured to Orcus' kingdom,
where the ghosts of his city and house now dwelt, including his
    father,
the noble-souled Anchises. He learned the laws of these places   120
and the will of the Fates for the future—what perils he had yet to
    face,
and what new trials and wars. Together they started back,
he and the Sibyl, climbing the steep ascent of the gloomy
path that wound its way upward and back toward the light.
To pass the time of the arduous journey, he spoke to his guide
his expressions of thanks for her help. "Whether you be indeed
a goddess, or merely a mortal woman who pleases the gods
and is given their special gifts, I am grateful to you and worship
you as no less than divine. I confess I owe you my life,
having escaped from the realm of the dead. When at last we
    emerge,   130
I shall build you a temple, erect an altar, and burn incense
there in your honor." The Sibyl, hearing him say this, sighed,

was quiet a while, and then chose to speak from the depths of her
    woe:
"No, I am not any goddess, but only a mortal, unworthy
of altars or incense. My story is this, that Phoebus Apollo
offered me endless life if I would accept his advances.
This was the blandishment, gift, or payment . . . whatever one
    calls it.
'Choose whatever you will, maiden of Cumae, and know
that it shall be yours,' he promised. Foolish I was then, and
    young,
and I looked to a heap of dust, pointed my finger, and asked   140
for as many years of life as were grains of dust in that pile.
What I neglected to ask for was endless youth, and the god
smiled and explained my blunder. He couldn't go back on his
    promise,
but thought he could bargain. He offered the gift I'd neglected to
    ask for
if I would submit to his lust. I told him no, and remain
a virgin still—but old, and the springtime of youth is long gone.
Each year that I totter through, I am older and weaker as time
itself turns to a burden. Generations of men are born
and die, as I watch in dismay. Seven, I've seen now, so far,
and what remains is appalling—three hundred springtimes, three
    hundred   150
harvest and vintage seasons. What I am now is a fragment
of what I was, but I'm flaking away, will be brittle and tiny,
a shrunken and wizened wraith, light as a feather the wind
blows this way and that. And the god, no longer love-struck,
will no longer recognize that girl he once cursed in his pique
to endure on this rack of time. What will be left then? A voice
the Fates will have left me to chirp the secrets of gods and the
    ages."
    While the Sibyl thus had been speaking, they made their way
        up the slope
to the world of light and emerged near Cumae, where they had
    started.
Aeneas made sacrifice here, then sailed to the next landfall,   160
a place Virgil tells us was called Caieta (as if
its clairvoyant natives knew that Aeneas one day would come
and they thought he'd be pleased that his nurse had thus been
    memorialized).
Whatever one calls it, this place was where Ulysses' companion

Macareus had stayed. He recognized Achaemenides,
the crew mate they'd left back at Aetna, whom Aeneas had taken
        aboard.
Astonished to see him alive, Macareus exclaimed, "Amazing!
Alive and well? I am glad! But what is a Greek like you
doing among these Trojans?" Achaemenides was gracious,
and, no longer dressed in rags that were held together with
        thorns,   170
he answered his shipmate thus: "I would confront once more
Polyphemus' gore-flecked jaws and his single evil
eye before I'd exchange these friends for my old home
on Ithaca. For my own father I feel no more reverence
and love than for Aeneas, to whom I owe thanks for my life.
Every breath that I take, I do so by his good gift,
and with every dawn and sunset my debt to this man increases.
And if I were now to drop dead, my dying words would be
        thanks
that I may expect to be buried with proper rites in a tomb
that isn't the Cyclops' disgusting maw. Can you even imagine   180
what I was thinking and feeling, watching you leave me? Your
        boat
had put out to sea, and I stared at the growing space between ship
and shore, and I felt a despair I cannot describe. I'd have called,
but that would have let the Cyclops know where I was. In a silent
nightmare I watched as he raged, tore a huge rock from the
        hillside,
and flung it out at your vessel, as if from some huge mangonel.
I held my breath lest the rock hit it, or, almost as bad,
I worried that waves it would cause might founder the boat. . . .
        I'd forgotten
I wasn't in danger aboard, but abandoned, alone, and in peril
greater than any that you were facing together. You made it   190
safely away and managed to get out of range. I was left
to cower and watch as this monster roamed around Aetna, raging
and pulling up trees with his huge hands as he cursed all Greeks,
and prayed that he might yet find one—Ulysses or one of his
        friends—
to torture a while, to rip pieces from out of his living
body and drink his blood, chewing on limbs that still quivered
with life and could feel the teeth that were tearing into their flesh.
Blinded, but hardly tamed, he was terrifying to watch
as he ranged like a crazed beast over his mountainside, gore

from his maimed eye still smeared on his face and into his beard,   200
where it mixed with the blood and gobbets of flesh of his latest
    victims.
I knew it was only a matter of time before he found me
and killed me, but that was by no means the worst of it.
    Somehow, my mind
fixed upon the notion that, after the monster ate me,
I should be part of his flesh, my flesh consumed or subsumed
into his and my spirit. . . . No corner in hell could be worse!
And I had to stand by and witness the show he put on when he
    captured
a couple of my companions, men I had known. I just stared
at this panorama of horror, watching him lift them up
and dash their heads on the ground, smashing their delicate skulls.   210
Then, like a beast, he crouched over their bodies and ravened,
ripping their organs out and their flesh from the bones and
    drinking
their blood, which was still warm. Along with this cannibal feast
he swilled some local wine straight from the barrel, but drank
too fast, too much. . . . God knows! In any event, he retched,
vomited, but then continued to eat, picking delicate
morsels from what was left of the corpses. Dreadful enough,
but I knew that what I was watching was sure to be reenacted
with me on the ground as his entrée. I managed to sneak away
and kept myself in hiding, subsisting on fallen acorns   220
and occasional succulent leaves, helpless, abandoned, alone,
and in utter despair. . . . And then a ship appeared, and the
    Trojans
rescued me. A Greek, I was welcomed among our erstwhile
foes. But tell me of your adventures! What did your company
suffer? What became of you after you left me?"
    Macareus then told of Aeolus, Hippotes' son,
and how he gave to Ulysses a gift of the winds, enclosed
in a leather bag—a handy thing for a sailor to have—
but the men supposed that the bag held treasure, and, after nine
days of splendid progress, with the coast they had sought in sight,   230
they undid the drawstrings and loosed the winds, which blew
    their vessel
all the way back to Aeolus' harbor. "A dismal business,"
Macareus said with a sigh, "and after that, we came
to the Laestrygonians' home in the city that Lamus built,
where Antiphates chased us, he and his mob. They hurled

timbers and heavy stones, and sank our ships, and our men
drowned in the sea. Only one vessel escaped—Ulysses
and I were aboard that lucky ship. We grieved for our losses
but carried on and arrived at last at that land you see
yonder. It's Circe's island. I warn you all to steer clear   240
of its dismal shore. We moored on that beach, but this time were
          careful,
and we drew lots to elect a party to go and explore.
I was chosen, with Polites, Eurylochus, Elpenor. . . .
He liked to drink, you remember. And eighteen others, I think.
We set out for Circe's city, where we found a thousand wolves,
bears, and lions—a zoo, but all of the animals tame
and wagging their tails and fawning, trotting along beside us.
At the gates of the palace, servants welcomed us in and led us
through marble halls to their mistress' presence. She sits on a
          throne,
splendid in purple and gold, and governs a magical realm   250
where nobody spins or cards or weaves. What they do is collect
and sort out plants and herbs, which they put in various boxes
and baskets. It isn't a kingdom as much as a giant drugstore
she's running there. She greeted us, seemed to be perfectly
          friendly,
and ordered a feast to be brought at once. She offered us wine,
or a punch she had made from wine, to drink one another's health.
The attendants she has are nymphs and nereids, gorgeous
          creatures,
and at once they produced great salvers of barley bread and
          elaborate
goblets and poured us drinks from beautiful serving vessels.
They had added spices and honey for sweetness and savor, and
          other   260
more baleful ingredients, too, from her pharmacopoeia, with other
surprising, dismaying results. We accepted cups from her hand,
raised them aloft, and drank, draining them down to the dregs.
Before we set down the cups, the goddess extended a magic
wand and touched our foreheads. I grew, I'm ashamed to say,
bristles. I lost the power of speech and could only grunt.
I'd been turned into a pig, and the others also were pigs. . . .
Instead of a mouth and a nose, I'd developed a definite snout.
I was down on the ground on all fours, and my friends were down
          beside me,
crawling about on the ground as snuffling, grunting beasts.   270

She drove us into a pen with the rest of her pigs, an enormous
collection of swine, I must say. And we still would be there, had
    not
Eurylochus somehow refused to accept her refreshment.
He had not been transformed, was still a man, and could still
speak, could go back and report in words to Ulysses, our captain,
who came forthwith to avenge us. This was how the great gift
of Mercury proved to be useful. That god who brings peace had
    given
our leader a little white flower with a black root, which the gods
have called by the name of moly. With this talismanic plant
Ulysses was able to come into Circe's palace, as we   280
had come before. The goddess offered him something to drink,
one of those terrible cocktails. . . . He held up the powerful
    charm,
this flower the god had provided, and with it could fend off the
    wand
she waved about and with which she was already trying to stroke
his hair. But nothing happened. Surprised and afraid, the queen
froze as he drew his sword. She had met her match, her master.
She wasn't at all dismayed, but pleased, even delighted,
in love with the man she had dreamt would come, and to whom
    she could look
for strength and dominion. She offered to share her throne and
    her bed,
and they pledged their faith with each other, clasping their hands
    as a sign   290
of union. Ulysses demanded from her, as a nuptial gift,
that his men should all be restored to human form. She consented
and sprinkled juices that she had concocted, muttering chants
and invocations to counteract the spells she had used
before, and she stroked our backs with the wand, which she now
    reversed
and held with its handle extended. She sang; we heard; and our
    souls
quickened. We stood erect as our bristles melted away,
and we felt our cloven hoofs return to their prior shape.
Our arms lengthened and straightened, and hands appeared at our
    wrists.
We wept for joy and in thanks, and embraced our captain, who
    also   300
wept to see us whole and hale, restored to ourselves
and to him. We stayed there a whole year, and in that extended

time in that strange island I witnessed and heard many things
the like of which it is hard to believe or to understand.
One of the stories I think of, one of Circe's attendants
told me one day. Ulysses was off somewhere with his mistress,
and she and I were left alone in the garden. She showed me
a statue, life-sized, and of snowy marble. A woodpecker, also
of marble, stood on his head. This wasn't a joke but enshrined,
and people had left before it the usual floral offerings   310
gods receive. I asked her who this was, and for what
reason this odd cult had arisen. And why a bird?
'Listen,' she said, 'and I'll tell you what Circe is able to do.
   "'Picus, the son of Saturn, who once ruled in Ausonia,
loved horses and fighting. A strong and a handsome man,
the statue is his. As fine as it looks, his living body
was even better, vital, vibrant, and more commanding.
He was at that perfect moment of youth's perfection. . . . His age
I can't say to the day, but I know that it couldn't have spanned
more than four of those ritual contests the Greeks put on   320
every fifth year at Elis. The dryads of woodlands pursued him,
eager to touch that remarkable body and bear his children,
and the nymphs of the fountains pined, burning for his embraces.
Yearning for him as well were the naiads—of Albula's river,
and the Numicus, Anio, Almo, the Farfar, the rushing Nar.
They all babbled and gushed of him, in the pools and the lakes,
but all these he spurned, for his heart belonged to one nymph
       alone.
This was the daughter Venilia bore on the Palatine Hill
to two-faced Janus. Their girl was a beautiful baby and, grown,
was a beautiful woman with many impressive suitors to choose
       from.   330
Picus, she much preferred, and he adored her for her beauty
and also her gift of song, which was even more rare and amazing.
She could move rocks and trees with her elegant trills and flutings,
tame the hearts of wild beasts, and stop the waters of flowing
rivers, which tarried to hear just a few more silvery notes.
They called her, therefore, Canens. Picus wholly adored her.
One day, however, he rode out to hunt wild boar in the nearby
meadows and groves—as if to prove to her and himself
that he could leave her singing, at least for a little while.
He was a handsome fellow indeed astride his remarkable   340
horse, with a brace of ashen spears in his hand and wearing
a splendid purple cloak, which was fastened closed at the neck
with a brooch of glistening gold. Circe, the Sun's daughter,

was gathering herbs in that fertile wood, where she saw the glint
of her father's light as it glanced off that bright brooch that he
     wore.
That may have first caught her attention, but then the young man
himself was something to see. She couldn't believe it or tear
her eyes away from this quite delicious creature. A fire
burned in her vitals and bones. She dropped the herbs from her
     hands
as if they were useless twigs and flowers and roots. This magic   350
was greater, and she was its victim. Or his. As he would be hers.
She would have accosted him then, but the pace of his steed was
     too swift,
and he and his train had gone by before she could get out the
     words,
but into the empty air he had left behind him she called,
"You think you've gotten away? But think again, for the wind
itself is not so fast or strong as my charms. You may try,
but you cannot escape my powers. I shall ensnare you yet,
for tricks and charms will always triumph over the strength
of simple virtue." She muttered an incantation and made
a gesture or two with her wand, creating a phantom boar,   360
an insubstantial simulacrum, which rushed through the trees
as bait, a delusional thing, a huge will-o'-the-wisp. . . .
And of course Prince Picus saw it and chased it at once through
     the bracken
and into the trees, through the deeper groves and the denser
     thickets,
until the trail had led where no horse could go. He dismounted
and followed along on foot, groping blindly behind
the figment he thought was his quarry. Circe, meanwhile, was
     weaving
more spells and charms, with incantations and prayers to the
     weird
spirits with whom she enjoyed her special connection. A mist
came up to obscure the face of her father, the Sun, in the heavens   370
and darken all the earth. The prince's servants and friends
were lost in the sudden ground fog and wandered about in
     confusion.
He was alone, undefended, and she now confronted him,
     speaking:
"O fairest of men, o handsome fellow! Your eyes have seared
my very soul. A goddess, I offer the gift of myself
to you, a perfect mortal. Accept as your father-in-law

the Sun that shines above us and sees all things. I am Circe,
his daughter, a goddess, a Titan. Do not reject me, I pray you."
"Whoever you are," he answered, "I must decline. I am not
for you, but belong to another to whom I have pledged my heart,   380
to Canens, the daughter of Janus, with whom I expect to remain
for the rest of my days." This wasn't what Circe was hoping to
        hear.
She clenched her teeth and pronounced numerous spells and
        curses,
but nothing at all happened. At length she challenged Picus:
"You think you can walk away and forget this? Your precious
        Canens
shall never see you again, nor shall you see her. That's finished!
A woman scorned, or a goddess, is something for man to fear.
You'll learn the wages of virtue." Then she fell silent or muttered
unintelligible sounds as she turned, twice to the West
and twice to the East, and then touched him, once, twice, and
        again.   390
He turned and began to run, faster than ever before,
as fast as his mind could imagine. . . . He wasn't running but
        flying,
as his body sprouted wings. Angry at what had happened,
he started to bang on the trees with his beak, to protest, to attack
whatever he could. His wings were the purple his cloak had been,
and the brooch of gold was still there at his neck in feathers of
        gold.
He was altogether transformed, and all that remained of the
        former
prince was his name, Picus ("woodpecker," in Latin).
     "'His friends who'd been searching and calling in vain for
        Picus found,
as the fog cleared and the cloud dispersed, the sorceress Circe,   400
whom they correctly accused of having committed some crime
against their lord. They demanded an answer. They wanted their
        prince
restored to them safe and sound, and prepared to attack the witch,
when she sprinkled her duppy dust into the air and touched them
with all of its noxious poisons. Night and the gods of Night
she summoned forth from hell; Chaos itself she invoked;
and Hecate, witchcraft's mistress. The woods quivered and
        groaned,
as the earth shook and rumbled. The trees turned white, and the
        plants,

wherever her dust had touched them, were crimson with drops of
  blood.
The stones groaned aloud, and from somewhere the baying of
  hounds   410
spooked the enchanted glade. Odd smells suffused the air,
while nasty beasties scuttled from underneath rocks or flew
through the suddenly fetid air. The young men were all afraid
and would have fled but couldn't. As if paralyzed, they stood
and endured the touch of her terrible wand, which turned them
  from men
to various kinds of feral beasts she thought they were.
    "'As the setting sun was fading on the farthest western
  shores,
Canens watched and waited for Picus' return, her love
now feeding her concern. Slaves and women-in-waiting
had gone with flaming torches to meet their master, welcome   420
him home, and light the last of his way. But nobody came.
Into the night she waited, and worry gave way to dread,
and dread to the dismal conviction that something awful had
  happened.
She wept of course, and she tore her hair, but that wasn't all,
for she set out to find her darling, her love, wandering madly
day and night, over hills and down the dales, wherever
chance beckoned her feet. Each dawn revealed her distraction,
her weariness, and her weakness, until at the sixth sunrise
her frail body collapsed by the banks of the Tiber, spent
and reduced to a vocalization of grief and a trickle of tears.   430
As a dying swan is said to sing its own funeral dirge,
so she poured out her plaint, for the lost love of her life,
and indeed for her life itself. Worn by woe to a shadow,
reduced to a wraith, she shimmered, melted, and disappeared
into thin air. And that place the ancient Muses would call
Canens in honor of her who there became her song.'
    "That was the kind of thing that went on. We were there a
  year,
had utterly lost our sea legs, and turned rather fat and lazy
when Ulysses ordered us back to the vessel to make it shipshape
and ready to put to sea. Circe warned him of danger,   440
warned us all with predictions of dire perils we'd face. . . .
True, or not? Who knows? But I believed her and stayed,
hiding out on the shore, which is why you find me here."
    Macareus, having completed his tale, fell silent.
This was the shore where Aeneas buried his nurse, Caieta,

with the epitaph he carved in hexameters there on her tomb:
AENEAS • MY • NURSLING • SAVED • ME • FROM • GREEKS' • CONSUMING •
    FIRE;
TO • FIND • HERE • ON • ITALIAN • SOIL • A • MORE • FITTING • PYRE.
They let slip the hawsers and put to sea, giving Circe's island
much leeway, and they headed up the coast to the mouth   450
of the Tiber, where its silt-laden waters flow to the sea.
There did Aeneas win Lavinia, who was Latinus'
daughter, fighting a war (again? over a woman?)
tribe versus tribe, and blood against blood, with the valiant
    Turnus
fighting to keep that girl whose hand he had been promised—
the girl, say, and his honor. Etruria, under Tarchon,
joined on Aeneas' side against the Rutulian forces
that Turnus led. On both sides, they sent out requests to their
    friends
for aid, supplies, reinforcements. Aeneas went to Evander,
who gave what he could. Turnus, in the other camp, dispatched   460
Venulus to the city of Argyripa, where great
Diomedes lived in exile on fertile holdings
that King Daunus had given as a marriage portion. To him
Venulus conveyed brave Turnus' request for aid.
Aetolia's hero listened but then declined—beyond
his general disinclination to fight, exposing to danger
his father-in-law's people, he said that his own forces
had been severely diminished. "Let me explain," the chieftain
said. "I will tell you the story I grieve to remember, much less
recite. But what can I do? You deserve to hear me explain.   470
After Troy was burned, Pergamon razed, and the Greek
appetite for destruction you'd think would be sated, Ajax—
the lesser Ajax, I mean—raped Cassandra. Such things
happen, of course; but he did this in Minerva's temple, displeasing
the goddess, who punished us all for the guilt of our one
    companion.
As we sailed back to our homes, the seas rose up, and the winds
scattered us this way and that. Lightning flashed, and the thunder
rolled in a terrible storm. Our disaster at Caphereus,
that terrible Euboean promontory, you've heard of. . . .
A dreadful business! Priam himself, if he had but known,   480
would have wept to hear the story of what happened there. I
    escaped,
having somehow found favor with well-armed Minerva, who
    spared me

to let me come home and find that my wife had taken up
    whoring.
Another goddess, Venus, was punishing me for offenses
she hadn't ever forgiven. I left that disgraceful scene
and put to sea again, again to find storms, adventures,
and terrible trials, which made me envy the drowned who were
    now
out of harm's way at last under those heaving waters
off the Euboean coast. I wished I were one of their number.
    "My companions also despaired, but Acmon pronounced
    aloud   490
those thoughts he ought to have kept to himself: 'What does it
    matter
what the gods may think? What further harm can they do us now?
It can't get worse! If Venus forgives us, I say, terrific!
But if not? Why should we fear her? This is the absolute worst,
and, in such an extreme condition, prayer is a crock, and the gods
are nonsense. Once you've touched bottom, there's no fear of
    falling farther.'
With such rash and impolitic words, Pleuronian Acmon
revived the goddess' anger. The rest of us told him to stow it,
but we were too late. He never replied, but his voice turned shrill
and higher, just as his hair was turning to feathers. His face   500
developed an avian beak, his arms were transformed to wings,
and his toes developed webs. In horror, Lycus watched him
as Idas did, too, and Rhexenor and Nycteus did, and Abas—
and I watched them as they also changed into great seabirds.
It happened to most of the crew, and they rose up into the air
to circle around the men who were left at the oars—not swans,
but something like a swan. A shearwater, or coot . . .
What does it matter? The point is that most of the men were lost,
and those I have left are barely enough to run this place
and keep it safe. I'm sorry, but that's how it is, my friend."   510
    Thus Diomedes, Oeneus' grandson, spoke to his guest.
Venulus then departed, leaving Messapian pastures
behind him. He passed on his way a place in Apulia, a grotto
darkened by forest shadows and hidden away by a stand
of reeds that concealed its mouth. Pan, half-goat and half-god,
claims the place now, but once nymphs lived there, and a
    shepherd—
crude even for shepherds—would come to scare them away,
or, later, when they returned, he'd tease them with boorish
    remarks,

vulgar jokes, insults, and apish dances until
the plants of the wood converged about him, grew up his body,   520
and covered his mouth, and he was changed from man to tree,
a nasty oleaster, or wild olive, whose fruit
is bitter still on the tongue as his words and thoughts were bitter.
　　Turnus' emissaries returned at last with their bleak
report that Diomedes had refused to give them aid.
The Rutulians, notwithstanding, continued their struggle, and
　　precious
blood on both sides was spilled in dismaying quantities. Turnus
contrived a desperate measure, bringing his fiery torches,
which set Aeneas' ships ablaze. . . . The resinous wood
caught at once and burst into tongues of flame as the pitch   530
and resin fed the burning. The masts smoldered, and sails
were about to go up in sheets of fire over the smoking
hulls of the beached ships, when Cybele, mother of gods
and goddesses, interfered. Those ships' timbers were pines
felled from the peaks of Ida, and precious to her. There was
　　music,
a thrill of flutes and cymbals, as the goddess approached through
　　the shimmering
air in her chariot borne by her tamed but still mighty lions.
"No, Turnus, no," she called out, "these ships may not be burnt.
These torches of yours will fail, for I shall rescue these trees
that grew in my sacred wood." She had barely completed her
　　sentence   540
when rain began to fall in torrents, with hail mixed in,
and the winds arose to churn the sea spray into the air.
In a sudden roughhouse of friendly brothers, the winds contended
and played with the ships as if they were toys lined up on a shelf.
One of the winds, the goddess encouraged to buffet with special
strength, and it broke the hawsers that tied the ships to their
　　mooring
there on the beach. They slid back into the roiling waters,
frisked and played in the waves, and dove and plunged like living
creatures. The wood, indeed, was softening now, and the prows
were turning to heads, as the oars were becoming toes and feet.   550
What had been keel was spine, the strakes were ribs, the cordage
was hair, and the yardarms were really arms—and the ships were
　　nymphs,
water nymphs that frolicked with girlish delight in the sea,
which only a moment before they had feared, as mountain
　　creatures

fear what is utterly foreign. But now they were quite at ease,
delighted with their adopted home in the sparkling water.
But still they remember their earlier fear, and they often assist
storm-tossed ships and support with their hands the keels of
    vessels
in trouble out there in the heavy weather—all but the Greeks',
for they share Aeneas' hatred of those who destroyed high Troy   560
and cannot be much concerned when Greeks get what they
    deserve.
Therefore they watched in delight as Ulysses' ship broke up,
and again rejoiced to see how the vessel Alcinoüs gave him
turned from wood to stone in the mouth of Ithaca's harbor.
        This transformation from ships to nymphs was an awesome
            portent,
and many hoped that Turnus and all his Rutulian soldiers
might take it as omen and warning, and cease their fighting, but
    no,
nothing remotely like that happened. The war continued,
with each side fighting, and gods assisting them both. They had
not only gods but courage, which sometimes is as good   570
as divine assistance (or may be another way of describing
the same natural force). The question was no longer that
of the girl, or territory, or power, but honor. Neither
side could yield or acknowledge the other as victor. The fighting
was therefore worse, or purer—depending on how you see it.
In the end, of course, the goddess Venus watched as her son
won, for Turnus fell and died by Aeneas' hand.
Ardea, Turnus' capital city, then fell, and the soldiers
set it ablaze. A terrible thing, as a powerful city
burns away into ashes. But out of the rubble, a bird   580
of a kind never before seen appeared in the air
to stir those still hot ashes with the flapping of its huge wings.
A gaunt and woeful bird with a mournful cry, the heron
(*ardea*, in Latin) keeps the city alive in its name
and the dismal tattoo of the death march its wings seem to be
        beating.
        At the end of a hero's life, what glory remains? Aeneas
had moved the gods—even Juno, who put her longstanding anger
aside at last. Iulus, his son, had grown to manhood,
and the son of Venus was ready to enter now into heaven.
Venus approached great Jupiter's throne, embraced his neck,   590
and asked of him: "O father and reverend lord, you have shown
        me
constant kindness, but now I pray your special indulgence.

I ask, on behalf of my son Aeneas, who is your grandson,
whatever measure you think may be meet and right of godhood.
He has already gone to the ghastly kingdom across the Styx,
and once is enough, I think, for any mortal." The gods
all gave assent together, even Juno nodding her head
agreeably. Then Jove declared, "You both are worthy,
the mother who asks, and the son for whom she asks, and we
      grant
this prayer of yours." He spoke, nodded, and Venus gave thanks   600
for his great gift. In the air, borne aloft by her team of doves,
she flew to the coast where Numicius' waters flow in its many
mouths in a delta of reeds. She ordered the god of the river
to lave the mortal part of her son, purifying, refining,
and carrying all the dross to the fathomless depths of the sea.
The river god did as she asked, flensing corruption away
and leaving only the godly. His mother aspersed him with
      fragrant
attars, touched his lips with ambrosia mixed with nectar,
and made him a god—Iuppiter Indiges, native, for now
he was born again in the place destiny always had promised.   610
      The joint state, both Latin and Alban, prospered and
      flourished.
Ascanius ruled, then Silvius, then his son Latinus, then Alba.
Epytus next, and Capys, Capetus, and then Tiberinus. . . .
(He was the one who drowned in the river that bears his name.)
His sons were Remulus (perished, hit by lightning) and warlike
Acrota, who passed on the scepter to Aventinus (he's buried
on the hill where he reigned and that bears his name). Then Proca
      followed.
      It was during his time on the throne that the wood nymph
      Pomona lived,
whose skill in the care of plants and trees has never been equaled,
which is why she was given that name. She hardly noticed the
      rivers   620
and forests, but loved the fields and orchards with lines of fruit
      trees,
each with its laden branches. These were her passion, her life.
She carried, instead of a javelin, one of those curved pruning
      hooks,
with which she would trim dead branches or shape the growth of
      a tree
to something pleasing and sound. She knew the secrets of
      grafting,
how to make the incision in a tree's bark and implant

in the one stock a foreign branch that would bear its own
fruit. Wherever she went she would water trees so that thirsty
roots could absorb their fill. Venus, she didn't disdain
so much as ignore—the oafish satyrs and dancing Pans   630
only made her laugh. She kept aloof from their antics,
avoiding Silvanus' crudeness, or Priapus' even more
assertive suggestions. She shut herself up in her orchards and
     tended
her more congenial friends, the stately and bountiful trees.
There was, however, one suitor, the god of springtime,
     Vertumnus.
He was in love with her—more than all the rest. He adored her,
but not even he could attract her attention or get her to smile.
He used to disguise himself, would put on the clothes of a farm
     hand,
a reaper, and bring her a basket of barley ears. In his own
ears he would stick hay stalks, to look like some storybook yokel.   640
He held in his hand an ox goad to pass himself off as a drover
or plowman. Or else with a pruner, he'd try to look like a field
     hand
who tended the grapes in their arbors. He'd come next time with
     a ladder
and seem to be bound for some nearby orchard to gather apples.
With wigs, costumes, and make-up, he tricked himself out as a
     soldier
back from the wars, or again, with a fishing pole on his shoulder,
and a creel on his hip, he would play a fisherman back with his
     catch.
The point was just to be near her, stand there, and gaze at her
     beauty,
and maybe to wish her good morning, good afternoon, or good
     evening
before he plodded on by. He lived for these trivial moments!   650
One day he put on an old woman's dress and a wig on his head
with strands that peeped out from beneath a faded and ratty
     kerchief.
Limping along the road and using a staff that he leaned on,
he stopped to admire her orchard, let himself in at the gate,
and looked around at the trees. "Lovely," he said. "Truly lovely!
But you, miss, are lovelier still." Then, in a moment of boldness,
he put his arm around her and gave her a kiss no old woman
was likely to give. She was puzzled perhaps, but not frightened or
     spooked.
The bent and aged creature looked around then and remarked

on an elm that supported a grapevine that had twined up its
      sturdy trunk.   660
"Just look at that, would you?" he said, "and think how that tree
and vine complement each other, complete each other. . . . The
      tree
without the vine is just leaves, gives shade perhaps, but that's all.
And without the tree, the vine would be crawling along on the
      ground,
where its grapes would rot. But together, they're splendid, and
      each one profits.
There's a lesson in that, my dear, one that you might consider.
The way you've been keeping yourself to yourself is no good, a
      sad
violation of Nature, as well as a waste. A lover is all
you need to make you complete as a woman. You'd have many
      choices,
as many, I think, as Helen or Queen Hippodamia had,   670
or Ulysses' wife, around whom that ungainly mob once gathered.
But you don't care, you avoid them all, in their scores and
      hundreds,
who've seen you and long from afar to address you, the humans,
      the gods,
and those creatures in between, the demigods living in comfort
down in the Alban Hills. Take my advice, young lady,
and pick from among this gaggle a single mate who would love
      you,
the best, the most ardent and true. The one I mean is Vertumnus.
I know that young man as well as I know myself, and I warrant,
I guarantee, that he loves you, absolutely adores you.
His eyes are for you alone—he's blind to all others—and you   680
are his first, as you will be his last and his only, love.
Consider that he is young, attractive, healthy, and strong.
Your tastes, too, are the same, for he likes trees and gardens
almost as much as you do. Besides, he's fun and takes on
various guises, can pass himself off as whatever you choose. . . .
It's a game he likes to play. But more than such pranks, even more
than the gardens and arboreta he cultivates, he adores you.
There is nothing else he wants as much in the whole world.
Pity him, dear. Believe me, you may take these words that I speak
as if they were coming from his own mouth, not to say his heart.   690
I urge you to think of the gods to whom you may give offense,
for these are most vengeful spirits and punish whoever may cross
      them.
Venus, for one, is well known to detest indifference to lovers'

earnest and honest prayers. And Nemesis stands behind her
to punish those who are proud and those who, asserting their
        private
wills, display a contempt for the natural order of things.
You should worry about annoying such goddesses, darling.
        Believe me,
for I have lived a long time and have seen many things. Let me tell
        you
a story I heard in Cyprus. It has an instructive lesson.
        "There once was a youth named Iphis, poor, as they say, but
        honest.   700
He happened to see and of course to fall in love with a princess—
Anaxarete, descended from Teucer's blue-blooded line.
He realized this was absurd, acknowledged the chasm between
        them,
and tried to get on with his life. . . . But reason goes only so far,
and beyond all reason, in spite of good judgment and common
        sense,
he adored this girl, he burned, yearned for her, just couldn't help
        it.
After a time, he gave in, confessed to himself he was crazy,
and might as well try. For what was there left to lose, if his mind
was gone? He approached the princess' nurse and explained his
        hopeless
and absolutely pointless passion. He asked for nothing   710
but pity. The love that he felt for her nursling was malapropos,
but surely she could understand how her darling's astonishing
beauty had driven him mad. . . . The lesser servants, he bribed
with gifts and small sums of money to deliver messages, trinkets,
and various tokens of love—corsages damp with his tears.
The princess was mildly amused, then mildly annoyed, and then
        not
so mildly. The man was a pest, a joke, and her heart was not
moved the least little bit. She spurned him, laughed at his love,
and then no longer laughed but looked away in disdain,
not even deigning to show him any reaction whatever.   720
What could the young man do? He waited until she passed by
and then called out, 'You win! I shall not trouble you ever
again. The triumph is yours, to enjoy or ignore as you choose.
I am undone. I die—which ought to afford you some small
satisfaction. How many girls whom you know can take credit
for the suicides of the suitors they spurned? Whatever you think
of me, the proof of my desperate love will be indisputable,

final, and absolute. No one can shrug it off,
not even you, my lady! You'll see with those lovely eyes
my corpse, their terrible trophy. And the world will know how
      your beauty   730
must have been splendid and awful to drive a young man to prefer
death to a life without you as his reason to keep on breathing.
What I lose in length of days, I shall gain in fame, for my story
will move lovers' hearts for generations, not for my sake
but for yours and that of your beauty as well. And we shall be
      joined
forever in the minds of those who hear my story.' He stopped
speaking and looked above him at the frame of the door where
      he'd loitered,
on which he had hung his notes, presents, and bunches of flowers,
and he threw a rope over the crossbeam and made it fast
with a noose at one end, through which he stuck his head. 'It's my
      last   740
garland,' he said, 'and I hope it pleases you more than the others.'
Having contrived this extravagant show, he was bound to
      continue.
He kicked away the stool on which he'd been standing. He hung
      there,
jerking and twitching a while, as his feet, kicking in spasm,
banged on the door and seemed to ask one last time for
      admittance.
Then he was still, and the servants, horrified, cut him down
and carried him home to his widowed mother. She cradled the
      stone-
cold body, and wept and wailed. . . . She did all the things that
      bereaved
mothers do. But at length she acknowledged the truth of his
      death.
A funeral then was arranged, a modest cortege to deliver   750
the corpse to its pyre. The route passed Anaxarete's street
and her house, and the sounds of the chanting and wailing floated
      up
to the hard-hearted princess' window. 'Whose funeral is it?'
she asked. 'Let us look down and see!' She went to stand at her
      room's
high window and peer through the curtain and down to the street,
where the bier was at that moment passing below her, and there
was Iphis, stretched out in his shroud, cold and white, and her
      eyes

were frozen, her face was frozen, her voice and her sight were
   gone.
She tried to step back, but her powers of movement were also
   gone.
She attempted to turn her face, but her neck was stiff as if   760
the muscles were stone, as her heart had been hard as any stone,
and the rest of her now was transformed in that terrible
   petrification. . . .
They say one can see it still, in Salamis, there in a temple,
a marble statue that is no mere excellent likeness
but the princess herself, now changed and worshiped, a holy
   image
people invoke in despair. They call it, because of its gaze,
the Prospicient Venus. I urge you, think of these things and
   consider
how you should order your life. Do not be so hard, like her,
but yield to your lover's passion. The gods will be pleased, and
   Nature,
and no late frosts will come to bother the delicate buds   770
of the trees you adore, and the winds will be gentle on all their
   blossoms."
   But that story got Vertumnus nowhere. The god then put by
his crone costume, and stood revealed in his own true form,
as handsome a youth as ever a maiden beheld. He dazzled,
as the sun after a storm can amaze the world by recalling
its true splendor, which we and it had all but forgotten.
He was ready to rape her, but there was no need—for his beauty
   ravished
the nymph, whose passion for him was now a match for his own.
   But back to the list of kings. The false Amulius rules;
then Numitor and his grandson regain the Ausonian kingdom;   780
and the walls of Rome are built. They start the work on the feast
that shepherds offer to Pales, the goddess of herds and flocks.
Tatius and the Sabine fathers, out for revenge
after the rape of their women, now make war on the city.
Tarpeia betrays her people, throwing open the gate,
but her payment is more than she'd hoped—instead of the
   soldier's bracelets,
they pile up their heavy shields on her body and crush her to
   death.
The men of Cures, that Sabine city, attempt a foray
at night through the gates that Romulus checked and secured. . . .
   But Juno

herself has undone one gate, and even greased the hinges   790
to let them open in silence. Venus has seen this, would lock
the gate that the other unbarred, but gods cannot cancel actions
of brother and sister divinities. All she can do is consult
with the water nymphs who preside over a spring near the temple
of Janus, not far from that gate. It isn't a geyser or torrent
but only a trivial bubbling up of innocuous water.
The nymphs, however, put sulfur into the spring, and pitch,
and now what comes up is live steam that reeks with a chemical
    stench.
The posts of the gate are smoking with hot fumes, and the gate
opens now onto a cauldron of bubbling pitch no human   800
could ever attempt to wade through. The Sabines stand there
    dismayed,
and the Romans have time to sound the alarm, put on their armor,
grab their weapons, and seize the offensive advantage. The
    fighting
is fierce, and the Roman plain is thick with the corpses of Sabines
and Romans, too, as the blood of friends and foes runs together,
making a gory lake. At length, a truce is arranged,
and a joint reign is decreed, with Romulus sharing the power
with Tatius—who dies, so Romulus then rules alone,
handing down laws and meting out justice to both the tribes.
It is in this time of peace that Mars takes off his shining   810
helmet and comes to address the father of gods and men.
"The time has arrived," he announces, "when Rome can stand on
    its own
strong foundations. The fate of the city is now assured
and no longer depends on the force of a single hero.
Grant, therefore, the reward that was promised to me and your
    grandson
long ago. Let us take up this man from the earth and install him
here in the heights of heaven. Thus shall we see fulfilled
the words we all remember hearing you pronounce.
Jupiter nodded his head in assent as the sky grew dark,
lightning flashed, and thunder crashed in evident portent,   820
confirming that this would be done, and the god's promise
    fulfilled.
Mars mounted his splendid car and, lashing his great
steeds, hurried down through the air to the top of the Palatine
    Hill,
where Romulus held his court, dispensing right and justice.
Mars caught up his son in a father's embrace, and the mortal

part fell away, dissolving as lead bullets will melt
in the heat of their flight from the sling. And all that remained was
    divine—
the god Quirinus, fit to recline on a couch in some heavenly
alcove, splendidly robed to attend to the prayers of mortals.

    Romulus' wife, Hersilia, grief-stricken, assumed   830
her husband was lost, was dead, but Juno sent Iris to tell her
to cease her tears of mourning. "Worthy to be his queen,
you are worthy to be his consort now in the heavens. Your
    husband
lives still, is a god, and longs for you. Trust me, follow,
and come to the king's temple that stands on the Quirinal Hill
so that you may behold once more the face you love so dearly."
Hersilia lowered her eyes, not afraid but modest
before a divine presence, and answered, "Goddess, I hear
and shall of course obey. I delight to see him again.
Lead me, and I will follow only too gladly. To gaze   840
on Romulus' face before I die would be heaven indeed."
Rainbow's daughter then took the queen by the hand and led her
to the top of Romulus' hill, where a bright star from the heavens
came down to earth. Hersilia's hair at once caught fire,
burst into flame so she was transformed, was a star, and ascended
herself into the air, climbing the firmament, rising
until the founder of Rome could receive her in his embrace.
She felt the familiar arms enclose her and change her body
from the mortal that it had been to something new and immortal,
just as her name changed from Hersilia to Hora—   850
the goddess of time and seasons—joined to her husband,
    Quirinus.

BOOK XV

Who now shall assume the burden, follow so great a king,
and lead the people? The finger of Fame indicates Numa,
picking him out for the throne—an awesome duty, but how
shall he discharge it? Familiar with Sabine ways, he yearns
to know yet more. He wonders what is the nature of things,
and how are men to live? With such questions in mind,
he leaves his native Cures and makes his way to Crotona,
where once Hercules stopped. There, Numa addresses
an aged citizen versed in the local lore and asks him
to speak of the city's beginning. The elder gives him this answer: 10
"Hercules, Jove's son, was returning from Spain with Geryon's
herd of cattle as prize. By happy chance he arrived
here at Lacinium's coast, where he stopped to allow his beasts
to graze on the rich grass while he waited in Croton's house,
resting and taking his ease after such arduous labors.
In gratitude, he announced, as he took his leave of his host,
'In generations to come, a great city will rise
here with your name in your honor.' This prophecy proved to
      be true.
Myscelus, Alemon's son, was born, to the gods' delight
and favor. Once, as he slept, the god Hercules appeared,   20
loomed over the bed where he lay, and spoke to his dream:
'Arise and leave this land. Settle yourself near the channel
where the rocky Aesar flows. Obey my command or brave
catastrophe!' The young man woke, appalled, as the god
vanished, leaving a nightmare from which there was no escape,
for the laws of that land were clear—all who attempted to leave
would surely die, and yet to stay would be daring disaster.
What could he do? In fright, he stared out into the darkness,
the thick clouds and the murk that arose from the sea, and he
      thought
he might try to sneak away. Possibly, no one would notice.   30
He packed a few belongings, but the walls have eyes and ears

and mouths, and the rumor spread of his plan. He was charged
      with intent
to break the laws, was arrested and taken to court for trial.
The prosecution's case was open and shut. In defense,
what could he say? He raised his hands to heaven and prayed
to the god at whose command he had thought to leave. 'Help me,'
he called to the hero who'd grown to divinity. 'I did your bidding.
Will you abandon me now to suffer death at their hands?'
The local custom was voting with pebbles dropped in an urn—
black for condemning and white for freeing the person accused.   40
One by one the jurors dropped in their pebbles, all black,
but then, when the urn was turned over, the pebbles that spilled
      forth had changed
from black to white, for the god had heard his suppliant's prayer
and interceded to save him. Alemon's son was discharged
and allowed to leave. He expressed his thanks to his great
      protector,
Hercules, and then, when a favoring wind had arisen,
set sail and crossed the wide Ionian Sea. He passed
Neretum, the Sallentines' city, and then the land
where the indolent Sybarites live, and then Tarentum, the hardy
Spartans' outpost. He passed the Bay of Siris, then headed   50
up the Iapygian coast to the Aesar's mouth and the mound
of earth piled up on the sacred bones of Croton. He landed,
laid out his city walls, and named it as he had been bidden."
This, at least, is the legend, and what they believe to this day.
      There was a man in that town, Pythagoras—born elsewhere,
on the island of Samos, but he had fled its tyrant and lived
in exile, thinking, as exiles often do, of the gods
in their heavenly thrones, and the freedom of thought by which
      man, too,
can share their splendid soaring. The mind has its own life,
and he could assess all things, could visit all possible worlds,   60
and then, coming back to himself, could speak of those things he
      had found,
learned, or excogitated, and explain to the people who heard
in respectful silence his teachings on the causes of things, their
      nature,
and their lessons in how to behave: what every man should do,
and what he deserves. Who—or, if you prefer it, what—
are the gods, and what do we owe them? Does Jove bring thunder
      and lightning,
or do these come from the natural churnings of things in Nature?

Are there laws that govern the snows, the winds, the high-
        scudding clouds,
and even the quakings of earth? What keeps the stars in their
        courses?
What is the secret of things? Or *is* there a secret to learn?   70
How do we know what we know? How does our knowing affect
the thing that is known? Such questions he was the first to
        consider,
as he was the first to condemn the eating of animal flesh.
These are the words that he spoke to the crowds, who were
        always impressed
but often merely amused by the oddness of what he proposed:
        "O men, o women, do not eat meat, which is cruel and
        polluting.
The earth provides us with fruits and nuts, berries and grains. . . .
The trees are laden with apples, and grapes hang thick on the
        vines.
We ought to be more than content with such foodstuffs, and
        delight
in milk with honey the bees have gathered, in which you can taste   80
the clover or thyme of those fields they cruised for nectar. The
        earth
provides for us in abundance. We have no reason to slaughter
like savage beasts—and some, cattle and horses, for instance,
and sheep, can live on grass. If others, the predators, raven
on flesh and take delight in the warm blood of their victims,
we're not compelled. With what shall the soul be fed, affronted,
offended by pointless violence and pain of flesh like our own?
What kind of creatures subsist on flesh? Wild tigers, lions,
wolves, and bears . . . and the Cyclops, that utterly monstrous
        creature
whose teeth delight to chew on the flesh of those he has killed.   90
Earth is the best of mothers and provides for us, her creatures,
with ways to appease our hunger without this destruction of life.
If the belly calls out for meat, the heart and soul object
to this unacceptable manner of filling our primitive maws.
        "There once was a better time we can barely recall but miss
as the homesick exile longs for the scenes of his childhood . . . the
        golden
age we know is past but in which our natures and Nature
were not yet at odds. In that blessed time, the fruits of trees
were plenty for us, and we never defiled our tables with blood
or feasted on death. Then in untroubled skies birds could fly   100

tranquil and safe. Then rabbits strolled unafraid in the fields,
and the fish could swim in unruffled lakes that no anglers' guile
had strewn with baited hooks. No trappers lurked in the woods
to snare unwary creatures. But then, perhaps on a dare,
an adventurous fellow who'd seen some lion bring down a gazelle
wondered what it was like to chew and swallow the flesh
of that poor beast. . . . That speculation then led to crime,
crime upon crime, the bite of steel into muscle and bone,
bellows and shrieks of pain, and the mess of our mastications
of the bodies of living things, which a part of us knows to be
     sacred.   110
If a wolf attacks you, you're right (and you have every right) to
     kill it,
but not to eat its carcass—for then you would be a wolf.
    "They say that the pig was our first victim because of
     its snout
and the way it would root up the seeds and young shoots of
     the crops
we labored so hard to grow. And the goats destroy our
     grapevines,
which we take as reason to kill them and eat their flesh. But
     the sheep
do nothing to harm mankind! Alive, they give us their milk
and share their wool for our clothing. How do we thank them
     for these
enormous favors? I speak in the name of simple justice
to say that it's wrong—as it's heinous to have your oxen work,   120
those strong and placid beasts that toil for us all in the fields,
and what does the farmer do in recompense for this faithful
service? He takes off the heavy yoke from the neck of the ox
and brings down his cruel axe! Why not murder your field hands
and serve them up at table garnished with crops they have tended?
A bad business indeed, and we make it worse by involving
the heavenly gods in these crimes, as if they took pleasure in
     blood.
And what beast do we choose for the rites we perform, but the
     best,
the fairest, whose beauty should speak on his behalf but instead
condemns him? The poor dumb creature can't understand the
     reason   130
the priest decorates his horns with ribbons and sprinkles the
     barley

over his head (that grain he himself worked in the field
to plant and then to harvest). He supposes we're giving him
     thanks,
but then he sees the flash of the knife, and he feels his blood
spilling out on the ground before the indelicate priest
rips away at the entrails and tries to predict the future
from how the offal appears. Then we sit down and feast
on the broilings of what remains of the corpse of our erstwhile
     partner.
I pray you, gentlemen, ladies, think what you do, repent,
and resolve to amend your lives to conform to reason and justice.   140
     "I speak as the god is prompting—as the Pythia does at
          Delphi—
and the words that come from my lips resound with their
          holy truth
in a way my inadequate voice can scarcely suggest, but, I beg you,
imagine a cave, the smoke, the special effects, and believe
that these things I say are the answers to questions that only
          children
are brave enough to ask. I've soared through the heavens, have
          ridden
the clouds as they float through the skies, have stood upon Atlas'
          shoulders,
and seen from a dizzying height the scurrying hither and thither
of men who had no idea whither they went and how
they lived their lives. And I wept to think how they needed to
          read   150
in the arcane scrolls of the Fates the secrets of life and death.
"Death is what men most fear. Their dread of that crossing over
the Styx hangs over their every waking hour. The poets'
stories of some dim, bloodless existence in shadows' kingdom
scare us as if they were true. It's only the body that dies,
disappears into ash on a pyre, or rots in the ground or the sea.
And after a death, that body, the mere meat, is beyond
hurt or harm, but the soul or spirit, the anima, deathless,
survives, moving on to another situation and body,
taking up residence there. . . . It's true. I remember clearly   160
other lives my spirit has gone through—at Troy in the war,
I fought. I was there as Euphorbus, the Trojan, a son of Panthoüs.
A spear that Menelaus threw pierced my sternum and killed me.
Not long ago, I traveled to Argos and saw there in Juno's
temple a relic, or battle trophy, a shield from that war

I recognized as the one I had worn on my own left arm—
Euphorbus' shield. Things change, but the soul continues. It
  wanders
from body to body, human or sometimes a beast's. Like wax,
it takes whatever impress the world at that moment imposes,
but then, in the fire, it melts, returning to pristine blankness.   170
And this is another reason to abstain from meat—that steak
or chop on your plate could well be some person you might have
  admired,
or knew, or perhaps loved, maybe your aunt or uncle,
for all our souls are kin, and therefore deserve respect.
  "As long as I'm going on this way, I may as well do
the whole paradoxical notion of change as the only constant,
for all things change. The cosmos itself is flux and motion.
Time is the measure of how things turn from one state to another.
Its course rolls on like a river, gentle or rapid, but pushed
by the weight of the water upstream. A river may look the same   180
but at every instant is new, a dying and reincarnation,
which dazzles the mind. You blink, and then open your eyes to
  behold
another river that flows through another landscape, another
universe. What was in the world is gone, and a new
world has been conjured up to take its place. . . . Amazing,
or it ought to be. But children learn to accept these wonders,
as day gives way to night, and night speeds on to another
dawn of a brand new day. And each time we take for granted
what is miraculous, awesome, and strange. Lie on the ground
at night and stare at the stars to watch how they wheel in their
  tracks.   190
The sun at morning is red, and red as well in the evening,
but somewhere along the way it was blazing white. . . . What
  happened?
The air overhead is purer, and the sun, more truly itself,
but then, when it nears the horizon, the contamination of earth
affects its appearance, its size and color, its very being.
And the moon, at night, is changing, has become our symbol of
  change,
waxing or waning, crescent, gibbous, or full, but . . . different.
  "The seasons come and give way to the next, in an imitation
of the seasons of human lives. Springtime is earth's childhood,
young but not yet with strength or assurance. Then summer
  arrives   200

with blossoms of meadow flowers and fertile fields with
     their crops
in the vigor of young manhood. The months slip away, and that
     strength
of youth disappears, giving way to autumn's ripeness and mellow
moments of contemplation of what one has been and done
(or failed to do). And the gray on the temples is like a frost
that comes to portend the winter, faltering steps in the cold,
the shivering, doddering end that comes in time to us all,
that time of snows and ice on the rock-hard frozen ground.
     "Our bodies are also changing, those instruments of our
          selves
that are not ourselves. We lay in our mothers' wombs, small
     helpless   210
concatenations of hopes and fears, and perhaps ambitions,
as Nature worked with her craftsman's cunning those tiny fingers
and toes and even tinier nails to amaze our parents.
And then, in the first enormous change we must all adjust to,
our mother's bodies expel us into the light and air.
The newborn infant just lies there, blinking, eating, peeing,
but look close and you think you can see him growing, his eyes
focus with new understanding, his fists clench with intention,
and hark at the babble that changes day by day into phonemes,
more and more recognizable words, and then plausible phrases,   220
that give way in turn to sentences. Pudgy wrists and ankles
turn into useful joints, as the baby creeps and crawls
and then with effort stands, then cruises and then . . . he walks.
These, we assume, are blessings, even though we know that
     their end
is a series of further changes, a giving back of these favors,
which turn out not to be gifts but loans. The child grows up,
grows old, and then that strength or beauty of which he was proud
deserts him, leaving him dazed and weeping. Milon, the athlete,
looks in the glass at those forearms, as strong as Hercules' once,
and now, with the wasted muscle and sinew that hangs from
     the bone,   230
a scrawny display of ruin, as Helen, too, is undone
to see her face that men were willing to die for dying,
her looks now gone into hiding, crawling in furrows and creases,
the ditches of no man's land. Time is a cannibal; age
is a vandal; and both together defile, deface, destroy
whatever we think of as fine in the lives of women and men.

"Even the elements change: earth and water, the heavy
sinking parts of the world, and air and fire, the light
and floating parts of it, mix and mingle, merge and divide
over and over again, in a series of endless cycles   240
of churning and roiling, a seething soup of energy, matter,
and restlessness. As the solid ice will melt to water,
and then boil away into steam or simply evaporate
to rise up into the sky, and then, in the clouds, condense,
so everything changes, yields to another guise of itself . . .
or is it another self? Our notions are primitive, crude,
and cannot encompass the tremulous truth that our eyes may see
but our brains can hardly dare admit. We suppose a birth
is an utterly new beginning, but it may be only a step
in a long and mysterious journey. And likewise, death is no end   250
but only another step on this epic and involuted
path we can hardly guess we are moving along. The self
encounters a random series of openings-up and closings-
down, but the world remains the same in its grand design
and even in weight and size—as if some celestial clerk
were taking stock and checking the figures in massive ledgers.
    "We ought not therefore worry at the signs of change
            and decay
that can trouble a cautious person. I have seen in my own lifetime
solid land that was washed away or submerged to become
a part of the sea. Elsewhere, the sea, I am sure, heaped up   260
sandbars, tide flats, marshes, expanding some headland or beach.
These stories we hear from time to time are true, of sea shells
in the rocks on the sides of mountains, far from the ocean's bed.
Such change is the way of Nature. Ages give way from gold
to silver and bronze and so on. . . . But not in a steady decline.
Think of it not as progress or regress but merely process,
neutral when all is said and done. A fountain springs up,
and somewhere else a fountain dies, or a river dries up,
but the same volume of water continues to flow to the sea.
How else could the Lycus dwindle away as it does and then spring   270
back to continue its journey, the same indisputable river?
The Erasinus also behaves this way, diving down,
flowing for miles underground, and then, in the Argolid plain,
emerging again to flow to the sea. Likewise, the Mysus
they say is ashamed of its source, dives down, and then reappears,
but now to be called the Caïcus. In Sicily, there is a river,
the Amenanus, that sometimes flows as a river, and sometimes

vanishes, leaving a empty ditch. The Anigrus' water,
which once was wholesome and pure, now is nasty and poisoned,
the centaurs, having bathed their wounds from Hercules' arrows,   280
polluted the stream forever, or this is what poets tell us.
The Hypanis, in Scythia's mountains, once was fresh and sweet
but now, as all of the guidebooks tell us, flows brackish with salt.
    "Antissa, Pharos, and Tyre were all once islands, surrounded
by water, but then the channels dried up, and now we can walk
from any of them to the mainland. Leucas, meanwhile, was
        connected
but now is cut off, an island, and the water flows and surrounds it.
Zancle (or, as we call it, Sicily) once was connected
by land to Italy; now, of course, it is separate, an island.
Helice, off in Achaia, and Buris were cities: they're gone,   290
washed away, and water covers their houses and streets.
Sailors look down and see parts of buildings below their keels.
The ground upon which we walk, the solid earth, can heave up,
change shape and form, and remind us that nothing is solid and
        lasting.
Near Troezen, out in the plain, is a hill, an abrupt excrescence.
They say that the winds were shut up somehow underground and
        raged,
seeking escape, a way to express and fulfill their natures.
They looked for some fissure or crack but, finding no outlet
        whatever,
huffed and puffed in their fury and thereby swelled up the ground
as if it were a balloon, or a pig's bladder that children   300
bat about—that hill is what they produced, and it lasted,
hardened, and passers-by would think it had been there forever.
    "These are not exceptions or marvels, for that would suggest
a rule, and an ordinary reliable norm, but the world
is arbitrary, abrupt, astounding. We have an expression
that things are as much alike as two drops of water—but water
isn't reliably like itself. I think of the Ammon,
cold at noon, but warm in the morning and evening. They say
the Athamanians kindle their fires by pouring its water
onto the wood, and it lights it. Cicones, meanwhile, have a river   310
with water that, if you should drink it, turns your organs to stone.
Closer to home, the Crathis' and Sybarus' waters produce
an odd effect in that those who drink of it find that their hair
will change color and lighten to amber or even gold.
There are other waters that have their effects not just on the body

but on the mind. The Salmacis water will put one to sleep,
as the Ethiopian lakes are also supposed to do.
One passes out or else, as some report, goes mad.
The Clitor's waters are said to have the peculiar power
to turn all those who taste it into teetotalers. How? 320
No one can say for sure, but the story is that Melampus,
after he cured Proetus' daughters of madness, threw
his herbs (among them hellebore) into the water; since then,
their sobering power remains to affect all those who partake.
On the other hand, the Lyncestian River does the reverse:
any who happen to drink its water stagger and reel
as if they were blitzed from guzzling wine at some all-night party.
There is even water that changes from moment to moment: I hear
in Pheneos there is a lake that is perfectly safe in the daytime,
but the same water at night can be lethal. A tricky business, 330
but everything is. The world is tricky, shifty, surprising
all the time. Ortygia drifted once on the ocean's
surface but now is a fixed island. The Symplegades, likewise,
floated, crashing together to threaten ships like the *Argo,*
but now they are quite secure and as solid as other islands.
Aetna, now alive with sulfur and fire, was once
just another hill; one day it may cool again,
for the earth is alive, and its moods and passions rise and fall.
People who live there report that its fissures are always changing,
that now this place may seethe and smoke, and then subside 340
as somewhere else breaks out. Who knows how volcanoes work?
Some say that the winds can get caught underground, and then
    they fan
the fires that rage below. When those winds have spent their force,
they fall back in exhaustion. Or maybe it's pitch and sulfur
that burn down there, but the fires deplete their fuel and gutter
and die—and that could happen. Nothing in Nature is constant
but continual change and process, which seem to be Nature's
    nature.
    "What is not too bizarre to happen? I'm told there are men
who live far to the North and bathe in some sacred pool
Minerva has graced. They do this nine times, and then on their
    bodies 350
the down and feathers of birds sprout out. Who knows if it's true?
There are also accounts of Scythian women who use some
    ointment
or emollient oil on their skins with the same peculiar result.
    "Sober and trustworthy men of science report observations

we all accept as true of things that are no less amazing.
A carcass will rot—we know this—and, out of the putrefaction
and heat this process entails, new life can be engendered
of maggots and such small creatures. We all have read about bulls
sacrificed to the gods and buried in ditches in which
their entrails rot and great swarms of bees are produced. These
      insects   360
have the same love for the meadows the oxen had in their lives,
and their habits are similar, too, for they also work for their keep.
Horses, however, are different. Bury a horse, and you get
high-spirited hornets and warlike wasps. Or a sea crab,
and out of its claws in the ground stinging scorpions come.
The worms that eat our corpses creep on the ground and spin
cocoons on the leaves of trees, from which will emerge in time
the butterflies that sculptors chiseled once on our tombs
as symbols of how the soul, transformed, may emerge again.

     "From out of the slimy mud, tadpoles appear and frogs.   370
How does this happen? And why do their hind legs grow much
      longer
to give them their power to leap? How can a she-bear know
to lick the amorphous mass of flesh she's produced and make it
a recognizable cub? These inconceivable things
happen every day! These creatures follow some blueprint
that instructs them what to do—it's not in their own brains
but the brain of the world's body. Otherwise, how could bees
transform the globby larvae born in their waxen cells
and perform the delicate task of sticking on legs and wings
to complete the creatures and make them a whole new generation 380
of functioning and productive bees? But such miracles happen
all the time. It is we who are dull and lacking in vision,
for we have forgotten the wonder of things. Can children believe
the improbable stories we tell them of how a glorious peacock
with all those eyes on its tail comes out of a simple egg
that looks exactly like that of the warlike eagle that Jove
loves, or that of the dove of Venus? That birds of all different
colors, sizes, and habits hatch out of eggs . . . is absurd
but perfectly true, as it's true that a man's backbone, when it rots
in earth, will produce, from the marrow, a snake that creeps from
      his tomb.   390
     "These creatures are generated from others' deaths, but
      one bird
contrives to renew himself, perishing, then, from his ashes,
amazingly reappearing. Assyrians call him the phoenix,

and say that he does not live on seeds or insects but feeds
on the gum of frankincense and balsam resin. This bird,
after he lives his allotted span of five hundred years,
builds a nest for himself in the heart of a towering palm tree,
using his talons and beak, and contriving a kind of a bier
with cassia bark and spikenard, cinnamon pieces, and myrrh.
He settles into this fragrant nest and, among these precious   400
odors, embalms himself, expires, and then, from the body
of the father phoenix that was, arises the fledgling son
with a new allotment of years in which he may live and thrive.
When the bird has attained the size and strength he needs for
        flight,
he gathers up from the tree the nest that his predecessor
carefully put together and carries this object away—
his father's remarkable tomb and his own cradle—to bring it
to the end of the world in the place where the lord of the Sun
        holds court.
There, before the sacred doors of the gleaming temple,
he offers up this marvel, in honor and gratitude.   410
        "There are wonders enough to extinguish wonder itself.
        We need
to accept the strangeness of things as they are. Think of hyenas!
The female mates with the male and becomes, herself, a male!
Or think of that little reptile, the chameleon, changing its color
according to what it rests on. Indians boast of a beast,
the lynx, I think—its urine turns into solid stone
as soon as it touches the air, as coral does when you pluck it
soft and bring it up from the water and into the air.
I could go on all day and into the night with this list
of strange and remarkable creatures, sports of the gods and
        Nature,   420
but just as much to the point—the demonstration of change
as the only constant—I offer the panorama of man,
the rise and fall of our cities and nations, their growth and decline.
Consider how Troy was great in wealth and in martial power
but now is destroyed, a ruin, with nothing to show the tourist
but barren fields and a beach. Sparta was rich and famous,
and what is it now? Mycenae flourished and now is a squalid
hamlet of farmers and goatherds living in huts near a hill
that once boasted a palace. Have you been to Athens? Or Thebes?
You suppose they have taken the names and carried them off
        elsewhere,   430
because nothing you see is impressive, or rich, but it's all that
        remains

of wealth, power, and glory; hovels and broken columns,
and gnarled old men drinking ouzo and gossiping under a tree.
Rome, meanwhile, was nothing but fields and is growing and
        thriving,
and the Tiber is lined with buildings from which one might think
        to rule
the world for a thousand years! That's what the oracles promised,
as I very well remember from that other life in Troy.
Helenus, Priam's son, one night exhorted Aeneas,
'Do not despair, great son of a goddess, but only believe
and you shall see my prophetic vision come true—high Troy   440
shall live as you continue to live. Although fire and sword
may try to stop you, you shall prevail, survive, and succeed
in finding a new land and founding another city
in which the heirs of our Phrygian blood shall know even greater
and more enduring grandeur. Iulus, your son, shall beget
a line of distinguished princes, who shall add to her wealth and
        power.
Rome shall thrive beyond anyone's dreams until one shall appear,
a prince, who shall rule the world and whom all shall obey and
        adore.
At the end of his days, the gods will gather him up and bear him
into celestial glory that he shall have earned.' These things   450
I remember Helenus telling pious Aeneas, who carried
his household gods from the ruins. . . . And I see with my own
        eyes now
those walls going up that turn his words into stones of truth.
    "But where was this discourse going? Ah, yes, that we
        change. All things
under the heavens change. The earth, its creatures, its people—
for we are a part of creation ourselves—go from form to form
and body to body. Our souls migrate from creature to creature,
human or even beast. Which is why we should hold in reverence
any body that housed, or may house, a soul and abjure
the eating of flesh as disgusting and wrong. It's the sin of
        Thyestes,   460
for who knows what soul of a brother or parent or child may
        inhere
in the body of that poor calf whose throat the sharp knife cuts?
Whose heart can endure the piteous sound of his agonized
        bawling?
Who can go out and spread grain on the ground for his chickens
        to eat,
call them by name as if they were children, and then, one day,

turn on them, turning monstrous, kill them, pluck them,
        eat them?
We are all in this together, the birds, the beasts and us. . . .
Let the poor ox go on as long as he can with his heavy
burdens; let sheep give wool in exchange for their grazing; let
        she goats
give us their foaming milk. But draw a line somewhere   470
and give up the nets and snares and traps and the arrows and
        spears.
Let blood not be on your hands. Give up the tricky feathers
you hang in the woods from the trees to frighten the deer toward
        the brake
where hunters wait. Stop baiting the cruel hooks that deceive
the endlessly stupid fish, whose pain is profound as your own.
Defend yourself against wolves and tigers, but do not become
a wolf or tiger yourself, gobbling gobbets of bodies
and gnawing the bones of those creatures with whom we should
        share the earth."
    Filled with these teachings, inspired, Numa returned to Rome
to assume the throne and rule the state. He married a nymph,   480
Egeria, and the Muses blessed their household. He led
a warlike people to ways of peace, and observance of holy
rites of reverence for gods and the earth. In the ripeness of years,
he laid down his scepter and died, and Roman mothers and fathers
mourned for the loss of Numa, their leader and inspiration.
His wife, bereft, abandoned the city, returned to the woods,
and hid herself in a glade, where she moaned, wept, and
        complained,
the sound of her lamentations disturbing the women who
        worshipped
at the famous woodland shrine of Diana Nemorensis
that Orestes built in Aricia. Her sister nymphs consoled her   490
and tried to calm her—at least to get her to quiet down.
From out of that shrine, great Theseus' son Hippolytus came
to tell her, "Restrain yourself! Your grief is by no means unique.
Loss, I'm afraid, is the lot of us all. If it helps you bear
your burden, I'll tell you my troubles. We'll console each other
        and mourn
together in that company misery's said to prefer.
    "I am Theseus' son, of whom you have no doubt heard.
Mine was a terrible death—my gullible father believed
that unspeakable woman, his wife, therefore my stepmother,
        Phaedra.
She wanted me to defile their bed. I refused. She accused me   500

of having tried to rape her. I was utterly guiltless, I swear
and swore, but my father couldn't suppose she was totally mad
or vindictive and calculating. Believing her testimony,
he banished me. As I fled in rage, shame, and chagrin,
and was making my way along the Bay of Corinth, the sea
rose up in a fury, a tidal wave like a mountain that bellowed
as if alive, and from out of its churning depths it produced
an actual beast, a bull with water that spewed from its mouth
and spurted out of its nostrils. My friends and servants were
    frightened,
but I was indifferent to danger, my soul being full of the grief   510
of exile, as well as the sense of injustice's terrible triumph.
My horses, twitching their ears, spooked by this monster, broke
into a frenzy and dashed. . . . I tried my best to restrain them,
control their course with the reins as we bounced along on that
    beach,
and thought I might yet subdue them and bring them back to
    their senses,
but the axle of one of the wheels of my car hit a large boulder
that wrenched the hubcap off. We lost our wheel, and the car
flipped and threw me over. A tangle of reins and traces
caught my legs and held me fast as the horses continued
to run in their freshened terror, dragging my body behind them.   520
I could hear, at least at first, the sounds of its bones breaking,
could feel my flesh as it snagged and tore on pieces of driftwood
and anchors of fishermen's dories hauled up there on the shingle.
A terrible thing it was, but every agony ends,
and my spirit at last broke free of those pieces of mangled meat
that no one could recognize anymore as parts of a body.
All that remained was a wound and pinkish stains on the beach.
Can you, dear lady, compare your grief with mine? Can you think
your suffering, bad as I'm sure it must feel, is unique in the
    world?
My death was as bad as it gets. And I saw that shadowy kingdom,   530
the gloom of which, I promise, would break your heart afresh.
I bathed those shreds of flesh that still hung from my frame
in Phlegethon's soothing waters. And there I should be, even still,
if not for Aesculapius, Phoebus Apollo's son,
who, with his charms and potent cures, restored me to life.
Pluto, cheated, was angry and would have prevented my leaving,
but Diana interceded, conjured a cloud to enfold me,
and hide me from envious eyes, which watched from the hushed
    shadows.
Then to keep me safe, she changed my looks to this aged

form you see before you. She thought about Crete and Delos,   540
but then conceived the idea of putting me here in Aricia.
To finish it off she changed my name, which was
        burdensome now,
with its equine associations she thought I'd as soon forget.
A hero, she said, and alive, she gave me the new name: thus
I am Virbius now, and I live in this grove as a lesser god,
following her who saved me as one of her congregation."
        A sad story, indeed, but what good are others' stories
when one is bereft and grieving? Egeria still was undone,
continued to sob and weep. She lay there prone on the ground
until she dissolved into tears and became her tears, a spring.   550
Diana is said to have done this in pity and love, and the spring
flows still in a modest trickle in that sad glade.
        The nymphs were, of course, astonished. Hippolytus—
        Virbius now—
was also amazed, but amazing transformations can happen.
At almost that same time, a farmer some way up the coast
who was plowing his field called out to his ox to stop as he
        watched,
stared at a clod of earth that seemed somehow to be . . . moving?
Yes, it was, and it changed its form, becoming a creature,
a human, who opened his mouth to prophesy and instruct
the Etruscans in what the future held in store. The people   560
of the region speak of this still and remember his name as Tages.
Of Romulus, too, there's a strange if not quite impossible story
of sudden change—it is said that he planted the shaft of his spear
in the ground on the Palatine Hill, where it put forth roots and
        leaves
and became a tree again. You can go to this hill even now,
see the tree, and touch it, and sit in its shade in wonder.
Strange, too, was the transformation of Cipus, who saw
his reflection one day in a pool: there, on his head, were horns.
He couldn't believe his eyes, and he reached up his hands to
        confirm
what the water's reflection suggested. There they were on his
        forehead,   570
these antler things. . . . He was calm as a man can possibly be
at a moment like that and figured it had to be some sort of
        portent.
But good, was it, or bad? He raised his arms to the heavens
and prayed to the gods to grant that if it were omen of good,
that benefit should befall the people; but if it were evil,

he prayed whatever misfortune impended should be his alone.
He constructed then an altar of turf and charged the priest
to perform the sacred rite, pouring the wine's libation
and sacrificing a beast. When the priest consulted the quivering
entrails, he couldn't be sure what meaning the message held.   580
But then, looking up, he saw on Cipus' head those horns,
and it all came clear at once. "All hail King Cipus!" he said.
"Those horns on your head are a crown, and all shall acknowledge
          your rule.
To you, the Latins will bend their knees and bow their heads.
Enter the gates of the city, and it shall be yours, o king!
Your throne is there, and your scepter. The people await their
          prince."
But Cipus turned his back on the city's walls and its gates.
"May the gods prevent such a thing!" he exclaimed. "It is better
          to live
in exile among strangers than here at home on a throne,
ruling over those who ought not to be ruled that way."   590
He summoned the people, the Senate, and called them together in
          conclave,
first having decked those horns on his head with fronds of pacific
and scared laurel. He mounted a nearby knoll, where he prayed
again to the gods for a time and then addressed the people,
civilians and soldiers alike, saying to them: "Fellow Romans,
I call you together to warn that one of us here will be king—
unless you combine and act to prevent it. Drive him forth
from the city we love. Do whatever you must. It may be
that you even have to kill him. Do not shrink or shirk
your duty, but do it. The risk to Rome, otherwise, is grave—   600
that he could enslave you all. The augur warns me that this
is not beyond the realm of what could come to pass.
There is, however, a sign by which you may know this man:
he has, on his forehead, a pair of horns and shouldn't be hard
to discover. Bind him with fetters, I say, or put him to death
as befits a would-be tyrant. For the sake of your children's
          children,
I urge you all to keep your freedom and dignity. Rise,
rise up together against him, whoever he is, and prevent
this dreadful and disgraceful thing." He was done, and a murmur
arose from the crowd as if a wind has sprung up to roil   610
a grove of trees that groaned in complaint, or waves of the sea
were pounding against a shore somewhere in the middle
          distance. . . .

From out of this babble, one voice pronounced the question
      they all
had been trying to frame: "Who is this? Which is this man?" They
      looked,
inspecting one another's foreheads for the telltale
mark, as Cipus spoke again, "The one whom you seek,
you have." They looked in wonder as he then uncovered his head
and showed them the horns. The populace wouldn't at first
      believe him,
but there were the growths on his temples. They muttered among
      themselves
and then fell silent. At length some brave soul stepped from the
      throng,   620
approached the podium, snatched the wreath from the ground,
      and put it
back on Cipus' illustrious head. There were echoing cheers,
and the Senate voted him land outside the city's walls,
as much as he might circumscribe in a day with a plow and a team
of oxen. There on the gates of his villa, those horns were carved
as the proud symbol of him who once had refused to be king.
      O Muses, help me now, for I see the end and need
the assistance all of us bards and poets are always begging.
If what I have done so far has pleased you, help me conclude,
I pray, with the story of Aesculapius, son of Coronis,   630
and how he came to the Tiber's banks and became a god.
      There once was a terrible plague that afflicted Latium. Men
were dying; bodies lay rotting in streets and alleys; the living
were weary with caring for those who were sick and digging the
      graves
of those whom the sickness had taken. Doctors were utterly
      helpless,
and people turned to the gods for relief, dispatching to Delphi
a delegation to pray for the oracle's aid. They watched
in awe and amazement as the laurels began to shake, and the
      shrine
itself commenced to tremble. From the tripod on which she sat
in the sanctum, the Pythia spoke the words of the mighty god: 640
"What you seek here, you shall find, but closer to home. Go there
to that nearer place, and demand of the son of Apollo what you
have asked here of his father. From him, shall you have a reply."
This answer was brought to the Senate in Rome, which in its
      wisdom
discussed the oracle's meaning. These elders agreed to send back

to Greece—to Epidaurus, where Aesculapius dwelled.
Off to that shrine they sailed, and once they had beached
        their keels
they went straightaway to the elders and leaders of this Greek
        temple
to ask for their god, for the rescue of Rome from its terrible
        plague.
Some were willing, for men in need should not be denied;   650
but some were not, for their own livings depended on this
thriving cult, and how would the place survive if its business
were snatched away? They debated all day and into the evening,
as fires were kindled and died down to beds of embers. The
        shadows
had come to reclaim the world, but the question was not yet
        resolved.
The men crawled to their beds to sleep, and that night, in a
        dream,
the spirit of Phoebus' son appeared to the Roman envoy,
as clear and as vivid as waking figures would seem at noon.
He held a staff in his left hand, stroked his beard with his right,
and, in resonant tones, announced, "Be not afraid. I shall come   660
to Rome with you and leave these figures and temples behind.
Look and remember this serpent coiling around my arm.
Recognize it as me, for in it shall you see me again,
but larger, huge, celestial, as heavenly bodies should be
whenever they condescend to be transformed." He vanished,
leaving behind him a silence that also had been transformed
and was richer and larger. The night also withdrew, and at
        daybreak
the men reassembled to speak with the priests in their lavish
        temple.
They had barely resumed discussing the question when eerie
        hisses
stopped all talk. The god had appeared, astonishing, splendid,   670
in the form of the golden serpent with a plume on his head,
        and eyes
that flashed with dazzling fire. The building shook, but the men,
quaking in fear, could barely take notice. The priest, their leader,
with his hair in the ritual ribbons, held up his arms and declared,
"Behold, your god has come! Pray, give homage, implore
the deity's bountiful blessings, and offer your thanks and
        praise. . . ."
Then, having closed his eyes, he continued, addressing the god,

"Holy, beautiful, strong, and good, bless, we pray,
these people who serve you and worship here at your shrine.
        Amen!"
And all fell down and prayed as they had been bidden and shown,   680
repeating exactly the words they had heard the high priest
        pronounce.
With their lips, their minds, and their hearts, they begged for
        divine grace,
and the god heard and nodded. They watched in awe as his
        glittering
crest waved in the air, and his flicking tongue appeared
once, twice, and thrice in a sure sign of assent.
The serpent then uncoiled and slithered along on the floor
among the garlands of flowers the pious had strewn, taking leave
of the sacred shrine in which he had dwelled so long. Outside
he continued to snake his way down the well-raked paths of the
        enclave,
out through the city streets, and down the slope to the harbor.   690
He turned once more in farewell to the place over which he'd
        presided
and then resolutely boarded the ship of the heirs of Troy.
As if stevedores had maneuvered some heavy cargo aboard,
the ship settled deep in the water, supporting the weight of the
        god.
The Romans, moved and amazed, gave thanks with a sacrifice
of a bull on the beach. They wreathed the ship's spars and the
        rigging
with sprays of fragrant flowers. At last, they cast off the lines
and caught the gentle breeze that bore them out of the harbor
and into the blue water. Around the mast, the serpent
had coiled his splendid body; he basked and gazed out to sea   700
like a happy tourist watching the wake break from the bows.
With a favoring wind behind them, they crossed the Ionian Sea
in six days to arrive at Italy's shore, where they saw
Juno's temple gleaming high on that bluff at Lacinium.
Then it was all familiar: Scylaceum, Iapygia,
the Cocinthian cliffs, Rometheum, Caulon, Narycia, the straits
that separate the Italian mainland from Sicily's bulk.
They headed for Leucosia, and Paestum—the temple and gardens
are worth the detour, the guidebooks tell us—and on to Naples,
Capri, Sorrento. . . . You've read the brochures, or maybe have   710
        been there.
Get out an atlas and trace with a finger their route up the lovely

coast, and you pass by Cumae, Caieta, and reach at last
Anzio, where the god debarked—for the weather had turned
bad, and he entered the temple built in his father's honor
there on the sandy beach to wait out the storm's fury.
When the weather cleared and the seas were calm again, the god
emerged from his father's sanctum to wriggle his way to the ship
(his scales left, on the sand over which he traveled, an odd
pattern you still can see there). He coiled his way up the rudder
and over the poop. He lay on deck with his head to the stern   720
and enjoyed the rest of the voyage, up the coastline to Castrum
and the mouth of the River Tiber, where crowds had gathered to
     greet him,
mothers and fathers, boys and girls, and the Vestal Virgins,
those chaste priestesses watching over the Trojan goddess'
holy flame. All gave him a grateful welcome and offered
the fragrant aromas of incense perfuming the votive fires
that burned all along the way in altars set up for the day.
Various victims fell to the bloody knives of the priests
who offered their sacrifices to him they hoped would deliver
their city from such affliction. The ship progressed upstream   730
and hove into view at last in the greatest of all great cities,
the world's heart and its brain. The serpent ascended the mast,
craned his powerful neck, and peered one way and another
at his new home. Where the river comes down into the city,
it separates to form two channels, as though two arms
were embracing the land in the middle, that small attractive island.
That was the place he chose, the serpent son of Apollo,
at last to disembark and resume his natural form—
or, better, to reappear in his supernatural splendor.
There, ensconced and at home, he brought the plague to a prompt   740
end, the city's savior and its grateful people's help.
    If that god came from elsewhere to settle here, Rome now
can boast of native deities, who earned their places in heaven.
Caesar, splendid in war and peace as well, achieved
great things for us all, and his glory, so well-deserved, showed
     bright
in the new star in the sky that he became. His godhood
his son declared and proved—for nothing he did in this life
was a greater blessing than this, that he left us his son, Augustus,
to rule in his stead and continue the care of a grateful people.
Schoolboys study his life, make his forced marches, and cross   750
his bridges-resting-on-piles; we admire his conquest of Britain,
his sallies up the treacherous mouth of the Nile, his battles

to subdue the Numidian Juba and annex the lands of the Pontus,
where Mithridates ruled. His triumphs became redundant,
although he permitted observance of only a few. But none,
no triumph, could compare to the blessing he left us—a worthy
heir in his son, Augustus. Their greatness reflects both ways,
for no such ruler as he could come from a merely mortal
man. The son is the proof of the father's divinity. Venus,
Aeneas' mother, saw how the plotters were talking treason   760
against her most reverend priest. She blanched in fear and anger
and cried out to her brother and sister gods: "Behold!
A terrible thing is about to happen! The life is in danger
of the heir of Dardanian Iülus. Against him, whom I love,
they conspire, impious, violent, and vile. How can I bear it?
I am the most insulted of gods—Diomedes' spear
wounded my side, and since then my life is a series of wounds.
My son was driven from Troy to toss on the sea like flotsam.
He fought with Turnus—or let us be frank and admit it was Juno
who checked him at every turn as long as she possibly could.   770
But who has the time to rehearse old woes when new
          dangers lurk?
Now, again, there are knives they are honing to strike at the breast
of one whom I have favored, loved, and tried to protect.
Vesta's sacred fires must not be extinguished in blood.
We must strive together somehow to prevent this criminal action."
          The poor, beautiful goddess wailed, inveighed, complained,
from one end of the sky to the other, but all in vain,
for if the gods were moved by the justice of her complaint,
what could they do? How could they cancel or change what
          those stern
sisters the Fates had decreed? No help, no hope, no answer . . .   780
except to complain, joining in with Venus to warn and mourn,
protest and express their outrage in serious portents of woe.
Lightning flashed in the sky, and battle horns resounded
in baleful bellows, which came from nowhere to charge the air
with shivers of awe. The Sun's bright face turned dim and sickly,
as if the ills of earth had infected his golden light.
The skies at night were aglow with ominous flashes. At dawn
the morning star was spotted and blotchy. Strange dark clouds
drifted above, and it rained, not water but drops of blood.
The moon at night shone red as a wound, and owls complained   790
and warned in their agitation. Everywhere, holy statues
in temple shrines and on household altars dripped with tears
as marble or ivory wept at the outrage about to take place.

There were many reports of moaning and wailing in sacred
        groves,
voices perhaps from the trees themselves. There were sacrifices,
but none of the victims was right: livers were badly formed
and blotchy, and entrails were fouled. People hid in their houses
and listened dismayed to the howls of enormous hounds, who
        belled
and bayed all night near the temples. Ghosts of the dead rose up
to meet in the marketplace and compare their accounts of woe.   800
With such a series of warnings, you'd think there would be
        some way
for men to take care, combine, prevent, avert. . . . But no,
none of it did any good. The implacable Fates had spoken.
The earth trembled with rage and disgust as the horror unfolded,
and the plotters assembled with swords they brought to the curia's
        precincts—
an outrage all by itself. Venus tore at her hair
and beat her breasts in grief and anger, but could not erase
a word of the terrible script the players below were enacting.
A cloud, like the one in which she had once wrapped Paris at Troy
to save his life, or like that she had used to deliver Aeneas   810
from Diomedes' wrath, she conjured up for Caesar,
but then, her father, Jove, restrained her with these grave words:
"Will you, all by yourself, presume? Can you budge the Fates'
fixed purpose? I share your sadness, but go and see
for yourself where the Fates maintain their tablets of iron and
        brass,
and read what is there inscribed. Nothing in heaven or earth,
warfare's din or lightning's crash, can change a jot
or tittle of those decrees. Your beloved descendant's life
and death must be fulfilled. In what he does and suffers,
he realizes himself. We cannot offer relief   820
or any comfort but only wisdom—his years are finished,
his allotted time is over, and now he may enter heaven
and join with us as a god, with temples on earth at which men
may worship. His work shall continue, with you and his
        splendid son
taking good care of the city we love. He shall share the name,
bear the oppressive burden, and avenge his father's murder.
We shall aid his righteous cause. The band of Mutina rebels
shall be put down, Pharsalia shall reel from his terrible might,
and Philippi shall reek with blood. The pomp of Pompey
shall drown in Sicilian waters, and Cleopatra shall learn   830

from Actium's horrid lesson how foolish a choice she made.
But why go on to list young Caesar's triumphs? The world
shall all be his as the cosmos bows to his power and justice.
It is peace he brings and the rule of law that men shall remember.
He shall, by his fine example, show men how rightly to live;
he shall teach and inspire his son, who shall follow him, ruling
    also.
Tiberius, too, will ascend to the seat of power and bear
the weight of the state's cares—but only when Caesar's years
are as numerous as his acts of virtue and loving kindness.
Then shall the gods receive him, too, as one of our own.   840
Meanwhile, attend to Julius Caesar's spirit, receive it
from his poor body, and take it up to shine in the sky,
that he may look down forever on the Capitol Hill and the Forum
he served so well and so long, to continue his vigilant care."

    Jove spoke, and Venus sped to the Senate chamber
to catch up Caesar's soul and carry it into the heavens.
She felt its fiery heat as she clutched it tight to her bosom,
and she let it go. She watched as it rose on its own to the heights
above the moon. It mounted higher and left a blazing
comet's tail in its wake as it reached its assigned position,   850
where it shines now as a star and beams in paternal approval
of what his son and heir is achieving. The son may protest
or even forbid that men should compare him with his father,
but fame may do as it will, opposing his wishes in this
singular case—for Atreus yields to his son Agamemnon;
Theseus surely outshone Aegeus, his father; Achilles
was greater than his own father. And Saturn was less than his son,
the almighty Jove we worship as lord of heaven and earth.
And so is Augustus the ruler and father of all the earth.

    I pray to the gods who led Aeneas and his companions   860
here from ruined Troy and who care for us, his descendants,
to the gods who protected Romulus' Rome and looked after
    Caesar's
burgeoning city—to Vesta, Apollo, Mars, and almighty
Jove, who sits on his lofty throne on Tarpeia's rock,
to grant that Augustus may rise one day in the far-off future,
leave this world he rules behind, ascend to the heavens,
and, like his father, reign as a god who will hear our prayers
and care for us in the future as he has cared in the past.

    And now is my poem finished, which not even Jupiter's rage,
or fire and sword, or even the greedy gnawings of age   870
shall ever undo. I await my death at some random hour,

but all it can take is my body. Over this, it shall have no power.
My work, my fame, will continue, ascending as high as the sky,
and among the stars the name of Ovid shall never die
but twinkle on forever—wherever the eagle has spread
its wings and as long as the Latin language is written and read.
If the words of poets have any truth or worth, they give
this hope to me, who wrote them—that I shall become them,
     and live.

INDEX

Ànius, king of Delos and priest of
Apollo, 272, 273

Antìgon-e, daughter of Laomedon, 93

Antìphates, king of the Laestrygonians,
288

Aphìdas, a sleeping Lapith, 246

Apòllo (Phoebus), son of Latona, god
of the sun, 12–15, 20, 21–24, 29, 34,
36, 37, 44, 68–71, 94, 110–12, 115,
149, 181, 198–99, 220–21, 224,
253–54, 266, 272, 286, 324

Aràchn-e, Lydian weaver, 105–9

Arcàdia, a region in the central Pello-
ponnese, 18, 31, 178

Àrcas, son of Jupiter and Callisto,
32–34

Àrdea, city of the Rutulians, 298

Arethùsa, a nymph who became a
spring, 96, 101–3

Argo, Jason's vessel, 124, 125, 157

Àrgonauts, Jason's crew, 124, 125–29

Àrgos, a city in the Peloponnese, 27,
116, 311

Àrgus, creature with a hundred eyes,
17–19, 34

Ariàdn-e, daughter of Minos, deserted
by Theseus, 153

Àrn-e, woman who betrays her home-
land, 138

Àsbolos, one of Actaeon's dogs, 49

Ascàlaphus, son of Acheron and
Orphne, 100

Astÿanax, son of Hector and An-
dromache, 266

Atalànta (1), an Arcadian girl loved by
Meleager, 157–59, 160

Atalànta (2), swift-footed daughter of
King Schoeneus, 210–14

Àthamas, husband of Ino, 75–77

Àthens, capital of Attica, 39, 103,
116–18, 138, 155, 318

Àthis, one of Phineus' men, 87–88

Àtlas, a giant, the son of Iapetos, and
also a mountain, 28, 80–81, 84, 109,
311

Augùstus. *See* Caesar, Augustus

Auròra, goddess of the dawn, 24, 97,
147, 184, 271–72

Autòlycus, son of Chione by Mercury,
224

Autòno-e, aunt of Pentheus, 63

Avèrnus, a lake in Campania, the en-
trance to the underworld, also the
underworld itself, 100, 196

Bàcchus, son of Jupiter and Semele,
god of wine, 52, 58–63, 64, 94, 108,
133, 218–20, 272

Bàttus, a dishonest peasant, 38–39

Baùcis, wife of Philemon, 165–68

Bo-òtes, a constellation in the northern
sky, 25

Bòreas, the north wind, a god, 123–24

Bỳblis, twin sister of Caunus, 185–90

Càdmus, son of Agenor, founder of
Thebes, 44–47, 78–79

Caènis/Caèneus, a girl, and then a boy
of Thessaly, 157, 242–43, 250–52

Caesar, Augustus, emperor of Rome at
the time of the writing of the *Meta-
morphoses,* 6, 184, 327–29

Caesar, Julius, predecessor of Caesar,
Augustus, 6, 327–30

Càla-is, son of Boreas and Orithyia,
125

Callìop-e, chief of the Muses, 94

Callìrho-e, daughter of Achelous and
wife of Alcmaeon, 184

Callìsto, a nymph, 31–34

Càlydon, a Greek city in Aetolia, 116,
156, 163, 177

Calydonian boar, quarry in the famous
hunt, 156–60

Canàch-e, one of Actaeon's dogs, 49

Cànens, a river nymph, wife of Picus,
291–94

Càssiopea, wife of Cepheus, 87

Càstor, twin brother of Pollux, and son
of Leda, 157, 159

Caùnus, twin brother of Biblys,
185–90

Càyster, a river in Lydia, 27

Cècrops, founder of Athens, 35

Cènchre-is, wife of Cinyras, mother of
Myrrha, 207

Cèntaurs, creatures, half-man and half-
horse, 175, 243–52

Cèphalus, husband of Procris, 123, 138,
143–48, 149

Cèpheus, king of Ethiopia, father of Andromeda, 81–83, 86–91

Cephìsus, a river god and father of Narcissus, 10, 44, 53, 137

Ceràstae, a group of Cypriots with horned heads, 200–201

Cèrberus, three-headed guard dog of Hades, 75, 77, 136, 195, 197

Cèrcopes, people turned into monkeys, 284–85

Cères (in Greek, Demeter), goddess of agriculture, mother of Proserpine, 94, 103, 108, 169–70, 207

Cè-yx, son of Lucifer, husband of Alcyone, 223, 225, 226–36

Charỳbdis, a whirlpool, 127, 275, 284

Chimaèra, a fire-breathing monster, 78, 190

Chìon-e, daugher of Daedalion, loved by both Apollo and Mercury, 224–25

Chrỳsaor, a horse, brother of Pegasus, 84

Cicònians, murderers of Orpheus, 215, 315

Cìnyras, son of Pygmalion and father of Myrrha, 203–8

Cìpus, a Roman praetor, 322–24

Cìrc-e, an enchantress, a daughter of the Sun, 282–84, 289–94

Cithaèron, a mountain in Boeotia, 26, 63

Clỳmen-e, mother of Phaethon, 20, 22, 25, 29, 69

Clỳti-e, a girl loved by Pheobus, changed to a sunflower, 69–71

Corònis, Princess of Larissa, mother of Aesculapius, 34–36

Crete, island of which Minos was king, 137–38, 150–53, 190–91, 274, 322

Cròcus, a youth changed to a flower, 71

Cròton, benefactor of Hercules, 307–8

Crotòna, a city named after Croton, 307

Cùpid, god of love, son of Venus, 12, 72, 83, 95, 186, 203, 209

Cỳan-e, a Sicilian fountain-nymph changed to water, 96–97

Cyàne-e, a nymph, daughter of Maeander, who marries Miletus, 184

Cỳbel-e, mother of the gods, 214, 297

Cỳcnus, son of Neptune, 240–42, 243, 253

Cỳgnus, son of Apollo, 370

Cỳgnus, son of Sthenelus, 30

Cỳllarus, a handsome centaur, 248–49

Cyparìssus, a youth loved by Apollo who becomes a cypress, 198

Cỳprius, one of Actaeon's dogs, 49

Cyprus, the island, 200, 212, 302

Daedàlion, brother of Ceyx, 223–25

Daèdalus, Athenian inventor, father of Icarus, and uncle of Perdix, 153–56, 192

Dàna-e, mother of Perseus, 79, 110

Dàphn-e, daughter of Peneus, changed to a laurel, 12–15

Dàphnis, a shepherd boy turned to stone, 71

Deianìra, sister of Meleager, wife of Hercules, 173, 176–78

Dèlos, island birthplace of Apollo and Diana, 12, 110, 114, 155

Dèlphi, a city in Phocis, site of Apollo's Oracle, 14, 199, 227, 311, 324

Demòleon, a centaur, 247–48

Dercètis, Babylonian woman changed to a fish, 65

Deucàlion, husband of Pyrrha, 9–11

Diàna (Phoebe), virgin-goddess of the hunt, also goddess of the moon, Apollo's twin, 13, 18, 32, 47–51, 72, 95, 110–11, 156, 224, 239, 320, 321

Dìctys, a centaur impaled on a tree, 247

Dìdo, queen of Carthage, lover of Aeneas, 284

Dìomedes, Greek hero at Troy, 254, 258, 262, 295–97, 328, 329

Dis. See Plùto

Dòrceus, one of Actaeon's dogs, 49

Dòris, wife of Nereus, 21, 27, 275

Dòrylas, a centaur, 248

Dòrylas, a rich landowner, 89

Dròmas, one of Actaeon's dogs, 49

Drỳas, a centaur, 245–46

Drỳop-e, daughter of Eurytus, changed to a lotus, 181–83

Ècho, a nymph in love with Narcissus, 53–57

Ìol-e, daughter of Eurytus, 176, 180–82

Iphigenìa, daughter of Agamemnon, 239, 261

Ìphis, Telethusa's daughter, 191–94

Ìphis, a young man of Cyprus, 302–3

Ìris, goddess of the rainbow, messenger of Juno, 7, 76, 232–33

Ìsis, an Egyptian goddess, associated with Io, 191, 193

Ìtys, son of Tereus and Procne, 121–23, 135

Ixìon, father of Pirithous and of the centaurs, 76, 159, 176

Jàson, leader of the Argonauts, husband of Medea, 125–29, 131, 133, 135, 157, 158, 159

Jove. See Jùpiter

Jùno, sister and wife of Jupiter, queen of the gods, 16–17, 31–34, 51–53, 54, 75–76, 107, 110, 116, 139, 176, 177, 180–81, 186, 231–32, 306

Jùpiter (Jove), son of Saturn, king of the gods, husband and brother of Juno, 14, 16–20, 28, 30, 31–32, 37, 42–43, 44, 51–53, 54, 75, 77, 79, 80, 81, 86, 99–101, 107, 108, 109, 141, 165–68, 179–80, 186, 189, 200, 224, 253, 256, 260, 266, 271, 277, 307, 308, 329–30

Justice, personified, 5, 87

Làbros, one of Actaeon's dogs, 49

Labyrinth, Daedalus' maze in Crete, 153

Làchn-e, one of Actaeon's dogs, 49

Làdon (1), one of Actaeon's dogs, 49

Làdon (2), the river where Pan catches up with Syrinx, 18

Laèlaps (1), Cephalus' dog, 146

Laèlaps (2), one of Actaeon's dogs, 49

La-èrtes, father of Ulysses, 255, 260

Laestrygònians, Cannibal tribe in Campania, 288

Lampètides, a musician, killed at Cepheus' palace, 89

Laòmedon, father of Priam, king of Troy, 107, 221, 236

Làpiths, a Thessalian tribe who fought the centaurs, 243–52

Latòna (also Leto, from the Greek), mother of Diana and Apollo, 109–12, 114–15, 272

Làtreus, a centaur, killed by Caeneus, 250–51

Leàrchus, son of Athamas, who kills him, 77

Lèda, mother of Castor and Pollux, 108

Lèlex, a companion of Theseus, 157, 164, 168

Lèmnos, an island in the Aegean, 266

Lèsbos, an island in the Aegean, 217, 260

Lèth-e, river of forgetfulness in the underworld, 232

Lèto. See Latòna

Leucòtho-e, daughter of Orchamas, changed to a frankincense shrub, 69–71

Lìbya (Africa), 80, 88

Libys, one of Acoetes' crew, 60–62

Lìchas, Hercules' servant, 178–79

Lìgdus, father of Iphis, 191

Lirìop-e, a river nymph, mother of Narcissus, 53

Lòtis, a nymph changed to a lotus, 182

Lùcifer, the morning star, father of Ceyx, 223, 231, 328

Lucìna, goddess of childbirth, 180–81, 209

Lycabas, Lycian murderer, one of Acoetes' crew, 60, 62

Lycàon, father of Callisto, changed to a wolf, 5, 6–7, 33

Lýcia, country in Asia Minor, 72, 262

Lycìsc-e, one of Actaeon's dogs, 49

Lycòrmas, the Aetolian river, 27

Lycòrmas, a fighter of Cepheus' party, 89

Lýncus, a king of Scythia, changed to a lynx, 103

Màcareus, a centaur, 250

Màcareus, a companion of Ulysses, 287–94

Maeànder, a river of Phrygia (Turkey), 27, 153, 184

Mars, god of war, 45, 47, 68, 305, 330

Màrsyas, a Phrygian satyr flayed alive, 115

Medèa, an enchantress, daughter of Aeetes, wife of Jason, 125–36

Mèdon (1), a centaur, 246

Mèdon (2), one of Acoetes' crew, 62

Medùsa, a gorgon, 83–84

Mègara, city between Athens and Corinth, 149

Melàmpus, one of Actaeon's dogs, 49

Melanchaètes, one of Actaeon's dogs, 49

Melàneus, one of Actaeon's dogs, 49

Meleàger, son of Oeneus and Althaea, 156–63

Meleagrides, sisters of Meleager who are turned to guinea-hens, 163

Melicèrta, the infant of Athamas and Ino who is transformed to Palaemon, 77–78

Mèmnon, Tithonius and Aurora's son, 271–72

Memnònides, birds sprung from the ashes of Memnon, 271

Menelàus, king of Sparta, brother of Agamemnon, husband of Helen, 261, 311

Meno-ètes, a Lycian soldier killed by Achilles, 241

Mèrcury (in Greek, Hermes), son of Jupiter and Maia, messenger of the gods, 18–19, 38–40, 42, 71, 94, 165, 224, 260

Mèrmeros, a centaur, 246

Mèrops, king of Ethiopia, husband of Clymene, 25

Mèstra, daughter of Erysicthon (not named in Ovid's text), 169–72

Mìdas, king of Phrygia, 218–21

Milètus, father of Caunus and Biblis, 184

Mìlon, an athlete of Crotona, 313

Minèrva (or Pallas; in Greek, Athena) daughter of Jupiter, goddess of wisdom, 35, 40, 46–47, 65, 83, 84, 87, 92–94, 105–6, 156, 247, 264

Mìnos, son of Jupiter and Europa, king of Crete, 137, 149–53

Mìnotaur, half-bull half-man, 152, 153

Mìnth-e, nymph turned to a mint plant, 215

Mìnyans, daughters of Minyas, changed to bats, 74

Mìnyas, father of Alcithoe and the other Minyans, 64, 74

Mòly, plant Mercury gives Ulysses that renders Circe's magic harmless, 290

Mònychus, the smart centaur who figures out how to kill Caeneus, 251

Mòpsus, Lapith soothsayer, 158, 250, 252

Mòrpheus, son of Sleep, 233–34

Mulciber. See Vùlcan

Mùnichus, king whose sons became birds, 274

Mùses, the nine patronesses of the arts, of whom only Urania and Callipe are mentioned by name, 92–104, 324

Mýrmidons, men created from ants, 142–43

Mýrrha, daughter of Cinyras, mother and half-sister of Adonis, 203–9

Mýscelus, son of Alemon, founder of Crotona, 307–8

Naì-ads, water nymphs, 18–19, 29, 57, 71, 72, 114, 117, 164, 175, 190, 217, 291, 297, 305

Nàp-e, one of Actaeon's dogs, 49

Narcìssus, son of Cephisus and Liriope, 53–58

Nàxos, the island, 61, 62

Nèbrophones, one of Actaeon's dogs, 49

Nèmesis, Greek goddess of punishment, 55, 302

Nèphel-e (1), one of Diana's nymphs, 48

Nèphel-e (2), wife of Athamas, 221

Nèreus, a sea god, husband of Doris, 27, 223, 225, 240, 275

Nèssus, a centaur, 157, 158, 175–76, 246

Nèstor, king of Pylos, famous for his sagacity, 151, 252–53, 257

Night, personified, 75, 293

Nile, Egyptian river and god, 11, 19, 27, 91, 193, 327

Nìleus, an opponent of Perseus who claimed descent from the river god, 91

Nìnus, founder of Niniveh at whose tomb Pyramis and Thisbe arrange to meet, 66

Nìob-e, wife of Amphion, mother of seven sons and seven daughters, 109–13

Nìsus, father of Scylla, 149–53

Nònacris, an Arcadian city and mountain, the home of Callisto, 18

Nùma, a king of Rome, 307, 320

Numitor, a king of Alba, 304

Nycteus, companion of Diomedes, 296

Nyctìmen-e, daughter of Epopeus, changed to an owl after having had sexual relations with her father, 296

Ocean (or Ocèanus), personified, a god, husband of Tethys, 33, 186, 281

Ocýrho-e, daughter of Chiron, changed to a mare, 37

Odýsseus. *See* Ulýsses

Oèdipus, king of Thebes, father and half-brother of Antigone, 145

Oèneus, king of Calydon, father of Meleager, 156, 163

Oèta, mountain range in Thessaly, site of the death of Hercules, 8, 26, 177–79

Olýmpus, a mountain in Thessaly, the home of the gods, 5, 26, 131, 276

Onètor, Peleus' herdsman, 225

Òrchamus, king of Babylon, father of Leucothe, 69–70

Òresitrophos, one of Actaeon's dogs, 49

Oribàsos, one of Actaeon's dogs, 49

Orithýia, sister of Procris, wife of Boreas, 123–24, 143

Òrpheus, son of Apollo and Calliope, husband of Eurydice, the proto-poet, 195–98, 216–18

Òssa, a mountain in Thessaly, 5, 26, 131

Òthrys, a mountain in Thessaly, 26, 131, 135, 242, 251

Òvid, 135–36, 183–84, 196, 330–31

Palamèdes, a Greek accused of spying at Troy, 257, 264

Pàllas. *See* Mìnerva

Pamphàgus, one of Actaeon's dogs, 49

Pan, god of the woods and of shepherds, 18–19, 220–21, 296, 300

Pandìon, king of Athens, father of Procne and Philomela, 116, 123

Pàndrosos, a daughter of Cecrops, 35, 39

Pàphos, a city on Cyprus named after Pygmalion's daughter, 203, 209

Pàris, son of Hecuba and Priam, husband of Helen, 238, 261, 329

Parnàssus, a mountain near Delphi, home of the Muses, 9, 13, 26, 80, 93

Pasìpha-e, daughter of the Sun, wife of Minos, mother of the Minotaur, 152, 192

Pèdasus, companion of Phineus, 89

Pègasus, a flying horse, born from the blood of Medusa, 84, 92

Pèlates, a companion of Phineus, 89

Pèlates, Lapith fighter, 244

Pèleus, father of Achilles, 138, 157, 222–26, 247–48, 260

Pèlias, half-brother of Aeson, 133–35

Pèlion, a mountain in Thessaly, 5, 131, 135, 240

Pèlops, son of Tantalus, 116

Penèlop-e, wife of Ulysses, 269

Penèus, a river and its god, father of Daphne, 12, 13, 14, 15, 27, 131

Pèntheus, king of Thebes, son of Echion, ripped apart by Bacchantes, 58–63

Pèrdix, nephew of Daedalus, changed to a partridge, 155–56

Periclýmenus, brother of Nestor, 253

Perimèl-e, a nymph loved by Achelous, changed to an island, 164

Periphètes, Vulcan's criminal son (not named in Ovid's text), 137

Persèphon-e. *See* Prosperpìna

Pèrseus, son of Jupiter and Danae, 79–92

Petraèus, a centaur, killed by Pirithous, 246

Phaèdra, second wife of Theseus, who fell in love with her stepson Hippolytus, 320

Phaèocomes, a centaur, 249

Phà-ethon, son of the Sun and Clymene, 20–29, 70

Phà-ethusa, sister of Phaethon, 29

Phìlammon, Chione's son, by Phoebus, half-brother of Autolycus, 224

Philèmon, husband of Baucis, 165–68

Philoctètes, friend to whom Hercules leaves his arrows, 179, 257, 264, 266

Philomèla, Pandion's daughter, Procne's sister, 117–23

Phìlyra, a daughter of Ocean whom Saturn loved, changing her into a mare and himself into a horse, 37

Phìneus, brother of Cepheus, fiancé and uncle of Andromeda, 86–92

Phlègethon, a river of the underworld, 100, 321

Phlègyas, a companion of Phineus, 88

Phòcis, land between Boeotia and Aetolia, 8, 9, 35, 93

Phòcus, son of Aeacus, half-brother of Telemon and Peleus, 138, 143, 146, 223

Phoèb-e. See Diàna

Phoèbus. See Apòllo

Phoènix (1), a bird that is reborn from its ashes, 317–18

Phoènix (2), companion of Achilles at the Calydonian boar hunt, 157

Phòrbas (1), a Lapith fighter, 246

Phòrbas (2), one of Phineus' fighters, slain by Perseus, 88

Phòrcys, daughters of, Gorgon sisters who share an eye, 84

Pìcus, king of Latium, turned to a woodpecker, 291–93

Pi-èrides, the nine daughters of Pierus, who were changed to magpies, 93–94

Pirìtho-us, son of Ixion, friend of Theseus, 157, 159, 243, 247

Plèiades, the seven daughters of Atlas and Pleione, now stars, 18, 109

Plùto, brother of Jove and Neptune, king of the underworld, 95–101, 195

Poemènis, one of Actaeon's dogs, 49

Pòllux, Castor's twin brother, 157, 159

Polydèctes, skeptical ruler of Seriphos, turned to stone by the Medusa's head, 92

Polydòrus, son of Priam, 267, 269–70

Polymèstor, king of Thrace, son-in-law of Priam, 267

Polyphèmus, a one-eyed giant, lover of Galatea, 275–79, 287–88

Polýxena, daughter of Priam and Hecuba, wedded to the dead Achilles, 267–68

Pomòna, a wood nymph, 299–304

Prìam, the last king of Troy, 236, 238, 261, 266

Priàpus, god of lust, 182

Pròcn-e, sister of Philomela, wife of Tereus, 117–23

Pròcris, wife of Cephalus, 123, 143–48

Procrùstes, robber who fitted his victims to the size of his couch, 137

Pròetus, Acrisius' usurping twin brother, 92

Promètheus, father of Deucalion, 3, 10

Propoètides, prostitutes of Amathus, 201

Pròreus, one of Acoetes' crew, 61

Proserpìna (in Greek, Persephone), daughter of Ceres, wife of Pluto, 95–101, 195, 215

Protesilà-us, first of the Greeks to fall at Troy, 240

Pròteus, a sea-god able to change form, 21, 168, 222, 280

Ptèrelas, one of Actaeon's dogs, 49

Pygmàlion, a Cypriot sculptor, father of Cinyras, 201–2

Pýlos, the city in Elis, 38, 116, 252

Pýramus, Thisbe's lover, 65–68

Pyrèneus, king of Thrace who attacked the Muses, 93

Pýrrha, wife of Deucalion, 9–11

Pythàgoras, Greek mathematician, philosopher, and vegetarian, 308–20

Pýthia, the spokeswoman at Delphi, 324

Pythian games, held in honor of Apollo, 12

Python, serpent Apollo kills, 12

Quirìnus, Romulus' name as a god, 306

Rhadamànthus, brother of Minos, 184

Rhèsus, king of Thrace, killed by Ulysses, 258

Rhexènor, companion of Diomedes, changed to a bird, 296

Rhòdop-e, a woman changed to a mountain in Thrace, 26, 107

Rhoètus (1), a Lapith fighter, 245

Rhoètus (2), one of Phineus' victims at Cepheus' palace, 87

Rome, 6, 304–7, 323–24, 327, 330

Ròmulus, later Quirinus, son of Mars, father of Rome, 304, 305–6, 322, 330

Rumor, personified, 176, 239

Sàlmacis, a pool and its amorous nymph, 71–74, 316

Sàmos (1), an Ionian island, 274

Sàmos (2), an island off the coast of Asia Minor, Pythagoras' birthplace, 155, 308

Sàturn, father of Jove, Neptune, and Pluto, 4, 108, 186, 291

Scìron, an Attic bandit, later a cliff, 137

Scorpio, the constellation, 26

Scýlla (1), daughter of Nisus, changed to a bird, 149–53

Scýlla (2), a nymph loved by Glaucus, changed to a monster, 275, 279, 282–84

Sèmel-e, mother of Bacchus, 51–52

Semiràmis, queen of Babylon, wife of Nisus, 65, 88

Sìbyl, Apollo's priestess at Cumae, 285–86

Silènus, a satyr, friend of Bacchus, 64, 218

Sìnis, a bandit, 137

Sirens, the, daughters of Achelous, 100–101, 284

Sìsyphus, son of Aeolus, 76, 196, 256

Sleep, personified, 232–33

Smìlax, nymph loved by Crocus, 71

Sparta, 116, 199–200

Sphynx, the, 145

Stìct-e, one of Actaeon's dogs, 49

Styx, the underworld river, 5, 19, 22, 52, 57, 75, 99, 214, 229, 246, 299, 311

Sýrinx, a nymph loved by Pan, 18–19

Sýros, an island, 138

Tàges, Etruscan seer, born from a clod of earth, 322

Tagus, a river in Lusitania, 250

Tàmasus, the field in Cyprus, where the tree of the golden apples grows, 212

Tàntalus, father of Niobe, 76, 109, 196

Tàrtarus, 254. See also Underworld

Tàtius, king of the Sabines who ruled jointly with Romulus, 305

Tèctaphos, a Lapith, 249

Tèlamon, brother of Peleus and Phocus, father of Ajax, 138, 142, 157, 159, 256

Tèlemus, a seer who warns Polyphemus, 276

Tèlephus, son of Hercules, wounded at Troy and then healed by Achilles' spear, 241, 260

Telethùsa, mother of Iphis, 191–94

Tèmpe, the valley of the river Peneus, 15, 131

Tèreus, king of Thrace, Procne's husband, 117–23

Tèthys, wife of Oceanus, 23, 25, 33, 186, 237, 281

Teùcer (1), king of Troy, 274

Teùcer (2), son of Telamon and Hesione, 260

Thebes, capital of Boeotia, 63, 65, 75, 78, 109, 273, 318

Thèmis, oracular goddess of justice, 9, 10, 80, 183

Thèridamas, one of Actaeon's dogs, 49

Thèron, one of Actaeon's dogs, 49

Thèrses, a king of Thebes whose gift to King Anius (q.v.) is given to Aeneas, 273

Thèseus, son of Aegeus, father of Hippolytus, 136–37, 153, 156, 159, 163–64, 173, 244, 320, 330

Thètis, mother of Achilles, 222–23, 226, 260

Thìsb-e, Babylonian girl, loved by Pyramus, 65–68

Thò-os, one of Actaeon's dogs, 49

Thrace, a land in the northeast, where the Cicones live, 93, 178, 216, 218, 267, 269–70

Tìgris, one of Actaeon's dogs, 49

Tirèsias, Theban seer, 53, 58

Tisìphon-e, one of the Furies, 76–77

Tithònus, husband of Aurora, 184

Tìtyus, a giant, 76, 196

Tmòlus, a Lydian mountain and its god, judge of the contest between Pan and Apollo, 26, 218, 220–21

Triptòlemus, king of Eleusis, 103

Trìton, a sea-god, 9, 21, 280

Troy, 158, 179, 221–22, 238–42, 249, 254, 256–67, 269, 271–74, 298, 319

Tùrnus, king of the Rutulians, defeated by Aeneas, 295, 297–98

Typhoèus, a giant beneath Mount Aetna, 95

Ulýsses (Odysseus), king of Ithaca, 256–66, 274, 276, 286–91, 294

Underworld, 27, 95, 96, 99, 100, 101, 195, 233. *See also* Tàrtarus

Vènus (in Greek, Aphrodite), goddess of love, 12, 47, 68, 94, 95, 186, 201–2, 209–15, 282, 296, 298, 305, 317, 328–30

Vertùmnus, god of the seasons, 299–304

Vùlcan, the blacksmithing god, husband of Venus, 21, 23, 68–69, 254, 263

Zàncl-e (Messina or, generally, Sicily), 275, 282, 315

Zètes, son of Boreas and Orithyia, 124, 125

Poet, novelist, critic, and journalist DAVID R. SLAVITT has published more than forty books. His translations include the *"Eclogues" and "Georgics" of Virgil, Ovid's Poetry of Exile, Seneca: The Tragedies, Volume 1,* and *The Fables of Avianus,* all available from Johns Hopkins.

LIBRARY OF CONGRESS CATALOGING-IN-PUBLICATION DATA

Ovid, 43 B.C.–17 or 18 A.D.
  [Metamorphoses. English]
  The metamorphoses of Ovid / translated freely into verse by David R.
    Slavitt.
       p.   cm.
  Includes index.
    ISBN 0-8018-4797-4 (hc : acid-free paper).—ISBN 0-8018-4798-2
  (pbk : acid-free paper)
    1. Metamorphosis—Mythology—Poetry.   2. Mythology, Classical—
  Poetry.   I. Slavitt, David R., 1935–   .   II. Title.
  PA6522.M2S55   1994
  873'.01—dc20   93-31580